# A THEORY OF SYNTAX FOR SYSTEMIC FUNCTIONAL LINGUISTICS

# AMSTERDAM STUDIES IN THE THEORY AND HISTORY OF LINGUISTIC SCIENCE

General Editor

E. F. KONRAD KOERNER

(University of Ottawa)

Series IV – CURRENT ISSUES IN LINGUISTIC THEORY

*Advisory Editorial Board*

Raimo Anttila (Los Angeles); Lyle Campbell (Christchurch, N.Z.)
Sheila Embleton (Toronto); John E. Joseph (Edinburgh)
Manfred Krifka (Berlin); Hans-Heinrich Lieb (Berlin)
E. Wyn Roberts (Vancouver, B.C.); Hans-Jürgen Sasse (Köln)

Volume 206

Robin Fawcett

*A Theory of Syntax for Systemic Functional Linguistics*

# A THEORY OF SYNTAX FOR SYSTEMIC FUNCTIONAL LINGUISTICS

ROBIN FAWCETT
*Cardiff University*

JOHN BENJAMINS PUBLISHING COMPANY
AMSTERDAM/PHILADELPHIA

∞ TM  The paper used in this publication meets the minimum requirements of American National Standard for Information Sciences — Permanence of Paper for Printed Library Materials, ANSI Z39.48-1984.

**Library of Congress Cataloging-in-Publication Data**

Fawcett, Robin
   A theory of syntax for systemic functional linguistics / Robin Fawcett.
   p.     cm. -- (Amsterdam studies in the theory and history of linguistic science. Series IV, Current issues in linguistic theory, ISSN 0304-0763 ; v. 206)
   Includes bibliographical references and index.
   1. Grammar, Comparative and general--Syntax. 2. Functionalism (Linguistics) 3. Systemic grammar I. Title. II. Series.
P291.F33     2000
415--dc21                                                                                                00-063105
ISBN 90 272 3713 1 (Eur.) / 1 55619 732 2 (US) (alk. paper)

© 2000 – John Benjamins B.V.
No part of this book may be reproduced in any form, by print, photoprint, microfilm, or any other means, without written permission from the publisher.

John Benjamins Publishing Co. • P.O.Box 75577 • 1070 AN Amsterdam • The Netherlands
John Benjamins North America • P.O.Box 27519 • Philadelphia PA 19118-0519 • USA

# Acknowledgements

There are many people who have contributed to my ideas about language in many different ways — including many generations of students — but I would like to express first my particular gratitude to two friends. The first is Michael Halliday, the 'father' of Systemic Functional Linguistics and the linguist to whom I, like many others, owe the overall shape of my theory of language. This, of course, does not prevent me from differing from him on a number of important points, as this book will show. Nonetheless, my debt to Halliday's pioneering concepts will be evident throughout this book.

The second linguist to whom I owe a particular debt is Gordon Tucker. He has been the main co-developer with me of the Cardiff Grammar, the syntax of which is presented in Part 2 of the book. At the same time he is also a friendly but ever-challenging critic. Thus he has filled the role for me that all linguists should try to provide for each other. I could not have a better colleague.

I am also indebted, of course, to many others with whom I have discussed the nature of language and/or whose works I have read with gratitude. These are too numerous to list, but the list of References gives some idea of those to whom I feel most grateful. With respect to the historical dimension of Part 1 of the book, I would like to express a particular debt to those who have provided earlier pictures of the development of Systemic Functional Linguistics — especially Kress (1976), Martin (1981), Butler (1985) and Halliday (1993).

I am also grateful to the two reviewers of this book for their encouragement and their wise counsels, and to Anke de Looper of John Benjamins for her editorial support throughout. The remaining infelicities — of which there are no doubt many — are, of course, my responsibility.

The research reported here is ultimately part of the COMMUNAL Project at Cardiff University. COMMUNAL is or has been supported by grants from the Speech Research Unit at DERA Malvern for over ten years as part of Assignment No. ASO4BP44 on Spoken Language Understanding and Dialogue (SLUD), by the University Research Council of International Computers Ltd (ICL), by Longman, and above all by Cardiff University. For all this support — and for the continuing loving support of my family — I am deeply grateful.

# An invitation

The subject of Linguistics is conducted in the main by busy academics with teaching and administrative loads that have grown significantly heavier over the last few decades. The result is that time for research — let alone time for the exploration of theoretical frameworks other than that in which one is currently working — is severely limited. But there is a second major group of working linguists: the postgraduate and undergraduate students who are being shepherded into the subject by these over-worked academics. And the members of this second group should have more time for exploring alternative approaches to understanding language — and indeed, as an intrinsic part of their work, an obligation to undertake such explorations. And there is perhaps a third group: those who regard themselves as 'users' or 'appliers' of Linguistics. But these linguists, I shall argue in the Preface, should not regard themselves as being different in kind from 'theoretical' and 'descriptive' linguists.

This invitation is addressed to linguists of all these types. But before we come to the invitation itself let me give you a little of the background to it.

During the last thirty years I have looked at many different approaches to understanding the nature of language. I have done so as a constant check on the rightness of my original decision (which I made around 1970) to work within the broad framework of Systemic Functional Linguistics (SFL). These alternative theories have included the following: Stratificational Linguistics; Tagmemics; Categorial Grammar, Transformational Generative Grammar (TGG) and its string of successors, culminating in the Minimalist Program; TGG's occasional interesting spin-offs (such as Lexical Functional Grammar, Generalized Phrase Structure Grammar and its successor Head-driven Phrase Structure Grammar, all of which I regard as still essentially 'Chomskyan' in their orientation despite the belief of those working in each that they represent a significant alternative to Chomsky); connectionist approaches to modelling language; Starosta's Lexicase Grammar and Hudson's Word Grammar; and other explicitly 'functional' grammars such as Dik's Functional Grammar, Langacker's Cognitive Linguistics, and van Valin's Role and Reference Grammar.

However, I still consider that Systemic Functional Linguistics has the greatest potential as a framework for understanding the nature of language and its use. An important part of its value — but only a part — is that it is a tolerant framework, with open boundaries, so that one can use it to develop a version of the model that fits one's own perception of the forms and functions of language. Even more importantly, it is a theory that enables one to keep an appropriate balance between such fundamental pairs of concepts as language and text, form and meaning, and paradigmatic and syntagmatic relations in language.

If I had thought that one or other of the alternative theories really was a better prospect, I would long ago have stopped working in the framework of SFL and devoted my time to exploring the nature of human language in that other framework. In other words, I have looked at many alternatives, and the fact is that I still find that SFL — despite the occasional frustrations that one encounters in working in this or any other theory — the most promising of all current theories of language.

We come now to the invitation. If you have not yet taken a serious look at SFL, perhaps this is the moment to dip a toe in the water? This book provides an introduction to the theory as a whole, as well as a full examination of the problem of the representation of the structure of language at the level of form. It will introduce you to the basic principles of this fascinating and sometimes elusive theory, and also to some of the theory's major current issues.

# Table of Contents

| | |
|---|---:|
| **Acknowledgements** | v |
| **An invitation** | vii |
| **List of Figures** | xiv |
| **Preface** | xv |

**1 Introduction**    1

    1.1    The scope and purposes of this book    1
    1.2    What is "a modern, large-scale systemic functional grammar"?    4
    1.3    The structure of the book    9

## PART 1: PROLEGOMENON TO THE THEORY    13

**2 SFL's original theory of syntax: Scale and Category Grammar**    15

    2.1    The impact on Linguistics of Halliday's "Categories" (1961)    15
    2.2    Levels of language in "Categories"    17
    2.3    The categories in "Categories"    18
    2.4    The scales in "Categories"    21
    2.5    The rarity of structural representations in "Categories" terms    24
    2.6    Some later additions to the S&C model: 'parataxis', 'hypotaxis', 'depth' and 'type'    26
    2.7    Forward from the Scale and Category model    31

**3 The place of syntax in a modern Systemic Functional Grammar**    33

    3.1    'Form' and 'meaning'    33
    3.2    'Language' and 'text' as 'potential' and 'instance'    35
    3.3    'Paradigmatic' and 'syntagmatic' relations    42
    3.4    Why a systemic functional theory of syntax is not an 'autonomous' theory of syntax    43

## 4 Halliday's later changes to the Scale and Category model — 45

- 4.1 The status of the changes: addition, evolution or revolution? — 45
- 4.2 Privileging the concept of 'system' — 46
- 4.3 Systems as choice between meanings — 47
- 4.4 The emergence of the multifunctional view of meaning — 50
- 4.5 The problem of the limited availability of Halliday's system networks — 51
- 4.6 The problem of Halliday's two positions on 'meaning' — 53
- 4.7 Two possible effects on the overall model of adopting the second position on 'meaning' — 60
- 4.8 Why a model of language requires a separate component for the realization rules — 64
- 4.9 A pivotal paper: "Text as semantic choice in social context" — 70
- 4.10 Summary: the implications of the changes — 74

## 5 Syntax in a generative systemic functional grammar — 77

- 5.1 "Systemic theory" (1993) and related works — 77
- 5.2 The 'theoretical-generative' and 'text-descriptive' strands of work in Systemic Functional Linguistics — 78
- 5.3 The "basic concepts" of "Systemic theory" — 81
- 5.4 A summary of the differences between "Categories" and "Systemic theory" — 91
- 5.5 The common ground between the Sydney and the Cardiff Grammars — 92

## 6 The major concepts of *An Introduction to Functional Grammar* — 95

- 6.1 Preview of this chapter — 95
- 6.2 In search of the "basic concepts" of *IFG* — 95
- 6.3 Summary of the differences between "Categories", "Systemic theory" and *IFG* — 101
- 6.4 The significance of the contrast in the concepts of "Systemic theory" and *IFG* — 102
- 6.5 The need for theories of both 'syntax potential' and 'instances of syntax' — 103
- 6.6 Summary of the argument so far — 106

# CONTENTS

## 7 The problem of the representations in *IFG* (and an alternative approach) — 107

- 7.1 Levels of language and the representation of the multifunctional nature of language — 107
- 7.2 The representation of a text-sentence in *IFG* — 111
- 7.3 The *IFG* representations in relation to other possible levels of representation — 117
- 7.4 How the Sydney Grammar works: the two models and their implications — 123
- 7.5 The status of *IFG*-style representations — 139
- 7.6 The availability of Sydney Grammar descriptions of English — 144
- 7.7 Summary of the answers to the two questions — 145
- 7.8 A comparison: the two levels of representation in the Cardiff Grammar — 146
- 7.9 The alternative ways of representing functional structure in the analysis of a text — 151
- 7.10 The need for a theory of syntax for SFL: the argument summarized — 152
- 7.11 The implications of the argument — 157

## 8 "Some proposals for systemic syntax" — 159

- 8.1 The situation in Systemic Functional Linguistics at the time of Fawcett's "Some proposals" (1974-6 and 1981) — 159
- 8.2 The purpose of "Some proposals" — 161
- 8.3 The 'categories' of "Some proposals" — 163
- 8.4 The 'relationships' of "Some proposals" — 165
- 8.5 The role of "Some proposals" in developing a modern SF theory of syntax — 166

## PART 2: THE NEW THEORY — 169

## 9 A theory of syntax potential — 171

- 9.1 Towards a 'new' theory of syntax for systemic functional grammar — 171
- 9.2 Syntax potential as both realization operations and potential structures — 175
- 9.3 A theory of instances of syntax: the plan for the rest of Part 2 — 185

## 10 A theory of instances of syntax: (1) the categories of syntax   187

10.1 A model without a 'rank scale' of 'units'   187
10.2 Classes of unit   193
10.3 Elements of structure   213
10.4 Places and potential structures   220
10.5 Items, the concept of 'word class' and morphology   226
10.6 Summary of the categories in a modern systemic functional grammar   231

## 11 A theory of instances of syntax: (2) the relationships between 'categories'   233

11.1 From 'rank' to 'constituency' and beyond   233
11.2 Probabilities in filling as a replacement for 'rank'   238
11.3 Componence   244
11.4 Conflation   249
11.5 Filling   251
11.6 Exponence and variation in depth of exponence   254
11.7 Continuous and discontinuous relationships between 'sister' elements   261
11.8 Recursion: co-ordination, embedding and reiteration   263
11.9 How embedding and co-ordination can replace 'hypotaxis' and 'parataxis'   271
11.10 Summary of the relationships between categories in a modern systemic functional grammar   272

## 12 Summary, conclusions and prospects   273

12.1 Towards a 'new' theory of syntax for systemic functional grammar   273
12.2 The categories of syntax: a summary and comparison   277
12.3 The relationships of syntax: a summary and comparison   280
12.4 A comparison of the two frameworks as integrated wholes   285
12.5 'Autonomous syntax', 'grammaticality' and 'probability'   287
12.6 The importance of clear and usable representations   288
12.7 A final evaluation of the significance of "Categories" for a modern systemic functional grammar   291
12.8 From theory to description: some prospects   293

## Appendix A:
## A fragment of a generative systemic functional grammar — 297

| | | |
|---|---|---|
| 1 | The purpose and scope of this appendix | 297 |
| 2 | The system network | 298 |
| 3 | The realization component | 299 |
| 4 | Summary | 301 |

## Appendix B:
## A summary of English syntax for the text analyst — 303

## Appendix C:
## The 'rank scale' debate — 309

| | | |
|---|---|---|
| 1 | The first phase of the debate: the 1960s and 1970s | 309 |
| 2 | Hudson's *de facto* contribution to the debate | 313 |
| 3 | The second phase of the debate: the 1980s and 1990s | 315 |
| 4 | The third phase of the debate: the 2000s | 333 |
| 5 | A possible end point to the debate: from 'rank' to 'filling probabilities' | 336 |

**References** — 339

**Index** — 353

# List of Figures

| | | |
|---|---|---|
| 1 | The representation of a clause in the "Categories" style | 25 |
| 2 | The representation of 'hypotaxis' in Halliday (1965/81) | 28 |
| 3 | A simplified model of any sign system | 34 |
| 4 | The main components of a systemic functional grammar | 36 |
| 5 | 'Realization' as 'instantiation': the re-arrangement of Figure 4 that is demanded by Halliday's second position on the grammar | 62 |
| 6 | An analysis by Halliday with an integrating syntax | 72 |
| 7 | A Sydney Grammar representation of a simple clause | 112 |
| 8 | The main components required in a systemic functional grammar that provides for 'structure conflation' | 125 |
| 9 | Matthiessen & Bateman's "output structure of an example" | 131 |
| 10 | The Cardiff Grammar analysis of a simple clause | 148 |
| 11 | The realization operations in the Cardiff and Sydney Grammars | 180 |
| 12 | The relationships of logical form to semantics and syntax | 210 |
| 13 | The use of the concept of 'place' to handle 'raising' phenomena | 225 |
| 14 | Two notations for representing 'componence' | 246 |
| 15 | A 'box diagram' representation of componence (as used in *IFG*) | 247 |
| 16 | The notations for representing 'componence' and 'conflation' | 250 |
| 17 | The notation for representing 'filling' in drawn diagrams and in print | 252 |
| 18 | The notations for representing 'componence', 'conflation' and 'filling' | 253 |
| 19 | The notations for 'exponence' in drawn diagrams and in print | 256 |
| 20 | Variation in the depth of exponence of a quantifying determiner | 257 |
| 21 | The notations for 'componence, 'filling' conflation' and 'exponence' | 260 |
| 22 | The complete syntactic analysis of a text-sentence | 260 |
| 23 | The discontinuity of a quality group that fills a modifier | 262 |
| 24 | An example of complexity in the nominal group | 266 |
| 25 | The analysis of a sentence with an embedded clause | 289 |
| Appendix A: 1 A highly simplified system network for 'thing' in English | | 298 |
| Appendix A: 2 Some simplified realization rules for the 'thing' in English | | 300 |
| Appendix B: The clause | | 305 |
| Appendix B: The nominal group, the prepositional group and the text | | 306 |
| Appendix B: The quality group, the quantity group and the genitive cluster | | 307 |

# Preface

## 1 Systemic Functional Linguistics as a major current theory of language

From some viewpoints, Systemic Functional Linguistics would not be considered one of the major theories of language of our time. If one judges the importance of a theory by the evidence of papers given at conferences of the Linguistic Society of America, the Linguistics Association of Great Britain and other such events, and by its representation in the journals associated with these societies and associations, then this inference is understandable. But it is an inference that would be seriously misleading.

Let us accept that a linguistic theory includes not only (1) a set of assumptions about the essential nature of language but also (2) assumptions about the goals of linguistics, (3) assumptions about the methods by which it is appropriate to try to achieve those goals, and (4) assumptions about the relations between theory, description and application. In this broad definition of a theory, there is a continuum of theories stretching from standard Chomskyan and para-Chomskyan linguistics at one end to Systemic Functional Linguistics (SFL) at (or near) the other — with theories such as van Valin's Role and Reference Grammar and Dik's Functional Grammar somewhere in the middle. Thirty years ago, in the heyday of what Smith & Wilson (1970) hailed as "the Chomskyan revolution", there was far less tolerance for non-Chomskyan approaches than there is today, and those of us who wanted to be able to explore the value of the still quite new theory of SFL found that we had to create our own conferences, summer schools, newsletters, book series, and ultimately journals in order to have an academic forum in which to pursue alternative interpretations of what the task of linguistics is. It really was that bad.

Nowadays, of course, there is a rather less prescriptive atmosphere in linguistics, and most conferences and journals are open to a rather wider spectrum of types of contribution. But the legacy of that period is the series of 'alternative' forums that were created at that time, such as the annual meetings of the Linguistics Association of Canada and the United States (LACUS) in North America, the regular conferences of Dikian functional linguists, and the International Systemic Functional Congresses (ISFCs) that take place annually in one or other of Europe, North America, Australasia, and the Far East, attracting attendances of 2-300 or more — and with annual local workshops in many countries as well. The picture is similar in the domain of publications. There are certain journals that are known to give a warmer welcome than others to papers with a functional perspective, so that many functional linguists have long since stopped offering papers to journals which are thought — perhaps quite wrongly — to be less interested in functional theories of language than they are in formal theories. In any case, there is so much going on within SFL (the functional theory which I know best) that those working within the theory find that they do not have the time and money to present systemic functional work at all of the wider linguistics conferences that they no doubt should — and this can in turn lead other linguists to think that 'not much is happening in Systemic Functional Linguistics'.

What this means is that, if the base from which you set out on your exploration of language is a department of linguistics in which the 'core' of linguistics is seen as lying within formal syntax (i.e., in what we might characterize as the 'S -> NP VP' paradigm, invoking 'X-bar theory' and so on), then you would probably have to make a considerable effort to find out about Systemic Functional Linguistics. My claim, of course, is that SFL is a far more interesting — and so far more important — theory of language than it may at first appear to be to someone whose initial standpoint is anywhere that is at all far away from it on the continuum of theories that I mentioned earlier.

An alternative approach to evaluating the importance of a theory is to ask what effect it has on the various fields in which a model of language is required — i.e., the various areas of 'applied linguistics'. The first level of 'application' of a theory is one that is usually not thought of as an application at all — but it is. This is the use of a theory of language in the description of a language. It is descriptions of languages — not theories — that get used to help solve problems of various sorts in fields such as the teaching and learning of languages, translation between languages, studying how children learn their mother tongue, analyzing literary style, critical discourse analysis, and the like — these being what are usually thought of as the 'applications' of the theory. But the fact is that you cannot apply a theory of language directly to a problem; you can only apply a theory-based description of a particular language (or languages).

# PREFACE

Over the last forty years or so, the ideas of Systemic Functional Linguistics (SFL) have influenced the description of many languages, and through this many other fields of applied linguistics. While the ideas of Noam Chomsky and other formal grammarians have dominated the conferences and publications in theoretical linguistics, descriptive linguists who have been concerned to provide usable descriptions of language such as Quirk, Leech, Sinclair, Huddleston, Biber and their colleagues have also drawn, directly or indirectly, upon the ideas of SFL — a theory whose principal architect is Michael Halliday (e.g., the treatment of 'given' and 'new' and 'theme' and rheme' as separate pairs of concepts in Quirk *et al.* 1985). And there are numerous other scholars working in the various fields of 'applied linguistics' who have found the ideas of SFL useful.

Indeed, the belief in SFL is that the division between theory, description and application is ultimately an artificial one, since the influences can work fruitfully in both directions (e.g., as emphasized in Halliday & Fawcett 1987b). When a theory is used in a challenging field of application such as syllabus design, literary stylistics or modelling the computer generation of text, inadequacies in the description may be revealed, and an improved version of the description — and so sometimes also the theory — may then be developed. Indeed, it can be argued that any theory of language that has been found useful in as wide a range of fields of application as SFL has should for this reason alone be of interest to the theoretical linguist.

However, SFL can claim a considerable theoretical status in its own right. A major reason is its pre-eminence in the field that is the most demanding formal test-bed of all for a theory of language. This is the field of natural language generation in computers. This is both an application of the theory — which is why it was included in the list above — and, when the work is carried out in a principled, theory-based manner, a highly demanding formalization of the theory. In the 1980s and 1990s broad-coverage systemic functional grammars have been formalized and tested more fully than most (if not all) other current theories in the field, and my involvement in this work over the last fifteen years has convinced me that this is indeed the most stringent of all types of formalization. Each of the two major alternative versions of SFL to be described here have satisfied this demanding test of their 'generativeness' to an impressive extent, these two models being "among the largest grammars existing anywhere in computational form" (Halliday 1994:xii). Butler in fact goes further, saying of the grammar in the COMMUNAL Project at Cardiff that it "currently operates with the largest computer-based systemic grammar in the world" (Butler 1993b:4503). Although it is notoriously hard to make comparisons between the coverage of grammars, I believe that he is right. Moreover, the Cardiff Grammar is still growing, as further areas are added and as existing areas are re-written to include the awkward and untidy bits that are omitted from so many published grammars (especially generative grammars).

In sum, then, we can say that Systemic Functional Linguistics has its own sets of assumptions about the essential nature of language, about the goals of linguistics, about the methods through which they should be pursued, and about relations between theory, description and application. These assumptions may only in part with those of theories of language at other points on the continuum mentioned earlier, but it can be argued that even from the standpoint of those other theories SFL deserves be regarded as a major current theory, because of its successful formalization in computer models of language.

## 2  What this book is about

This book proposes a new theory of syntax for SFL. In doing so it examines and evaluates some of the major differences between two current versions of SFL, focussing in particular on the way in which they model syntax.

We shall find that there are also important alternative positions within Halliday's theory, and — most pertinently — that he gives us no adequate statement of a 'theory of syntax' in either of the two major recent publications in which we might expect to find one: his paper "Systemic theory" (1993) and his widely influential *Introduction to Functional Grammar* (1985, second edition 1994). Moreover, we shall find that this leads us to draw unexpected conclusions about the theoretical status of the representations of clauses in *IFG,* and so about what a theory of syntax for SFL should be like.

Indeed, it is one of the most surprising facts about SFL that, after forty years of fairly widespread use in various fields of application, there is no general agreement as to how best to represent the structure of language at the level of form. This book makes clear proposals for a (partly) new theory of syntax, and in particular for the replacement of the method of representing structure that is used in Halliday's *Introduction to Functional Grammar* (1994) by a simpler method. Moreover, the new theory of syntax is one that is equally relevant, I shall argue, to a model of language in which Halliday's current representations are retained.

# PREFACE

This book therefore addresses a major current issue in a major current theory of language. The questions that it discusses and the concepts that it proposes are ones that are potentially relevant to any functional grammar, so that the exploratory journey on which it takes the reader should interest any linguist who takes a functional approach to understanding the nature of language.

## 3 The book's two parts

The book has two main parts: a 'prolegomenon' to a theory of syntax, and the presentation of the theory itself.

The 'prolegomenon' provides the framework of ideas that is necessary in order to understand why the theory to be presented in Part 2 is as it is. Theories have histories, and the founding document of systemic theory is Halliday's "Categories of the Theory of Grammar" (1961/76) — a paper that was essentially a theory of syntax. It is fascinating to trace the way in which the original seven main concepts of "Categories" have developed into the two current alternative accounts of what is required in the syntax of "a modern systemic functional grammar" (a term that will be defined in Chapter 1). I have therefor chosen to begin Part 1 with a summary of Halliday's seminal paper "Categories". I then sketch in the major components of a systemic functional (SF) model of language that has the two levels of 'meaning' and 'form', going on to show that it provides a framework that can be used for evaluating the two major alternative approaches to syntax being considered here. Specifically, I identify the place of a **theory of syntax** within this overall model — both for the grammar itself and for the outputs from the grammar. Then in the following chapter I sketch in the major stages through which the theory of language presented in "Categories" has been transmuted into the new theory of language that is Systemic Functional Linguistics.

Against this historical background, the later chapters of Part 1 describe and summarize the three major 'post-Categories' sources for establishing a modern theory of syntax for SFL. The first is the 'theoretical-generative' approach to systemic functional syntax exemplified in Halliday's "Systemic theory" (1993), but also in works by Matthiessen & Bateman (1991) and by Fawcett, Tucker & Lin (1993). The second is Halliday's *An Introduction to Functional Grammar* (second edition 1994, henceforth *IFG*). The third 'updating' of "Categories" is my "Some proposals for systemic syntax" (1974-6/81) — together with the later revisions to it, as described in Fawcett (1980), Tucker (1998) and Fawcett (in press). I shall try to provide a clear explanation as to (1) what the differences between these three current models of syntax are, (2) why these differences exist, and (3) the extent to which each work is a useful source for establishing a modern theory of syntax for SFL. Taken together, these three 'post-Categories' accounts of systemic syntax provide most — though not quite all — of the concepts needed for the new version of the theory presented in Part 2.

In evaluating these alternative theories of syntax, we shall find it useful to distinguish between two broad strands of scholarly work that are found in each of the two versions of SFL theory that are being compared. Indeed, these two strands can be found in many theories of language — though by no means all. They are what we shall call the 'theoretical-generative' and the 'text-descriptive' strands, and these terms will be explained more fully when they are introduced in Chapter 5.

However, there is a second set of distinctions that is equally useful. When we look at a theory from the viewpoint of a reader who is trying to discover what a given theoretical statement actually involves, it is useful to be able to consult published descriptions of languages that exemplify those concepts. In Chapter 7 we shall distinguish three major levels on the 'scale of availability' of a theory — and we shall find that both versions of SFL are currently inadequately provided for in these terms (as indeed are most if not all other theories of language). I then summarize the prospects for rectifying this situation.

With these points in mind, Part 2 presents the full set of categories and relationships that are required in a theory of syntax for a modern systemic functional grammar — i.e., a model of language that can be used for both the generation and the analysis of texts (including generation and analysis by a computer). At the same time, Part 2 evaluates the relationship between what is proposed here and the earlier major writings within the theory — including, as well as the works mentioned above, those by Halliday's colleagues in the 1960s who contributed to the theory of syntax, and those who implemented his version of the grammar in the computer.

While the concepts being presented in Part 2 are, in their very nature, abstract, they are illustrated at every point through a description of the syntax of English — with occasional comments on the requirements of markedly different languages.

The book has three appendices. Each of the first two illustrates an aspect of the theoretical model described in the main text. Appendix A provides a simple but fully explicit example of the model of a SF grammar presented in Part 1 — a model, it is suggested, which can be said to be common to both of the current modern SF theories of language. Appendix B provides, in just three pages and a key, summary diagrams of the central units of English syntax and their structures. Finally, Appendix C provides a fuller account of the 'rank scale debate' than it seemed appropriate to include in the main text, for those with a particular interest in this topic.

Appendix B is taken from my *Functional Syntax Handbook: Analyzing English at the level of form* (Fawcett in press), a work which consists of a full description of English in terms of the theory of syntax presented here. It is designed for use both as a 'fast track' course book and as a reference work that can be consulted by those analyzing the structure of text-sentences in functional terms. This 'syntax handbook' will be complemented in due course by my *Functional Semantics Handbook: Analyzing English at the level of meaning* (Fawcett forthcoming a), and this will provide an equivalent framework for the analysis of texts in terms of their various types of meaning.

## 4 The relationship of the new proposals to Halliday's representations of structure

In what I have said so far, I have been writing as if the theory of syntax to be presented here is an **alternative** to Halliday's approach to structure. And this is indeed what it is, in that the method of representing the syntax of a text-sentence to be described here is ultimately an alternative to his 'multiple structure' method rather than a complement to it. However, I shall also suggest that even a user of Halliday's approach who remains unconvinced by my argument **also needs the set of concepts proposed here** (or a fairly similar set). This statement is likely to come as a surprise to many readers, i.e., to those who are familiar with Halliday's proposals for representing the structure of a clause by a set of several different structures — proposals which have not until now been publicly questioned by other systemic linguists. The reason why Halliday's model needs to incorporate the concepts proposed here is that his current structural representations in *IFG* and elsewhere are not, as he himself would agree, the final stage in the process of generation in his framework, but an intermediate one. In the final stage, the five or more different structures that he distinguishes must be integrated into **a single represent-**

ation. And it is this integration into a single structure that the theory of syntax presented here provides.

To express matters in this way seems at first sight to provide a neat way to reconcile the two models of structure. To my considerable regret, however, I have to point out that this is not what I am proposing. This is because, once one recognizes the need for this final type of representation, it leads on to further questions. If this final integrated representation is required — as it undoubtedly is — we have to ask questions such as:

1. What is the status in the theory of the intermediate 'multiple structure' representations of clauses in *IFG*?
2. Do they represent some sort of 'intermediate' structure between the representation in terms of systemic features and the final integrated representation?
3. If so, are the 'multiple structures' needed at all?

If the answer to the third question is "Yes", so that 'multiple structures' of the type shown in *IFG* are indeed to be treated as an integral part of the model of language, this entails the addition to the model of a new component. Its function would be to convert the 'multiple structure' type of representation into a single representation. But this leads in turn to further questions, such as:

4. Is such component used in the computer implementations of Halliday's theory, e.g., is it described in Matthiessen & Bateman (1991)?
5. Is there any indication anywhere else in the literature of SFL as to what this component would be like? Indeed, we must also ask:
6. Is there, in fact, any way in which it is possible to 'integrate' several different structures (as opposed to integrating their elements, which is already standard practice in the theory)?

Chapter 7 asks these questions, provides the answers, and then discusses the implications of these answers for the theory.

Where does this leave the representations of clause structure in *IFG* and the many derived works? It may be argued by some that the main value of such 'multiple structure' representations is that they provide the best available description of a language that foregrounds the concept that each clause is the realization of several different broad types of meaning (or 'metafunctions', in Halliday's terms). On the other hand, a representation of the clause that shows (1) the various different types of meaning that it expresses **at the level of**

**semantics** and (2) a single structure **at the level of form** provides an equally insightful representation of this important aspect of language, and presents no additional problems for the theory. Moreover it is in fact easier, in a fully generative SF grammar, to generate the final structures directly from the system networks than it is to do it via a 'multiple structure' representation. Chapter 7 includes an example of the alternative way of representing the many meanings in a clause, i.e., by showing the semantic features in their 'strands of meaning'. In this approach, then, there is no 'intermediate' structure, and the representation of syntax at the level of form is the final structure.

Thus, whether or not one retains the intermediate level of 'multiple structure' representations of *IFG* in one's model of language, every systemic functional grammar requires a representation of syntax in a single, integrated structure, underpinned by a set of theoretical concepts such as those set out in Part 2 of this book.

# 1
# Introduction

## 1.1 The scope and purposes of this book

The title of this book can be read as implying that Systemic Functional Linguistics (SFL) does not currently have an agreed theory of syntax, and that it is therefore in need of one. This is precisely the interpretation that I intend.

There certainly was a theory of syntax at the inception of SFL, because the core of Halliday's "Categories of the theory of grammar" (1961) consists of just that. But later developments in Halliday's thinking have left most of the concepts presented in "Categories" with a curiously peripheral status, as we shall see in due course. And the concepts which have superseded them in Halliday's current model for use in representing structure at the level of form seem to hover — insightfully or unsatisfactorily, depending upon your viewpoint — somewhere between the levels of meaning and form. As we shall see in Chapter 5, Halliday's most recent restatement of the theory (Halliday 1993) has virtually nothing to say about structure at the level of form — i.e., syntax — and his recent major functional description of English (Halliday 1985 and 1994) similarly fails to provide a summary of the theory that underlies it.[1]

This book makes clear proposals for a new theory of syntax for a modern, comprehensive, computer-implementable SFL. It is one that is relevant, it will be argued, to all versions of SFL, including — perhaps surprisingly — that of Halliday. The book therefore addresses a fundamental issue in what is being increasingly recognized as one of the major current theories of language. For an objective evaluation of SFL in relation to other leading 'functional' theories of language, see Butler (forthcoming a and b).[2]

---

1. However, there are some explicitly theoretical statements and, as we shall see in Chapter 6, it is possible to infer from the description much of the rest of the underlying theory.

2. Butler (forthcoming a) first characterizes the major differences between a 'formalist' and a 'functionalist' approach to understanding language, and then goes on to discuss six major current theories that are explicitly 'functionalist'. These are (following closely his summarizing descriptions): (1) the 'generative functionalism' of Prince and Kuno, (2) Functional Grammar, as initially proposed by Dik, (3) Role and Reference Grammar, developed mainly by

However, most of the questions that this book discusses and the concepts that it proposes are potentially relevant to all functional linguists, whatever theory they work with. The book assumes no prior knowledge of SFL, and it can therefore be read by newcomers to the theory as an introduction to current issues within SFL. Note, however, that the focus is mainly on issues that relate to the representation of structure at the level of form, and that other current issues receive rather less attention.

This book seeks to answer the following major question:

1. What theoretical concepts are required for the description of syntax in a modern, large-scale systemic functional grammar?

And, as an interesting side issue:

2. How far are the founding concepts introduced in Halliday's "Categories of the theory of grammar" (1961/76) still valid in such a model?[3]

As we shall discover, there are some surprising twists in the answers to both of these questions.

---

van Valin, (4) Systemic Functional Grammar, associated principally with the name of Halliday, (5) the rather loose collection of approaches sometimes called West Coast Functionalism, and (6) Cognitive Grammar, developed primarily by Langacker. From these six he selects Functional Grammar, Role and Reference Grammar and Systemic Functional Grammar (SFG) as the ones that are sufficiently well formalized to be termed, in his words, 'structural-functional' grammars. And within SFG he gives a generous amount of space to the proposals in the Cardiff Grammar framework, alongside those of Halliday, so that it is presented at times almost as a fourth alternative 'functional-structural' grammar.

3. This book therefore takes "Categories" as the starting point of the new theory. This theory, like all others, is built upon the work of earlier scholars, and Halliday himself writes that "its primary source was the work of J.R. Firth and his colleagues" (Halliday 1993:4505). A close reading of Firth (1957 and 1968) shows that most of the concepts in "Categories" can be found at some point or other in Firth's writings, but Halliday's achievement — as so often in influential innovatory work — was to perceive an overall theoretical framework within which they could be insightfully related to each other. Thus, while all systemic functional linguists would join with Halliday in honouring Firth as a revered predecessor, it is "Categories" that is regarded as the founding document of the theory. For summaries of Firth's views on language, see Firth's own "Synopsis of linguistics theory 1930-55"(1957/68), and for historical perspectives on the theory that include its other antecedents in the ideas of Malinowski, Hjelmslev, Whorf, the Prague School and Chinese linguistics, see Kress (1976), Monaghan (1979), Steiner (1983), Butler (1985), Hasan & Martin (1989) and Halliday (1993). For the influence of Saussure on SFL see Fawcett (1983).

Apart from this introductory chapter, the book has two main parts. Part 1 is a 'prolegomenon' to the theory, and Part 2 is presentation of the theory itself — this being exemplified at every point, typically through a description of the syntax of English but occasionally referring to other languages with markedly different syntax. Readers who are wary of theory that is exemplified predominantly through English will understandably be critical, and I can only invite them to note that SFL has been used for the description of other languages from its earliest days — though this dimension of linguistic research has perhaps less zealously than in those theories in which the search for formal language universals is a major goal.[4] The emphasis in SFL is on first describing languages in their own terms, and then looking to see what the description has in common with descriptions of other languages. And there is a longstanding suspicion of claims for 'universals' — other than those concerning the overall characteristics of language (e.g., as discussed in Chapter 3). However, throughout its history SFL has been used to describe other languages than English, and the version of the theory whose syntactic component is presented in Part 2 has similarly been used to describe other languages than English (including Chinese and Japanese).[5]

Before going any further, I should try to clarify the senses in which I am using the terms "grammar" and "syntax". In "Categories", the term "grammar" has a meaning close to a combination of the usual senses of the terms **syntax** and **morphology**. Here, however, I shall use the term "grammar" in the sense of 'a model of the sentence-generating component of language' — a description that will be amplified in Section 3.2 of Chapter 3. And I shall use **syntax** in the sense of 'syntagmatic relations at the level of form, including inflectional morphology'. Like Halliday (1961/76:65) and Firth before him (1957/68:183), I see no strong justification for setting up two components of a general model of language, one for structure above the 'word' ('syntax') and one for structure below it ('morphology') — even though 'inflectional' languages may appear to

---

4. Indeed, Halliday's first published description of a language was an account of Chinese.

5. Some linguists — and perhaps especially those who have been influenced by the assumptions of formal language theory — would wish their theory to provide in advance for all of the possible characteristics that any human language might turn out to have. The approach to theory-building that is taken in SFL is more pragmatic, interleaving the construction of theory with the description of languages and texts.

invite this distinction.[6] See Section 10.5 of Chapter 10 for the way in which the morphology of English is handled here, and for a comment on the application of the theory to 'agglutinating' languages such as Japanese and Swahili.

This book has one major limitation, which should be stated straight away. This is that its focus is on just one part of a modern **systemic functional grammar** (a SF grammar), i.e., the **syntax**, as defined above. There are three reasons for not trying to cover the full model of language in a single book. Firstly, this topic is sufficient for one book, so that to try to present a full discussion of the whole theory would make the book more than twice as long. Secondly, this component of a modern SF grammar has received far less attention that it deserves in the recent literature of SFL. Thirdly, it is this level of language that is the subject of Halliday's well-known *Introduction to Functional Grammar* , a work that will be referred to regularly throughout this book. (The first edition was published in 1985 and the second in 1994; most references will be to the latter, which I shall refer to as *IFG*.) We shall find that there are a number of theoretical problems with *IFG* which need to be addressed if we are to develop an adequate theory of syntax for a modern SF grammar. Part 1 of the present book therefore also functions as a friendly critique of that work from within a framework of shared basic assumptions. However, the argument that I shall present here concludes with a demonstration that the representations in *IFG* cannot serve as the 'final' representation at the level of form, and that this fact requires us to reconsider the theoretical status of the 'multiple structure' representations in *IFG* itself — and so in the many derived works. Part 2 therefore specifies the concepts that are needed for a modern, large-scale systemic functional grammar.

## 1.2 What is "a modern, large-scale systemic functional grammar"?

Clearly, it is important that I should explain what I mean by the expression "a modern, large-scale systemic functional grammar" (which I shall normally

---

6. It makes even less sense to make a distinction between 'syntax' and 'morphology' in agglutinating languages such as Japanese, Swahili and Mohawk than it does in English, since it can be argued that in such languages many of the morphemes realize 'event-related' meanings and function directly as elements of the clause. For a discussion of this matter, see Section 10.5.2 of Chapter 10.

refer to hereafter as "a modern SF grammar"). We shall come to the questions of what it means for a grammar to be **systemic** and **functional** in Chapters 3 and 4 respectively. Here I wish to explain what I mean by a "modern, large-scale grammar".

Firstly, such a grammar should be capable of providing a descriptive framework of a language that can be used for the **large-scale analysis of texts**. Typically, such text analysis are carried out for one of the many 'applications' of linguistic theory; for surveys of the applications for which SFL has been used, e.g., as described in Butler (1985), Fawcett & Young (1987) and Butler (1993b). However, text analysis can also be undertaken simply as the exploration of the nature of language, as a source of information for the construction of models of language. Since the 1980s there has been an increasing use of corpora of texts stored in computers as a significant input to the construction of grammars, e.g., Sinclair (1990); Francis, Hunston & Manning (1996 and 1998); and Biber *et al.* (1999).

The second requirement of a "modern, large-scale grammar" reflects one of the major developments in Linguistics of the last few decades: the construction of computer models of language. Such models are being developed for use, within Artificial Intelligence, in the two complementary fields of Natural Language Generation and Natural Language Understanding (NLG and NLU) — and there has a great deal of work on making systemic functional grammars sufficiently full in their coverage and sufficiently explicit in their formalization to be incorporated in **computer models of language** — mainly in NLG but also in NLU. But this work is not simply yet another area of application. The principled implementation of a theory of language in a computer model is the most demanding of all possible formal tests of a theory of language. The implementation of a theory in natural language generation is particularly testing, as the literature of the area demonstrates. The reason is that the output from the system is a string of words, and every little flaw in the implementation can immediately be noticed by any user of the language. This is in contrast with a system for NLU, often called a "parser", where the output can only be evaluated in terms of the theory that is used in the processing of the text.

Thus, when a theory of language has demonstrated its value through its use in both the large-scale analysis of texts and in a large-scale, principled computer implementation for NLG and NLU, it has met three of the most demanding of all possible tests of a theory. As will be clear, the reason why the computer implementation of a theory of language is to be valued highly is that responding to these challenges in a principled manner provides an extremely rigorous formal test of the theory's concepts.

Within the broad family of systemic functional theories of language, there are what we may term (1) the "Sydney Grammar" (with two 'sub-dialects' associated with Hasan and Martin concerning differences in their models relating to the higher levels of '(discourse) semantics', 'register' and 'genre'), (2) the "Cardiff Grammar", (3) the "Nottingham Grammar", (4) the "Leuven Grammar", and perhaps others. Halliday has made the interesting suggestion that we should think of these alternative versions of SFL as being related to each other in the way that the dialects and registers of a language are.[7]

However, the only two SF grammars that have been formalized to the point where they can be implemented in a computer are the Sydney Grammar and the Cardiff Grammar.[8] These have been implemented in the Penman and COMMUNAL Projects respectively. Both versions of SF grammar have been used predominantly for modelling English, but both have also been used for Chinese, Japanese and other languages. The major component of Penman is a computer model of Halliday's SF grammar; it incorporates minor modifications

---

7. It was Michael Halliday who first suggested the metaphor of 'the Cardiff dialect', 'the Nottingham dialect' etc, during the International Systemic Functional Congress held in Beijing in 1995. However, he has also suggested the metaphor of 'register variation' — originally for thinking about the differences between Martin's and Hasan's different approaches to genre and register. He calls the difference between those two models a "kind of variation in 'metaregister'", saying that this is "one of the ways in which systemic theory appears as a metaphor for language itself" (Halliday 1993:4507). In some ways the concept of 'register variation' provides a more insightful metaphor than that of 'dialectal variation'.

8. The Cardiff Grammar is a model of language that exists both in the form of a computer model of language and as a description of English for use in text analysis. It is called "the Cardiff Grammar" because it has been developed by a group of linguists associated with Cardiff University. These currently include (besides myself): my fellow lexicogrammarian Gordon Tucker (see especially Tucker 1998), Paul Tench, a specialist in intonation (see especially Tench 1996), and several postgraduate students. Earlier there have been valuable inputs from David Young (e.g., as reported in Fawcett, Tucker & Young 1988), Joan Wright, and Yuen Lin, and from a number of distinguished scholars who it has been our good fortune to have as visitors to Cardiff — including, among others, Professor Huang Guowen of Zhongshan University, Guangzhou, Professor Erich Steiner of the University of the Saarland, Saarbrucken, and Professor Masa-aki Tatsuki of Doshisha University, Kyoto. Versions of the Cardiff Grammar have already been developed for central portions of two languages other than English, i.e., Chinese and Japanese (small but significant computer implementations having been built for both), and further work is planned on other languages. Finally, there have been valuable contributions to the overall model from many postgraduate students. For a fairly full bibliography of work in the Cardiff Grammar framework, see Fawcett (1998).

by Matthiessen, and it is described in Mann & Matthiessen (1983/85), Matthiessen & Bateman (1991), Matthiessen (1995) etc. COMMUNAL is the computer implementation of the Cardiff Grammar, and it is described in Fawcett (1988a), Fawcett & Tucker (1990), Fawcett, Tucker & Lin (1993), Tucker (1998), etc.[9] Halliday describes the two computer SF grammars as follows (referring first to the one that implements his own grammar):

> the current version of this grammar was [...] developed by Christian Matthiessen. A closely related grammar, with some descriptive differences but based on the same systemic functional theory, has been developed at the Computational Linguistics Unit of Cardiff University, under the direction of Robin Fawcett. These two are among the largest grammars existing anywhere in computational form. (Halliday 1994:xii)

The Penman Project led in due course to a number of spin-off projects, e.g., Patten's SLANG (1988), and the KOMET Project in multilingual text generation, as reported (for German) in Teich (1999), and to work in NLU by Kaspar (1988) and O'Donnell (1994). The COMMUNAL Project, however, is a later but completely new computer implementation of a SF grammar for English, derived from the earlier descriptive work of Fawcett and colleagues (while learning from the perceived strengths and weaknesses of the 'Nigel' grammar in Penman). The three most important innovations of COMMUNAL for our present purposes are the facts (1) that the system networks were explicitly developed to model the level of semantics; (2) that the realizations of meanings in lexis, intonation and punctuation have all been integrated with realizations in syntax and morphology from the inception of the project; and (3) that the concept of probability is built into the model at many different points. One spin-off application of Fawcett's work has been its use in modelling TRANSITIVITY in the EUROTRA Project in Machine Translation (e.g., Steiner *et al.* 1988). The syntax framework introduced here has also been successfully tested in the field of Natural Language Understanding. See Weerasinghe & Fawcett (1993) and Weerasinghe (1994) for a description of the probability-based parser that constructs tree diagrams from an input string of words, and O'Donoghue (1994) for an account of his complementary semantic

---

9. The acronym "COMMUNAL" stands for "COnvivial Man-Machine Understanding through NAtural Language". This is a long-term project in building a computer model of how we generate English text. At its heart lies GENESYS, a sentence generator that is so named because it GENErates SYStemically, i.e., using a systemic functional grammar. For an account of how a sentence is generated in this grammar, see Fawcett, Tucker & Lin (1993).

interpreter, whose task is to recover the semantic features selected in generating the functional structure, and so to provide a feature-based semantic representation.

Here we shall limit ourselves to the Sydney and the Cardiff 'dialects' of SF grammar, since it is only these two that have been subject to development and testing in the environments of both extensive text description and large-scale computer modelling.

Despite the real and important differences between the two models (which this book will bring out at the relevant points), Halliday is right in saying (as he does in the passage cited above) that the grammar in the COMMUNAL Project is "based on the same systemic functional theory" as that in Penman. In other words, while there are important differences between the two models, as this book demonstrates, there is sufficient common ground between the two models for us to be able to treat them as variants of the same theory (as we shall in Chapter 3).

What we need, clearly, is a recent statement by Halliday in which he summarizes his current theory of language, in the way that "Categories" did for Scale and Category Grammar. Fortunately, his contribution on "Systemic Theory" to the *Encyclopaedia of Languages and Linguistics* (Asher 1993) goes a long way to providing this, and it can be usefully supplemented by his "On grammar and grammatics" (1996). However, the orientation of "Systemic theory" is 'theoretical-generative' rather than 'text-descriptive' (to employ two terms whose implications will be explained more fully in Section 5.2 of Chapter 5), and the perhaps surprising result is that it has rather little to say about the syntactic structure of texts. We shall therefore also need to make use of Halliday's major recent descriptive work, *An Introduction to Functional Grammar*, and this provides, as we shall see, a significantly different picture of language. I shall also draw occasionally on Matthiessen (1995), a work that complements *IFG* invaluably by providing the system networks that are largely missing from that work, and which also sometimes provide a hint of an interestingly different perspective on the Sydney Grammar.

However, for reasons which will be explained at the relevant points, the fact is that Halliday has nowhere made a comprehensive statement as to the nature of syntax in a modern SF grammar that is comparable in its scope with that in "Categories" — and nor has Matthiessen or any other exponent of the Sydney Grammar. One would expect that the enormous changes made to the model as it was developed from the Scale and Category Grammar of the 1960s into the Systemic Functional Grammar of the 1990s would have led to changes in the representation of structure at the level of form. And indeed they have, as Chapter 7 will clearly demonstrate. But Halliday has provided only the most general of justifications for the immense changes that he has made in the way that formal structure is represented in his model (e.g., in Chapters 1 and 2 of *IFG*). The only reasonably full statement by a systemic functional grammarian whose purpose is to reflect the major changes in the theory referred to above has been that of Fawcett (1974-6/81) — this being probably best known through the summary provided in Butler (1985:94-102).

It is important to emphasize that the 'ground rules' that guide my work on syntax differ from Halliday's in one important way. This is that the aim is to show only the minimal necessary structure at the level of form, and to provide for the explicit representation of meanings — and so also the representation of the broad types of meaning corresponding to Halliday's 'metafunctions' — at a second level of representation, i.e., at the 'systemic-semantic' level of representation. The model of syntax presented in Fawcett (1974-6/81) has developed, with a small number of major changes and many minor ones, into the theory of syntax that has become an integral part of the current large-scale Cardiff Grammar — as described in Fawcett, Tucker & Lin (1993), Tucker (1998), Fawcett (in press and forthcoming a), and the various other works listed in Fawcett (1998). In setting out a modern theory of SF syntax in Part 2, therefore, I shall inevitably draw to a significant extent on this work as well as on that of Halliday and his close colleagues.

## 1.3 The structure of the book

The overall structure of the book is as follows. Part 1 provides a prolegomenon to a modern theory of systemic functional syntax, summarizing the history of this aspect of SFL theory and raising a number of important issues. Part 2 then presents the theory itself — and, at the same time, it exemplifies it through a description of the syntax of English (with occasional remarks about its application to other languages).

The main purpose of Part 1 is to show why Part 2 is needed. In other words, it is only if I can convince you that there is a need for the type of representation at the level of form presented in Part 2 that those proposals become relevant. Part 1 begins with a summary of the history of the central concepts of the theory, partly to enable us to understand which of the current central concepts have always been in the theory, and partly because the earlier versions of the theory constitute a 'quarry', as it were, in which ideas may be found which will help in building the new theory of syntax that is required.

We shall begin, in Chapter 2, with a summary of Halliday's seminal paper "Categories of the theory of grammar" (1961/76) — which is itself essentially a theory of syntax. After outlining Halliday's overall model of language as it was in 1961, I shall summarize the seven main concepts in what was at that time an exciting new theory of syntax (or "grammar", as Halliday would term it). However, during the sixties Halliday developed what was essentially a theory of syntax into the rich theory of language as a whole that is known today as Systemic Functional Grammar. The purpose of Chapter 3 is to outline the major concepts that underlie a modern systemic functional grammar, and so to specify the context in which a systemic functional theory of syntax has to operate. This provides the basis for the rest of the book. This chapter also explains why, in SFL, it is not possible — or even desirable — for such a theory of syntax to be 'autonomous'. Chapter 4 then briefly describes the major innovations made by Halliday and his colleagues in the 1960s, which progressively transformed the theory into Systemic Functional Grammar — i.e., into the model of language described in Chapter 3. Interestingly, however, neither Halliday nor any of his close colleagues has made a detailed statement about a modern theory of SF syntax that can be compared with that in "Categories". The best summary of the "basic concepts" of the theory as Halliday sees them today is in his paper "Systemic theory" (1993), and this is summarized in Chapter 5. A second obvious source of insights is the major description of English that he provides in *IFG*), and this is examined in Chapter 7. Surprisingly, there are considerable differences between the theoretical concepts presented in these two works by Halliday, both of which were published in the early 1990s, and this clearly requires comment and explanation. But it is the analysis of texts in *IFG*, of course, that constitutes the major evidence as to how Halliday sees the structure of what we shall later call 'instances of syntax'. And in evaluating these representations we shall find — contrary to what you might expect — that they raise serious theoretical problems. Moreover, in the course of Chapter 7 it becomes clear that, even if you feel completely happy about the representations of structure in *IFG*, Halliday's model additionally needs an integrating syntax of the sort proposed here in Part 2. However, there is a third document that 'updates' the concepts in "Categories" in the light of the development of Scale and Category Grammar into Systemic Functional Grammar, i.e., Fawcett (1974-6/81), and this is summarized briefly in Chapter 8. (The summary is brief, because there is a considerable overlap between that work and the proposals made in Part 2.) Taken together, the discussions of these three 'post-Categories' accounts of systemic syntax provide, together with the discussion of "Categories" itself, the necessary basis for understanding why the theory to be set out in Part 2 is as it is.

Part 2, then, constitutes a full statement of what is required in a theory of syntax for a modern systemic functional grammar — i.e., for a theory that provides the concepts that are needed when making descriptions of languages that can be used both as (1) a generative systemic functional grammar of a language (e.g., in a computer) and (2) a framework for the systematic description of texts. Chapter 9 describes the specification of structure provided by the grammar itself — which we shall term its **syntax potential** — and Chapters 10 and 11 specify respectively the **categories** and the **relationships** between these categories that are required in a model of the **instances of syntax**. Thus the "categories" presented here correspond in general terms to the "categories" of Halliday (1961/76), while the "relationships" presented here correspond — though with considerable differences — to his "scales". The final chapter of Part 2 — Chapter 12 — provides a summary of the differences between (1) Halliday's current model of syntax and (2) the new theory of syntax presented here, and also between "Categories" and the latter.

Thus the book both starts and ends with "Categories". In this way it acknowledges the vital place of this remarkable document in the history of Systemic Functional Linguistics in general, and in particular in the representation of syntax in such a theory.

There are also three appendices. Appendix A is a small example of a generative grammar, and its purpose is to illustrate the 'core' model that is introduced in Chapter 3 and that forms the basis of the comparison between the Sydney Grammar and the Cardiff Grammar that runs through the book. Appendix B is a description of the major syntactic units of English, summarized in three pages, as developed through very large amounts of text-descriptive work in the framework of the Cardiff Grammar. It describes the central portions of English syntax, and it consequently exemplifies most of the concepts introduced in Chapters 10 and 11. Appendix C provides a fuller account of what has been termed 'the rank scale debate' than is required in the main text, for readers with a particular interest in this topic.

Is it necessary, you may ask, to read all of Part 1, in order to understand the presentation of the theory in Part 2? The answer is that, strictly speaking, it is not. However, it is in Part 1 — and in particular in Chapter 7 — that I explain why the theory presented in Part 2 is needed.

But there is a further reason to read Part 1. It is that Halliday describes Systemic Functional Linguistics as a theory of language that has remained essentially unchanged in its lexicogrammatical 'core' over the last forty years, with the developments in the theory coming through "expansion" rather than change (e.g., 1993:4507). However, Chapters 3 to 7 of Part 1 demonstrate clearly that he has in fact introduced a whole series of changes between the sixties and today. Thus the fact that I am proposing certain further changes to the theory in Part 2 is not so revolutionary as it might at first appear. This further stage in the evolution of the theory is necessary, I believe, in order to enable it to meet the demands that will be made on Systemic Functional Linguistics in the 2000s.

# Part 1

# Prolegomenon to the theory

# 2
# SFL's original theory of syntax: Scale and Category Grammar

## 2.1 The impact on Linguistics of Halliday's "Categories" (1961)

In 1961 the journal *Word* published a paper that is arguably one of the most influential that has ever appeared in it: Halliday's "Categories of the Theory of Grammar". This 51-page paper set out what quickly came to be regarded as the definitive version of a set of concepts that had made a quiet first entrance on the public scene some five years earlier in Halliday's "Grammatical Categories in Modern Chinese" (1956/76).[1] This publication was followed closely by Halliday (1957), but it was "Categories" (as the paper quickly became known) that was effectively the founding document of the new theory of language — i.e., Scale and Category Grammar, and so in due course Systemic Functional Linguistics. It was soon reprinted in the prestigious Bobbs-Merrill Reprint Series, and excerpts from it have been included in quite a number of other volumes. (These include Halliday (1976), and the page references given here will normally be to this work, because it is probably the version of "Categories" that is the most widely available.)

Descriptions of languages that use the framework of concepts set out in "Categories" have had a considerable influence on both **descriptive** and **applied** linguistics. Their influence can be clearly seen in the great eclectic grammars of Quirk *et al.* (1972) and Quirk *et al.* (1985), and so in the many derived works that re-use their categories such as Biber *et al.* (1999). However, the explicit presentation of these concepts probably reached its widest audience in the extended summary of the theory that Halliday provided in *The Linguistic Sciences and Language Teaching* (Halliday, McIntosh & Strevens, 1964). This work was highly influential, particularly in the fields of language teaching that were its intended audience. The book was itself republished two

---

1. It could therefore be argued that the date of the founding publication of what later grew into Systemic Functional Grammar was 1956. Indeed, a major work of monograph length also appeared before "Categories", namely Halliday (1959).

years later in the USA.[2]

Chomsky's influential work *Syntactic Structures* (1957) was published a year later than Halliday's first theoretical statement (Halliday 1956) but four years before "Categories". While *Syntactic Structures* had a greater influence on **theoretical linguistics**, it was "Categories" that was the more influential in the various fields of **applied linguistics**. These included mother tongue and second language teaching, literary stylistics, translation, and studies of discourse structure and language variation. Moreover, the publication of "Categories" also led to the use of Scale and Category (S&C) Grammar in **descriptive linguistics**, and S&C descriptions for languages other than English include Chinese, Swahili, Russian and French.[3] Since theory, description and application are (or should be) all mutually influential — e.g., as argued in Halliday & Fawcett 1987b) — the arrival of Scale and Category Grammar in 1961 had a very considerable effect on linguistics as a whole.

However, it is perhaps the most important single fact about S&C Grammar that, in less than five years, Halliday himself changed the theory in a manner which was, in its ultimate effects, revolutionary. This work led in due course to a new name for the theory: **Systemic Grammar**. However, this label was soon changed in its, by the inclusion of a second modifier, so that it became **Systemic Functional Grammar** (SFG). This name reflects the changes to the theory in the 1960s to be described in Chapter 4, and it has been

---

2. It was in this version that I first encountered Halliday's proposals for the categories of the theory of grammar. I can still recall vividly the satisfying sense of insight that I received when, in 1965, I worked my way through those densely written paragraphs — and came to understand how categories such as 'noun' and 'subject' can be related to each other in the overall framework of a unified theory of grammar. This experience was later matched by the similar sense of insight that I got from attending Halliday's lectures in London in 1970, when I first encountered his helpful matrix diagram — beautifully drawn on a traditional London University blackboard with coloured chalk. On this occasion the insight was into the 'multifunctional' nature of the various grammatical units, through the cross-classification of the 'functional components' of language (later called "metafunctions") with the major grammatical 'units', such as the clause and the nominal group. Examples of that diagram can be found in Halliday (1971/73b:141), Halliday (1977/78:132), Martin (1992:18), etc., and I have adapted it for the presentation of my own version of SFG, e.g., in Fawcett (1980:95).

3. It can be argued that the widely accepted — and firmly institutionalized — dichotomy between theoretical and applied linguistics works against the goal of improving our linguistic theories. The grounds for making this claim are the experience of many linguists that the demands on a theory from undertaking extensive work in description and application are likely to be a better source of useful innovations than ideas that arise when the proponents of a theory are only interested in theorizing. (See Halliday & Fawcett 1987b.)

the standard name for the 'grammatical' part of the theory ever since. These changes of name reflect Halliday's transformation of the theory from being a theory about the level of 'form' — and specifically about 'grammar' — into a theory about the levels of both 'form' and 'meaning'.

The final change of name has been the growth in the use of the broader term **Systemic Functional Linguistics** (SFL), alongside "Systemic Functional Grammar". However, this does not mark a further change in the theory. Rather, it reflects the fact that the theory is no longer simply a theory of grammar, but a holistic theory of (1) language (including all the levels that it is deemed necessary to recognize) and (2) its use in social contexts.

## 2.2 Levels of language in "Categories"

When Halliday's "Categories of the Theory of Grammar" was first published (in 1961), it was rightly regarded as an unusually comprehensive framework for thinking about language. However, its major focus was on 'grammar', in a sense that is roughly equivalent to a combination of the traditional senses of the terms "syntax" and "morphology". Here, however, we shall use the term "syntax" in a broad sense that includes the 'grammatical' aspects of morphology (for which see Section 10.5 of Chapter 10).

Halliday begins "Categories" by outlining the overall theory. The central concept is that of **levels** of language. Halliday states that "the theory requires that linguistic events should be accounted for at a number of different levels", and he then goes on to claim that "the primary levels are 'form', 'substance' and 'context'" (1961/76:52-3). Notice, then, that there is no level called "semantics", "context" being defined as "the relation of the form to the non-linguistic features of the situations in which language operates, and to linguistic features other than those of the item under attention". A few lines later he comments that "contextual meaning [...] is an extension of the popular — and traditional semantic — notion of meaning", and that "the contextual meaning of an item is its relation to extratextual features". These general remarks certainly leave plenty of scope for the expansion in Halliday's future writings that they receive over the next forty years.

The focus in "Categories" is on the level of 'form', of which Halliday states (1961/76:53) that it "is in fact two related levels, 'grammar' and 'lexis'."

Thus 'grammar' — complex though this component of the overall model is — is simply a 'demi-level' (as it was later termed) within the level of 'form'. In "Categories", therefore, the meaning of the word "grammar" is far more restricted that the other widely used sense of the term, in which a grammar means something like 'model of language'. (Indeed, this is the sense in which I shall normally use the term in this book — except when quoting Halliday — most notably in Chapter 3.) In "Categories" the meaning of the term "grammar" covers the combination of what have traditionally been separated as 'syntax' and 'morphology'.

It is within the demi-level of 'grammar', then, that we find the four 'categories' and three 'scales' that together define the "Categories" theory of grammar. Let us take the categories first.

## 2.3 The categories in "Categories"

The major categories in Halliday's earlier paper "Grammatical Categories in Modern Chinese" (1956/76) were those of **unit**, **element** and **class**. Kress (1976:33) comments that "one is impressed by the lowly status of both *system* and *structure*" in that earlier framework of concepts.[4] In "Categories", however, the influence of Firth's 'system-structure' theory (Firth 1957/68:173) is made fully explicit. Firstly, Halliday promotes the concept of **system** from its apparent subservience to **class** in the earlier work, so that it becomes one of the four "fundamental categories" (1961/76:55). Secondly, the concept of **element** from Halliday (1956/76) is presented as subservient to the slightly more abstract concept of **structure** (an element being a component of a structure). The major categories of "Categories", then, are **unit**, **structure**, **class** and **system**. We shall begin with the concept of 'unit', just as Halliday does in "Categories".

Halliday defines the **unit** as "the category set up to account for the stretches [of "language activity"] that carry grammatical patterns" (1961/76:57). But what are these "grammatical patterns"? From Halliday's wording at this point one might expect them to be the patterns found inside the unit — but this is another type of 'patterning' as we shall see shortly. For Halliday, the

---

4. Here we see the influence of Firth's concepts on Halliday. As Halliday himself frequently acknowledges, his theory is a development from Firths 'system' and 'structure' theory (e.g., Halliday 1993:4505).

concepts of 'unit' and 'rank' are inseparable, and the "patterning" that Halliday has in mind here is the patterning of the 'consists of' relationship which, in Halliday's theory, holds between the different 'ranks' of unit. Thus clauses are said to 'consist of' groups, and groups to 'consist of' words — to exemplify from the three central units of Halliday's 'rank scale' for English . (See Section 2.4 of Chapter 2 for 'rank'.) The full set of units proposed for English in "Categories" is: sentence, clause, group/phrase, word and morpheme.

Halliday describes the unit as "the pattern carrier" (1961/76:59), and the patterns that are "carried" inside units are accounted for by the concept of **structure**. Thus Halliday states that "the category set up to account for likeness between events in successivity is the 'structure'" (1961/76:59). Thus the following would all be said to have the same 'structure' (at least at the 'primary' degree of 'delicacy'; for 'delicacy' see below):

| *Ivy* | *cooked* | *a Spanish omelette* | *yesterday evening* |
| *We* | *ate* | *it* | *with great enjoyment.* |
| *The cat* | *watched* | *us* | *rather enviously.* |

Halliday then goes on to introduce the concept of **element** (which was presented as one of the basic concepts in his earlier paper), saying that what enables us to recognize "likeness" between "structures" is the fact that they are "made up of 'elements' which are represented as being in linear progression" (1961/76:59). Thus each of the four examples above has the structure (in "Categories" terms) of S P C A, i.e., Subject + Predicator + Complement + Adjunct. The concepts of 'element' and 'structure' are, it will be clear, mutually defining; there can be no structure without the potential for having two or more elements, and there can be no element without there being a structure of which it is a component (including, in the limiting case, the sole component). And, as we shall see, it is the concept of 'element of structure' (or "element" for short) that will emerge as one of the two dominating categories of later theories of SF syntax, including the theory underlying *IFG* and the theory to be described in Part 2.

Within this section of "Categories" Halliday also introduces the related concept of **place**. He writes that "a structure is [...] an arrangement of elements ordered in 'places'" (1961/76:60). While this is not one of Halliday's four "fundamental categories", it is nonetheless one that will be important for a modern SF grammar, as we shall see in Section 10.4 of Chapter 10.

Halliday's third "fundamental category" is that of **class**. Interestingly, this concept is always used in relation to units (and never to elements), so that in SFL the term "class", when used in its technical sense in the field of grammar, always means **class of unit**. Halliday defines 'class' as "that grouping of members of a given unit which is defined by operation in the structure of the unit next above" (1961/76:64). For example, the class of the unit 'word' that is called a "noun" operates as the head of a nominal group. Halliday claims that the class of the unit 'group' that he has called the "nominal group" is recognized in the description of English on similar grounds, i.e., because it operates (typically) as a Subject or a Complement in the higher unit of the 'clause'. His second major class of group is the 'verbal group' which in S&C Grammar always and only operates at the clause element 'Predicator'. For Halliday, then, "a class is not a grouping of members of a given unit which are alike in their own structure" (1961/76:65).[5]

Finally, Halliday introduces his fourth "fundamental category", i.e., **system**. He states that its role is to account for "the occurrence of one rather than another from among a number of like events" (1961/76:67). For example, the concept of 'system' would be said to account for the occurrence of *this* rather than *that* as the deictic determiner in the nominal group *this boy*. This is in fact the direct incorporation into Halliday's theory of Firth's concept of 'system', as defined in Firth (1957/68:173). Notice that there is no hint in "Categories" that the concept of 'system' is not at exactly the same level of language as the three other fundamental categories, i.e., at the level of form. It is presented as simply one of the four fundamental categories of the demi-level of grammar. It was in fact Halliday's later changes to the status of this concept that fundamentally altered the theory set out in "Categories" into Systemic Functional Grammar — as we shall see in Chapter 4.

These changes may have seemed at the time to be merely evolutionary. But their cumulative effect was, as many systemic functional linguists realized in the early 1970s, revolutionary. They in fact resulted in a completely new theory of language.

---

5. In Section 10.2.2 of Chapter 10, however, the value of defining a **class of unit** by Halliday's criteria will be challenged and alternative criteria will be proposed. The concept is particularly relevant with respect to groups. In Section 10.5 of Chapter 10 a different status for the concept of a 'word' will be proposed, so that its relationship to units such as clause and group is no longer simply that it is the unit below 'group' on the 'rank scale'. Finally, the concept of the 'verbal group' will be abolished in favour of treating all of its elements as direct elements of the clause, as Appendix B shows. (See Fawcett 2000 and forthcoming b for the full set of arguments for this, and Appendix C for a summary of them.)

## 2.4 The scales in "Categories"

We turn now to the three 'scales'. The first — and the most fundamental of the three in understanding the "Categories" framework — is the scale of **'rank'**. Halliday states that "the relationship among the units [...] is that, going from top (largest) to bottom (smallest), each 'consists of' one, or more than one, of the unit next below (next smaller)". And he goes on to state that "the scale on which the units are [...] ranged may be called 'rank'" (1961/76:58). The units for English that he recognizes in "Categories" are the **sentence, clause, group (phrase), word** and **morpheme**.[6] Halliday then points out that "the theory allows for downward 'rank shift': the transfer of a [...] given unit to a lower rank" [i.e., it allows a unit such as a clause to occur at an element where, in the unmarked case, a lower unit such as a group or a word would occur]. Moreover the theory "does not allow for upward 'rank shift'", i.e., a word cannot function directly as an element of a clause. The claim that elements of a clause must be filled by groups rather than by words (which Halliday expresses as "no upward rank shift") has attracted particularly strong criticism, both from outside SFL (e.g., Matthews 1966) and from within it (e.g., Hudson 1971 and Fawcett 1973/81). Indeed, the value of the concept of the 'rank scale' will be strongly challenged in Part 2, and an alternative approach will be proposed that modifies the original 'rank scale' principle so fundamentally that it is effectively a proposal for a new way of thinking about relations between units. (See Section 11.1 of Chapter 11.)

We turn now to the scale of **exponence**. Halliday defines it as "the scale which relates the categories of the theory, which are categories of the highest degree of abstraction, to the data" (1961/76:71). It encompasses any relationship that relates any of the categories to each other and to the data, where "data" is to be understood in the sense of the representation that is closest to what Halliday calls the "phonic" or "graphic substance". In "Categories", then, "exponence" is a term with a very broad coverage. Halliday then goes on to claim that, while he recognizes that each of the four categories stands in a different relationship to the data, "exponence can be regarded as a single scale".

---

6. Halliday states that 'group' and 'phrase' are two "fundamental" sub-classes of 'group' (Halliday 1961/76:253. This makes the difference between them sound very important, but he gives no reason for this in "Categories'. (Indeed, this section was omitted by Kress when editing "Categories" for inclusion in Halliday 1961/76.) See Section 10.1 of Chapter 10 for Halliday's explanation for why he introduced the two terms.

The concept of 'exponence' when put like this, is so broad as to be of very little practical use, and it is not surprising that it later underwent very considerable changes. The first change resulted directly from Halliday's change in the concept of 'system'. In a footnote in Halliday (1966/76:90), he substitutes the term **realization** for "exponence". This term was borrowed from Lamb's 'stratificational grammar' (Lamb 1966), and it quickly came to be used in Lamb's sense, i.e., to mean the "relationship between the 'strata', or levels, of a [...] semiotic system" (Halliday 1993:4505). We shall return to the concept of realization at various points in this book, notably in Section 3.1. of Chapter 3, Section 4.6 of Chapter 4, Chapter 5 and Section 9.2 of Chapter 9. The original term "exponence" was later re-defined in Fawcett (1974-6/81) and later publications, in a sense that is close to Firth's original formulation (1957/68:183). See Section 11.5 of Chapter 11 for a full discussion of this term.

Finally, Halliday defines the scale of **delicacy** as "the scale of differentiation, or depth in detail" (1961/76:72). The concept is intended to account for the fact that two descriptions of a piece of text may differ from each other in "depth of detail", depending on how far the analyst wishes to go in describing a text, or how far the fullest available grammatical description allows one to go. When the concept is described in these terms — as it is in "Categories" — it seems to be a reflection of the practical problems of describing languages rather than a matter of theory. In "Categories" the concept is applied very widely, i.e., (1) to 'classes' of 'units', in order to set up 'primary' and 'secondary classes', etc.; (2) to 'structures' to provide for 'primary' and 'secondary' structures; and (3) to 'systems' to set up systems whose entry condition is a feature in another system. Indeed, it was the combination of the concepts of 'system' and 'delicacy' that was to lead in due course to the concept that a whole language can be represented in one large **system network**. (For a system network for a small part of one unit, the nominal group, see Figure 1 in Appendix A.) We shall encounter the concept of 'primary' and 'secondary' structures again in Chapter 7, since it is used in the analysis of texts in *IFG*.

In later years the concept of 'delicacy' came to be associated primarily with the concept of 'system', and so to find its true place in the theory. For example, Berry, in her standard introduction to systemic linguistics, introduces the concept of 'delicacy' by explaining that as we traverse a system network we are "making finer and finer distinctions in meaning; that is, we [are] gradually making more *delicate* distinctions in meaning. [...] This scale is called the scale of delicacy" (Berry 1975:177). This concept is illustrated in the little system network in Figure 1 of Appendix A. There, the feature [count] in the system of [mass] vs. [count] is the entry condition to the system of [singular] vs. plural], so that the second system is dependent on, and so more delicate than, the first.[7]

While Halliday continues to use the derived concept of 'secondary structures' in *IFG* (as we shall see in Section 10.3.4 of Chapter 10), he took the innovatory step in "Categories" of interpreting 'secondary classes' as 'systems' (1961/76:67) — and so of relating the two paradigmatic concepts of 'class' and 'system' on the scale of delicacy. Thus, the elevation of the concept of 'system' to the level of 'meaning' (which we shall discuss in Section 4.3 of Chapter 4) also implies the elevation of the concept of 'class'.

However, the concept of 'delicacy' in the system network was to lead in turn to another of Halliday's great insights — and so in turn to the rejection of what we may call the 'two books' model of language. This is the view of a language in which it is seen as being modelled by the equivalent of a 'grammar book' and a 'dictionary'. Unlike the important innovations to be introduced in Chapter 4, this concept is already stated clearly in "Categories" (1961/76:69). Here Halliday wrote, with great foresight, of "the grammarian's dream" of extending the systems by which we handle **grammar** so that they cover **lexis** as well. The crucial point is, as he said there, that "the theoretical status of the move from grammar to lexis is [...] not a feature of rank but one of delicacy." He then went on to express the hope that one day we would be able to show "that lexis can be defined as 'most delicate grammar'." How does that hope stand today? The fact is that Halliday's early hypothesis has now been developed and tested by a number of other SF linguists (especially by those working in the framework of the Cardiff Grammar). Such system networks show both (1) the relationships to each other of the meanings of lexical items (i.e., of 'word senses'), and (2) their relationships to the choices in the syntactically-realized part of the grammar to which they are related. See, for example, Fawcett (1987), (1980:151-4 and 217-20), (1994b) and (1997),

---

7. In creating and interpeting system networks, the concept of 'dependency' is in fact more fundamental than 'delicacy', as I have shown in Fawcett (1988b). It is quite widely assumed that systems that are realized in lexis are inherently more 'delicate' than systems that are realized in syntax, and that syntactically-realized systems are therefore never dependent on lexically-realized systems. But see Fawcett (1996) for a demonstration that this assumption is wrong in relation to certain classes of lexical verb, and Tucker (1998) for a similar demonstration in relation to certain adjectives and manner adverbs.

Hasan (1987) and especially Tucker (1996a and b), (1997) and (1998). Thus we can now claim to have demonstrated that the "grammarian's dream" of "lexis as most delicate grammar" can indeed be made a reality. In a modern SF grammar, then, what is being modelled is not just the **grammar** of a language, but what Halliday has aptly termed the **lexicogrammar**.

## 2.5 The rarity of structural representations in "Categories" terms

Reading "Categories" is demanding work, and the reader's task is not eased by the fact that only rarely does Halliday illustrate the abstract concepts that he is presenting with examples. Ironically, by far the fullest exemplification of the concepts comes in the 'grammar' of meals (viewed as another social construct) that is presented in Section 9! There are occasional indications as to what the elements of the units of the clause in English would be like (e.g., in Section 4.3), but there is no attempt to provide a full set of descriptive categories for any aspect of the grammar of English or any other language, other than the list of units on the 'rank scale' of English. For example, there is no indication of what Halliday considered at the time to be the full set of classes of group.

Perhaps the most surprising omission is that there is no visual representation of the full structure of a clause-length text that has been analyzed in terms of the categories proposed in this key paper. One direct result of this is that there is no indication as to how the various units in a the description of a clause are to be related to each other in an integrated representation of structure.

One possible reason for the lack of specificity in "Categories" may be that Halliday wished to avoid using tree diagram representations, since these might be read as implying inappropriate parallels with Chomsky's "phrase structure" approach to analyzing syntax. By the mid-1960s, however, Halliday's colleagues Huddleston and Hudson were publishing representations based on the Scale and Category framework described in "Categories", and Figure 1 illustrates this type of representation of a text-sentence.[8]

---

8. The term "sentence' is normally used in this book with the same meaning as "text-sentence", but I shall use the fuller term every now and then in order to make the point that a 'sentence' is, from the viewpoint taken here and described in Chapter 3, a 'text with the structure of a sentence'. The quite limited role of the concept of 'sentence' in the present theory of syntax will be explained in Section 9.2.1 of Chapter 9.

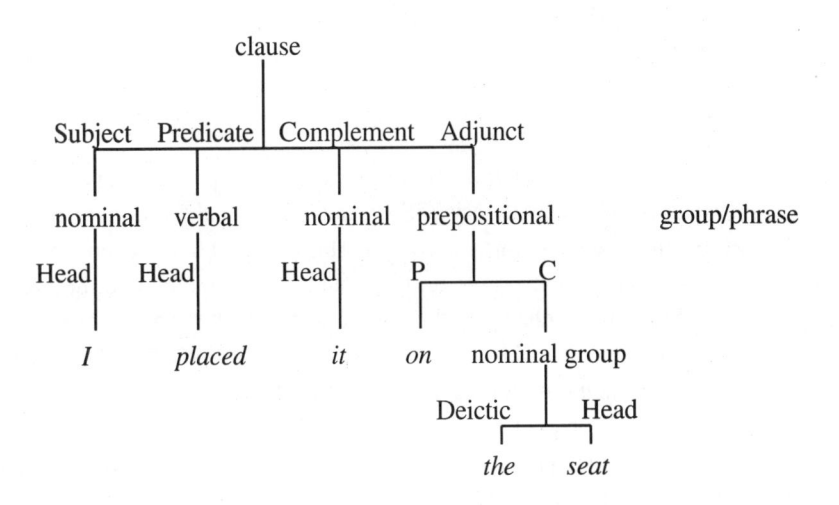

```
                        clause
                          |
    Subject   Predicate | Complement   Adjunct
       |         |            |           |
     nominal   verbal       nominal    prepositional              group/phrase
       |         |            |         |      |
      Head     Head         Head       P       C
                                       |       |
       I      placed         it       on    nominal group
                                           |           |
                                        Deictic       Head
                                           |           |
                                          the         seat
```

*Figure 1: The representation of a clause in the "Categories" style*
*(from Huddleston 1965/81:45)*[9]

This particular example is taken from the section on "Notational conventions" at the start of Halliday & Martin's *Readings in Systemic Linguistics* (1981:12). Interestingly, it is adapted from one of the only two 1960s papers in that volume that actually illustrate their points with examples of the analysis of sentences (Huddleston 1965/81:45) — the other being Hudson (1967/81).

If you look at the two collections of papers that chart the development of SFL to 1980 (Halliday 1976, and Halliday & Martin 1981), you will find that the illustrative analysis of a text-sentence continues to be a rarity well into the 1970s. Hudson (1971) is an honourable exception. Even in introductory textbooks such as Berry (1975), there are relatively few examples of what the analysis of a text should be like. It was only with the eventual publication of the first edition of *IFG* in 1985 that large numbers of examples of analyses in SF terms became generally available. By then, however, Halliday had introduced a completely different type of representation, as we shall see in Chapter 7.

Even so, *IFG* has the same lack of integrated representations of structure as "Categories", i.e., representations that shows how the analysis of, let us say, a nominal group fits into the analysis of a clause.

---

9. Here the letter "P" stands for "Preposition" (or 'little predicator') and "C" for "Prepositional Complement" (or "little complement"), as is explained in Halliday (1965/81:39).

## 2.6 Some later additions to the S&C model: 'parataxis' and 'hypotaxis', 'depth' and 'type'

### 2.6.1 'Parataxis' and 'hypotaxis'

In the next chapter we shall meet the set of ideas that were to change the S&C framework into the new theory of Systemic Functional Grammar. But in the early sixties there was important work by Halliday and his new colleagues Huddleston and Hudson that significantly refined and supplemented the S&C framework — but without changing the overall shape of the theory. Indeed, a series of introductory textbooks continued to present the S&C view of syntax well into the 1970s, including Strang 1962/68), Leech (1966), Scott, Bowley *et al.* (1968), Turner & Mohan (1970), Sinclair (1972), Muir (1972), Benson and Greaves (1973) and Berry (1975 & 1977). This was in spite of the alternative, 'multiple structure' approach to representing structure that Halliday was already developing, as described in Halliday (1969/81), Halliday 1971/73a), etc.[10]

Here I shall foreground four concepts that were proposed in this period as additions to the "Categories" framework, each of which is of interest to us in the task of constructing a modern theory of SF syntax.

The first two concepts are a pair of ideas that have come to play a major role in Halliday's later model of grammar — and especially in the framework that he uses for analyzing text-sentences in *IFG*. These are **'parataxis'** and **'hypotaxis'**.

In what follows, I shall use 'scare quotes' around these terms as a sign that they — or rather one of them, i.e., 'hypotaxis' — will have no role to play in the framework presented here. However, since the two terms are so closely bound up together in Halliday's theory, it will be safer to avoid 'parataxis' too. The types of relationship between units that 'parataxis' provides for are essentially the same as those covered by **co-ordination**, in a broad sense of the term that includes 'asyndetic co-ordination' (as described in Quirk *et al.* 1985:918) as well as co-ordination with overt markers such as *and*. I shall therefore normally use the term "co-ordination" rather that "parataxis".

Halliday's first distinction is in fact between two broad types of structure that he calls "univariate" and "multivariate" structures. A "multivariate" struct-

---

10. Benson and Greaves (1973) acknowledge their debt to Michael Gregory's *English Patterns*, an excellent Scale and Category Grammar of English that was widely circulated in photocopied form but which unfortunately never reached full publication.

ure is simply a unit that is composed of one or more of a set of different elements of structure, such as a clause or a nominal group, essentially as distinguished in "Categories" and as recognized here. The term "multi-" is intended to mark the fact that the sister "variables" (as Halliday calls the 'elements', in what seems an unnecessarily abstract terminology) are different from each other. So for our present purposes we can set the concept of 'multivariate structure' on one side, since it does not introduce a new concept to the theory.

It is within the category of 'univariate' structures that a new pair of concepts are to be found. The question is whether their introduction leads to better descriptions of languages, or whether they cause difficulties. I shall argue that one of them — the concept of 'hypotaxis' — is a source of problems in three ways. Firstly, it is not in fact as easy as one at first thinks to work out what it actually means in structural terms to say that one unit is hypotactically related to another. Secondly, Halliday has given it great prominence in his theory, and this prominence has been at the expense of another concept — that of 'embedding'. The concept of embedding is of course tied to the general concept of 'constituency', but it is not necessarily linked to formal grammars, and its use in SFL leads to the insightful analysis of long and complex texts. The third problem with 'hypotaxis' is related to this: in practical terms, it has often led to analyses of text-sentences that are plainly counter-intuitive (e.g. treating *He said* as a clause in *He said that he would be there*).

A 'univariate' structure, then, is said to be a 'structure' that is composed of two or more categories that are the same. More specifically, the 'taxis' is between two or more **classes of unit** — predominantly between clauses, but also between groups, words and even morphemes. As we shall see when we meet the concept of 'co-ordination' in Section 11.8.2 of Chapter 11, the Cardiff Grammar models a 'paratactic' relationship between two or more units, as in *cats, dogs and horses*, as three co-ordinated **units** that jointly **fill** an **element of structure** in a higher unit in the tree. There are a number of problems to consider in relation to co-ordination, but we shall delay the discussion of these to Section 11.8.2 of Chapter 11. We can therefore set aside the concept of 'parataxis' (as we have already done with 'multivariate' structures).

This leaves just the concept of 'hypotaxis'. Halliday describes 'hypotaxis' as "a chain of dependencies [between units]" (Halliday 1965/81:34). In Halliday's example *I'd have come if you'd telephoned before I left*, the clause *before I left* is said to be 'dependent on' *if you'd telephoned* — but not to be embedded within it and so not to fill one of its elements. And the clause *if you'd telephoned* is similarly said to be 'dependent on' *I'd have come* without being embedded in it as an element. This concept of 'dependence without embedding' is shown by the use of letters from the Greek alphabet, i.e., "α β γ" etc. to represent the 'elements' of such structures. In Halliday (1965/81:35) the illustrative diagrams take the form shown in Figure 2. This shows the influence of the traditional 'tree diagram' representations of structure that were used in S&C Grammar in the 1960s, as in Figure 1.

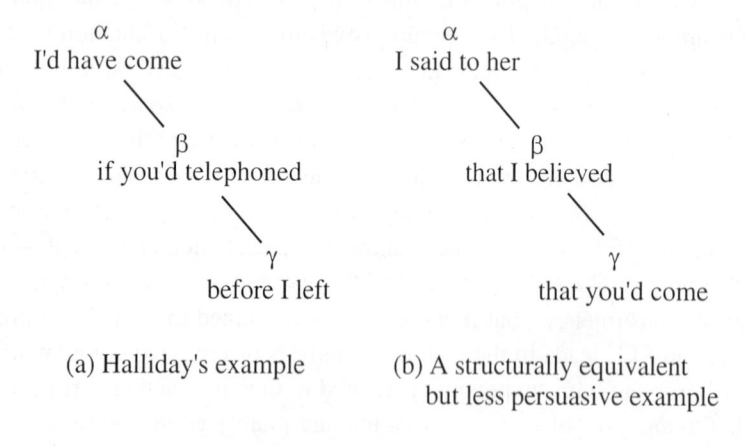

α
I'd have come
　＼
　　β
　if you'd telephoned
　　　＼
　　　　γ
　　before I left

(a) Halliday's example

α
I said to her
　＼
　　β
　that I believed
　　　＼
　　　　γ
　　that you'd come

(b) A structurally equivalent but less persuasive example

*Figure 2: The representation of 'hypotaxis' in Halliday (1965/81)*

In *IFG*, however (e.g., pp. 375-81) Halliday shows the relationship of 'hypotaxis' as a set of horizontally linked boxes below the text, each labelled "α β γ" etc., exactly as in the 'box diagram' representations of structure in Figure 7 in Chapter 7. In these diagrams the relationship looks like sister constituency, the only remaining expression of 'dependence' being the Greek letters.

Halliday's claim is that the introduction of the 'hypotactic' relationship avoids what he describes, revealingly, as "a somewhat artificial increase in 'depth' in number of layers [in the tree structure]" (Halliday 1965/81). Indeed, it seems that the desire to avoid the embedding of units within units of the same or a lower 'rank' (i.e., 'rank shift') was the major motivation in the rapid extension of the use of 'hypotactic' relations to analyze a wide range of phenomena in the structure of language (as is shown in Section 4 of Appendix C).

In my view, however, examples of 'hypotaxis' such as those in Figure 2 are more insightfully analyzed as cases of embedding, where a unit fills an element of the unit above. Indeed, in using Example (a) in Figure 2 to illustrate the concept of 'hypotaxis' Halliday has chosen the most favourable type of example. It is one in which it is possible to interpret the 'main' clause in each 'hypotactically' related pair as a complete clause. And it is this that enables one to think first of each such pair as two separate clauses, and then to go on to ask how they are related to each other. However, Halliday also treats clauses that report speech or thought in the same way, and his analysis of Example (b) in Figure 1 would be as shown there. And here the line of reasoning used to justify the hypotactic analysis of Example (a) is simply not possible. In other words, *I said to her* is clearly an uncompleted clause that is "expecting" (to borrow Firth's metaphor) another element (which we may call a Complement). And *that I believed* similarly expects a Complement. In the Cardiff Grammar — as in virtually all grammars other than Halliday's — these would be treated as cases of embedded clauses that fill an element of a higher clause. Figure 25 in Chapter 12 shows a full analysis of an example similar to (b) above, and there is a short further discussion of such cases. See Fawcett (1996) for how to handle 'complementation' of the type found in Example (b) in a SF generative grammar, and Section 11.9 of Chapter 11 for a summary of how the Cardiff Grammar handles the full range of 'hypotactic' relations between clauses.

In the light of the discussion of Example (b), we can see that the difference between Examples (a) and (b) is the difference between a Complement and an Adjunct. To put it in explicitly SF terms, it is the difference between a Participant Role (a role that is 'expected' by the Process expressed in the Main Verb), and a Circumstance (a role that is not). In Example (a), therefore, the Cardiff Gram-mar would model *before I left* as a clause that fills an Adjunct in the clause *if you'd telephoned before I left*, and this longer clause would be shown as filling an Adjunct in the clause *I'd have come if you'd telephoned before I left*.

In pages 35-39 of Halliday (1965/81), Halliday discusses the complexities of alternative interpretations of Example (a) and similar examples, with the intention of showing that 'hypotaxis' represents the structural relationships more clearly than an analysis with embedding would. However, that discussion does not throw up any problems that are not equally well represented in the framework proposed in Part 2. Indeed, in many cases such relations are better represented by embedding. Thus the analysis of *If you'd telephoned before I left, I'd have come* would simply show *if you'd telephoned before I left* as a thematized Adjunct. And examples such as *If before I left you'd telephoned,*

*I'd have come* can be handled equally straightforwardly (though they would cause discontinuity in Halliday's model). See Section 11.9 of Chapter 11 for my analyses of the set of examples for which Halliday uses 'hypotaxis', and see Fawcett (in press) for the full presentation of this alternative approach.[11]

There is a further problem about the proposed relationship of 'hypotaxis'. This is the question of what it actually means to say that the relationship is one of 'dependency without embedding'. The answer lies in Halliday's use of the terms 'modifier' and 'head' (*IFG* p. 217) to describe the relationship. Essentially, the relationship of 'hypotaxis' is the same the traditional 'modifier-head' relationship in a unit. The only differences are that Halliday narrows the definition, such that (1) each element must be filled by the same unit, and (2) the relationship between each element and the sister elements on either side of it is always the same. (And neither of these is the case, it can be argued, for the relationships between the modifiers and the head in the English nominal group, for which see Section 10.2.5 of Chapter 10.) Thus, despite this narrowing of the definition, 'hypotaxis' is still a relationship between sister elements — and this, you will recall, is essentially what a 'multivariate' structure is. So the distinction between 'multivariate' and 'univariate' structures is not in fact very clear.

Another approach to the problem to ask how the concept would be formalized for implementation in the computer. It was Matthiessen who, with Mann and others, implemented Halliday's grammar in the Penman Project, and he has stated (personal communication) that hypotactic relations such as those exemplified above are handled in Penman essentially as if they were embedded units. And this, as will be clear, is precisely how they are handled in the Cardiff Grammar, and in the theoretical framework described in Part 2.

### 2.6.2 'Depth' in layers of structure

A second important concept from the 1960s is that of the **depth** of the **layering** in the tree diagram representation of a text-sentence. The concept of

---

11. For a demonstration that the concept of the 'hypotactic verbal group complex' is not needed, and for an account of how the Cardiff Grammar provides for the phenomena for which Halliday sets up the concept of the 'verbal group complex', see Fawcett (forthcoming c). That paper also shows why the concept of a 'paratactic verbal group complex' is not needed, as well as showing, incidentally, how most types of text-sentence that Halliday would analyze as showing 'hypotactic' relations between clauses can be handled elegantly as embedded clauses.

'depth' is introduced and discussed in Huddleston (1965/81). This enables us to say that a particular unit is at a depth of three (or whatever) below the topmost clause in a structure. However the concept of 'depth' is ultimately **not** a part of the theory. Instead, it is a valuable metric (among other such metrics) for establishing and comparing the structural complexity of texts. (See Section 11.8.4 of Chapter 11 for some further remarks on the depth of layering in a structure, from the viewpoint of cognitive processing.)

2.6.3 The concept of 'type' of unit

Finally, we should note that Halliday introduced the concept of 'type' of unit in Halliday (1963/76). He introduced this as a complementary concept to 'class of unit' — such that the 'class' of a unit was said to be determined by its potential for operation at given elements in the unit next above it on the 'rank scale', and the 'type' of a unit was said to be determined by its internal structure. Berry (1975:76-7) explains the term and the concept, but it never came into general use. When we consider the change in meaning that the term "class of unit" has undergone in Section 10.2 of Chapter 10, we shall see that the significance of 'type' was that the concept that it expresses has become one of the key concepts in a modern theory of SF syntax — though still, it seems, not for Halliday. Instead, he continues to use the concept of 'class of unit' in *IFG* in its original "Categories" sense, and he makes no use at all of 'type'.

## 2.7 Forward from the Scale and Category model

We can summarize this chapter by saying that the set of four categories and the three scales described above defines Halliday's theory of grammar as it was in 1961, but that the theory was supplemented by the concepts summarized in Section 2.6 in the early and middle 1960s. Further excellent summaries and discussions can be found in Kress (1976), Martin (1981), Steiner (1983, in German) and, for a particularly full account, Butler (1985).

However, between 1961 and the present there have been significant changes in most of these concepts. When we consider the nature of these changes in the next few chapters, we shall find that some of them are changes in the extent to which the concept remains central within the theory, and some are changes in the term's meaning — and sometimes, of course, there are changes in both. Moreover, while some of these changes are recognized overtly in Halliday's own writings, they typically are not. In Chapter 12 we shall examine the question of just how great these changes have been, and so also the question of what relevance the 1961 categories and scales have today. Surprisingly, perhaps, we shall find that the concepts of "Categories" appear to be more relevant to the theory of syntax found in the Cardiff Grammar than they are to Halliday's presentations of his own version of SF grammar.

In the next chapter we shall jump in time from 1961 to the present, in order to ask "What are the major components of a modern SF grammar, and how do they relate to each other?" We need the answer to this question in order to provide the setting in which a modern systemic functional theory of syntax operates. While there are important differences between the Sydney and the Cardiff Grammars, we shall find that the overall model to be presented here is at a sufficiently general level of abstraction to be able to encompass them both. It can therefore provide a framework within which it is possible to make useful comparisons between the Sydney Grammar and the Cardiff Grammar.

Then in the following chapter — Chapter 4 — I shall summarize the changes which brought this new model into being.

# 3
# The place of syntax in a modern Systemic Functional Grammar

## 3.1 'Form' and 'meaning'

What are the major components of a modern SF grammar? A good way to approach the answer to this question is to consider three pairs of concepts that were introduced to modern linguistics by Saussure). Saussure's ideas have influenced most theories of language developed in the twentieth century, though this is not always overtly acknowledged by their progenitors. His influence on the set of concepts to be presented here will quickly become obvious. (For a full discussion of the relevance of Saussure's concepts to the present model see Fawcett 1983, and for a somewhat different SF viewpoint see Thibault 1997).

Saussure's central concept is the 'linguistic sign'. As is well known, he emphasizes that a 'sign' consists of a 'signifier' and a 'signified', and we shall interpret this as saying that a sign has both a **form** and a **meaning**. And to this we can add the important concept — which is long familiar to functionally oriented linguists — that form and meaning are mutually defining.[1]

Consider, as an analogy, the type of simple traffic control system that has just two 'forms' of display — a red disk and a green disk. It also has just two 'meanings' — which are, in crude terms, 'stop' and 'go'. A human language is of course very much more complex than this in both its forms and its meanings — and indeed in the relationships between the two. But it is nonetheless helpful to recognize that the two primary levels of a language — as in any semiotic system — are those of meaning and form.[2]

---

1. This book assumes that the reader is likely to be sympathetic to a broadly functional approach to the problem of how best to understand the nature of language. Clearly, formal grammarians who work in the 'autonomous syntax' approach would not accept this concept quite as wholeheartedly as most functional grammarians would.

2. Here I am inviting you to adopt a position that involves a fundamental rethinking of the traditional view of levels of language that is found in most of the standard introductions to linguistics, i.e., the view that the two primary levels of language are (1) the layer at which

The concept of a language as a 'sign system' summarizes neatly the vital point that we should not expect to be able to understand the forms of a language without considering at the same time the meanings of the language — and vice versa.

It follows from this that, if our goal is to model language, we need to model a very large **set** of linguistic signs. In other words, just as an individual **sign** (such as a red 'stop') sign has both a form and a meaning, so too a **sign system** such as a natural human language has the two levels of form and meaning. Figure 3 can therefore be seen as a very simple model of **a language as a whole**.

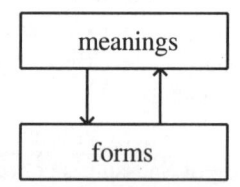

```
        ┌──────────┐
        │ meanings │
        └──────────┘
           ↓    ↑
        ┌──────────┐
        │  forms   │
        └──────────┘
```

*Figure 3: A simplified model of any sign system*

The two levels of 'meanings' and 'forms' in Figure 3 are linked by two arrows. These indicate that a sign system is not a static object, but a device for turning meanings into forms, and forms into meanings. I have argued that a language is best thought of as a 'procedure' (Fawcett 1980:54f.) or, in computing terms, as a 'program' (Fawcett 1993).

The relationship between the set of meanings and the set of forms is one of **realization**. Thus the arrow pointing downwards shows that the meanings of a language are 'realized by' linguistic forms, and the arrow pointing upwards shows that forms 'realize' meanings.

However, contrary to what some formal language theorists think, the two processes are not the reverses of each other. This is because the problems faced by someone who is trying to produce a text that will be effective and appropriate to a particular point in discourse are not the same as the problems that face

---

we find **phonemes** and the structures into which they can combine, and (2) the layer at which we find **morphemes** and the structures into which they can be built. In the current model, however, 'segmental phonology' is regarded as being **the internal specification of items**, i.e., as a phenomenon that occurs **within the level of form** (rather than being a 'realization' of (part of) it). See (Fawcett 1980:59) for a fuller statement of this position.

someone who is trying to work out the meaning of an incoming text. (It is only in a very impoverished, form-based view of language that grammars may appear to be 'reversible'.) This principle applies both to abstract psychological models of how humans process incoming and outgoing language texts and to computer models of language processing ( 1993 and 1994a, Weerasinghe & Fawcett 1993). Thus, while the fuller model of language that we shall develop in the next two sections may appear to be oriented more to the 'production' of text than to analyzing it, the term "realization" is in fact directionally neutral.

It is also too general to be useful, so that we need to build a picture of the steps by which this model turns 'meanings' into 'forms'. For this we need to move on to a second pair of concepts.[3]

## 3.2 'Language' and 'text' as 'potential' and 'instance'

In extending the concept of a 'sign' to that of a 'sign system', I have in fact already introduced this second vital pair of concepts (for which Saussure's nearest equivalents are "langue" and "parole"). This is the distinction between a language taken as a whole (i.e., a **language** as a resource for communicating meanings to our fellow human beings) and a **text** (i.e., an 'output' from the language when it is used on a given occasion). Thus a text is defined here as 'an instance of language in use', and texts may of course be spoken or written. A 'text-sentence' is therefore a text whose internal structure is that of a sentence.

---

3.  Halliday often writes in a way that implies that the reason why human languages are more complex than many other semiotic systems is that grammar 'intervenes' between meanings and phonological and graphological forms (e.g., Halliday 1996:29), whereas it does not in simpler systems (such as a traffic light system). One difficulty about this view is that he also sees the grammar as having its own 'meaning potential' inside it, and this gives us a model in which the 'meanings' of the higher semantic level are detached, as it were, from their realizations in forms, such that they have to be mapped first onto the meanings within the grammar (or 'lexicogrammar', as Halliday prefers to call it). I take a different view, as this book shows, in that I regard the level of meanings within the 'lexicogrammar' as the key level of linguistically-realized meaning, such that it is realized in any one of (1) syntax, (2) intonation or punctuation (depending on the medium of discourse) and (3) items. (Notice that it is only one of these, namely items, to which the supposed 'third level' of segmental phonology/graphology is relevant, and this fact raises serious questions about its traditional status as a 'level of language'.) In my approach, therefore, any 'higher' meaning — such as those that Halliday includes under the umbrella concept of 'grammatical metaphor' — is to be accounted for by one or other of several different concepts. See Fawcett (1993) for a brief indication of some of these, and Fawcett & Huang (in preparation) for a much fuller picture. Many of the concepts introduced in this footnote will be amplified in later parts of this book.

(The question of what may occur inside a 'sentence' is taken up in Part 2.)

In systemic functional linguistics this distinction between a language and a text is also described in terms of a more abstract pair of concepts. These are language as **potential** and language as **instance**, where an 'instance' is the part of the potential that is currently activated. The relationship between 'the potential' and an 'instance' of that 'potential' is one of **instantiation**.[4]

To the concepts of 'meaning' and 'form', then, we can now add 'potential' and 'instance'. It is only when we combine these two dimensions of contrast that we have an adequate framework for thinking about the nature of language — and any other semiotic system.

The diagram in Figure 4 brings together these two pairs of concepts to define the four components that are essential for modelling any semiotic system. It provides a framework for thinking about language in terms of (1) the potential and (2) the many possible instances of that potential, and to do so at the two levels of (a) meaning and (b) form. The four components of the model are defined by the intersections of these two pairs of concepts.

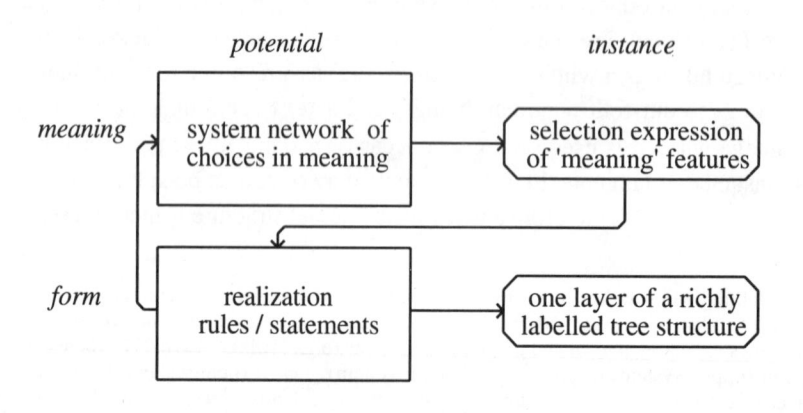

|  | *potential* | *instance* |
|---|---|---|
| *meaning* | system network of choices in meaning | selection expression of 'meaning' features |
| *form* | realization rules / statements | one layer of a richly labelled tree structure |

*Figure 4: The main components of a systemic functional grammar*

---

4. In the past SF linguists have usually referred to instances as "instantiations". But since we need the term "instantiation" to refer to the relationship between the 'potential' and the 'instances' that it generates, as here, it is preferable to use a different term for the 'product' of the 'process' of instantiation. Hence my introduction here of the term "instance". Note that some SF linguists (e.g., Matthiessen & Bateman 1991) have used the term "actualization" in place of "instantiation". One reason for preferring "instantiation'" to "actualization" is the fact that English has the corresponding noun "instance", which can be used to distinguish the 'product' from the 'process'. It is this pair of terms, then, that is used in the present theory.

At this point I should clarify the sense in which I am using the terms "grammar" and "meaning". Let us take "grammar" first, since it is used in the caption for Figure 4. In "Categories", "grammar" was the name of a sub-component of the level of form, but here its meaning has been extended in two ways. The most obvious is that a grammar now includes a level of **meaning** as well as a level of **form**. Thus a 'grammar' is essentially a model of the sentence-generating component of a full model of language and its use. The second extension — which is less obvious — is that the term "grammar" is regularly used as a short form for "lexicogrammar". Strictly speaking, the term "lexicogrammar" is preferable as the name for the resulting component of language, because the concept of the system — and so the concept of the system network — has now been extended to cover meanings realized in lexis as well as meanings realized in syntax and in grammatical items (as we saw in Section 2.4 of Chapter 2). So in what follows the term "grammar" is typically to be understood as a short form for "lexicogrammar" (as in most current SFL writings).[5]

However, there is a problem about using the term "lexicogrammar" (or indeed "grammar") in a sense that includes the level of meaning. The problem is that Halliday has explored two different positions on the issue of what we might call 'levels of meaning', and when he uses the term "lexicogrammar" it is typically in a sense where it is equated with the level of form, such that this is in a relationship of realization to the level of "semantics". (See Sections 4.6 to 4.9 of Chapter 4 for a full account of Halliday's two positions, and for the reasons why I think that his first position is greatly preferable.) In using the term "lexicogrammar' here, then, I am starting from the concept that a grammar is a 'model of language' (which is not the way that Halliday uses the term 'grammar") and I am then incorporating into it, by prefixing it with "lexico", Halliday's important point that 'lexis' must be integrated with 'syntax' (or 'grammar') in any such model. But I have to point out that this is a hybrid term that does not correspond to Halliday's normal use of the term "lexicogrammar' — and, having made the point that the model must include lexis (and indeed intonation and punctuation), I shall normally use the shorter term "grammar" in the rest of the book, when referring to the concept of a model of the sentence-

---

5. The point in Halliday's developing model of language that corresponds most closely to the model represented in Figure 4 is that represented in Halliday (1970/76b) and Halliday 1977/78), which were probably written at about the same time. See Section 4.9 of Chapter 4 for a summary of the implications of these two important papers.

generating component of language.

Now let us consider the term "meaning', as used in Figure 4. Throughout this chapter I have been careful to use to use the term "meaning" rather than "semantics" — even though I have happily used it elsewhere as the label for this level of language. Many systemic functional linguists (including Halliday in most of his writings) are understandably reluctant to use the term "semantics", because of the conceptual baggage that it brings with it from other disciplines and, within linguistics, from other theories of language. The types of 'meaning' that are covered in SFL by the system networks of TRANSITIVITY, MOOD, THEME and so one are much more comprehensive than the sense in which the term "semantics' is used by many linguists and philosophers. Nonetheless Halliday has till fairly recently allowed himself to use "semantic" (as a modifier) to refer to phenomena at this level of 'meaning'. And some systemic functional linguists — including Halliday himself in his important paper "Text as semantic choice in social contexts" (1977/78) and myself — have regularly used the term "semantics" in the systemic functional sense of 'meaning potential'. We have done so because it is one way of expressing the theory's important claim that all of the different types of meaning covered by the system networks have to be included in any adequate theory of 'meaning', if only because the various sub-networks of TRANSITIVITY, MOOD, THEME and the others are partially interdependent on each other. SFL offers a particularly rich and powerful way to model the level of 'meaning' in language, and I have always felt it right to refer to this level of language by the term "semantics". Thus, in Figure 4, I would be happy to replace "choice between meanings" by "semantic choices" and "meaning' features" by "semantic features".[6]

Let us now consider each of the four parts of the diagram in Figure 4, and their specific relationships to each other. (The two components of language are shown as a box with right-angled corners, and the outputs from those components are shown in a smaller box with cut-off corners.)

First, our model of language has, at the level of meaning, a component that specifies the **meaning potential** of the language — as Halliday has aptly named it (e.g., Halliday 1970:142). This is the core of a systemic functional

---

6. When Halliday was writing the 1985 edition of *IFG*, he would probably have been reasonably happy with my use here of the term "semantic features". By the 1994 edition, however, he had changed his position on when it is and is not appropriate to use the terms **semantics** and **semantic**, changing the wording at some points in the second edition to reflect this.

grammar, and it consists of a vast **system network** of choices between meanings. In other words, the system networks model the language's **potential** at the level of **meaning**. Figure 1 in Appendix A introduces a simple system network for 'things', thus exemplifying the standard way of representing a system network in diagram form.

Since there is a **potential** at the level of meaning, we should logically expect that there will also be **instances** at this level — and indeed there are. On each traversal of a system network, a set of semantic features is colleced, and the grammar then makes a copy of these, which is called a **selection expression**. There are two reasons for collecting the features as a set. The first is that they constitute the systemic description — and so, I would argue, the semantic description — of that unit in the text-sentence that is generated. The second is that the realization rules (to which we shall come in a moment) need to be able to refer to the whole set of the selected features, because many of the rules require two or more features to have been co-selected in order to 'fire', i.e., to be triggered into operation. In Figure 4, then, the two top boxes show (1) that the meaning potential is a system network of choices in meaning (i.e., 'semantic features', in my view) and (2) that an instance of that potential consists of the set of features that have been (or might be) selected on any given traversal of the network. Since the topic of this book is syntax rather than semantics, I shall say no more about these. However, the little grammar in Appendix A gives you a clear introductory picture of what a system network is and how it operates. It can be used to generate a variety of selection expressions, and then to use the 'realization rules' to build a structure.

We turn now to the level of **form** — and it is at this level that we require a theory of syntax. The term "form" is used here in a wider sense than that in "Categories" (or indeed any of Halliday's later writings) because it includes, as well as **syntax** and grammatical and lexical **items**, components for **intonation** or **punctuation** (depending on whether the medium is speech or writing). This is an approach to the concept of 'form' that looks at language 'from above', i.e., intonation and punctuation are here considered to be types of 'form' because, like syntax and items, they directly realize meanings.[7]

---

7. There is a difference from Halliday's model in the way in which the term "form" is being used here. He uses "form" in a sense that includes (1) grammatical structures and items and (2) lexical items, but not intonation or punctuation. However, the Cardiff model of language integrates intonation and punctuation with syntax and lexis as the co-realizations of the meaning potential of the language, so that these too are regarded as types of 'form'. The effect

Figure 4 shows that at this level too — as we would logically expect — there is both a potential and an instance. The two levels of form and meaning are connected to each other, in a generative model of language, through the fact that the **output** from the level of meaning is the **input** to the level of form — more precisely, to the **form potential**. The form potential of a language consists principally of the **realization rules** (or, as Halliday calls them, 'realization statements').[8]

The key point is that, just as it is the activation of parts of the system network that specifies the output at the level of meaning (i.e., the selection expression), it is the activation of some of the realization rules that specify the structural outputs from the grammar. It is the realization rules — together with the 'potential structures', a concept that we shall meet in Section 9.9.2 of Chapter 9 — that specify the structures, and that therefore constitute the 'form

---

is that **intonation** is not treated as 'below' the level of syntax and items, but as **a parallel form of realization**. The Cardiff Grammar recognizes that it is only **items** that require expression in **segmental phonology** (which includes inherent word stress). One effect of this is that the two major aspects of phonology — intonation and segmental phonology — are treated as two separate components. They may look like one component when you view language 'from below', but if you look at intonation and segmental phonology 'from above', i.e., from the viewpoint of the meaning potential of the system networks, and if you then ask how meanings are realized in language, it becomes clear that the two are very different from each other: intonation realizing meanings directly, while segmental phonology does not. In the COMMUNAL Project we have implemented in the computer a lightly adapted version of Tench's development of Halliday's approach to intonation (e.g., Tench 1990, 1996). Tench's work stands in relation to Halliday's very much as does Tucker's and my work on grammar and lexis. In the implemented computer model, then, intonation and punctuation are alternative 'forms' of language — alongside syntax and items. For a fairly full description of this approach to intonation and of how this integration is achieved, see Fawcett (1990), and for an illustration of it in the generation of a sentence see Fawcett, Tucker & Lin (1993).

8. At various points in his writings, Halliday contrasts the systemic functional view of 'language as a resource' with the Chomskyan view of 'language as a set of rules'. Hence his strong preference for the term "realization statement" over "realization rule". Like many other systemic functional linguists, however, I take the view that, in defining the 'resource', we necessarily use a type of 'rule'. Thus a system network is itself a set of 'rules' about what features may be chosen under what conditions. This was first demonstrated in a fully explicit manner in the appendices to Hudson (1976), and similar 'rules' are found in the representation of the system network in a computer implementation in Prolog (as described in Fawcett, Tucker & Lin 1993). And realization statements are even more obviously a type of 'rule'. In other words, while a systemic functional grammar does not have 'phrase structure rules' and 'transformational rules', it does have other types of rule. In other words, while a systemic functional grammar does not have 'phrase structure rules' and 'transformational rules', it does have other types of rule. Here, then, we shall treat the terms "realization rule" and "realization statement" as interchangeable.

potential' in the grammar. It is the task of Chapters 9, 10 and 11 (which constitute the bulk of Part 2) to specify the concepts that are needed in the two components in Figure 4 that are the 'form potential' and the 'form instance' — i.e., the realization rules and their outputs.

If you wish to observe the realization rules at work in a simple example of the process of generating text, please consult Appendix A. In brief, we can say that the role of the realization rules is to convert the selection expression of semantic features that is generated on a traversal of the network into a layer of the tree diagram representation of the sentence that is being built up. This concept is illustrated in Figure 2 of Appendix A, which has the potential to generate just eighteen different nominal groups.

In a fuller grammar the first unit to be generated would be a clause, and then one or more realization rules would specify re-entry to the system network of meaning potential (as shown by the loop-back arrow on the left side of Figure 4), in order to generate one or more nominal groups (or even an embedded clause) to fill the relevant elements of the clause (as described in Fawcett, Tucker & Lin 1993). The 'tree structures' in the bottom right box in Figure 4 are labelled sufficiently richly to express the various functions that each element serves, and they are, it will be clear, the **instances** at the level of **form**.

The prototypical instance at the level of form is a 'sentence' — and a sentence frequently consists of a single **clause**, e.g., *I've been discussing that new student with Peter.* Since the grammar is part of a fuller model for the generation of texts, we may also refer to the output as a **text-sentence**, and this has the value of reminding us that sentences do not occur singly, as formal linguists sometimes appear to assume, but within longer texts in which they themselves function as elements. (Note, however, that we can also treat a **group** of words such as *that new student* as an instance, exactly as is done in the little grammar in Appendix A.)

At this point I must make it clear that Halliday sometimes writes in a way that implies a substantial change to the model represented in Figure 4, and the effects of this will be explored in Sections 4.6 and 4.7 of Chapter 4. I shall nonetheless argue there that Figure 4 does indeed represent a general model that applies to all systemic functional grammars.

Let us return to Figure 4. Its significance is that it brings together, in a single diagram, two key pairs of concepts that correspond, broadly speaking, to two pairs of Saussurean concepts: **meaning** and **form**, and **potential** and

**instance**. In a systemic functional grammar, meaning and form are related by the general relationship of **realization** but, as we have seen, this relationship does not operate directly. Instead, it operates via the concept of **instantiation**. Instantiation occurs first at the level of 'meaning, when a traversal of the system network generates a selection expression of features, i.e. what Halliday has called an 'act of meaning' (Halliday 1993:4505). Then the realization rules that specify the 'form potential' come into play and act upon the selection expression to realize it, and the final output from the grammar is the generation of a second 'instance', i.e., one unit that adds a layer of structure to the 'tree' representation of a text-sentence that is being built.

Taken together, these concepts model the basic components of a systemic functional grammar, so that Figure 4 represents, at a fairly high level of abstraction, the main components of the model of language within which the alternative current theories of syntax in SFL can be set.

### 3.3 'Paradigmatic' and 'syntagmatic' relations

However, Saussure made a third crucial distinction between two pairs of concepts: that between **paradigmatic** and **syntagmatic** relations in language.[9] This distinction is a particularly important one for systemic functional linguistics, because it introduces the concept that is the most central of all in understanding how Systemic Functional Grammar differs from other functional approaches to language, such as those of Dik (e.g., 1997 a and b), van Valin (e.g., 1993) and Givon (1993a and b).

**Paradigmatic relations** are relations of contrast. There are two key points that must be made about them. Firstly, paradigmatic relations are unlike syntagmatic relations in that they exist only in the **potential** and never in an **instance**. From the viewpoint of the text analyst, they express a contrast between (1) the meaning (and so the form) that was chosen for use in the text and (2) the one or more meanings (and so forms) that might have been chosen (but were not). In other words, paradigmatic relations exist only in the **language** that is used to produce a text-sentence — and not in the sentence itself.

The second key point is that, while it is incontestable that there are rel-

---

9. Saussure himself did not use the term "paradigmatic", but the French equivalent of the term "associative".

ations of contrast at the level of **form**, and while Halliday's concept of 'system' in "Categories" was, like that of Firth, a system of contrasts at the level of form, in a modern SF grammar the system networks model choices between **meanings**. And it is these that are seen as the generative base of the grammar. The result is that the purely formal contrasts in a language play no role in how the grammar operates in the generation of a sentence. See Figure 1 in Appendix A for a simplified system network of some of the choices between meanings that must be made when generating a nominal group. As you will see, the choice between classifying the referent as a 'mass' thing or a 'count' thing is one of the primary systems (in this small simplified grammar), and the choice in the system of 'singular' or 'plural' is dependent on it. Thus **choice between meanings** is the key concept in a systemic functional grammar. However, the focus of this book is on the level of form, so I shall have very little more to say about the system networks.[10]

This book, then, focuses on **syntagmatic relations**. There are in fact two aspects to syntagmatic relations in language: **part-whole relations** and **sequential relations**. The more fundamental concept is that of part-whole relations, and while syntagmatic relations are usually thought of in terms of the level of form, part-whole relations are found at both the level of semantics and at the level of form. But it is the level of **form** that we shall focus on here, i.e., as shown in Figure 4 in Section 3.2.

We can summarize this chapter so far by saying that, in terms of Figure 4, the place of **syntax** in a model of language is in the **syntagmatic** relations at the level of **form**. At various points in the rest of this book, therefore, we shall find ourselves thinking in terms of either (1) **instances of syntax** or (2) the **syntax potential** that specifies those outputs from the grammar.[11]

---

10. If you are not a systemic functional linguist, you may be asking at this point: "Why do systemic functional linguists give priority to paradigmatic relations between meanings rather than forms?" It is a good question, and it may be helpful to say briefly what my answer is. Ultimately, it is because generating a text involves making choices, and it is clearly the contrasts between alternative **meanings** between which we choose — rather than the contrasts between the **forms**. For example, if two outputs from the grammar display a contrast in form, as between *that student* and *those students*, the importance of the contrast is that the two forms express a contrast in meaning which the Performer wishes to communicate to the Addressee. In other words, the difference between 'singular' and 'plural' is ultimately a difference of meaning rather than form. (But there is, of course, no meaning without form.)

11. The other parts of the 'form potential' are the 'lexis potential', the 'intonation potential' and the 'punctuation potential'.

## 3.4 Why a systemic functional theory of syntax is not an 'autonomous' theory of syntax

It will now be clear why an account of a systemic functional theory of syntax is not an 'autonomous' theory of syntax, and why it should not try to be one — even though this is assumed to be desirable in formal theories of language. In such grammars the rules of syntax are held to be independent of the meanings that they express — and this is not, of course, the position taken in systemic functional linguistics. It follows, therefore, that the theoretical framework for syntax to be set out in Chapters 9, 10 and 11 is just one part of a model of language as a whole. It is therefore not its goal to try to provide a full specification of which strings of words are 'grammatical' and which are 'ungrammatical'. In so far as this is a useful goal, it is one that is to be shared among all the components of the grammar, including the system networks themselves. See Section 12.5 of Chapter 12 for a further brief discussion of the concepts of 'grammaticality' and 'probability', in the light of the theory of syntax that is set out in Part 2.

Now that we have established the overall framework within which a modern systemic functional model of syntax must be located, we turn to examine the new ideas of the 1960s which were to turn the Scale and Category Grammar that we met in Chapter 2 into Systemic Functional Grammar — i.e., into a model of language that is essentially the same as the one that I have just outlined here.

# 4
# Halliday's later changes to the Scale and Category model

## 4.1 The status of the changes: addition, evolution or revolution?

In the first half of this chapter I shall briefly chart the three stages by which, in the late 1960s and early 1970s, Halliday transformed Scale and Category Grammar into Systemic Functional Grammar. As we shall see, each of the three is quite closely related to the other two. Then in the second half of the chapter I shall describe how, in the 1970s, Halliday tentatively explored two contrasting approaches to meaning — one of which adds a second level of meaning — and how in the 1990s he finally decided in favour of what we may call the 'two-level model of meaning'. Although I shall not present here the full set of arguments against his decision (which deserve a paper or even a book of their own) I shall show why, even if you accept Halliday's position, it does not seriously affect my claim that the model of language presented in Figure 4 of Chapter 3 is common to all systemic functional grammars.

I have already suggested that the first three changes to the "Categories" model introduced by Halliday in the late 1960s and early 1970s were revolutionary. Interestingly, however, Halliday himself writes about these momentous developments in the theory as if they were, in large measure, simply additions to it — rather than changes that might involve re-assessing the existing concepts. Thus he writes (1993:4507) that "systemic work [...] has tended to expand by moving into new spheres of activity, rather than by re-working earlier positions". The difference between expanding a theory and changing it is an important one. The term "expand" typically implies additions rather than alterations, so that the 'expansion" of a theory does not necessarily require one to rethink the concepts of the earlier version. But any changes to the existing concepts in a theory should be followed by a thorough check to discover whether they lead to the need for any further changes. In a theory of language, as in language itself, *tout se tient* (Meillet 1937). It is certainly true that the theory has expanded greatly, in the sense that it now covers many additional aspects of language and additional languages, and that is has been used in additional areas of application. But many of the innovations — including the three to be summarized here — have had an effect that is ultimately revolutionary. And such changes do indeed demand the "re-working [of] earlier positions". It is a nice irony that Halliday should have written the words cited above in his 1993 paper "Systemic theory", because it is there that he spells out most clearly the revolutionary effect of the changes from "Categories" — as we shall see in due course. (Perhaps this is part of the general phenomenon that it is often easier for others to see the significance of a new idea than it is for the innovator.)

During the period of almost forty years since 1961, Halliday has proposed a great many new ideas. Some, such as the three to be outlined here, have been highly insightful and extraordinarily influential. Others have quietly grown into becoming part of his theory and have been accepted by some scholars, while leaving others (such as myself sometimes) unpersuaded of their value. And some have been simply floated and then quietly forgotten.

In this chapter I shall summarize Halliday's three most significant changes to the framework outlined in "Categories", and their effects on the type of syntax that is appropriate for such a model. The first change led immediately to the second — though it was not logically necessary that it should do so — and the second led a little later to the third — though again it did not necessarily follow that it would.

## 4.2 Privileging the concept of 'system'

As we saw in Chapter 2, Halliday takes the position in "Categories" that everything within 'grammar' is part of the same level of language, i.e., 'form' 1961/76:53). The four "categories of the theory of grammar" and the three "scales" that relate them were therefore all presented as belonging within 'grammar', and so as all being at the same level of language.

However, in "Some notes on 'deep' grammar" (1966/76) Halliday began to explore, initially quite tentatively, the possibility of elevating the category of 'system' to a the predominant position in the theory. He wrote:

> Systemic description [i.e., the description of a piece of text in terms of features derived from system networks] may be thought of as complementary to structural

description [i.e., a description in terms of grammatical units and their elements, etc], the one concerned with paradigmatic and the other with syntagmatic relations. On the other hand, **it might be useful to consider some possible consequences of regarding systemic description as the underlying form of representation, if it turned out that the structural description could be shown to be derivable from it** [my emphasis]. In that case structure would be fully predictable. (Halliday 1966/76: 93-4)

In a series of key papers in the middle and late sixties (many of which are reprinted in Halliday & Martin 1981), Halliday and his colleagues Henrici, Huddleston and Hudson begin the long process of demonstrating that it is indeed possible to "derive" structural representations from systemic representations. Through this, the "possible consequences" quickly became the founding principles of the new version of the theory: **Systemic Grammar**. By 1969 paradigmatic relations had become so important in the theory that Halliday could write:

> The grammar is based on the notion of choice [...] The speaker of a language, like a person engaged in any kind of culturally determined behaviour, can be regarded as carrying out [...] a number of distinct choices. [...] The grammar of any language can be represented as a very large network of systems. (Halliday 1969/76:3)

In this way the concept of **system** is developed into the more complex concept of a **system network**, i.e., a network of systems in which systems are related to each other by a finite set of 'and' and 'or' relationships (as set out in Halliday (1970/76b:15) and in most standard systemic writings). For a simple example see Figure 1 of Appendix A.

It was this same body of work that also addressed the problem of showing that systemic grammar could also be a **generative grammar** (cp. Hudson's paper 'Systemic generative grammar' (1974/81). However, this concept needs to be interpreted and expanded in terms of the second and third great changes in the theory, and it is to these that we now turn.

### 4.3 Systems as choice between meanings

We come now to a second and equally important change to the theory. It has already been hinted at in Halliday's use of the terms "deep" and "underlying" in the passage cited above to describe the level of the systemic representation. But it was signposted more clearly when Halliday wrote a few pages later (1966/76:96) that "underlying grammar is 'semantically significant' grammar".[1] By 1970 Halliday had begun to describe the system networks of TRANSITIVITY, MOOD, THEME and so on as the **meaning potential** of a language, and so as being at a separate level from that of the structures that are 'predicted by', and so 'derived from', the semantic features in the system networks. For example, he wrote in one classic passage:

> A functional theory of language is a theory about meanings, not about words or constructions. [...] Where then do we find the functions differentiated in language? They are differentiated **semantically**, as different areas of what I call the **'meaning potential'** [my emphasis]. (Halliday 1971/73b:110)

And he then went on to describe these "areas" as the "networks of interrelated options that define, as a whole, the resources for what the speaker wants to say", and to identify them as the networks for TRANSITIVITY, MOOD, THEME and so on.

Ten years later, Halliday was still writing in similar terms — but only at times, as we shall see in Section 4.6. Here, for example, is an excerpt from his "Introduction" to *Readings in systemic linguistics* (Halliday & Martin 1981). Notice that he distinguishes and defines the two relationships of 'instantiation' and 'realization' in very similar terms to those used in Sections 3.1 and 3.2 of Chapter 3. (Here he characterizes the relationships as "processes", because he is thinking in terms of a generative model of language.)

---

1. To understand fully what is at stake here, we must recognize the fact that linguists employ two main metaphors for thinking about the **levels of language**. In the longer established metaphor, the more abstract phenomena such as 'meanings' of various types are regarded as 'higher', and the more concrete phenomena, such as the spoken and written forms of language, are thought of as 'lower'. But in the metaphor implied in the use of Hockett's terms "deep structure" and "surface structure" (as later taken over by Chomsky and others) this model is inverted. In this metaphor, the extension of the model of syntax to take account of 'semantics' involves the addition of a 'deep' or 'underlying' representation, this being seen as the 'level' within syntax that is nearest to meaning. In other words, in choosing to give "Some notes on 'deep' grammar" the title he did, Halliday was adopting the terminology of the then dominant theoretical model of language. In contrast, he had presented in "Categories" a diagram in which the relationships are horizontal, in which "context" is on the left, "form" is in the middle" and "substance" is on the right. After Halliday (1966/76), however, he quickly moved to the use of the model of language in which 'context' and 'meaning' are higher than 'form' and in which 'substance' is lower. It seems that he was influenced in this — at least in part — by the way in which the relationships between the strata of language are represented in Lamb's Stratificational Grammar (from which Halliday took the word "realization" for its use in denoting the relationship between levels). So in Halliday (1977/78:128), for example, we find a model in which 'meaning' is above 'form' and 'phonetics' is below.

'Instantiation' is the process of selecting within the sets of options (the systems) that make up the meaning potential (the system). It is the process of choosing. By this step particular paths are traced through the network of paradigmatic alternatives. [...] 'Realization' is the process of making manifest the options that have been selected. It is the process of expressing the choices made. By this step **meanings** are encoded in **wordings** [my emphasis]. (Halliday 1981:14)

Here Halliday is characterizing 'instantiation' at the level of meaning, in terms of Figure 4 in Chapter 3, but there is also, of course, as we saw in Chapter 3, a process of instantiation at the level of form.

It was passages such as the two cited immediately above that led many systemic functional linguists — including myself — to interpret Halliday as suggesting that the system networks of TRANSITIVITY, MOOD, THEME and so on should be regarded as the **semantics** of a language. We accepted this as a major insight, and used it as the basic assumption for a re-interpretation of the earlier system networks. I myself first expressed this position publicly in Fawcett (1973/81), writing that

'Meaning' is concerned with the intra-linguistic level of **semantics**. [...] A network may therefore be regarded as a summary of a complex area of **meaning potential** [my emphasis] (Fawcett 1973/81:157).

And Berry, in her classic introduction to systemic linguistics, writes that

the terms in a system [...] are distinct **meanings within a common area of meaning** [my emphasis] (Berry 1975:144).

In a similar vein Kress, in his insightful account of the development of Halliday's ideas, states that

the freeing of system from surface structure has a consequence that systems are now made up of terms which are **semantic features** [my emphasis] (Kress 1976:35).

Today, very many systemic functional linguists would take it as axiomatic that system networks such as those for TRANSITIVITY, MOOD, THEME etc. model choices between meanings, i.e., semantic features. These linguists include those who work in the framework of the Cardiff Grammar (including those in China and Japan), those working with the Nottingham Grammar (as described in Berry (1975, 1977 and 1996:8-9), those who are applying systemic functional grammar to other semiotic systems (e.g., Kress & van Leeuwen 1997, van Leeuwen 1999 and probably O'Toole 1994). Moreover, Halliday himself continues to write in a similar manner at times, e.g., in *IFG*:

> In a functional grammar, [...] **a language is interpreted as a system of meanings** [my emphasis], accompanied by forms through which the meanings can be expressed (Halliday 1994:xix).

In this view of the basic architecture of language, then, the **meaning potential** constitutes the level of **semantics**. More precisely, it is the task of the system networks to model those 'meanings' that are expressible through realization rules at the level of form (Figure 4 in Section 3.2 of Chapter 3).[2]

On this basis, many systemic functional linguists have assumed that the networks of TRANSITIVITY, MOOD, THEME and so on, do (or should) represent choices in meaning, and that they therefore do (or should) constitute the level of semantics. And for at least some of us who were working in SFL in the 1970s, the corollary of this was that, when we saw Halliday's system networks as still reflecting contrasts that were formal rather than semantic (e.g., his MOOD network, which has remained virtually unchanged since the 1960s, in contrast with his TRANSITIVITY network) we revised them by 'pushing' them towards the semantics — exactly as Halliday himself had done with his networks for TRANSITIVITY during the 1960s.

However, it is not the case that all systemic linguists took this position, and it is certainly not the case that Halliday himself consistently did so, as we shall see in Sections 4.6 and 4.7. First, however, we shall note the third of the three main stages in the revolution that transformed Scale and Category Grammar into Systemic Functional Grammar.

## 4.4 The emergence of the multifunctional view of meaning

If the word *semantic* had not been associated with the narrow definition of 'meaning' that it had for most linguists in the 1960s and 1970s, it is possible that Halliday's revised model of language might have been called "Systemic Semantic Grammar". Instead, it is **Systemic Functional Grammar** — and the chief significance of the term "functional" is that it serves as a useful

---

2. The view that language is most usefully thought of as consisting essentially of the two levels of meaning and form is of course not unique to SFL. It suffuses the work of many of the most useful grammars of the last half century (e.g., Quirk *et al.* 1985, Sinclair 1990, Francis, Hunston & Manning 1996 and 1998, and Biber *et al.* 1999), and it is explicitly evoked in the title of Bolinger's *Meaning and form* (1977). What makes the approach to meaning in SFL unique is the coupling of the concept of meaning with that of choice between features in system networks.

## LATER CHANGES TO THE S&C MODEL 51

reminder of the third of Halliday's great innovative concepts. This is the insight that every piece of text (such as, for example, a simple clause) realizes several different types of meaning, often in the same element. In other words, it serves for the expression of 'representational' meaning or, to use Halliday's term, **experiential** meaning; **logical** meanings such as the relationships expressed in the words *and* and *or*; **interpersonal** meanings of various types (which for Halliday includes what I would distinguish as **affective, validity** and **polarity** meanings); and at least two kinds of **textual** meanings, i.e., **thematic** meaning and **informational** meanings (the latter including the meanings of 'Given' and 'New', as realized in intonation).[3] The recognition of the 'multifunctional' nature of language — and so of equivalent system networks that model the 'meaning potential' of each "strand of meaning" in a text (*IFG* p. 34) — has become one of the defining characteristics of the contemporary systemic functional approach to understanding the nature of language. See Figure 7 in Section 7.2 of Chapter 7 and Figure 10 in Section 7.8 for two contrasting ways of representing this concept in the diagrams that represent the analysis of a clause. And see Chapter 7 also for the suggestion that the concept of 'strands of meaning' was over-extended when it came to be equated with the concept of 'multiple structures'.

### 4.5 The problem of the limited availability of Halliday's system networks

At this point, let us note a surprising problem that the newcomer to SFL enounters. We saw in Section 4.3 that many systemic linguists, including myself, welcomed Halliday's suggestion that we should regard the system networks of TRANSITIVITY, MOOD, THEME and so on as constituting the level of semantics, and that where the networks had not yet been pushed to the semantics, we developed new networks that were explicitly semantic. This leads in turn to the question: "What changes did Halliday make to his own

---

3. In fact, Halliday recognizes four 'metafunctions': the **experiential, logical, interpersonal** and **textual**. I have long advocated the value of recognizing the eight major types of meaning listed in the main text (and three minor ones), e.g., as described in Fawcett (1980), (in press) and (forthcoming a). This difference in the degree of 'delicacy' between the Sydney and Cardiff Grammars — a metaphor explored in Gregory (1987) — will be reflected in the descriptions of texts in Sections 7.2 and 7.9 of Chapter 7, but it has no direct consequences for the theoretical concepts discussed in the present book.

system networks in the late 1960s and early 1970s, as a result of the realization that they should be regarded as 'meaning potential' of the language?"

It is actually rather hard to find out. The irony is that, while Halliday is the chief architect of systemic theory, he himself has published only highly simplified diagrams of the overall system network and small fragments of sub-networks — with one exception, which I shall return to in a moment. Thus, despite the fact that the concept of the system network lies at the heart of the grammar, the fact is that, even today, we still have only secondary evidence as to what Halliday himself thinks the system networks for English should be like.

Examples of introductory 'toy grammars' by Halliday can be found in Halliday (1969/81), Halliday (1971/73a:40) and, for a slightly fuller picture, Halliday (1977/78). And there are fragments of early networks for specific areas of meaning in Halliday (1967-8) and, for two pictures of his changing views on 'modality', Halliday (1970/76a:189-213) and Halliday (1994:360).

The one major exception was the publication of a very full set of Halliday's system networks for English as they were in 1964 (i.e., over a third of a century ago), in Halliday (1976:101-135) — and without the editorial encouragement of Kress it seems doubtful that we would have even these.

When *IFG* first appeared in 1985, many of its readers will have hoped to find at least some simplified system networks — only to find that this major work by the architect of Systemic Functional Grammar included hardly any. Halliday's reason for omitting them, he explains, is that the purpose of the book is to present "not the systemic portion of a description of English, with the grammar represented as networks of choices, but the structural portion in which we show how the options are realized" (1994:xv). And he goes on to say, disarmingly, that "the systemic portion of the grammar is in the computer" (i.e., as part of the Penman Project described in Section 1.2 of Chapter 1).

Finally — but not until 1995 — Halliday's close collaborator Matthiessen brought the networks out of the computer and made them available in Matthiessen (1995). As Matthiessen says (1995:i-ii), "the interpretation of English [in this book] is based on Halliday's work and [... it] is intended to be read together with his 1985/1994 *Introduction to Functional Grammar.*" It is clear that the system networks are in fact Matthiessen's re-working of Halliday's original networks, incorporating minor improvements and suggestions from other systemic linguists (including, in a small way, myself: see Matthiessen 1995:655).

However, while it is certainly useful to have access to these more recent networks, the reader who is hoping to find explicitly semantic system networks in Matthiessen (1995) is likely to be disappointed. Most of the networks are essentially as they were in the late 1960s and early 1970s — or, where they are different, they are not noticeably more semantic. Despite this caveat, it is extremely valuable to have, at last, a reasonably complete set of system networks for the Sydney Grammar. (However, see Section 7.6 of Chapter 7 for a critical view of the value to the text analyst of these networks as they stand.)

## 4.6 The problem of Halliday's two positions on 'meaning'

We saw in Section 4.3 that in the mid-1960s Halliday changed the theoretical status of the system networks, so that they came to be seen as modelling choices between meanings. And yet a close study of the system networks in Matthiessen (1995) shows that many are essentially the same as Halliday's 1964 networks (as published in Halliday 1976). In other words, system networks that Halliday had originally developed on the assumption that they were at the level of form were re-interpreted as being at the level of meaning. Is it really possible, one has to ask, that networks that were developed for one level of representation should be able to be transported, unchanged, to function at another level of representation? After major theoretical changes of the sort described above, the next logical steps should surely be a critical re-examination of the existing networks to discover where they were and where they were not already sufficiently 'semanticized', followed by the careful semanticization of those parts that needed it, in order to turn a brilliant insight into a practical reality.

So why, we may wonder, did Halliday not carry out such a programme of semanticizing his system networks? We may make a number of guesses at the possible reasons. These might have included:

1. The enthusiastic welcome already given to the existing networks by new converts to systemic linguists;
2. the lack of serious criticism of the networks by his immediate colleagues — a lack that is perhaps not surprising, given that Halliday's main collaborators at the time were Hudson and Huddleston, both of whom were more 'form-centred' than Halliday

himself (as they have continued to be);
3. Halliday's preoccupation in that period with various other aspects of the burgeoning work, both in the theory and its applications in many fields, to many of which he contributed personally;
4. the concern that the features in the new networks would be so much further removed from their realizations at the level of form that the new realization statements (to use Halliday's term) would be very hard to write;
5. sheer lack of time to undertake this task, given its size and his other commitments.[4]

Whatever the reason, the fact is that Halliday felt justified at the time in presenting the existing networks as at least a first approximation to what was needed for a representation of the meaning potential of English. Thus the existing system networks had an ambivalent status between being at the level of form (for which they had been developed) and being at the level of meaning (which they were now said to represent).

It may have been the ambivalence of the status of the system networks of TRANSITIVITY, MOOD, THEME and so on that allowed Halliday **both** to think of his existing networks as 'semantic' **and** at the same time to explore the alternative approach to the representation of meaning to which we shall come shortly. But the point to note here is that Halliday himself never embraced fully the revolutionary change described above in Section 4.4 — despite the fact that it was his own proposal.

In evaluating the lack of specificity that is sometimes found in Halliday's writings — which at times risks being interpreted as indecisiveness — it is important to understand the spirit in which he 'does his linguistics'. Essentially, he is an explorer. His typical practice is to suggest some new idea, and then to explore its possibilities in text-descriptive terms to see how far it fits in with other concepts in the theory, rather than to present the world with new 'truths'.

The idea that the system networks of TRANSITIVITY, MOOD, THEME and so on are choices between **meanings** — and that they are therefore essentially **semantic** choices — was initially just one such tentative proposal,

---

4. Halliday's output in that period was, by any standards, prodigious in the number of innovatory concepts that he produced, the breadth of coverage of his work, and in its sheer quantity.

as we saw in Section 4.3, but the warmth of its reception by many systemic linguists at the time (though not all; compare Hudson 1971) did not prevent Halliday from exploring, in parallel, an alternative approach to the representation of meaning. It is significant that his 1973 book, in which the two alternative positions on 'meaning' are discussed, was entitled *Explorations in the Functions of Language*. From the early 1970s onwards, then, Halliday has consistently held open the possibility of exploring two alternative models of the stratification of meaning. But the fact that each makes 'meaning' central to understanding language means that they can easily be confused and the distinctions blurred.

In the first approach, then, the system networks of TRANSITIVITY, MOOD, THEME and so on are held to be choices in meaning, and so "the semantics" — very much as in the model proposed here.

In the second approach, which we shall call the 'two-level model of meaning', the existing networks are held to be choices **within the grammar** (or the 'lexicogrammar') — albeit in a grammar that is described as having been "pushed [...] fairly far" towards the semantics, and whose networks Halliday still describes as modelling "meaning potential" (Halliday 1994:xix). These **lower** level choices in 'meaning' are said to be "preselected" by choices in a **higher** system network, which is itself the level of semantics.

For very many years the major new component of the second possible model of language was represented in Halliday's writings solely by the use of the term "semantics" as a placeholder in his summaries of what a language is like (e.g., in Halliday 1977/78:128). His nearest related work in this period was on the development, with Bernstein and Turner, of the concept of "sociosemantic" system networks (e.g., Halliday 1973:48-102) — but these only applied in very specific contexts of situation and consequently did not constitute a generalized semantics, as I pointed out in Fawcett (1975). In this period Halliday also expanded the theory into other areas, such as child language development and historical linguistics, and wrote his most significant paper on literary stylistics (Halliday 1971/73b).

In just one area of meaning Halliday provided a small "semantic" network which 'preselected' options in what has always been the rather 'form-centred' MOOD network (Halliday 1984:13). This little network for the semantics of MOOD only had eight pathways through it, but Hasan & Cloran (1990) and Hasan (1992) have developed very much fuller system networks which can be regarded as expansions of it for use in describing children's language, all within the Sydney Grammar framework.[5]

However, the major effort to provide system networks that could function as the 'higher semantics' in the framework of the Sydney Grammar has been Martin's development of what he calls a "discourse semantics", as described in his valuable *English Text* (Martin 1992). Martin's theory of language constitutes a separate 'sub-dialect' of the Sydney Grammar that is significantly different from that of Hasan and indeed Halliday — but he too, like Hasan and Cloran, works on the assumption that his 'discourse semantic' system networks will be 'realized' by a grammar such as that of Halliday (1994) and Matthiessen (1995). However, even Martin's 620-page work does not provide a full coverage of the proposed higher level of system networks. This is understandable, both because of the size of the task and because the focus of *English Text* is not on the grammar as a whole, but on providing a much more complete coverage of the topic of 'cohesion' than the limited coverage in Halliday & Hasan's *Cohesion in English* (1976).[6]

As will perhaps be obvious, the position taken here is that the semanticization of the system networks for TRANSITIVITY, MOOD, THEME and so on that constitute the meaning potential should incorporate many of the types of meaning covered in Martin's 'discourse semantics', so enabling the overall model of language to remain as it is in Figure 4 of Chapter 3, rather than becoming increasingly complex.

Thus Halliday himself did not take on the task of a thorough re-working of

---

5. See Fawcett (1999:247-9, 258-9) for a discussion of some of the differences between Halliday's 'grammatical' network for MOOD and my much richer MOOD network, which is explicitly at the level of semantics. See Fawcett (forthcoming a) for the full version of the computer-implemented network for MOOD (which replaces that in Fawcett 1980:103).

6. The reason why the coverage in *Cohesion in English* was limited was not, of course, that the authors were unaware that other factors also contribute to the 'cohesion' of a text, but because they explicitly confined their goals in that work to covering those aspects of 'cohesion' that are not realized in structures — and Halliday takes the position that TRANSITIVITY, MOOD, THEME and so on are all meanings that are indeed realized in structures. (But see my discussion of the reasons for disagreeing with this view in Chapter 7.) Yet the fact is that TRANSITIVITY, MOOD, THEME etc. can also contribute to the 'cohesion' of a text, as Martin (1992) clearly demonstrates. Perhaps one of the reasons for the popularity of *Cohesion in English* is the fact that its ideas can be applied to the analysis of texts without having a full understanding of the SFL approach to understanding language. The reult is that most studies of cohesion do only part of the job. This has in turn had an unfortunate effect on work in some areas where SFL can usefully be applied, such as psychiatric linguists, where the two major areas of study are cohesion and syntax (the latter being of the 'phrase-structure' type).

the existing systemic descriptions that the revolutionary new model logically called for. However, the few new networks that emerged from that period such as those for 'modality' (Halliday 1970/76a) are more clearly oriented to meaning than most of the 1964 networks reproduced in Halliday (1976). The position remains that some of Halliday's networks (e.g., TRANSITIVITY, the network for generating Participant Roles, etc.) have been pushed very much further towards the semantics than others (e.g., the MOOD network).

In recent years, however, Halliday appears to have reached the decision that it really is necessary to add a second and higher level of 'meaning'. This is the position that is expressed in Halliday (1996), Matthiessen (1995) and in Halliday & Matthiessen (1999) — the latter being the exploration of a possible 'experiential semantics'. As a consequence of this decision, Halliday now uses the term "semantics" for this new level of 'meaning' — while continuing, however, to describe the system networks of TRANSITIVITY, MOOD, THEME and so on as "meaning potential" (e.g., Halliday 1993:4505).[7]

Since our purpose in this book is to establish the theory that is required for modelling syntax at the level of form, we must ask the question: "Does Halliday's adoption of the second position on the levels of meaning in language mean that the general framework within which we are comparing the Sydney and the Cardiff approaches to analyzing syntax, as summarized in Figure 4 of Chapter 3, becomes invald?" The answer is that it might in principle have been invalidated by Halliday's recent decision, but that in practice it does not. The reason is that, whether or not we add a higher layer of 'meaning' to our model of language, there is still a level of **meaning potential** within the grammar. It is a level of description that Halliday describes as having "been pushed [...] fairly far [...] in the direction of the semantics" (Halliday 1994:xix). From the

---

7. In my view the addition of this new level of meaning is an unnecessary complication to the theory. It has the considerable disadvantage that it requires a whole new level of system networks, which together must cover the same broad range of types of meaning as the existing ones. We need to be absolutely sure that this very large new level of system networks really is needed, before we commit ourselves to a vast amount of new work, the result of which will be to complicate even further what is already a very rich and complex model of language. I believe that the evidence is that this vast extension of the theory is neither desirable nor necessary — so long as we actually carry out the implications of Halliday's proposal that the system networks of TRANSITIVITY, MOOD, THEME and so on should model choices between meanings. I consider that the phenomena that have led Halliday to adopt his latest position are to be explained in other ways (one being to further semanticize some of Halliday's networks, e.g., that for MOOD). See Fawcett (forthcoming a) for a set of such semantic system networks.

'theoretical-generative' viewpoint (a concept that will be introduced in Section 5.2 of Chapter 5), there seems to be no very significant difference between the mode of operation of a grammar in which system networks that have been pushed "fairly far in the direction of the semantics" and one in which the system networks have been pushed all the way.

Notice, moreover, that the **outputs** from any grammar with system networks of either type must be considered to be at the level of **form**, because they specify the sequence of the items that constitute the 'final' output ("final", that is, apart from specifying the output's spoken or written shape). And this is true of both the Sydney and the Cardiff Grammars, despite the differences between the types of representation that are found in each. (However, there are theoretical problems about the status of the Sydney Grammar representations, as we shall see in Chapter 7.) For the purpose of a general comparison between the two models, then, we may treat the level of 'meaning potential' in Halliday's grammar (i.e., the level at which TRANSITIVITY, MOOD, THEME and so on are located) as roughly equivalent to the semantic system networks of the Cardiff Grammar. In other words, Halliday's adoption of the second position on levels of meaning makes no significant difference to the components of the model of language that we shall assume to be common to all of those who work in the framework of SFL. (But see the next section for a caveat to this claim.)

In terms of the change from "Categories" to a modern SF grammar, we may say that the effect of the fundamental change in the theory in the late 1960s was that the concept of 'system' was removed from the account of language at the level of form, and made the central concept at the level of meaning. As a result there were now the two levels of 'instances' shown in Figure 4 of Chapter 3: the selection expression at the level of meaning and the richly labelled tree structure at the level of form.

The perception that the system networks of TRANSITIVITY, MOOD, THEME etc. represent the meaning potential of a language is, in my view, the most significant of all of Halliday's insights. As I pointed out above, one important result of accepting this major claim is that it challenges us to develop our system networks further, with the explicit goal of making them represent choices between meanings (rather than forms), and so to model the **level of semantics** in language.

In the work done over the last fifteen years by my colleagues and myself at Cardiff, one of our main goals has been to develop a new model of a SF grammar that tests the hypothesis that the system networks of TRANSITIV-

ITY, MOOD, THEME and so on are capable of being developed into a fully adequate model of semantics. Indeed, the very large computer implementation of a grammar (including lexis, intonation and punctuation) that we have built at Cardiff operates on precisely these principles. The first stage of this work was described in Fawcett, Tucker & Lin (1993) and related papers, and many aspects of the later stages have been reported in the many other papers listed in Fawcett (1998). As a result of all this work by the many members of the team, I am convinced that, in Halliday's own words (1994:xix), the "choices in the grammar [i.e., the system networks] can be essentially choices in meaning without the grammar thereby losing contact with the ground". The way in which a SF grammar keeps "contact with the ground", is to ensure that it has explicit realization rules that are capable of generating a full range of realizations in structures, items, intonation and punctuation at the level of form (while conforming to certain agreed limitations on their complexity). I am therefore as confident as it is ever possible to be in science that it is indeed possible to make a reality of Halliday's original proposal that the system networks of TRANSITIVITY, MOOD, THEME and so on should be, to adapt Halliday's metaphor (1994:xix) "pushed all the way to the semantics". We who work in the framework of the Cardiff Grammar — together with all of the many other systemic functional grammarians who take the view that the system networks of TRANSITIVITY, MOOD, THEME etc. constitute the major level of meaning in language — have therefore come to a different conclusion from Halliday on this matter.

From the viewpoint of our concerns in this book, however, this major difference of view about what is required 'above' the meaning potential that belongs within the grammar is relatively unimportant. As I have argued in this section, both of the two models have networks for TRANSITIVITY, MOOD, THEME etc. that are at the level of 'meaning potential'. Moreover, the features in both are realized by essentially the same types of 'realization operation', as we shall see in Chapters 5 and 9.[8]

---

8. I should point out that, when Halliday adds a further level of system networks above the existing level, he necesarily also add a further component to the model, to enable the grammar to 'map' the choices made at one level onto the choices available at the lower level. However, he does not describe what this extension to the model entails, so I shall attempt to provide a summary of this in the next section. A further problem is that Halliday uses the term 'preselection' in two senses. The first is the standard sense of the 'preselection' that occurs in a realization rule which 'pre-selects' a feature to be chosen on a subsequent traversal of the network (as we shall see in Chapters 5 and 9). But his second use is for the 'preselection' of a

Nonetheless, there has been a knock-on effect of Halliday's adoption of the second position which leads him to describe the grammar in a way that appears to be in conflict with the general SFL model of language proposed in Chapter 3 and in expressed in Figure 4. The next section describes this problematical change of position by Halliday, and the simple alternative.

### 4.7 Two possible effects on the overall model of adopting the second position on 'meaning'

I claimed in Chapter 3 that Figure 4 (in Section 3.2 of that chapter) represents the way in which both the Sydney and the Cardiff grammars operate. As we have seen, Halliday's more recent writings have increasingly strongly taken the position — which he first explored in the 1970s — that there is a 'higher semantics' as well as the 'meaning potential' within the lexocogrammar (e.g., Halliday 1993 and 1996). How would this affect the overall model of language?

It would be reasonable, if this higher level of system networks really is necessary, simply to add the higher level to the model illustrated in Figure 4 of Chapter 3. This would require the addition of the following sub-components: (1) a new higher system network (a second 'meaning potential'), which would generate its own set of features after each traversal of the network), (2) the selection expression of the 'instances' that have been chosen, (3) a 'realization component' that states what the effect of each choice is (i.e., 'preselection' rules, which would specify that if Feature X is chosen in the higher network, Feature Y must be chosen in the lower network) , and (4) the output from the operation of that component, i.e., the list of features to be chosen in the lower network. The result of this change would be to add the components decribed here above the model shown in Figure 4 of Chapter 3. This is the first of the "two possible effects" referred to in the title of this section.

However, adding to the model in Figure 4 in this way has **not** been Halliday's response to the situation. Instead, his later works present the view

---

choice in a network that results from a choice in a higher component. It is of course important to keep a clear distinction between the **levels** (or strata) of language and the **layers** of structure within syntax. In the Cardiff Grammar, therefore, we use "preselection" only in the established sense of the relationship between layers of the tree structure. We use the terms "predetermine" and "predetermination" for the relationship between any higher component in the process of generation and the choices in the system network.

that the system networks of meaning potential and their outputs at the level of form shown in Figure 4 are all **at the same level.**

Taking this position brings with it a serious problem. We shall address it now, because it is a problem which, like the introduction of the higher level of meaning, has the potential to make it impossible to compare the representations at the level of form of the Sydney and the Cardiff Grammars.

The problem is as follows. In his earlier descriptions of the grammar (1969/81) and (1970/76b), Halliday showed the relationship between the system networks and the output structures to be one of **realization.** But in his this second approach to the representation of meaning the relationship must logically be regarded as one of **instantiation**. This is because system and structure are presented in the new model as being **at the same level of language**. The specific problem is that, in the earlier stage of the development of the theory (when the system networks were regarded as being at a higher level than the structures that manifest them), Halliday had identified the set of operations that change the selection expression into the structures as 'realization statements'. So are the outputs from the system networks of TRANSTIVITY, MOOD, THEME and so on really at the level of form, or are they are the same level as the system networks, i.e., at a level that has been "pushed [...] fairly far [...] in the direction of the semantics" (Halliday 1994:xix)?

Passages in Halliday's recent writings such as the following two seem to be attempts to reconcile the two senses in which he now finds himself using the term "realization" — senses which in the new model have in fact become incompatible. Is the concept of 'realization' interstratal or intrastratal — or is it really possible that it can be stretched far enough to be used for both, without losing its integrity? In the first of the two passages Halliday writes:

> realization" is both "the relation between the 'strata', or levels [i.e .the original sense of "realization"] of a [...] semiotic system — and, **by analogy**, between the paradigmatic and the syntagmatic phases of representation **within one stratum** [my emphasis]. (Halliday 1993:4505)

And in a slightly later work Halliday describes the use of the term "realization" in the 'intrastratal' sense as an "extension" of the concept of 'realization', saying:

> Realization is [...] **extended** to refer to the **intrastratal** relation between a systemic feature and its structural (or other) manifestation [my emphasis]. (Halliday 1996:29)

If Halliday had not used the words "within one stratum" and "intrastratal" in these two passages, they could have been interpreted perfectly satisfactorily as describing the relationship of realization that holds between the two levels of **instances** in the model represented in Figure 4 of Chapter 3, i.e., (1) the selection expression of features and (2) the structure at the level of form. And in this case the use of the term "realization" would not be an "analogy" or an "extension". But Halliday did use those words, and under a strict interpretation of their meaning, the relationship must, in his current framework, be surely be said to be one of 'instantiation' rather than 'realization'.

The implications of the position that "the paradigmatic and the syntagmatic phases of representation" [i.e., the system network and the output structure] are "within one stratum" are illustrated in Figure 5.

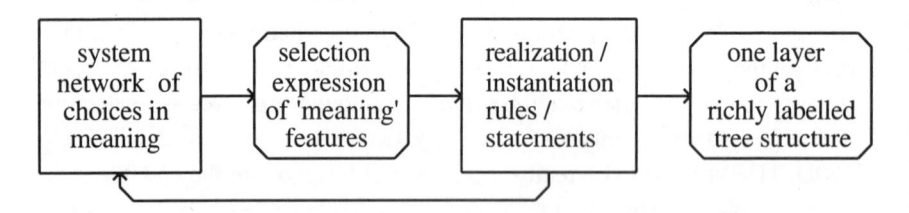

| system network of choices in meaning | → | selection expression of 'meaning' features | → | realization / instantiation rules / statements | → | one layer of a richly labelled tree structure |

*Figure 5: 'Realization' as 'instantiation': the re-arrangement of Figure 4 that is demanded by Halliday's second position on the grammar*

Figure 5 is essentially a re-arrangement of the two components and two outputs in Figure 4 so that they all appear to function within one level of language. Topologically, the two are equivalent, but this does not mean that they are "mere notational variants" of each other.[9] The disadvantage of Figure 5 is that it loses the important insights captured in Figure 4, which shows the places in the model of the central concepts of **realization** (relating the levels of form and meaning) and **instantiation** (relating the potential and the instances).

If the components and outputs shown in Figure 5 really did constitute a single level of language, it would be a level of a very unusual sort. This is because it still contains the same two levels of 'meaning' and 'form' that

---

9. Here I am borrowing the well-known words used by Chomsky to dismiss the difference between the position of the 'generative semanticists' and his own 'interpretive semantics' position within transformational generative grammar in the late 1960s. Notations are semiotic systems, and notational variants are seldom as slight as the use of the term "mere" implies.

Halliday's writings in the early 1970s proposed (as we saw in Section 4.3), and which suggest the model of language shown in Figure 4 in Chapter 3. The reason why the reinterpretations by Halliday of what "realization" means cited above are so problematical is that it is not logically possible to hold at the same time the two views that

(1) there are two levels of instances (as Figure 4 suggests that there are), and
(2) the two levels of instances are at the same level of language (as Figure 5 suggests).

It would only be possible to hold both views if one were to claim at the same time that the selection expression of features chosen from the 'meaning potential' and the structure that so clearly manifests it at a lower level are at the same level. Yet the system networks are patently more 'semantic' than the structures that are generated from them. Indeed, when Halliday first introduced the concept of 'realization', it was in precisely the sense of the relationship between two levels, i.e., between (1) the system networks at the level of **meaning potential** and — after first generating a selection expression and then applying the realization statements — (2) the output structures, which are necessarily at the level of **form**.

Interestingly, the symbol for the meaning of 'is realized by' in informal realization rules in a SF grammar is a small arrow pointing diagonally from the top left corner of an imaginary rectangle to the bottom right corner. And one could draw just such an arrow with a felt tip pen right across the diagram in Figure 4, so symbolizing that the relationship between the meaning potential and the realized instance is the same, both in individual cases and in the case of the model as a whole. Yet this relationship is in fact, as we can see, one that involves not just realization but both instantiation (twice) and realization.

There is a small further problem in adopting the position represented in Figure 5. This is that it is not clear what we should call this supposed 'level' of language. Halliday calls it the "lexicogrammar" and this makes it, in effect, an alternative term to "form".

Let me summarize the main point that is made in this section. This is that, even if Halliday turns out to be right about the need to add another level of system networks above those in the 'meaning potential' of the lexicogrammar (which I do not think he is), it does not necessarily follow that we must deny that there is also realization between the established levels of the generative apparatus that I have described in Chapter 3 (this generative apparatus being exemplified both in Appendix A and in Halliday's own early generative grammars). To assert that the only relationships involved in Figure 5 — and so in Figure 4 — are ones of 'instantiation' would be to sacrifice the great insight of the later 1960s and early 1970s that the system networks of TRANSITIVITY, MOOD, THEME etc. are choices in meaning.[10] And for what would this sacrifice be made? Ultimately, it would be for the abstract (and undesirably limiting) notion that the specification of the 'potential' at every level of language necessarily has the form of a system network. The more desirable alternative, as our work in the COMMUNAL Project at Cardiff has shown, is to allow that a full model of language in use may require different ways of specifying the 'potential'. Indeed this concept is illustrated in the outline proposed in Chapter 3, in that we saw there that it is the role of the realization rules to specify the 'form potential'.[11]

Thus Figure 4 expresses the powerful, theoretically well-motivated and computer-tested models of language that have been implemented in both the Sydney and the Cardiff Grammars. In contrast, the view of language summarized in Figure 5 (which is what Halliday's re-interpretation of his earlier insight entails) loses precisely the major insight of his revolutionary changes in the 1960s, as summarized in Sections 4.1 to 4.4 of this chapter — i.e., the insight that there is a relationship of realization between the system networks of meaning potential and the structural outputs.

## 4.8 Why a SFL model of language requires a separate component for the realization rules

Finally, we must consider the implications for the model of language summarized in Figure 4 of another interesting change in Halliday's represent-

---

10. It would not solve the problem to label them as 'formal meaning' in contrast with 'semantic meaning'; they are still patently more semantic than their syntactic correlates.

11. In any case, an adequate model of the full process of generation requires other ways of modelling decision-making in the higher stages of planning. System networks can be regarded as a special type of 'decision tree' that is incorporated within the semiotic system of language itself. See Fawcett (1993) for a brief account of some of the other types of specifying 'potentials' that are being implemented in the COMMUNAL Project, and Fawcett (1988) for a bibliography that includes accounts of work on 'higher components' of this sort.

ations of his model of language. It is a change that correlates with the view that we have just been examining, i.e., the view that the system networks of TRANSITIVITY, MOOD, THEME etc. belong at the same level as their outputs.

The reason why it is important to examine this change too is that it carries with it an implication that is even more drastic in its consequences for the model of language outlined in Figure 4 than the change discussed in the last section. This is because it implies that the grammar has **no separate component for the realization rules**. If this concept were to be sustained, there would be no 'form potential' in Figure 4 that corresponded to the 'meaning potential'. And this in turn would have serious consequences for the picture of language to be presented here, and especially in Chapters 5 and 9, where we shall make a major distinction in the theory of syntax to be presented there between 'syntax potential' and 'instances of syntax'.

There was no such problem with Halliday's early systemic functional grammars (e.g., 1969/81 and 1970/76b). Each contains two components: (1) the system network and (2) the realization rules — very much as in Figure 4 in Chapter 3. In Halliday (1969/81), for example, the system network is shown on page 141, and the 'realization statements' that convert any selection expression that is chosen in traversing the network into a structure are set out in a table on page 142. Thus the two figures illustrate each of the two components of the model. And the same pattern is found in Halliday (1970/76b) — with some minor changes in the detail of the realization rules, as is to be expected at this early stage in the development of generative systemic functional grammars. In other words, the components of these grammars and their outputs correspond directly to the two components and two outputs shown in Figure 4 of Section 3.2 of Chapter 3.

However, in some of Halliday's other writings, starting very soon after that time, he began using a representation of the system networks and realization rules that can be interpreted in a very different manner — though always in introductory grammars or fragments of grammars, as in Halliday (1971/73a:40 and 1977/78:208-22). The same pattern is found in his 1964 networks (which were published in Halliday (1976:135).[12] And the same pattern is found in his recent work e.g., in the network for the 'verbal group' in Halliday (1996:11).

---

12. These system networks may well date from the time before Halliday realized that they should be regarded as modelling the 'meaning potential' of the language.

Finally, this way of representing the realization rules is used throughout Matthiessen (1995). In the diagrams in all of these works, any feature for which there is a realization rule has the rule written immediately under the feature itself, almost as a footnote on the feature. In other words, the impression is given that the realization rules are **part of the system network itself**.

The initially attractive idea that this is intended to represent is that each feature in a system network contributes to the structure that is being built, and that each such rule should 'fire' as soon as its feature is chosen. Representing the realization rules in this way, then, fits in nicely with the idea that the lexicogrammar is simply all at one level of language — and this is precisely the concept that is required in Halliday's second approach to meaning.

Ultimately, however, this approach is unworkable. The problem with it is that it depends on the concept that there are no exceptions to the 'typical' effect of choosing a given feature. But if the 'firing' of the realization rule is dependent upon the co-selection of another feature (as is often the case), it cannot be allowed to fire as soon as the feature is chosen, because a 'conditional feature' may also be selected in another part of the network which might demand that the realization should be different. Let us look at a simple example, taken from the little grammar in Appendix B. Consider the realization rule for the feature [near] in Figure 2 of Appendix B. The rule states that, if either [singular] or [mass] is also chosen, the realization is that the deictic determiner (dd) will be expounded by the item *this,* but that if the feature [plural] is co-selected it will be expounded by *these.*

In this particular example, the conditional features happen to occur in a sub-network that is 'higher' on the page than the one in which the feature [near] occurs. This might lead you to think that this makes it possible for the realization rule for the feature [near] to fire as soon as it is chosen, on the grounds that the grammar already 'knows' whether the conditional features have or have not been chosen. However, the features that function as 'conditions' could equally well occur in a part of the network to be traversed later, so that we cannot proceed on this assumption.[13] In practice the simplest workable solution

---

13. Neither approach would be acceptable in the Sydney Grammar, however, because there is a strong insistence on the concept that, in principle, all systems are entered simultaneously. If this is the case, the grammar would not know whether a possible conditional feature had or had not been co-selected at the time when the feature [near] was chosen. (The computer implementation of the Cardiff Grammar currently operates on the assumption that the 'higher'

# LATER CHANGES TO THE S&C MODEL 67

is that no realization rules should be applied until the traversal of the network has been completed, and to make the resulting selection expression of features available to each realization rule, as it is applied. This is what is done in the Cardiff Grammar and, as we shall see in the next chapter, in the computer implementation of Halliday's grammar too.

There is an alternative solution, and we shall explore it here briefly in order to demonstrate that it is not a desirable answer to the question of how best to model conditions on realizations. It is to model the conditions by the use of the conventions of a system network. Continuing with the example from Appendix B, we would need to extend the existing relatively simple network in Figure 1 in the following ways.[14] We would need to add (1) a right-opening 'and' bracket after each of [mass], [singular] and [plural], and (2) a right-opening 'or' bracket after [near]. Then (3) a line would need to be drawn from each of the three 'and' brackets associated with [mass] and [singular] to a new left-opening 'or' bracket, with (4) a further line running from the latter to a new left opening 'and' bracket. This would also be entered by a line from the right-opening 'or' bracket by [near] (5). Then (6) a dummy feature (standing for the meaning 'near-and-singular-or-mass') would need to be inserted to the right of the left-opening 'and' bracket. This would be a case of what is termed a 'gate', i.e., a feature that is in the system network but which is not part of a system.[15] Next, we would need to draw a line from the right-opening 'and' bracket by [plural] to a second new left-facing 'and' bracket (7), and (8) this would also be entered by a line from the second branch of the right-opening 'or' bracket' by the feature [near]. Then (9) a second 'dummy' feature would be placed to the right of this left-opening 'and' bracket, standing for the meaning 'near-and-

---

system networks are traversed before the lower ones, but they could be reformulated if it ever became possible to apply the computational concept of 'parallel processing' to system networks.)

14. To appreciate fully the implications of the details that follow, and so to obtain the full picture of what is involved, you might like to sketch in the system network from Figure 1 of Appendix B, and then add the extensions specified in the main text above.

15. Clearly, this concept is an anomaly in a systemic grammar; see Fawcett, Tucker & Lin (1993:126) for a discussion of the concept of 'gate', which is widely used in the computer implementation of Halliday's version of SFG in the Penman Project to minimize the use of conditions on realization rules (e.g., Mann & Matthiessen 1983/85). However, its theoretical status requires further clarification, discussion and justification before it is given the status in the theory that is accorded to the concept of a system.

plural'. As a result of the addition of all this new 'wiring' it would be possible to insert two realization rules which would not have conditions attached to them, i.e., one that stated that the feature 'near-and-singular-or-mass' would be realized by the item *this*, and one that said that ' near-and-plural' is realized by *these*.[16]

This example of the alternative approaches to a relatively simple part of the grammar demonstrates clearly the value of the use of conditional features in realization rules. But it also underlines the value of respecting the distinction between the use of the system network notation for representing systemic relationships of choice, and the mis-use of them (as it seems to me to be) to represent conditions on realization. It is clearly preferable in the case we are considering here, as it is in any model, to have different notations for the two different concepts. This is why, in Appendix B, system networks are used to model choices in meaning (as in Figure 1) and tables are used to model the realization rules (as in Figure 2). Indeed, this follows the pattern established in Halliday's early grammars (e.g., 1969/81 and 1970/76b).

To summarize so far: the insistence that realization rules must not contain conditional features so that they can be simple enough to be written in on the system network makes the additional 'wiring' in the network quite complex, and the greatly preferable alternative is to place all of the realization rules together in a separate component — i.e., the component that specifies the 'form potential' — as shown in Figure 4 and demonstrated in Figure 2 of Appendix A.

This second approach is in fact the only one that is workable in a large-scale SF grammar. The reason is simple: it is that the number of realization rules that require conditions grows as the grammar is extended to cover the less frequent linguistic phenomena. Thus it often happens that an action in building a part of the structure is dependent on the co-selection of one or more other features.

As the coverage of the grammar grows fuller, then, it has to encompass more and more exceptions to the general rule, and the place of the general concept of 'conditions on realization rules' becomes correspondingly more important. It is interesting to study the nature of the realization rules presented in Fawcett, Tucker & Lin (1993) from this viewpoint. There are very few, other

---

16. It is only if you have actually draw in all of these additions to the network in Figure 2 of Appendix B that you can check that the replacement of the simple realization rules in Figure 2 of Appendix B really does need to be as complex as the above description makes it sound.

than those realized in lexical items such as nouns and adjectives, that have no conditions at all.[17]

To summarize: when simple realization statements are written under the features in network diagrams, these are best regarded as an informal version of the full realization rule. Such diagrams may have the laudable effect of focussing attention on the system networks themselves — but they bring with them the unfortunate side-effect that they make the realization rules appear to be relatively minor 'footnotes' to the features in the networks. And they are not. In a fully explicit theoretical model of how language works, therefore, it is necessary to show the realization rules as a separate component, as was done in Halliday's first generative grammars (as cited above), in other early systemic grammars such as the very large one described in Hudson (1971), and in all versions of the Cardiff Grammar (e.g., in Figure 2 of Appendix B). Including the conditions on realization within the system network has the further disadvantage that it muddles two aspects of language: (1) choices between meanings and (2) their realization at the level of form.

When the 'form potential' component of a systemic functional grammar is shown as the separate component that it undoubtedly is (as in Figure 4), this helps to make it clear that the system networks are a different component from the realization rules — and one that is at a higher level. But when the 'form potential' is not given a specific identity in overall diagrams of how language works, as is the case in diagrams where language is represented as a system network with the realization rules presented as 'footnotes' on the features, there is a temptation to see the processes described in Figure 4 and exemplified in Appendix A as all occurring within one 'level', as in Figure 5.

Halliday has written at different times in terms of both frameworks, and also in terms that suggest that the boundary between the two is indeterminate (Halliday 1996:29). While I recognize the 'indeterminacy' that is bound to be found in living systems such as natural human languages, I think that it is right to accept the challenge of trying to make the model sufficiently explicit to be incorporated in a computer model of language. And doing this in turn suggests the value of recognizing the component 'modules' of Figure 4 in Chapter 3.

---

17. Indeed, the rule for [near] in Figure 2 can be stated more economically than it is there if we introduce the possibility of 'negative conditions', e.g., "If plural then dd < "these", if not plural than dd < "this." " — or even "If plural then dd < "these" else dd < "this".". Both are used, as is appropriate, in the computer implementation of the COMMUNAL grammar.

## 4.9 A pivotal paper: "Text as semantic choice in social context"

We come now to a stage in Halliday's developing model of language which has a particular significance for the emergence of the alternative model of systemic functional grammar presented here, and so for the major alternative approach to representing structure at the level of form.

"Text as semantic choice in social context" (Halliday 1977/78) describes in semi-formal terms the generation of a sentence in the context of its 'co-text' — and in so doing it provided by far the fullest description of the systemic and structural representation of a clause that Halliday had yet published. This fact alone would have been sufficient to make it a pivotal paper in the development of the theory, but it has a further significance, as we shall see.

It is important to note its position in the series of works that Halliday produced in the 1970s. While it was not published till 1977 (and republished in part in 1978), the full version was in fact widely available in photocopy form for several years before that — and, judging by the very close similarities in terminology with Halliday (1970/76b), it was probably written at the same time, i.e., in or around 1970.[18]

The general picture that it gives of the nature of language and of how the grammar works is fully compatible with the picture given in Chapter 3. That is, the system networks of TRANSITIVITY, MOOD, THEME and so on are presented as being at the level of semantics, and their realizations are integrated in a single structure at the level of form. (However, Halliday there terms it the 'lexicogrammatical level'; this is a little confusing, since Halliday later uses the term "lexicogrammar" in a sense that includes the system networks.) Thus the paper begins with the words:

> Let us assume that the semantic system is one of three levels, or strata, that constitute the linguistic system:
>
> Semantic (semology)
> Lexicogrammatical (lexology: syntax, morphology and lexis)
> Phonological (phonology and phonetics).
>
> (Halliday 1977:176)

---

18. The only full version of "Text as semantic choice in social context" is Halliday (1977). Surprisingly — and disappointingly — when it was republished in 1978 in *Language as Social Semiotic* the part that showed all the detail of the description was omitted, and only the general description remained. In what follows, therefore, most references will be to Halliday (1977).

Halliday then makes the point that "these are strata in Lamb's sense", and the terms in brackets are intended to show the parallels with Lamb's multi-stratal model (Lamb 1966). Of the three levels distinguished here, it is the first two in which we are interested. Let us take the "semantic" level first. Halliday writes:

> Let us assume that the semantic system has four components: experiential, logical, interpersonal and textual (1977:176).

And two paragraphs later he suggests a third basic assumption:

> Let us assume that each component of the semantic system specifies its own structures, as the 'output' of the options in the network (each act of choice contributing to the formation of the structure). (1977:176)

Since Halliday never shows any structures that can be decribed as "semantic" other than the multiple structures of functional elements found in *IFG* (which we shall be examining in the next chapter), it is clearly these to which he is referring. In other words, choices in the system network in the experiential component result in 'structures' such as 'Agent + Process + Affected'.

What, then, is the role of the level labelled "lexicogrammar" in this approach? It is a role that is very different from that which it is assigned in Halliday's 'two levels of meaning' approach to language, in which the "lexicogrammar" includes everything from the system networks of TRANSITIVITY, MOOD, THEME etc. to as their final realization in form. Interestingly, Halliday writes in "Language as choice in social context" that

> it is the function of the lexiogrammatical stratum to map the structures onto each other so as **to form a single integrated structure** [my emphasis] that represents all components [of the semantics] simultaneously. (Halliday 1877:176)

As we shall see in Section 7.8 of Chapter 7, this is essentially the role of the realization rules in the Cardiff Grammar (though only if we allow ourselves to interpret "structures" as 'strands of meaning represented by features').[19]

The example analyzed in Halliday (1977) as an illustration of these

---

19. However, it must be said that one of the five introductory 'assumptions' in Halliday (1977/78) seems to reflect the second of the two positions on meaning identified in Section 4.6. This is when he writes: "Let us assume that each stratum [...] is described as a network of options." This view is clearly incompatible with that modelled in Figure 4 of Chapter 3, because there the component that specifies the 'potential' at the level of form is the realization rules — and so **not** a system network. Since the other assumptions are fully compatible with the model described in Figure 4 of Chapter 3, and since this one therefore appears to be at odds with those others, we shall take it that its inclusion in the paper is evidence that even as he wrote it Halliday was toying with the possibility of the second of his two models of meaning.

principles is fairly complex, i.e., *"I would as soon live with a pair of unoiled garden shears," said her inamorata.* Halliday's analysis of this text-sentence raises a number of interesting questions that would distract us from the main point, so we shall look instead at the simpler example from the second of Halliday's two papers that exemplify the type of analysis that reflects the above description, i.e, that in Halliday (1970/76b). This is shown in Figure 6.

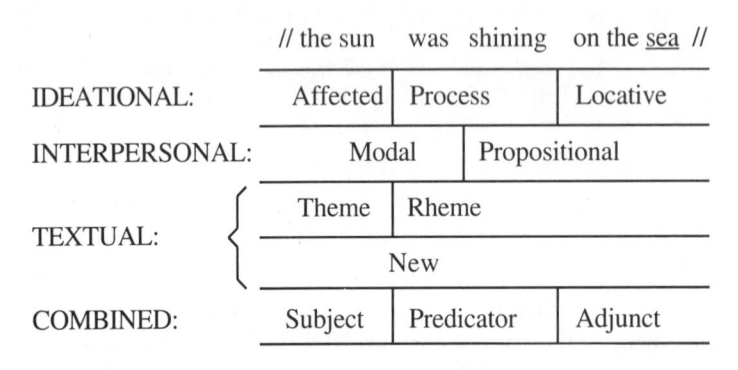

|  | // the sun | was shining | on the sea // |
|---|---|---|---|
| IDEATIONAL: | Affected | Process | Locative |
| INTERPERSONAL: | Modal | Propositional | |
| TEXTUAL: | Theme | Rheme | |
|  | New | | |
| COMBINED: | Subject | Predicator | Adjunct |

*Figure 6: An analysis by Halliday with an integrating syntax*

Notice first that there is a line of structure for each of the 'ideational' and the 'interpersonal' strands of meaning: with the usual two for the 'textual' meaning — i.e., one showing the 'thematic' structure, and one the 'information' structure.[20] But the key feature of the diagram is the single line of structure which comes below these four lines, and which uses the names of the elements of the clause which were established as part of Scale and Category Grammar — i.e, at the time when the assumption was that the whole grammar was at the level of form. Some of the labels for the 'functions' are different from those found in later representations such as those in *IFG*, e.g., "Modal" and "Propositional" are later replaced by "Mood" and "Residue", but we shall find in Chapter 7 that the first four lines of Figure 6 correspond closely to the type of analysis found in all of Halliday's work since that time.

Figure 6 is exactly as it occurs in Halliday (1970/76b), with the exception of the word "COMBINED", which I have added (borrowing it from the

---

20. Strictly speaking, the term "ideational" should be replaced by "experiential" (as it is in the diagram in Halliday 1977:222) since "ideational" is in Halliday's terminology the superordinate term that also includes the 'logical' metafunction, and this line of analysis shows only the 'experiential' meaning.

equivalent diagram in Halliday (1977). It is clear that, even though there are few explanatory comments on the diagram in either Halliday (1970/76b) or Halliday (1977), Halliday's intention is precisely that of showing that the structures represented in the four 'strands of meaning' above are "combined" in the single integrated structure shown below them. In Halliday's words (1970/76b:24): "any element [e.g., the Subject] may have more than one structural role, like a chord in a fugue which participates simultaneously in more than one melodic line."

However, despite the obvious attractions of the general model implied by the analysis in Figure 6, Halliday abandoned it after presenting it in just two papers. What replaced it was a representation in which the 'SPCA' elements shown in Figure 6 as integrating the four strands of meaning above them are reduced in status, so that they become merely the analysis at the second degree of delicacy of the 'interpersonal' strand of meaning. Indeed, just as the 'integrating' use of this type of structure was introduced with little more than a hint as to why it was being used, so too it was abandoned without any explanation. In Section 7.2 of Chapter 7, when we consider the *IFG* method of analysis in more detail, I shall summarize the reasons that Halliday gives for treating the 'SPCA-type' analysis as 'interpersonal' meaning. (However, that statement does not explain what structure will perform the vital integrating function.)

One reason why Halliday's "Language as choice in social context" is important, then, is that it is to this apparently aberrant stage of his developing model that the Cardiff Grammar is most closely related. In other words, if you compare Figure 6 above with Figure 10 in Section 7.9 of Chapter 7, you will see that, in broad terms, the two representations suggest the same overall model of language. There are still differences, of course. The most visually prominent one is that in the Cardiff Grammar representation the syntactic analysis is drawn above the text (this, however, being merely a matter of convenience and convention). A second difference is that in the Cardiff Grammar the strands of meanings are represented by semantic features from the system network itself, rather than by 'functional elements' that are generated from it. This, as we shall see in Chapter 7, is a much more fundamental difference.

Thus Figure 6 is more like the representation used in the Cardiff Grammar than the standard *IFG* analysis is, e.g., as shown in Figure 7 in Section 7.2 of Chapter 7. In that chapter I shall comment on the differences; here my purpose is simply to note the fact of this phase in Halliday's frequently changing model.

# 4.10 Summary: the implications of the changes

In Chapter 3 we built up a picture, at a somewhat abstract level, of the essential components of a modern, large-scale, computer-implementable systemic functional grammar — and we noted that Appendix A provides an example of these concepts at work in a small but fully generative SF grammar. Then in the first half of the present chapter we traced the key changes by which Halliday transformed the "Categories" model into a modern SF grammar. Taken together, these three changes — privileging the concept of 'system', recognizing that the choices in systems are choices between meanings, and recognizing the many functions that grammar simultaneously serves — have revolutionized the theory and created a new model of language.

Of these three changes, the most fundamental was Halliday's 1966 proposal that the system networks of TRANSITIVITY, MOOD and THEME should be regarded as modelling choices between meanings. Since the system networks were now regarded as being at a higher level of language than the forms that express them, their relationships to the other major categories are inevitably changed.

The new general concept that was needed to provide for these 'interstratal' relationships was **realization** (which was originally introduced, as we saw in Section 2.4 of Chapter 2, as a simple replacement for Halliday's earlier broad term "exponence"). As we shall find in the next chapter, this second change was to have a fairly drastic effect on the seven "fundamental" concepts introduced in "Categories". A second new basic concept was **instantiation** — and it is the fact that we find both a 'potential' and an 'instance' at each of the two levels within the lexicogrammar that demonstrates the presence, **within** the grammar, of the two levels of 'meaning' and 'form'.

Then, in the second half of the chapter, we surveyed the effect of Halliday's adoption of the concept that there is a higher set of system networks than those of TRANSITIVITY, MOOD and THEME. First we noted that this has led him to express increasingly strongly the view that the relationship between these system networks and the structures that are generated from them is only one of realization by "extension" or by "analogy". I then gave some of the reasons why I think he is wrong to dismiss his earlier insight that the system networks constitute the level of semantics, and I argued that the topological relationships between the different parts of the model of language summarized in Figure 4 remain intact — even when the diagram is redrawn in order to make them appear to occupy a single stratum of language, as in Figure 5. The key point is that, since the relationships remain the same, it is still possible to make a direct comparison between the output structures of the Sydney and the Cardiff Grammars.

Next, I showed why diagrams consisting of system networks in which the realization rules are shown as 'footnotes' on the features are not only inadequate for a large-scale grammar but that they also give a misleading picture of language. In other words, the existence of such diagrams should not be taken as evidence that the full set of components and outputs shown in Figure 4 is unnecessary.

Finally, I showed that there was one temporary phase in the development of Halliday's theory in which he showed the Scale and Category elements of the clause as serving the function of integrating the various strands of meanings that are always shown in any *IFG*-style analysis — very much as the Cardiff Grammar does, in general terms, and as this book argues that all systemic functional grammars should. Yet it is a model which Halliday quickly abandoned for reasons that are far from clear, inserting the 'intregrating' elements in the 'interpersonal' strand of meaning instead, as we shall see in Chapter 7. And, as we shall also see in Chapter 7, this leaves the considerable problem of how these semi-semantic 'multiple structures' are to be integrated into a single structure.

In the next chapter we shall survey the "basic concepts" presented in Halliday's important 1993 paper "Systemic theory". This short but densely packed paper is particularly important for understanding Halliday's view of language, because it is Halliday's most recent comprehensive summary of what he sees as the "basic concepts" of the theory. It therefore gives us a way of making a direct comparison between the "fundamental" categories and scales that he identifies in "Categories of the theory of grammar" and the concepts that he now considers to be the most important. In the next chapter I shall chart those concepts that remain intact form "Categories" (in so far as any do); those that have changed; those that receive no mention in the new framework; and — perhaps most importantly of all — those that have been added. Then in Chapter 6 we shall look in the same way at the "basic concepts" that are stated (or assumed) in *IFG*. And these, surprising though it may at first seem, are very far from being the same as those in "Systemic theory".

# 5
# Syntax in a generative systemic functional grammar

## 5.1 "Systemic theory" (1993) and related works

The main focus of this chapter is on Halliday's "Systemic Theory" (1993). In the final section, however, I shall introduce certain other works in SFL which specify the 'syntax potential' of language in a similar fashion — and this will include work in the framework of the Cardiff Grammar as well as other work in the Sydney Grammar framework.

"Systemic Theory" consists of just four large, densely-packed pages in the *Encyclopaedia of Languages and Linguistics* (Asher 1993). Indeed, because it provides an overview of the theory as a whole, less than half of it has any direct bearing on our interests here. Luckily, there are fuller accounts of some of the concepts discussed there in Halliday's "On grammar and grammatics" (1996), and almost all of the concepts presented in "Systemic theory" are discussed in Matthiessen (1995). I shall therefore also draw on these works from time to time.

The picture of the nature of language that one gets from "Systemic theory" is fascinatingly different from that given in "Categories" — and indeed, as we shall see in the next chapter, from the picture of language given in *IFG*. It is of course to be expected that it should be different from "Categories", since that paper appeared over thirty years earlier, but it is at first sight surprising that "Systemic theory" is so different from *IFG* (whose second edition was published just a year after it, in 1994).

We can take the view of language presented in "Systemic theory" as broadly representative of three closely related bodies of work: (1) the work in the mid-1960s by Halliday, Henrici, Huddleston and Hudson that was to develop into the set of concepts presented in "Systemic Theory"; (2) the formalization and computer implementation of these concepts by Mann, Matthiessen and others, as first described informally in Mann & Matthiessen

(1983/85) and later more fully in Matthiessen & Bateman (1991) and (less formally) in Matthiessen (1995); and (3) — with some differences — the set of concepts used in the Cardiff Grammar, as first described in Fawcett (1973/81 and 1980) and defined most clearly in Fawcett, Tucker & Lin (1993). It is the first two bodies of work that "Systemic theory" reflects most closely.

Interestingly, we shall find that, in what we shall term the 'theoretical-generative' aspect of a SF theory of syntax, there are fewer important differences between the Sydney and the Cardiff Grammars than there are in the 'text-descriptive' aspect. By the end of this chapter we shall see how it is that there can be a fairly close similarity between the two models with respect to one aspect of the theory, while there is not in the other.

## 5.2 The 'theoretical-generative' and 'text-descriptive' strands of work in Systemic Functional Linguistics

It is useful to recognize two strands of work in SFL. These two strands can also be found within other theories of language, but some theories give much greater prominence to one rather than the other. We shall call these two strands the 'theoretical-generative' and the 'text-descriptive' strands — and they can be found in both the Sydney and the Cardiff versions of SFL. Sometimes they both occur in the same paper or book, but some of the most important publications are clearly dominated by the one or the other. Some SF linguists — and perhaps especially those who are strongly oriented to 'text-descriptive' linguistics — are tempted to take up one strand of work and to consider the other to be beyond their area of responsibility, as it were, but in reality the two are mutually dependent, each gaining from advances in the other.

The origin of the important body of scholarship in the **theoretical-generative** strand of SFL was the work carried out at University College London in the mid-1960s by Halliday (e.g., 1969/81), Huddleston (e.g., 1966/81), Henrici (e.g., 1965/81) and Hudson (e.g., 1971). Their achievement was to lay the foundations for the expression of systemic theory as a **generative** model of language. While this was in part a response to the challenge of Chomsky's claim that grammars should be generative, their work was also conceived as a solution to the problem of formulating the model of language sufficiently explicitly to enable it to be implemented in a computer model that generated text-sentences. This is probably the most challenging of all ways of expressing a generative grammar (as I pointed out in Section 1.2 of Chapter 2), and the work of the four pioneers in generative SFL has led on to a number of computer implementations that have been important milestones in Computational Linguistics. The first was Winograd's major contribution to the sub-field of Natural Language Understanding (Winograd 1972), and this was later followed by the equally significant contribution to the sub-field of Natural Language Generation (NLG) by Davey (1978). His impressive achievement led in turn to the dominance of work in NLG throughout the 1980s and thereafter by work based on SF grammar — first by Patten (1988) and then by Mann, Matthiessen, Bateman and others through the Penman Project (which was introduced, with references, in Section 1.2 of Chapter 1). Finally, this was followed by work on other languages in the Komet Project at Darmstadt and on multilingual text generation in Sydney, and by the partly equivalent but more detailed work by my colleagues and myself at Cardiff. Much of this work continues in the 2000s.

The considerable extent to which the ideas developed by the original four researchers have remained the cornerstone of systemic generation ever since is an impressive tribute to the quality of their work. It is not the case that there have been no further developments, however. These further developments have included significant changes to the set of realization operations, developments in the role of **pre-selection** on re-entry to the system network and, most significantly of all in my view, the introduction of the use of **probabilities**. Yet the fact is that, apart from the "further developments" just mentioned, most of the set of concepts that are used today in generative SFL grammars can be traced back to their forerunners in the work of the 1960s.

I have called this body of work 'theoretical-generative', but it is of course possible to have work in linguistics that is **theoretical** but not **generative**. Indeed, "Categories" itself is one such example. Since the mid-sixties, however, there has been a strong correlation between work in SFL that specifies how a generative grammar works and work on the theoretical concepts of the theory.

From this viewpoint, what is most striking about "Systemic theory" is that the ideas that Halliday chooses to present as the "basic concepts" of the theory are precisely the ones that are central to the concerns of the theoretical-generative strand of work in SFL (as we shall see in the next section).

The second strand of work in SFL is the one that is more widely known: this is the **text-descriptive** strand of work. Like the term 'theoretical-generative', the term 'text-descriptive' is intended to evoke two types of work in linguistics that do not necessarily occur together, but which in SFL tend to be mutually supportive. The first is the **description of languages**, where the goal is to achieve a functional description of a language with a broad coverage (rather than, for example, the identification of particular syntactic phenomena as part of a search for syntactic 'universals', as in some other theories). Such descriptions typically have a strong functional orientation and are based on the evidence of real-life texts and/or evidence from computer corpora. Some examples are Quirk *et al.* (1985) and its various precursors and sequels, and, from the new generation of corpus-based grammars, the *Collins COBUILD English Grammar* (Sinclair 1990) and its derived works, such as Francis, Hunston & Manning (1996 and 1998), and also Biber *et al.* (1999). Works such as Halliday's *IFG* and Fawcett (in press) are also in the text-descriptive tradition.

It is a descriptive linguistics of this type that is needed by many researchers in many fields of 'applied linguistics' for use in the **description of texts**. These fields include language learning (mother tongue and second language), speech pathology, literary stylistics and critical discourse theory, and many of the researchers in such fields specifically require a usable, functionally-oriented description of language such as SFL claims to provide.

The term "text-descriptive" is therefore intended to cover both of these aspects of what is perceived here as one general strand of work: the text-based description of languages and the description of texts. But in terms of the numbers of users of text-descriptive work, most users require SFL for the analysis of texts for one purpose or another. However, SFL descriptions have also been used directly in educational work on curriculum development, etc.

The two editions of *IFG* (1985 and 1994) and the many spin-off publications (listed in a footnote in Section 7.1.1 of Chapter 7) are the main testimony to this strand of work in the Sydney framework. The main works in this tradition from the Cardiff group are Fawcett (in press) and Fawcett (forthcoming a). But a good example of a work in the Cardiff framework that comprehends both the theoretical-generative and the text-descriptive traditions is Tucker (1998).

Thus, when Halliday was asked to write an account of 'systemic theory' for the *Encyclopaedia of Languages and Linguistics*, it was natural that he should draw primarily on the theoretical-generative strand of the theory. However, this leaves unanswered the question of why the aspects of the theory that are relevant to the 'text-descriptive' work that is presented in *IFG* are so different from the aspects presented in "Systemic theory". (I shall return to this question in the next chapter, after we have considered the concepts that are foregrounded in *IFG*.)

It seems to me that, in cases where a theory has these two strands within its work — as both the Sydney and the Cardiff Grammars have — the publications that reflect one or other of these two aspects of the theory should not present **different models** of language, but **different aspects of the same model**. More specifically, any such "different aspect" should be a selection of a 'subset' of the concepts that make up the overall model, this 'subset' being selected for presentation to a particular audience in order to try to meet its particular needs. This is the case with the different presentations of the Cardiff version of SFL, e.g., in its 'theoretical-generative' aspect in Fawcett, Tucker & Lin (1993) and in its 'text-descriptive' aspect in Fawcett (in press). It is not a question of 'horses for courses', except in the sense defined above.

However, as we shall see in Chapter 7, it seems that two different positions on how a grammar works have been allowed to develop alongside each other in the Sydney version of SFL — and that in this case the two positions are **not** compatible with each other. This then raises the difficult question of which one is the 'correct' version of the theory — and, in relation to the other version, why it is different and what status it has in the theory.

With these issues in mind, we shall turn now to an examination of the concepts presented in "Systemic theory". Then in Chapters 6 and 7 we shall examine those in *IFG*.

"Systemic theory" has six sections, covering (1) the origins of systemic theory, (2) systems and their realization, (3) other basic concepts, (4) other features of the theory (the orientation to 'language as social process', and so 'register', etc), (5) the development of systemic theory, and (6) contemporary influences on systemic theory and current trends in the theory. Here, we are interested in the "basic concepts" of the theory, so we shall draw mainly on Sections (1) to (3).

## 5.3 The "basic concepts" of "Systemic theory"

Halliday begins "Systemic theory" by reminding us that "systemic theory" is short for "systemic-functional theory", and this establishes from the start that the "systemic" approach to explaining language is one that is inherently oriented to 'function' and 'meaning'. The fact that SFG is a different theory of language from S&C is underlined when Halliday describes it (1993:4505) as "a development of *Scale and Category Grammar*"; indeed, the encyclopaedia in which "Systemic theory" appears contains a separate article on S&C grammar (Butler 1993a).

The question that we need to ask is: "How far do the seven 'fundamental' concepts of "Categories" (as described in Chapter 2 of this book) coincide with the 'basic concepts' presented in "Systemic theory", thirty-two years later?"

Let us begin by looking for the four concepts from "Categories" of 'unit','class', 'structure' and 'system'. We shall find, as we would expect in a theory that has been re-named "systemic (functional) theory", that **system** is strongly fore-grounded, so let us begin with this concept. In Halliday's words (1993:4505): "the system takes priority," and he defines a system as a set of "options in **meaning potential** [my emphasis]". He then goes on to show how, because an option in one system can serve as an entry condition to another, large numbers of such systems combine to form a **system network**. Moreover, because the 'entry condition' to a system may consist of more than one option and because more than one system may be entered from one entry condition, the structure of a system network is more complex than that of a simple taxonomy. (For an example of a system network with such 'simultaneous' systems, see the simple example in Figure 1 of Appendix A.) Thus the first two "basic concepts" of "Systemic Theory' are 'system' and 'system network', where they model the "meaning potential" of a language.

One might be tempted to say that the concept of 'system' has been expanded from what it was in "Categories" rather than changed — if it were not for the vital fact that the system networks of TRANSITIVITY, MOOD, THEME and so on now model choices between meanings, as Halliday's use of the term "meaning potential" indicates. Thus the points being presented in this section of "Systemic theory" correspond to the two changes in the theory that were charted in Sections 4.2 and 4.3 of Chapter 4.

However, Halliday also uses the term **system** in a more general sense. In this second sense it denotes 'paradigmatic relations' (or 'options in meaning potential'), and it is in contrast with the term **structure**, which is itself to be understood in a broad sense that embraces all aspects of syntagmatic organization at the level of form. But we should notice this is not the sense in which the term "structure" was used in "Categories". There it was used in a quite specific sense, i.e., one in which it was mutually defining with the concept of 'element'. In other words, a second "fundamental category" is now being used in a different sense.

Perhaps, you might think, the concept of 'structure' in the "Categories" sense would still be reflected in "Systemic theory" through the presence of the term **element**, with which it is mutually defining? The term "element" does indeed appear in "Systemic theory", but once again it is used in a somewhat different sense (as I shall explain shortly). But the most surprising fact of all about the concept of 'element' in "Systemic theory" is that it is not presented as one of the "basic concepts". It is simply employed in defining other concepts — rather as if it was considered to be a non-theoretical concept whose meaning the reader is expected to interpret without guidance. In "Systemic theory", then, the concepts of both 'structure' and 'element' are used in different senses from those with which they were used in "Categories".

How, then, have the two other "fundamental" categories from "Categories" fared, i.e., **unit** and **class** (of unit)? Amazingly, these two terms are also missing from "Systemic theory". One reason why it is surprising that the concept of 'unit' is not listed as a "basic concept" is that it is a vital part of the 'rank scale' concept — and it is this concept which provides the main organizing principle in "Categories" (as we saw in Section 2.3 of Chapter 2). We shall discuss the curious treatment of the related concept of 'rank' shortly, when we ask what status is given in "Systemic theory" to the 'scales' that were introduced in "Categories".

The fourth "fundamental category" in "Categories" is 'class' — and this concept too is missing from the list of "basic concepts" in "Systemic theory". This absence is equally surprising, because the concept of 'class of unit' is essential to any generative SF grammar. The reason is that the way in which such grammars work is that each pass through the system network builds the structure of a given class of unit. For example, the class of unit that the simple system network in Figure 1 of Appendix A generates is the nominal group, and it cannot generate any other class of unit. The class of unit that is generated in all of the illustrative generative grammars that Halliday presents is the clause (e.g., Halliday 1969/81). "Systemic theory" is oriented to the use of the theory in generation so that the concept of 'class (of unit)' is, in a sense, presupposed throughout, yet the fact is that it is not presented as a "basic concept".

Thus, only one of the four "fundamental" categories of "Categories" appears in the list of "basic concepts" in "Systemic theory" (i.e.,'system') — and even then it has a significantly modified sense. Two are either used informally or presupposed (i.e., 'element' and 'class (of unit)'), but it is really surprising to find that they are not presented as "basic concepts". And one of the four original "fundamental concepts" ('unit') is completely missing.

How far, then, are the 'scales' of "Categories" still treated as "basic concepts" in "Systemic theory"? In the section headed "Other basic concepts" Halliday makes the claim that "systemic theory retains [from "Categories"] the concepts of 'rank', 'realization' [his 1966 replacement for 'exponence'] and 'delicacy'" (Halliday 1993:4505-6). But are these the same concepts that we met in the summary of "Categories" in Chapter 2?

Let us begin with **delicacy**. I suggested in Section 2.4 of Chapter 2 that this concept belongs essentially with that of 'system' (and so with 'system network'), such that one system is more "delicate" than another if its entry condition is a feature in that other system — and so on, across a chain of such dependencies (as illustrated on a small scale in Figure 1 of Appendix A). It follows, then, that the elevation of the 'system' to model contrasts in 'meaning potential' rather than contrasts between forms brings with it a similar change in the meaning of 'delicacy' — so that 'delicacy' has similarly become a partly different concept. It is therefore not simply "retained", as Halliday says (p. 4505); it has been adapted, just as the concept of 'system' has been adapted. However, there is what we might term a "second order" manifestation of the concept, i.e., its use to describe the relationship between 'primary' and 'secondary' structures'. (See Figure 7 in Section 7.2 of Chapter 7 for the presentation of MOOD as having both a 'primary' and a 'secondary' structure, and see Section 10.3.4 of Chapter 10 for a critical discussion of this concept.) With these substantial provisos, then, we may say that the term "delicacy" is used in "Systemic theory" in a roughly similar sense to that which it had in "Categories".

We turn now to the concept of '**rank**' — the 'scale' which, with 'unit', provides the major organizing principle of the grammar in "Categories". The definition that Halliday gives of it in "Systemic theory" is one of the more puzzling sections of the paper. Here he defines 'rank' in a somewhat opaque manner, writing:

> 'Rank' is constituency based on function, and hence 'flat', with minimal layering.
> (Halliday 1993:4505)

The meaning of "and hence flat" can be clarified by expanding the last part of Halliday's definition to "and hence represented by diagrams that resemble 'flat trees' rather than 'trees with multiple branching'". And such trees naturally have "minimal layering".

Notice that while Halliday introduces the word "rank" in "Systemic theory", the idea that it means a 'rank scale' of units with the associated concept of 'accountability at all ranks' is simply omitted from what is presented as a summary of the "basic concepts" of the theory. One reason why this is particularly surprising is that the concept of the 'rank scale' is still reflected quite strongly in *IFG*, as we shall see in the next chapter. Nor is there any help on this matter in Halliday (1996). On the other hand, Matthiessen uses the concepts of the 'rank scale' and 'rank shift' quite freely in his *Lexicogrammatical Cartography*, and he defines 'rank' in the standard "Categories" manner in the book's useful Glossary section (Matthiessen 1995:790). Thus it would be premature to interpret Halliday's failure to foreground the concept of the 'rank scale' in "Systemic theory" as a weakening of his commitment to the 'rank scale'. It is nonetheless a curious omission.

Whatever the reason for this omission, I should flag at this point that I shall argue in Part 2 that there are other principles than the concept of the 'rank scale' that lead one to adopt a 'flat tree' approach to constituency. So I wish to point out that Halliday's assertion here of the close relationship between 'rank' and 'flat tree constituency' does not necessarily imply that each of the two concepts entails the other. The two concepts are in fact clearly different, and while it may be true that having a 'rank scale' in one's grammar entails 'flat tree constituency' the reverse is not true. Indeed, I shall argue in Part 2 that it is not only possible for a grammar to have the 'flat tree' type of 'constituency' without at the same time using the concept of the 'rank scale', but that it is also desirable. I shall explain the many advantages of adopting this position when I introduce the new theory of syntax for SF grammar to be described in Part 2.

Finally, let us look at what has happened to the term **realization** (Halliday's 1966 replacement for the original "Categories" term "exponence"). Halliday originally brought the concept of 'realization' into use as a result of the elevation of 'system' to model 'meaning potential', as we saw in Figure 4 (in Section 3.2 of Chapter 3). However, the original "Categories" concept of 'exponence / realization' has now become the concept that denotes the relationship between two levels of language. In Halliday's words:

'Realization' is the relationship between the 'strata' (or levels) of a [...] semiotic system" (Halliday (1993:4505).

Thus the term has significantly changed its meaning as a result of the elevation of 'system' to model 'meaning potential', just as 'system' itself and 'delicacy' have — but in this case the change of meaning has been marked by a change of name.

However, there is a second major class of differences between the concepts of "Categories" and those of "Systemic theory". This is the introduction of three major new "basic concepts". These are: 'selection expression', 'instantiation' and 'realization statement'. The first and the third can be explicitly dated back to work in the mid-1960s, but the second, while being implicit in that work, has only come to the fore since the early 1980s.

While there are no equivalents for any of these three concepts in "Categories", we have already met all three in Chapter 3. This is because each is essential to a modern SF grammar. Indeed, the first and the third are labels for boxes in the model of language represented in Figure 4 in Section 3.2 of Chapter 3.

Let us begin with **instantiation**. In Halliday's words:

'Instantiation' is the relation between the semiotic system and the observable events, or 'acts of meaning'. (Halliday 1993:4505)

Even a **selection expression**, which is strictly speaking not "observable", is an 'instance', i.e., an 'instance of meaning', in that it is the set of features that have been chosen on one traversal of the system network. Thus the instance of meaning' chosen in Section 3 of the worked example in Appendix A is:

[thing, count, plural, student, nearness to performer, un-near]

(When features are listed formally, they are placed in square brackets, as here.)

The selection expression is the input to the **realization statements**. The function of each of these is to specify, for a given feature in the system network, the operation through which that feature contributes to "the structural configuration" that is being generated. In "Systemic theory" Halliday specifies seven types of realization statement, his claim being that every such statement conforms to one of the seven types. As we saw in Chapter 3, a theory of syntax must be concerned with how the grammar specifies both (1) the **syntax potential** and (2) the **instances of syntax**, i.e., the outputs from the grammar. In terms of Figure 4 in Chapter 3, then, Halliday's 'realization statements' belong in the box labelled "realization rules / statements".[1]

---

1. Halliday prefers the term 'statements' to rules', but there is no difference of substance here. Following Hudson's pioneering work on realization in Hudson (1971), I use the term "realization rules". Strictly speaking, what Halliday refers to here as "realization statements"

I shall now list the set of types of 'realization operation' given in "Systemic theory". However, I shall leave the full explanation and evaluation of each to Chapter 9 of Part 2, because they are relatively close to the set that is required for this component of a modern theory of syntax for a SF grammar — though the set to be introduced in Chapter 9 set is slightly fuller. They will therefore be explained and evaluated at that point, i.e., in Section 9.2.1 of Chapter 9. (In what follows I have highlighted the use of any concept that also occurs in "Categories" in boldface, for a reason that I shall explain in a moment.)

Halliday's seven types of 'realization statement' are, in his words:

(a) 'Insert' an **element** (e.g., insert subject);
(b) 'Conflate' one **element** with another (e.g., conflate subject with theme);
(c) 'Order' an **element** with respect to another, or to some defined location (e.g., order finite auxiliary before subject);
(d) 'Classify' an **element** (e.g., classify process as mental: cognition);
(e) ''Split' an **element** into a further configuration (e.g., split mood into subject + finite);
(f) 'Preselect' some feature at a lower **rank** (e.g., preselect nominal group);
(g) 'Lexify' an **element** (e.g., lexify subject : *it*).

(Halliday 1993:4505)

We can see examples of some of these operations in the realization rules given in Figure 2 of Appendix A. A realization rule such as "h < "water" " includes both Halliday's (a), where the rule inserts a head (shown in Appendix A as "h") in the structure, and his (g), in that the rule also states that the head is to be expounded by the item "water". On the other hand, Halliday's 'ordering' rule (c) is covered by the simplified 'potential structure' of "ngp: dd m h q", which is shown in Section 3 of Appendix A. This specifies that, if a deictic determiner (dd) is present in the nominal group that is being generated, it precedes any modifier (m) that may be present, and that both precede any head (h) that may be present, and that this precedes any qualifier (g) that may be present. (The potential structure for the nominal group in the large COMMUNAL grammar currently operates with seventy elements, so the potential structure shown in Appendix B is indeed, as is stated there, highly simplified.)

Earlier, we were considering the fact that the concept of 'element' was not

---

are 'realization operations', because it is possible for the realization statement for a given feature to include two or more such 'operations'.

presented as a "basic concept" in "Systemic theory". However, as you can see from the number of instances of the word "element" in boldface in Halliday's realization statements, this term certainly plays a central role in the process of building 'structure' in his theory. Notice, however, that the term "element" is being used here in a different sense from that in "Categories" — and also from that in which it is typically used in *IFG* and in Matthiessen (1995:23-5). In the Sydney Grammar, it is the word "function" that should, strictly speaking, be used to refer to concepts such as 'Subject' and 'Theme', e.g., in (a), (b) and (c) of Halliday's realization statements. The term "element" is typically used for the component of the clause into which such "functions" combine. Interestingly, Matthiessen makes no use at all of the term "element", using instead the informal term "bundle of functions".[2] Thus in "Systemic theory" Halliday uses "element" in Matthiessen's sense of "function" — such that the "conflation" (or 'fusion') of two or more such "functions" combines to constitute a single element of the clause, in the way to be described in Section 7.2 of Chapter 7. It is this unified sense of "element" that corresponds most closely to the meaning of the term "element" in "Categories". It may be thought that this is not a major difference, but it is nonetheless a significant one, because it reflects the addition to the theory of the concept that an element may carry several meanings at the same time — this being the third of the major developments in the theory that we noted in Chapter 4.[3]

Strangely, one vital operation appears to be missing from Halliday's list in "Systemic theory" — and it is also missing from the closely related lists given in Matthiessen & Bateman (1991) and Matthiessen (1995). This missing operation is 'Insert unit', and I shall comment on the possible reasons for its absence in Section 9.2 of Chapter 9.

We have seen that "Systemic theory" incorporates the first two of the three major developments to the "Categories" model, as described in Sections 4.2 and 4.3 of Chapter 4. In a later section of the paper (entitled "Other basic concepts")

---

2. The index in Matthiessen (1995) indicates that there are no uses of the term "element" (in the sense of 'element of structure' of a 'unit') in this comprehensive work of almost 1000 pages.

3. You may have noticed that the term "rank" is used in (f) above, but this is not significant. This is because, strictly speaking, Halliday should have used here a term such as "layer of structure" or "unit", since the unit that is 'lower' in the structure is not necessarily of a lower 'rank' (e.g., a clause or a prepositional group/phrase frequently functions as a qualifier in a nominal group).

Halliday introduces the third major innovation, i.e., the concept that "the content plane of a language is organized in a small number of functionally organized components" (p. 4505). These are the four 'metafunctions' within the Hallidayan lexicogrammar that we met in Section 4.4 of Chapter 4. But the concept is also expressed in the realization operation of 'conflation'. Thus, as Halliday's example of Operation (b) above shows, a 'Theme' (which realizes a 'textual' meaning) may be conflated with a 'Subject' (which realizes an 'interpersonal' meaning). We shall return to the topic of 'conflation' in Chapter 7.

We have already noted several surprising omissions of "Categories" concepts from the basic concepts of "Systemic theory". I shall now identify another omission — though it is one of a different sort. You will recall, from Section 4.6 of Chapter 4, that in recent years Halliday has shown an increasing commitment the view that we should recognize an additional layer of 'meaning potential' — i.e., a 'semantics' above the level of 'meaning potential' that is represented in the system networks for TRANSITIVITY, MOOD and so on. We called this the 'two-level' model of meaning. Interestingly, Halliday does not include this concept in "Systemic theory". If it is as central to his view of language as some of his recent writings suggest (e.g., 1996:29), why, one wonders, has it been left out?[4] One reason may be that he was not sufficiently confident of its place in the overall theory at the time of writing "Systemic theory" to give it this status. Another possible reason may be that he limited himself, in what was necessarily a short paper, to just those concepts that he believed to be common to all 'dialects' of SFL. In other words, he may have omitted the concept of a 'higher semantics' on the grounds that some other systemic functional linguists (including those working in the framework of the Cardiff Grammar) consider that the existing system networks (or replacements for them that are more explicitly semantic) are all that is needed to model those aspects of 'meaning' that it is appropriate to model as lying within language. Either way, the absence of this concept from this key summary of the theory seems to signal that at the time of writing Halliday was less confident of its centrality in his view of language than he appears to have become in subsequent

---

4. For example, Halliday contrasts his view and mine on the question of levels of language, when writing of the problem of "the nature and location of the stratal boundary between the grammar and the semantics" (Halliday 1996:29). He says: "One can, in fact, map it onto the boundary between system and structure, as Fawcett does, [...] whereas I have found it more valuable to set up two distinct strata of paradigmatic (systemic) organization". (Here he slightly misrepresents my position, because in the Cardiff Grammar there is structure at the level of semantics, in the sense of 'componence without sequence (except in co-ordination)'.

works, such as Halliday & Matthiessen (1999).

Let me summarize the "basic concepts' of "Systemic theory". These are: 'system', 'system network', 'selection expression', 'realization' and 'structure' — the latter, however, only being used in a highly generalized sense. In addition, Halliday makes a fundamental distinction between 'realization' and 'instantiation', exactly as we have done as in Chapter 3. However, he then he goes on to blur the distinction by saying that the term "realization" is not only used for "the relation between strata" but also, "by analogy", for "the relation between the paradigmatic and the syntagmatic phases of representation within one stratum". I find this an unfortunate formulation, because it suggests that there is an immediate relationship between the system networks ("the paradigmatic [...] phase") and the output structure ("the [...] syntagmatic phase"). In other words, this way of describing matters overlooks (1) the relation of instantiation between the system networks and the selection expression, (2) the selection expression itself, (3) the realization rules (which are triggered by the features in the selection expression), and finally (4) instantiation relation between these and the output structures that they generate. In other words, at this point in "Systemic theory" Halliday's second view of 'meaning' (as described in Section 4.6 of Chapter 4) appears to be dominant — i.e., the one in which the system networks are assumed to be at the same level as the final output structures. Apart from this short passage, however, the theoretical model of language presented in "Systemic theory", with its two components of the system networks and the realization statements, is essentially the same as the general systemic functional model proposed in Chapter 3.

Let us now summarize the place in "Systemic theory" of the more specifically 'structural' concepts from "Categories". The categories of 'unit', 'class (of unit)' and 'element' are not included in the presentation of the "basic concepts". Moreover, while the term "element" is used in presenting the realization statements, it has a different sense from that in "Categories". On the other hand, "Systemic theory" includes a set of seven 'realization operations'. While the latter are related to the "categories" that are missing in "Systemic theory" — in the sense that they generate the structures that exemplify the missing categories — the relationship is not self-evident. In Section 9.2.1 of Chapter 9 we shall see exactly how a revised set of realization operations can generate all of the specific categories and relationships that are needed to specify the instances at the level of form in a modern systemic functional grammar.

Thus two sets of concepts are required in a full theory of syntax: (1) the theoretical concepts that specify the syntax potential, and (2) the theoretical concepts that specify the instances. The theory of 'syntax potential' will be presented and discussed in Chapter 9 of Part 2, and the theory of 'instances of syntax' will be set out in Chapters 10 and 11.

There would be widespread agreement among systemic functional linguists — and especially among those who are interested in the theoretical-generative strand of work in SFL — that "Systemic theory" provides an excellent (though necessarily highly compressed) summary of the essential concepts of Halliday's SF grammar. Indeed, the model described in Chapter 3 and summarized in Figure 4 (in Section 3.2 of that chapter) can be seen as an alternative statement of broadly the same set of concepts — subject to the qualifications expressed above and in Section 4.7 of Chapter 4.

From the viewpoint of the topic of this book, this difference is not crucial, since we are focussing here on the theory of syntax, i.e., the theory of both the potential and the instances at the level of form. In Section 4.6 of Chapter 4 we established that the difference between the levels of the system networks in the Sydney and the Cardiff versions of SFL, while significant in some cases, did not invalidate the view that the two share the same general framework, and this view is supported by the broad similarity between the 'realization operations' in the two frameworks that we have noted. This means that we are indeed in a position to make a direct comparison between the theories of syntax presented in each of the two theories.

However, from this last perspective "Systemic theory" has one great weakness. This is that it does not provide a specification of the "basic concepts" of the part of the theory whose task it is to account for the status of the instances at the level of form. It is these concepts with which *IFG* is concerned.

## 5.4 A summary of the differences between "Categories" and "Systemic theory"

Let me now summarize the differences between "Categories" and "Systemic theory". They could hardly be greater. The fact is that "Systemic theory" presents an almost completely new set of "basic concepts". These are: 'system' and 'system network' (but both in the 'meaning potential' sense), 'instantiation', 'selection expression', 'realization' and 'structure' (the last being used in a highly generalized sense that is quite different from its precise sense in "Categories"). Thus the list of "basic concepts" in "Systemic theory" does not mention two of the four original "fundamental" categories at all ('unit' and 'class'), and the two that are included as "basic concepts" now have significantly different meanings ('system' and 'structure'). The concept of 'element' is referred to, as we have seen, but it is not presented as a "basic concept", and it has a significantly different sense from that of the term "element" in "Categories".

As for the three 'scales' found in "Categories", the concepts of 'delicacy' and 'exponence' (the latter now renamed "realization") have changed as a natural consequence of the elevation of 'system' to model 'meaning potential'. And the term 'rank' (which has no meaning without 'unit', in its "Categories" sense) is re-interpreted in "Systemic theory" as a general statement about 'flat tree constituency', with no statement at all about the concepts of a 'rank scale' and the associated limitations on 'rank shift'. According to "Systemic theory", then, it would appear that all of the concepts that are presented in "Categories" as "fundamental" have either been dropped or been changed — many quite drastically.

At this point in our exploration of Halliday's presentation of his ideas about syntax, we might reasonably conclude that Halliday has completely changed the "basic concepts" of his theory. This, however, would be a mistake, as we shall see in the next chapter. Indeed, before we draw our final conclusions about what sources it will be useful to consult in building a theory of syntax for a modern systemic functional grammar — and so before we draw our final conclusions about the extent to which the concepts of "Categories" are still valid today — we must bring certain other bodies of work into the picture. These are: (1) the theoretical concepts that underlie *IFG*, since this work constitutes the major manifestation of the 'text-descriptive' strand of the work in the Sydney Grammar framework, and (2) the fullest statement of the requirements of a theory of SF syntax yet made, i.e., Fawcett (1974-6/81), together with the subsequent revisions to that work.

But it is in our examination of the major concepts of *IFG* that the most fundamental problems will arise, and this gives rise to what I expect to be the most controversial chapter in the book — Chapter 7. There I shall examine and discuss the great theoretical problems that are raised by Halliday's representations of structure in *IFG* and elsewhere, and so demonstrate the need for a new — or partly new — theory of syntax for SFL.

## 5.5 The common ground between the Sydney and the Cardiff Grammars

However, before we leave the topic of "Systemic theory", it is important to bring out the impressive extent to which the set of concepts that it foregrounds are similar to the equivalent set of concepts in the Cardiff Grammar framework, e.g., as set out in Fawcett, Tucker & Lin (1993). There are differences as well as similarities between the two approaches, as we shall see in Section 9.2 of Chapter 9, but it is clear that the 'realization operations' in the two versions of the theory perform essentially the same general function in the generation of text-sentences.

As we saw in Section 5.2, the origin of the concepts presented in "Systemic theory" lies in the work carried out in the mid-1960s by Halliday, Huddleston, Henrici and Hudson. Early examples of their use can be seen in Halliday (1969/81) and especially in Hudson's major work *English Complex Sentences* (1971). One early published description of these 'realization operations' that resembles the modern sets of operations appeared in Berry (1977:18-35), and fairly similar sets have been presented in Fawcett (1973/81 and 1980), Matthiessen & Bateman (1991:95-6), Fawcett, Tucker & Lin (1993), Matthiessen (1995:23-6), etc.

Clearly, there is a direct line from the early work of the 1960s, through Halliday's role as the grammar consultant to the Penman project, to the work on the Penman Project described in Matthiessen & Bateman (1991) — and Halliday has drawn upon all of this work in writing "Systemic theory". However, there is a similarly direct line from the 1960s work, via Halliday (1969/81), Hudson (1971), to Fawcett (1973/81) and (1980) — and so to the theoretical-generative model found in the Cardiff Grammar today and implemented in the computer in the COMMUNAL Project. As we saw in Section 4.9 of Chapter 4, the stage in the develoment of Halliday's model at which it most resembled the current Cardiff Grammar was that reflected in Halliday (1970/76b) and what I have described as the "pivotal paper" of "Language as choice in social contexts" (1977/78).

The position, therefore, is that the generative apparatus in the two frameworks is broadly comparable. Or, to put it in terms of the diagram of language in Figure 4 in Section 3.2 of Chapter 3, the 'form potential' of the two models is fairly similar. Moreover, both models also recognize the importance of instances at the level of **meaning**, i.e., the concept of a 'selection expression'.

However, the specific 'realization rules' in each of the two versions are capable of being used to generate different types of structural output — and it is in the part of the theory that describes these outputs — or instances — that the major differences between the two models occur. As we shall see in more detail in Section 7.8 of Chapter 7, the output from the Cardiff Grammar is a single structure with a rich labelling of the nodes, while the output from the Sydney Grammar is — at least in principle — a set of several different structural representations. It is the task of the rest of Part 1 to explain just what these differences are, and to examine the extremely serious questions that they raise for the theory of syntax in SFL.[5]

5. Interestingly, the lack of a specification of a theory of 'instances of syntax' in "Systemic theory" cannot be the result of a general decision by Halliday to exclude any account of instances, because there is a short paragraph that describes the nature of instances at the level of **meaning** (i.e., the concept of a 'selection expression'). It would therefore have been logical if Halliday had also included an account of the theory of instances at the level of **form**.

# 6
# The major concepts of
# *An Introduction to Functional Grammar*

## 6.1 Preview of this chapter

In this chapter, like the last, the task is to summarize the "basic concepts" presented in a major recent work by Halliday. This time the work is *IFG* (using the 1994 edition). Surprisingly, perhaps, we shall find it quite difficult to establish the theoretical concepts that underlie the description of English structure given in *IFG*. And then, when we have identified them, we shall find a disquieting difference between these "basic concepts" and those that we found in "Systemic theory". This in turn raises questions about the relationships between *IFG* and "Systemic theory" and between *IFG* and "Categories", and so about how far the Sydney Grammar can be said to have a theory of syntax.

We saw in the last chapter that "Systemic theory" does not include in its list of "basic concepts" three of the four most central concepts from "Categories", i.e., 'unit', 'class (of unit)' and 'element (of structure)'. Moreover, it either omits or re-works each of the three 'scales'. Do the concepts of "Categories" fare any better in *IFG* ?

## 6.2 In search of the "basic concepts" of *IFG*

### 6.2.1 The evidence from the opening chapters

The "Introduction" of *IFG* provides twenty-two pages of wide-ranging discussion, taking in "natural grammar", "grammar and semantics", "sentence and word", "system and text", "the spoken language", "the unconscious language", "theoretical approach", "applications", "the 'code", and "possible grammars". However, while this "Introduction"includes many interesting passages (e.g., that concerning "grammar and semantics", which I have referred to in Chapters 3 and 4), and while it certainly gives the reader a general sense of Halliday's approach to language, it does not set out for the reader the set of theoretical categories that underlie the main body of the book.

Chapter 1 is entitled "Constituency". It is here, one might think, that we should find a set of statements about the type of theory of syntax that will be used in the descriptive chapters of the book. But what we are given instead is a highly generalized introduction to the concept of 'constituency', this being illustrated from the English and Chinese writing systems and from English intonation. Halliday then uses these to illustrate the concept of a 'rank scale of units'. It is only in Chapter 2 that we reach the application of the 'constituency' concepts discussed in Chapter 1 to grammar itself, and Halliday simply presents the concept of a 'rank scale' of units from 'sentence' to 'morpheme' as "strengthening this conception of grammatical structure" (*IFG* p. 23). The concepts are simply presented to the reader, with no attempt to justify them as preferable to alternatives by supportive arguments. This is understandable in a work that is presented as a textbook but it does not help us in our quest to understand the theory that underlies the description. In fact they are open to challenge, as we shall see in Section 11.1 of Chapter 11.

The next two sections of Chapter 2 describe the differences between "maximal bracketing" and "minimal bracketing" — i.e., what Hudson earlier (1967/81:103) called the "few-ICs approach" vs. the "many-ICs approach (where "ICs" stands for "Immediate Constituents"). Here, we should understand that the term "bracketing" refers to a concept rather than a notation, but it is derived from the ultimately misleading concept that 'constituency' in syntax can be adequately represented by a linear representation of a bracketed string of words and/or morphemes. (See Section 11.2 of Chapter 11 for a discussion of alternative notations for representing the 'componence' part of 'constituency'.)

However, Halliday makes a claim in this section that runs counter to the view of syntax to be taken here, and we shall address it at this point. The claim is that grammars which use "maximal bracketing" (e.g., most grammars in the tradition that uses 're-write rules' such as "S -> NP VP") tend also to use 'class' labels (such as "noun phrase") in their tree diagrams, while grammars that use 'minimal bracketing' (i.e., most grammars in the functional tradition) tend to use 'functional' labels (such as "Subject"). At first this may seem to be a neat matching of two pairs of concepts, but in fact it does not correspond to the way in which descriptions of structure are made in a modern SF grammar — even in Halliday's own version. The reason is that in all SF grammars —

including *IFG* — the concept of 'class of unit' is as central as the concept of 'element of structure'.

Indeed, the way in which the book itself is structured demonstrates this point — even though the concept of 'class of unit' is hardly mentioned outside the discussion in Chapter 2. Thus all of Part I of *IFG* is about the clause (a 'class of unit'), and each of the various chapters of Part II is defined in relation to the clause ("above", "below", "beside", "around" and even "beyond" the clause). And the sections of Chapter 6, which is about groups and phrases, are all identified in terms of the 'class of unit' that is being described. Thus, even though the concept of 'class of unit' is itself barely mentioned, the whole book is, in a sense, structured around it. As we shall see in Part 2, 'class of unit' is one of the two core categories, with 'element of structure', that are required in a modern theory of SF syntax.

Thus, while Halliday is right in pointing out that the formal, 're-write rule' tradition in linguistics typically ignores the concept of 'element' in favour of 'class', he goes too far in suggesting that 'functional grammars' necessarily foreground 'element' (or "function" in the sense of 'functional element') over 'class of unit'. On the other hand, it is true that functional grammars in general and SF grammars in particular tend to use 'minimal bracketing' — i.e., 'flat tree' diagrams with minimal branching (with the proviso that very many American functionalists have adopted the "S -> NP VP" pattern of the re-write rule grammarians).[1] 'Flat tree' diagrams are necessary in a grammar that integrates many different types of meaning (i.e., one that 'conflates' several different types of meaning (these being interpreted as 'structures' in Halliday's model) — but in Section 10.2.1 of Chapter 10 I shall suggest that there is a 'higher' governing principle that explains why the optimal representations of structure will be 'flat tree' structures rather than highly branching structures such as those currently used in theories such as Chomsky's 'minimalist program' (Chomsky 1995) and head-driven phrase structure grammars (Pollard & Sag 1994).

We shall now return to our search for a summary of the underlying concepts of *IFG*. The last two sections of *IFG*'s Chapter 2 are directly useful to the reader, as they introduce the second major concept — after the concept of 'class of unit' — that underlies the structure of the book: the 'multiple structure' that Halliday's model claims that each clause has. Here he introduces the

---

1. This originates, of course, in the traditional "Subject + Predicate" structure of traditional grammar; see Fawcett (1999) on the subject of the Subject in English.

concept that there are three structures that show "three strands of meaning" in the clause (*IFG* p. 34) — though in fact there are typically several more than three, as we shall see in Section 7.2 of the next chapter.

From the viewpoint of our purposes in this book, it is a matter of regret that Halliday did not use a greater proportion of the "Introduction" and the two introductory chapters to provide a guide to the theoretical framework that underlies the description of English in the rest of the book. Indeed, a number of readers of the book — and indeed reviewers of the book — have expressed the view that the general discussions of 'constituency' are not what the reader needs at that stage of the book (if at all).

Surprisingly, Halliday himself drastically downgrades the importance of 'constituency' at the end of Chapter 1 when he suggests that, "as one explores language more deeply, constituency gradually slips into the background, and explanations come more and more to involve other, more abstract kinds of relationship" (*IFG* p. 16). (Readers will only understand what Halliday is hinting at here if they are familiar with his idea that the meanings of the different 'metafunctions' are realized in different types of structure — a view that we shall explore in Section 7.1.1 of the next chapter.)

But what happens in practice, as we read on through *IFG*? Do "other, more abstract types of relationship" take over from 'constituency'? The fact is that they do not. The different structures that Halliday proposes for each strand of meaning are all represented in the same way, i.e., by the use of 'box diagrams'. It is true that in some cases the significant elements (such as 'Theme' and 'New') tend to be found at the beginning and end of their structures, but there are too many exceptions to the generalizations that he proposes for it to be worth setting up different types of structure for different types of meaning. Halliday's solution to the problem of finding an adequate notation is to use box diagrams for representing **all** of the various types of structure that he claims to find in the clause. But box diagrams, as Halliday himself makes clear (*IFG* p. 36), are just one of several ways of representing the concept of 'constituency'. (For a critical examination of the role of the concept of 'constituency' in a theory of syntax, see Section 11.1 of Chapter 11.) The picture twith which these chapters of *IFG* leave the reader with is one of a reluctant recognition that, after all, the 'flat tree' type of constituency provides the best way of representing structure. And, as we shall see in Chapter 7, there is a compelling reason for Halliday to represent each of the different lines of structure in the same way.

Thus, the twenty-two-page "Introduction" and the further two introductory chapters of *IFG* introduce many important and interesting ideas. And yet, even though much of the discussion is about 'constituency', there is no summary statement of the concepts that are required for the description of English in *IFG* that is in any way comparable to the earlier statement in "Categories".

6.2.2   The evidence from the index and the main text

So far we have looked for the "basic concepts" in the opening chapters of *IFG* — and without much success. (The one major concept that is clearly introduced there is that of 'multiple structures' in the clause, to which we shall return shortly.) However, there are two alternative approaches to locating the "basic concepts' of a book which turn out to yield more interesting results. These are to count the entries for each major concept in the book's index, and to read the text with a constant eye to the concepts that underlie it.

Let us take as out starting point the index entries for the four 'categories'. The concept of 'unit' has just six entries, all being in the first twenty-five pages of this 434-page book. As for the concept of 'class', the word-form "class" also occurs frequently in the early pages (pp. 25-30). However, it is usually being used in the context of the highly generalized discussion of the differences between 'class-oriented' and 'function-oriented' grammars that we noted above. The word "class" in fact only occurs once with the technical meaning of 'class of unit' (on p. 214), and even then the reference is to 'word classes', rather than to the more controversial issue of 'classes of group'. Indeed, the concept of 'class of group' does not appear explicitly at all. However, the terms "element" and "element of structure" have half a dozen mentions, scattered through the book. Finally, the terms "system" and "system network" both have a couple of entries. It is not surprising that they should not be much used, since the book is about structures rather than the system networks , as Halliday makes clear.

What about the three 'scales', and the additional 'relationships' that we met in Section 2.6 of Chapter 2?  Let us begin with 'rank'. While the word "rank" is used on only three pages of the two introductory chapters, it is also used on two later occasions (on p. 188 when referring to 'rank shift' in the nominal group and then, incidentally, on pages 351-3 during a discussion of nominalization). However, the term "embedding' is introduced on page 188 as a synonym for "rankshift', and the few important statements about this concept are all expressed in terms of "embedding" (see especially page 142).

Interestingly, the concepts of 'rank' and 'rank shift' (alias 'embedding') have only a relatively small role to play in *IFG*.[2] This is in large measure because the book focusses so strongly on the clause that groups and their internal structures are not fully explored — and the fact is that all classes of group frequently contain other groups and clauses within them, as Part 2 and the outline description of English in Appendix B both clearly illustrate. However, in *IFG* the theory itself is also responsible for the reduced role of 'rank shift', because it treats many relationships between units that would in other approaches be analyzed as cases of embedding as 'hypotaxis', i.e., as 'dependency without embedding'. (Halliday's concept of 'hypotaxis' was introduced in Section 2.6.1 of Chapter 2.) Interestingly, Halliday seems to be sounding a note of caution about the concept of the 'rank scale' when he writes that, while "the guiding principle [when one is describing a text] is that of exhaustiveness at each rank, [...]

> it is an integral feature of this same guiding principle that there is indeterminacy in its application. [...] The issue is whether, in a comprehensive interpretation of the system, it is worth maintaining the global generalization, because of its explanatory power, **even though it imposes local complications at certain places in the description** [my emphasis]" (Halliday 1994:12).

I shall delay a full examination of Halliday's approach to 'rank' and 'embedding' in *IFG* to the main discussion of these concept in Chapter 11(Sections 11.1, and 1.8.3 to 11.8.5). See also Appendix C on 'the rank scale debate'.

The term "realization" (formerly "exponence") is not prominent in *IFG* either (with half a dozen index entries), but this is not surprising in a book about the outputs from the grammar — i.e., the instances at the level of form — rather than about how they are to be generated from the system networks.

As for the concept of 'delicacy', it is not mentioned at all in *IFG*. However, it is illustrated at various points in the book in one of its two main "Categories" senses, i.e., in terms of the 'primary', 'secondary' and even 'tertiary' structures that are shown for the 'thematic' and 'interpersonal' structures that Halliday recognizes in the clause. (For a discussion of the relevance of 'delicacy' to a modern theory of SF syntax, see Section 10.3.4 of Chapter 10.)

In contrast with the scanty entries for the established "Categories" concepts, the index shows that most pages between 218 and 291 concern the

---

2. In contrast, this concept (under the name of "embedding"), plays a major role in the theory to be proposed in Part 2, and in the description of English that exemplifies it (Fawcett in press).

later concepts of 'parataxis' and/or 'hypotaxis'. In *IFG*, then, these two have become two of the major syntactic concepts — together, of course, with the concept that a clause contains several lines of structure.

To summarize; while the evidence of the index is that only one of the "Categories" concepts, i.e., 'element', is referred to throughout the description of English in *IFG*, the fact is that, if we supplement these references by all of the many other times when terms such as "constituent" and "function" are used to express essentially the same concept, we find that the concept of 'element of structure' occurs frequently throughout the book. And we saw in Section 6.2.1 that 'class of unit' is presupposed throughout the book, even though it is barely mentioned. We can therefore at least say that the two concepts that will be foregrounded in Part 2 as the central categories of syntax also play a central role in *IFG*. The only caveat — and it is an important one — is that we shall use different criteria for identifying the class of a unit from Halliday's — so that the concept itself is significantly different.

## 6.3 Summary of the differences between "Categories" and *IFG*

From the viewpoint of comparing the theoretical framework that underlies *IFG* with that of other works in SFL, *IFG* is disappointing. Despite the twenty-two pages of its "Introduction" and another thirty-three pages of two further introductory chapters that are largely about 'constituency', *IFG* does not provide even a brief summary of the theoretical framework that underlies the description of English given in the book.

We have seen that the influence of "Categories" on *IFG* does not at first appear to be very strong, in terms of the overt use of its concepts. But we have also seen that, if we read the descriptive chapters of *IFG* with "Categories" in mind, we find that the two concepts of 'element of structure' and 'class of unit' are present throughout the book (even though the latter is hardly ever referred to overtly). And the concept of 'units on a rank scale' (around which the "Categories" framework is structured) is also present, though it seems to be kept in the background except when it is brought in for the two purposes of (1) explaining the limitations on 'rank shift', and (2) providing the criterion by which the classes of group recognized in *IFG* are set up. Interestingly, however, Halliday injects a note of caution about the concept of the 'rank scale' (*IFG* p. 12), and we shall examine his words at this point more closely in the context of other such indications in the full discussions of 'rank' in Section 11.1 of Chapter 11 and of 'embedding' in Sections 11.8.3 to 11.8.5.

Thus all three of the 'categories' of 'unit', 'class of unit' and 'element (of structure)' are in fact alive and well in *IFG,* and the 'rank scale' is also there in the background for use when needed. Moreover, while the concept of 'delicacy' is never mentioned, it is illustrated throughout *IFG* whenever MOOD is analyzed, in the sense of an analysis in terms of 'primary' and 'secondary' structures. (For a discussion of the relevance of 'delicacy' to 'structure', see Section 10.3.4 of Chapter 10.)

We might say, then, that *IFG* is a description of English that is based on the concepts of "Categories" — but with the addition of the concepts of 'parataxis' and 'hypotaxis' from Halliday (1965/81).

However, there is one highly significant difference that is not covered by what has been said so far. It is that it is assumed in "Categories" that a clause has a single structure, where the typical elements were "S P C A", etc. But in *IFG*, as we shall see, a clause is seen as having simultaneously five or more different structures. The problems raised by these representations will be our major concern in the next chapter.

### 6.4 The significance of the contrast in the concepts of "Systemic theory" and *IFG*

Why should "Systemic theory" introduce so many concepts that have little or no role to play in *IFG*? And, if the concepts of 'unit', 'class of unit', and 'element of structure' are present in *IFG* — if only in the background — why should they be absent from "Systemic theory"? Or, to put the question in more general terms, why should there be this great disparity between the presentations of the theory in these two works of the early 1990s?

The answer, I believe, lies in the fact that the two works are intended for different readerships, so that Halliday foregrounds different aspects of SFL in each of the two works.

As we saw in Section 5.2 of Chapter 5, *IFG* is intended as an account of the outputs from the operation of the grammar, and not as an account of the grammar itself. It describes the **instances**, but only at the level of what is assumed to be the 'final' output at the level of form (in terms of the diagram in Figure 4 in Section 3.2 of Chapter 2). In contrast, the emphasis in "Systemic theory" is wholly on describing the **potential** of a language — and at the levels of both meaning (the system networks) and form (the realization operations). This contrast in goals explains why the concepts of 'system', 'system network' and 'selection expression' play so little part in *IFG*. And, at the level of form, it explains why the focus in "Systemic theory" is on the generative apparatus of SFL and so on the 'realization statements' that constitute the 'form potential', at the expense of the output structures that they generate. (Nonetheless, the lack of any mention of many of the categories and relationships that specify the outputs leaves a notable gap in what is intended as an account of the theory.)

It is because *IFG* is intended primarily as a grammar for students and others who are engaged in the task of **text analysis** that the emphasis is on the description of the outputs from the grammar, rather than on the grammar itself. This is probably also the reason why the focus in *IFG* is on the substantive categories of the description (such as Subject and Actor) rather than on the abstract categories of the theory that underlies the description, (such as 'functional element' and 'class of unit').

However, while this may be the reason for the differences between the two works, it is far from being a satisfying answer to the question with which this section began.

## 6.5 The need for theories of both 'syntax potential' and 'instances of syntax'

The fact that "Systemic theory" omits any specification of the part of the theory that would be used in a description of the outputs from the grammar leaves the reader in a highly unsatisfactory position. Since the paper is entitled "Systemic theory", this omission seems to imply that the theory does not need to specify these concepts. On the other hand, it is just possible that Halliday has omitted them on the grounds that if one specifies the 'form potential' in the realization statements, there is no need to specify the outputs, on the grounds that this is what the realization statements do.

Whatever Halliday's position on this issue, I wish to make clear that my view is that a theory does indeed have the responsibility to specify these concepts explicitly. In other words, **it is the task of a theory of SF syntax to specify both the apparatus that generates the text-sentences that are the outputs from the grammar (the realization**

**component) and the concepts that are required to model those outputs.** Moreover, both of these must be treated as intrgral parts of the theory, as the use of the theory for modelling the generation and understanding of language in computers shows clearly.

One might expect, in principle, that it would be sufficient to characterize the 'form potential', and that the theory required to describe the instances would follow automatically from this — and if this was so the approach taken in "Systemic theory" would be justified. But in practice this does not provide the framework of concepts that is required in the applications to which a model of language is put. In other words, it is not enough to model language in its generative mode (or 'at rest'); the theory must supply the concepts that are required for modelling the use of language in both the **generation** and the **analysis** of text-sentences — and it must do this for each level of language that is recognized in the theory.

For the purposes of analyzing a string of words in a text, it is necessary to be able to specify the concepts that are required for the structural description of that string of words — and to be able to do so, moreover, without drawing at every stage on one's knowledge of the procedures by which the string of words was generated. In other words, it must be possible to carry out the process of analyzing the syntax of a text (traditionally known as **parsing**) independently of the process of generation.

The reason why the two processes of generation and understanding cannot be treated as mirror images of each other is that each of the two processes of generation and understanding involves a different kind of 'problem-solving'. This arises because the two processes operate in different directions. More specifically, the evidence that is taken into account when deciding to make one analysis rather than another when parsing the syntax of a text is different from the evidence that is drawn on to determine the choices in generation. In parsing, the available linguistic data are those that are observable in the surrounding text **at the level of form**; in generation in the decisions are taken at the level of meaning (or in a higher component), so that the data that affect choices are **at the level of semantics** (or above it).

The practical demonstration of this fact (as I take it to be) is that this aspect of a systemic functional theory of syntax is needed in two important areas of application. The first is that of specifying what a computer needs to know, in order to analyze a string of incoming words into the syntactic structure that relates them. This need for a theory of the syntax of instances is demonstrated in Weerasinghe & Fawcett (1993), Weerasinghe (1994) and Souter (1996), and these works all illustrate the use of the concepts presented in Part 2. The second area of application is the analysis of texts by humans. It is not surprising that broadly the same set of concepts is required in both cases, and this is why a book that is written to help people to analyze texts invariably makes at least some use of a theory of instances. Indeed, this is precisely why we find Halliday making such frequent but informal use of the concepts of 'class of unit' and 'element of structure' in *IFG*, and it is why Fawcett (in press) can apprpriately be regarded as the direct complement to Part 2 of the present book.[3]

The fact that one cannot use a systemic functional grammar for parsing a string of words by making it run 'in reverse' is not simply a by-product of the nature of the Cardiff Grammar. It is in the nature of all systemic functional grammars that they are inherently adapted for the generation for texts. See Fawcett (1980:56) for the first statement of this claim, and see Fawcett (1993) and, less formally, Fawcett (1994) for fuller justifications.[4]

The fact that computer models of systemic functional grammars cannot simply be turned into natural language understanding machines by reversing them underlines this book's main argument, i.e., the argument that there is a need for an explict theory of systemic functional syntax. It provides evidence from this important sub-field of computational linguistics research that we can place alongside the less explicit evidence from the needs of the text analyst. In other words, it is a clear demonstration of the need for the sort of theory of 'instances of syntax' that is to be presented in Part 2 of this book.

---

3. See Fawcett (1993) for a statement addressed to linguists on the question of whether there is an inherent 'directionality' in language, and Fawcett (1994a) for the argument against assuming a simplistic concept of 'reversibility' in grammars, in a paper addressed to computational linguists. For illustrations of why a theory of instances of syntax is a necessary part of any adequate model of the process of understanding texts, see Fawcett (1994a), Weerasinghe & Fawcett (1993), Weerasinghe (1994) and Souter (1996). For an account of the component that is the nearest equivalent to a 'reverse' of the realization rules, see O'Donoghue (1994). In the COMMUNAL Project this is called the 'semantic interpreter', and O'Donoghue's important paper describes REVELATION, the semantic interpreter developed for COMMUNAL.

4. Thus, when Kaspar tried to build a language understanding system that corresponded to the sentence generator in the Penman Project (Kaspar 1988), he found that he had to build an additional component that would first parse the string of words to produce a syntactic structure, i.e., a component for which there is no equivalent in the generator, essentially as claimed in Fawcett (1994a). This structure then provides the input to the component that is, in a sense, the reverse of the realization rules (i.e., the 'semantic interpreter', in COMMUNAL terms).

## 6.6 Summary of the argument so far

We noted in Chapter 5 that what is missing in "Systemic theory" is an account of those concepts that are required to describe the **instances** of language at the level of **form** — i.e., the concepts of "Categories". But we have seen in the present chapter that, despite initial appearances, these concepts are still in use in *IFG* — if only in the background.

There are two main reasons for the very considerable differences between the concepts presented in "Categories" and "Systemic theory": (1) the changes to the theory in the 1960s (as outlined in Chapter 4), which have removed the concept of the system from the level of form, and (2) the unexplained lack in "Systemic theory" of a section on the outputs at this level. The lack of a specification of a theory of the 'syntax of instances' in *IFG* means that Halliday has not made a statement about this aspect of the theory since 1961. Yet, as we saw in the last section, this is an essential part of a full theory of syntax.

It is the task of Part 2 of this book to provide an integrated account of the full set of concepts that is required in a modern theory of systemic functional syntax, for both the potential and the instances.

However, before we come to Part 2 there is an important issue to be resolved. It is one that involves a serious criticism of the version of systemic functional grammar that is (1) the most widely known, (2) the most widely reproduced by others in introductory texts, and (3) the one in which most SF linguists have invested most time and effort. It is, of course, the version of the Sydney Grammar presented in Halliday's *IFG* and in Matthiessen (1995), but this fact means that the message of the next chapter is one that will be unwelcome to many.

To those readers of this book who have already made a large commitment of time and energy to the current Sydney Grammar — and I hope there will be many — I simply ask that you bring as open a mind as you can to the reading of the next chapter. When you have read it, I think it will be clear that the problems described there must be addressed. And it is surely better, from viewpoint of the long-term survival of the major insights of the theory, that these problems should be pointed out by one who wishes to resolve them within the overall framework of the theory — as is done here — rather than by someone who does not accept the core tenets of the theory, and who might therefore present these problems as ones that undermine the theory as a whole. That they do not do.

# 7
# The problem of the representations in *IFG* (and an alternative approach)

## 7.1 Levels of language and the representation of the multi-functional nature of language: two questions

7.1.1 Two questions to ask about the representations in *IFG*

In this chapter, we shall examine the ways in which the structure of a text-sentence is represented in *IFG* and in other works by Halliday. This will raise a major problem, namely that a concept that is central in the 'text-descriptive' strand of Halliday's work turns out to be incompatible with current work in the 'theoretical-generative' strand. We shall need to consider the strength of the argument to be advanced here, the question of how far its conclusions matter for practical purposes, and — assuming its validity — what course of action it should lead to.

The problem, then, is that of establishing the status in the theory of the **representations** of the structure of text-sentences in *IFG* (and so in the other published works of the Sydney Grammar).

It will probably be a surprise to most of those readers who are familiar with Halliday's writings that the way of representing functional structure in *IFG* should be seen as a problem for the theory. This is because the argument to be set out in the rest of this chapter has not been put before. Indeed, the 'multiple structure' method of representation used throughout *IFG* is widely assumed to be an integral part of the theory. However, as we shall see, the representations that are used in the 'text-descriptive' applications of the theory — e.g., as in *IFG* — are seriously at odds with the way in which the 'theoretical-generative' apparatus in the Sydney Grammar actually operates when generating text-sentences (as well as being at odds with the Cardiff Grammar approach).

I should begin by making it clear that this chapter assumes that the concept of a 'representation' is a substantive one for a theory, rather than a matter of 'mere notation'. However, even if a 'representation' was considered to be simply a notation, this would not make it a trivial matter. This is because notations are **semiotic systems**, and it is one of the responsibilities of a semiotic theory to ensure that it has appropriate forms of representation for the relevant media — in diagram form for flat surfaces, in computer program form, etc.

Indeed, the complex of problems that we must now tackle involves issues that reach far beyond the question of how best to represent the structure of language at the level of form. They involve such questions as whether our representations of text-sentences should represent one level of language or more than one, of where and how we wish to represent the multifunctional nature of meaning, and so on.

Let me begin by expressing our first question in relatively general terms (though we shall later divide it into three sub-questions):

1. What is the status in systemic functional theory of the representations of the functional structure of text-sentences given throughout both *IFG* and the various associated texts?[1]

Figure 7, which we shall come to in Section 7.2, illustrates a representation of this type, and we shall examine its detailed implications there. Here I simply wish to make the point that *IFG*-style representations of functional structure are not the only way of representing the multifunctional nature of texts in SFL. In particular, the representations used in the Cardiff Grammar (e.g., as in Fawcett

---

1. The publication of the first edition of *IFG* in 1985 was followed in the 1990s by a spate of helpful introductions to it, almost all of which use exactly the same 'box diagram' method of representing what is, in fact, constituency structure: Collerson (1994), Eggins (1994), Gerot & Wignell (1994), Bloor & Bloor (1995), Butt, Fahey, Spinks & Yallop (1995), and Thompson (1996). Lock (1996) allows himself to depart a little more from *IFG*, but is essentially also an introduction to it, while Downing & Locke (1992) take an even more independent but still clearly Hallidayan position. (Indeed, they incorporate bits of Fawcett (1974-6/81) in their treatment of the nominal group.) Martin, Matthiessen & Painter (1997) is a useful supplementary clarification and workbook. Matthiessen (1995) provides the system networks to complement *IFG* and describes structure very similarly. The publication of the second edition of *IFG* in 1994 further established the Sydney Grammar approach to representing structure as the 'standard' method. Yet, since forms of representation typically have implications for the theory itself, it is important to consider and evaluate alternative approaches, and then to justify the decision to use one method of representing structure rather than another. That is precisely the purpose of this book and of Fawcett (1999), (2000), (in press) and (forthcoming a). Interestingly, one recent introduction to SF grammar (Morley 2000) takes a broadly similar approach to the present one, i.e., it presents an updated version of the original Scale and Category as the representation at the level of form — as also does Young (1980).

1997 and 1999, Tucker 1998, etc.) are significantly different from those in *IFG*. In Section 7.8 we shall look at this alternative approach to representing texts, and then in Section 7.9 we shall compare the two methods.

We shall begin our search for the answer to our question about the theoretical status of the representations in *IFG* by examining Halliday's own writings. However, we shall find that in establishing the answer to this first question we shall encounter another (which, to be fair, we shall also ask about the Cardiff Grammar). This second question is:

2. Does the Sydney Grammar make available theoretically motivated descriptions of English that are at the levels of language that Halliday's theoretical statements state to be desirable? And does the Cardiff Grammar? If not, when will they be available?

This question needs to be answered in terms of what we shall term the **scale of availability** of a theory. (This is of course not a 'scale' as a concept within the theory, as the 'scales' in "Categories" are.)

7.1.2 The 'scale of availability' of a theory

If we are to evaluate a theory of language adequately, we need to see the exemplification of the theory in the description of one or more languages. It is here, in the theory-based description of specific languages, that the concept of a 'scale of availability' applies. Thus every systemic functional grammar — like every theory-based grammar — exists in at least the following three versions.

First, there is the **ultimate model** version — the 'vision' version. This is the idealized view of the comprehensive, fully explicit model of language that is the ultimate target of the research. In this, the theory has been fully developed and successfully applied to the description of a great variety of whole languages — including the awkward bits that do not fit easily into one's particular model — and it has proved its usefulness through being successfully used in a wide range of applications. No theory of language, of course, has ever attained this idealized goal, but it is a necessary mental construct in the development of both an adequate theory and a 'best possible description' of a language.

Secondly, there is the current **best possible description** of a language in terms of the theoretical model, such as may exist in a combination of one (or preferably more) of the following: (1) researchers' notes, (2) published papers and (3) computer implementations of the model. The current 'best possible description' may well fall short of the 'ultimate model'.

Thirdly, there is the **best available description**. This is the best description that is currently available in a usable form that can be obtained by anyone who wants it, e.g., for use in analyzing texts — and this typically falls short of the 'best possible description'. Within this section of the scale of availability there is scope for further variation. For example, long before the publication in 1985 of Halliday's *An Introduction to Functional Grammar*, some systemic linguists had access to versions of what was referred to at the time (e.g in Berry 1975:201) as "*An Outlook on Modern English* (forthcoming)". When this work did eventually 'come forth' as *IFG*, it was a rather different book.

Most published 'grammars' aim to achieve two goals. The first is to give at least a feel for the 'vision' version of the theory — which is helpful — and the second is to provide a description of the language in those terms. But the reality is that most grammars fail to provide more than a highly selective coverage of the language's grammar, and too often the aspects that are covered thoroughly are precisely the aspects which the theory was originally developed to cover. For example, many formal grammars seem to be particularly focussed on problems such as that of how to handle so-called 'raising' phenomena and other phenomena that present challenges for re-write rule grammars, such as some uses of the verb *seem*, e.g., *Patsy seems to be believed to be a suitable candidate* — to cite an example that includes both, taken from a recent generative grammar in the Chomskyan tradition (Haegeman & Guéron 1999: 206). Most SF grammars have much less to say about such constructions — emphasizing instead their ability to handle the many simultaneous types of meaning within one clause. However, SFL must cover such constructions, as well as those aspects of language that it was originally developed to cover.[2]

Clearly, Question 2 relates to the 'best available description' section of the scale of availability, and we shall return to it in Sections 7.6 and 7.8.

Finally, let us relate the scale of availability to the broad contrast between the two strands of work that we find within the two main SF models: the 'theoretical-generative' and the 'text-descriptive'. One would expect to be able to use the publicly available work from the 'text-descriptive' strand as a means

---

2. The Cardiff Grammar offers a complete text-descriptive framework for 'raising' phenomena, the verb *seem*, etc. The generative version of the grammar currently handles several major types of so-called 'rasing' phenomena (though not quite all of them yet). See Fawcett (in press) for the descriptive analyses of such structures.

of discovering the nature of the theory itself. But this, as we shall see, is not a simple matter in the case of Halliday's work. Indeed, it is not easy to discover how the theoretical model actually works, as we shall see later in this chapter.

### 7.1.3 How this chapter will approach the problem

Our first question is about the status in the theory of the representations of structure in *IFG*. The first step towards an answer must therefore be to make sure that we understand just what is being represented in such structures. After doing this in Section 7.2, we shall look in Section 7.3 at this type of representation in the light of Halliday's theoretical statements on levels of representation. And this will show, perhaps surprisingly, that Halliday in fact advocates the position that there should also be **a second type of representation** — i.e., one that lies above the one found in *IFG*. Furthermore, we shall also find that the status within the theory of the type of representation found in *IFG* is not what one might suppose. In other words, we shall find that there is a significant difference between (1) what we have called the 'theoretical-generative' version of Halliday's theory and (2) the 'text-descriptive' version. And, within the latter, we shall find that there is a serious shortfall between what Halliday rightly states to be theoretically desirable and the 'best available descriptions' of English and other languages that are is in fact available to help text analysts.

As a comparison, we shall then consider briefly the nearest equivalent representations in the framework of the Cardiff Grammar. And here we shall find that there is currently an even greater shortfall of 'best available descriptions' that describe the Cardiff version of SFL — but that in this case the situation is rapidly being rectified.

## 7.2 The representation of a text-sentence in *IFG*

In the text-descriptive strand of the work in the Sydney Grammar, the functional structure of a text that consists of a simple clause is modelled in the way shown in Figure 7. It is a set of box diagrams, each of which represents several simultaneous 'strings' of elements (using the term loosely). These 'box diagram' representations of structure represent a simple constituency relationship of the 'flat tree' type, i.e., of the type with only one layer of branching.

We should be clear from the start, then, that the use of 'box diagrams' for representing structure is not a 'structurally neutral' form of representation, such as Halliday's writings seem to imply would be desirable, but a type of constituency — as Halliday himself in fact recognizes (1994:16).

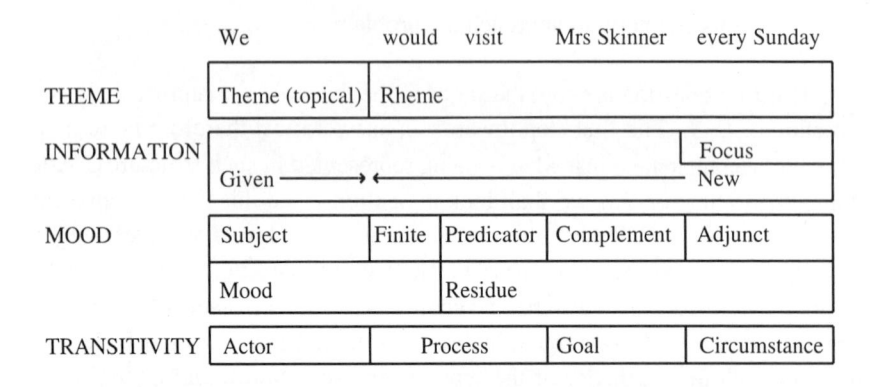

|  | We | would | visit | Mrs Skinner | every Sunday |
|---|---|---|---|---|---|
| THEME | Theme (topical) | Rheme | | | |
| INFORMATION | Given ⟶ ⟵ | | | Focus | |
| | | | | New | |
| MOOD | Subject | Finite | Predicator | Complement | Adjunct |
| | Mood | | Residue | | |
| TRANSITIVITY | Actor | Process | | Goal | Circumstance |

*Figure 7: A Sydney Grammar representation of a simple clause*

To the best of my knowledge, the first published use in SFL of the 'set of box diagrams' method of displaying the multifunctional structure of language was in Halliday (1971/73a:43).[3] However, its antecedents can be clearly traced in the sets of conventional 'tree diagram' constituency diagrams used to represent the different structures that Halliday associates with different metafunctions in Halliday (1967-8) and (1969/81).

In the latter paper, Halliday writes that

> the clause has a number of different but simultaneous **constituent structures** [my emphasis] according to which set of options [each of which corresponds to one 'metafunction'] is being considered. (1969/81:143)

This concept of "simultaneous structures" is the concept that underlies the representation in Figure 7, and all of the similar representations in *IFG* and the many derived works. Notice, however, that the words "simultaneous structures" in the description of the clause cited above make a very much stronger claim about the size of the 'simultaneous' units than do the 'realization

---

3. The beginnings of the 'box diagram' representation were there in Halliday (1970/76b), as we saw in Section 4.9 of Chapter 4, but the boxes were not complete at that stage. Moreover, that paper was not in fact published until 1976.

statements' on the immediately preceding page of the same paper. Table 1 on page 142 of Halliday (1969/81) simply show that pairs and trios of 'functions' are sometimes brought together by a conflation statement to form a **single element** of the clause, the meanings of such elements being derived from two or three different 'metafunctions'. (It gives no rule that conflates whole structures.) Halliday describes this second and less ambitious type of 'conflation' lower on the same page as the quotation above when he says that

> each **element** [my emphasis] of [the] structure is a complex of functions, a set of structural 'roles' specified as realizations of the options selected [in the system network]. (Halliday 1969/81:143)

These two statements correspond to two different models of 'conflation' that will be introduced later in this chapter, and we shall refer to them as the 'structure conflation' and the 'element conflation' models. The second concept could of course be included within the first, in principle — but we shall find that in practice this does not happen. This difference between the two types of 'conflation' will be crucial, as the argument to be presented in this chapter unfolds.

Let us now examine Figure 7 more closely. It show four clearly separated lines of box diagrams (one containing two lines of structure within it), such that each of the four major lines corresponds to one of four major types of 'meaning'. The two basic assumptions upon which such a diagram rests are (1) that there should be a separate structural representation for each major strand of meaning (including two completely distinct structures within 'textual' meaning), and (2) any one 'element' of the clause is likely to consist of the 'conflation' of two or more 'functions' from two or more different lines of meaning. For example, the description in Halliday (1994:30f.) of *the duke* in *the duke gave my aunt this teapot* states that, in his approach, the three 'functions' of 'Subject', 'Actor' and 'Theme' are typically — but not necessarily — mapped onto one another to form a single 'element' of the clause (just as the same three 'functions' are in Figure 7).[4]

Halliday's introductory writings often imply that each line of structure corresponds to one of his three (or four) 'metafunctions', i.e., broad types of

---

4. In the Sydney Grammar, the correct term for what we might informally call the 'sub-elements' of a clause is "grammatical functions" or, for brevity, "functions", e.g., Matthiessen (1995:23-5). However, Halliday refers to them as "elements" throughout the description of the realization operations in "Systemic theory" (1993), as we saw in Chapter 5. Matthiessen (1995:782) characterizes them as "micro-functions" (since the term "function" is used in too many senses), but this term is not in general use.

'meaning'. There are four such metafunctions when he splits the 'ideational' metafunction into the 'experiential' and the 'logical', e.g., as described in Halliday (1977/78:128), but in his introductory writings he frequently omits the 'logical' and only illustrates three (as in Figure 7). The interesting point here, then, is that the four 'strands of meaning' shown in Figure 7 — and in all equivalent representations in *IFG* — do **not** correspond to Halliday's four 'metafunctions'. Thus the THEME and INFORMATION lines of analysis both belong in his 'textual' metafunction; the MOOD analysis (which itself contains two lines) is the 'interpersonal' metafunction; and the TRANSITIVITY is 'experiential'. The fourth 'metafunction' (i.e., the 'logical') is omitted in Figure 7, because Halliday only introduces it when there is a 'logico-semantic relationship' between two or more clauses.

However, there are in fact at least three other lines of representation in the analysis of a typical text-sentence in Halliday (1994:368-5), in addition to the four shown in Figure 7.

The fifth is the analysis of the logico-semantic relationships between clauses that Halliday introduces to represent 'paratactic' or 'hypotactic' relations, as in *I'll come when I'm ready* (see Section 2.6.1 of Chapter 2.)

The sixth line of representation arises from the fact that Halliday always shows two lines of structure for the 'interpersonal' strand of meaning. At the **primary** degree of **delicacy** the structure is 'Mood + Residue'. Here I am using the term "primary" that was introduced to the theory for this purpose in Halliday 1961/76), in order to make explicit the nature of the relationship between the two lines. Then at the **secondary** degree of delicacy the structure within the 'Mood' element is divided into 'Subject + Finite'. This is not a matter of constituency relations, Halliday emphasizes, but of a more delicate analysis at the same layer of structure, as we saw in Section 2.4 of Chapter 2.

Halliday's reasons for including this line of analysis as part of the interpersonal component are dependent on the fact that the Subject and Finite are involved in the expression of MOOD meanings. While I agree that these two elements contribute to the clause's interpersonal meaning (Fawcett 1999), I see no reason to include the other elements here. Halliday's stated reason for including Complements and Adjuncts in this line of analysis is that a Complement is an element that (typically) can become a Subject (though not in examples such as *clever* in *Ivy is clever*, as Halliday admits) and that an Adjunct is one that cannot. While this is largely true it does not seem a sufficient justification for including them in the analysis of every clause, and nor does it explain why the 'Predicator' is included there. In fact, this line of analysis does not explain anything about the particular text that is currently being analyzed, since these elements patently do **not** carry the meaning associated with the Subject in the clause currently being analyzed. (The Complement might, if the concept of the syntactic transformation were to be introduced to the theory, but Halliday would clearly not wish to do that.)[5]

It is interesting to note that the inclusion of the clause elements "Predicator", "Complement" and "Adjunct" as 'secondary' elements in the "Residue" is the last remaining trace in the descriptive framework found in *IFG* of a set of concepts that were central in the Scale and Category description of English. Indeed they, together with "Subject" were the primary elements of clause structure in "Categories". Interestingly, these elements are not referred to in the explication of "The 'silver' text" (*IFG* pp. 368-85). So what is their role?

In *IFG*, their role seems to be little more than a way of labelling another row of boxes that would otherwise remain empty, like the "Residue" (of which they are said to be the corresponding more delicate analysis) and the Rheme. But in Halliday (1970/76b) and (1977/78) they played a far more important role, as we saw in Section 4.9 of Chapter 4.

We come finally to the seventh line of analysis shown in the standard analyses of texts in *IFG*. This shows textual 'cohesion', but as Halliday does not propose it as a type of structure we shall pay no further attention to it here.

Halliday's analysis of a clause therefore typically involves at least **seven** lines of analysis. It is as if the variation in the structures of the various lines of analysis is seen as a phenomenon of language that is to be celebrated. But we must ask: "Is it a linguistic phenomenon rather than a metaphenomenon, i.e., a product of Halliday's version of the theory?". I shall argue in Section 7.4 (1) that it is indeed a metaphenomenon; (2) that this approach to representing the multi-functional nature of language brings with it enormous problems; and (3) that there is a preferable approach that achieves the same goals.

It may come as a surprise to some readers that an *IFG*-style analysis in fact requires seven separate lines of representation (six of these being structural). This is because the writings of the Sydney grammarians regularly present the view that there are either three or at most four strands of meaning, each

---

5. In contrast, the concepts of 'Complement' and "Adjunct" — but not 'Predicator' — have a central role in the Cardiff Grammar. Here, a Complement is an 'experiential' element of the clause that is 'predicted' by the Process (i.e., a Participant Role), while an Adjunct is one that is not (i.e., a Circumstantial Role) — or an element expressing a different type of meaning.

corresponding to one of the metafunctions. In Chapter 2 of *IFG*, for example, Halliday introduces the concept that a clause has multiple structures under the beguilingly simple section heading of "Three lines of meaning in the clause" (p. 33). Yet, the fact is — as I have just demonstrated — that a analysis of a sentence in *IFG* terms regularly requires seven lines of analysis (and sometimes even more, as we shall see shortly).

In *IFG*, therefore, the task of analyzing a text — and so the model of language that underlies it — is rather more complex than we are at first led to expect. Indeed, in the analyses of "The 'silver' text" on pages 368-85 of *IFG* there are often **eight** or more lines of analysis, because Halliday adds an extra line for the analysis of the 'unpacked' interpretation of examples that contain cases of what he terms "grammatical metaphor". (See Chapter 10 of *IFG* for an overview of this important set of phenomena — for many of which, however, the Cardiff Grammar suggests rather different solutions.)[6]

The two examples on pages 375-6 of *IFG* provide a final example of how complex Halliday's representations can become: each has **ten** lines of analysis. The reason is that Halliday shows three lines of analysis within the THEME line, on the grounds that there are three degrees of structural delicacy in them. However, it should be said that Halliday's analysis of 'multiple theme' in this way is one with which many other systemic functional grammarians disagree — as also do other grammarians (e.g., Huddleston 1988).

For our present purposes, however, the main point to notice is that a diagram such as that in Figure 7 embodies a very significant extension of the concept that a single element such as *we* in Figure 7 is the 'conflation' of three 'functions'. In such diagrams the whole clause is presented as the 'conflation' of five or more functional structures (as well as also involving 'more delicate' layers of analysis). In Sections 7.4 and 7.5, I shall challenge Halliday's concept that it is whole structures that are conflated with each other, rather than individual elements. Moreover, this central proposal of Halliday's is also challenged, as I shall show, by the actual practice in the theoretical-generative strand of work in the Sydney Grammar, i.e., in the computer implementations of Halliday's model by Mann, Matthiessen and Bateman — and even, surprisingly, by Halliday's own writings on generation.

---

6. I should point out that the seven or eight lines of structure found in an *IFG*-style analysis do **not** correspond to the eight major types of meaning that I consider to be present (if only by their non-realization) in a typical clause. See Section 7.8 for a brief introduction to the eight strands of meaning that are recognized in the Cardiff Grammar.

## 7.3 The *IFG* representations in relation to other possible levels of representation

7.3.1 Three sub-questions and the issues that they raise

Now that we have examined the nature of representations such as that in Figure 7, we are ready to consider their theoretical status. We shall do this by breaking down the first question that we asked in Section 7.1 into three sub-questions:

1a. Is it desirable — or indeed necessary — to have representations of a text at the levels of both form and meaning?
1b. In a model with representations at the level of both form and meaning, is it desirable — or indeed necessary — to show explicitly the multifunctional nature of language at both levels?
1c. In the representation at the level of form, is the conflation that occurs between the realizations of the various strands of meaning a conflation of whole structures or a conflation of individual elements?

In answering these questions, we shall make two discoveries about the status of the representations of texts in *IFG* which are likely to surprise most readers.

In the rest of this section I shall suggest answers to the first two of the above three questions, in terms of the Sydney Grammar. Then in Section 4.7.1 I shall address Question 1c.

In the light of the answers to these questions, Section 7.5 will discuss the precise status in the theory of such representations, and the question of how far they may have a value that is not dependent on their status in the theory. Then in Section 7.6 I shall assess how far the Sydney Grammar is currently able to supply descriptions of English that enable text analysts to describe texts in its terms.

After that, I shall ask the same testing set of questions about the Cardiff Grammar (in Section 7.8) — and there we shall find that the answers can be given more briefly.

Finally, in Section 7.9, I shall summarize the problems of developing adequate representations for multifunctional models of language.

## 7.3.2 The desirability of having two levels of representation

Let us begin with Halliday's own description of the status of the analyses offered in *IFG*. He writes:

> This book [...] presents the structures which are the 'output' of the networks — which collectively realize the sets of features that can be chosen. (Halliday 1994:xxvii)

So far so good; this is indeed what the analyses of texts in *IFG* does, in Halliday's terms. But a few lines below that he adds that

> all the structural analyses [given in *IFG*] could be **reinterpreted in terms of the features selected** [my emphasis]. (Halliday 1994:xxvii)

The significant thing about these passages is that they show that Halliday recognizes that there are, in principle, **two types of representation for each clause**. The first type corresponds to those in *IFG*, and these are presented to us as instances at the level of form. However, since these "realize the sets of features than can be chosen" (in the 'meaning potential'), it is clear that there is also, in principle, a second type of representation — one that is expressed in terms of the systemic features from which the structure is generated. It is a pity that Halliday does not give an example of what he thinks such representations might be like, but I shall give an example of one possible way of such showing such representations in Section 7.8.

However, Halliday's words in "Systemic theory" go even further, clearly implying that it is not only **possible** to provide this second level of representation, but that it is also **desirable**. He states that

> in systemic theory **the system takes priority** [my emphasis]; the most abstract representation [...] is in paradigmatic terms. [...] Syntagmatic organization is interpreted as the 'realization' of paradigmatic features, the 'meaning potential'. (Halliday 1993:4505)

And a few paragraphs later he foregrounds the importance of the representation of the systemic 'meaning potential' more strongly still, writing that

> the selection expression constitutes the grammar's description of the item [e.g., a clause]. (Halliday 1993:4505)

This is heady stuff. However, the ambitious view of the essential nature of a semiotic system expressed in the above quotations is shared by all of those who work in the framework of the Cardiff Grammar, and by many other systemic functional linguists. There are two important consequences that follow directly from accepting this position for our present concerns. Firstly, Halliday's words suggest that the diagram of language shown in Figure 4 in Section 3.2 of Chapter 3 can indeed stand as a summary of the framework that is common to both the Sydney and the Cardiff Grammars. Secondly, they show that Halliday believes that, if we are to make a full analysis of a clause, we must give equality — and indeed "priority" — to the features that have been selected in generating it — i.e., to the features that specify its 'meaning potential'. All this is, we should note, is what should happen "in principle"; we shall come shortly to what is currently done in practice.

It therefore seems that Halliday's answer to Question 1a above is, in principle, that there should be representations at the levels of **both** meaning **and** form. Moreover, this principle should clearly be applied to the analysis of texts as well as to the generation of texts. Indeed, the concept of 'priority to the system' is precisely what is implied by the fact that the name of the theory is "**systemic** functional grammar" — and not "**structural** functional grammar". So what, one might reasonably ask, does Halliday consider that the systemic representation of a clause would be like? The answer is that we do not know.

7.3.3 Why there are no systemic representations in *IFG*

Perhaps the most surprising fact of all about Systemic Functional Grammar as a theory of language is that that there is no generally agreed way of showing, in the representation of the analysis of a text, the features in the system network that have been chosen in generating it. What makes this fact even stranger is that all of the SF linguists who engage in the 'theoretical-generative' task of building such grammars recognize that it is not merely **desirable** to have a representation of the features; it is **necessary**. This is because the 'selection expression' is an integral part of the operation of the grammar, as we saw in Chapter 3 and as is demonstrated in Appendix A.

The recognition of this situation leads us to ask a new question. This is: "Since the grammar is is systemic as well as functional, why doesn't Halliday show representations of the features in *IFG*?" Halliday gives a partial answer to this question when he writes in the "Foreword" to *IFG* that, because he wrote this book "specially for those who are studying grammar for text analysis purposes, I did not include the systemic part" (1994:x). Later he explains that "structures are less abstract; they are so to speak 'nearer the text'" (1994:xxvii). In other words, the clear implication is that Halliday decided that *IFG* should present the structural representations of texts rather than the systemic representations, on the grounds that the structural representations are likely to be easier for the reader to understand. Notice, however, that here Halliday is describing a strategy for overcoming the difficulties of communicating the theory's concepts for a particular class of readers, not making a statement about the status in the theory of the structural representations shown in *IFG*.

There are in fact three further practical reasons why *IFG* does not provide the reader with systemic analyses. The first is that if Halliday had included the systemic analyses too — and so also the system networks and realization statements that would make that possible — the book would have had to be two to three times as long (Halliday 1994:xv). The second reason is that Halliday has never published full sets of his current system networks, and it would have been odd if their first public appearance had been in what was intended as a text book. As we saw in Section 4.5 of Chapter 4, it was only through the publication of Matthiessen (1995) that the system networks which accompany *IFG* were finally published. And the third reason is that it is not obvious how best to represent, in a readily interpretable diagram, the analysis of a clause in terms of its features. A simple list of all the features that have been chosen is clearly inadequate, because it may include the names of thirty or forty features, not all of which are immediately interpretable. There have in fact been very few published attempts — in any version of the theory — to develop any such method of displaying the systemic features of a text. The diagrams in Fawcett (1980: 195 and 231) are early forerunners of the method of presentation currently used in the Cardiff framework, an example of which is presented in Section 7.8. So far as I know, Fawcett (forthcoming a) will be the first work to introduce a method of analyzing texts in terms of their systemic features.

### 7.3.4 A summary of the argument so far

To summarize so far: Halliday recognizes that texts should in principle be represented in terms of their features in the 'meaning potential' as well as their functional structures. Indeed, he states that "the system takes priority". However, the fact that *IFG* is written "specifically for those who are studying grammar for text analysis purposes" ((1994:x) has led him to focus on representations of texts that display the functional structure rather than the more abstract systemic features, one reason being that it is easier to understand such analyses. The answer to Question 1a is therefore that Halliday, like me, believes that in a SF model of language a text should, in principle, be analyzed in terms of both its meaning potential and its structure — this being the model summarized in Figure 4 of Section 3.2 of Chapter 3 (or perhaps for Halliday the topological variant in Figure 5 in Section 4.7 of Chapter 4, with its unsatisfactory representation of 'instantiation' and 'realization').

Indeed, when Halliday is writing in theoretical-generative terms, he always writes with the assumption that there will also be a representation in terms of the systemic features. He cannot but do so, because if there is no selection expression of features there can be no input to the realization rules (as we saw in Chapters 3 and 5). However, for text-descriptive purposes such as those for which *IFG* is intended, Halliday seems to take a different position. This is that, while it may in principle be desirable to represent the systemic features as well as the functional structures, it is either not possible or not necessary to provide this level of description. Section 7.8 will discuss the question of when it will become possible to provide a systemic description of English..

The implications of the argument so far for the representations given in *IFG* is that their status is somewhat diminished in importance. This is because they represent the grammatical **structure** of language — even though, to cite Halliday's words once again, "in systemic theory the system takes priority".


7.3.5 Where should we show the multifunctional nature of language?

We shall now turn briefly to Question 1b, i.e., "Should the representation show the multifunctional nature of language?" The answer to this question goes a long way to explaining why the representations in *IFG* are as they are — and it is as follows. Given (1) that the multifunctional nature of language is a central principle of the systemic functional model of language, and (2) that the representation of functional structure is the only type of representation that has so far been developed to the point where it can be made generally available through publication (for use in describing texts, etc), it is useful that it should show, if it is possible to do so without misrepresenting the model, the multifunctional nature of text.

However, as we shall see in Section 7.8, the picture of what is both possible and desirable changes when we have the option of showing the multifunctional nature of language in the representation of the meaning potential, i.e., at the level of meaning. The question then becomes: "If the multifunctional nature of language is shown in the representation at the level of meaning, is it also necessary — or even appropriate — to show it at the level of form too?" My answer is that the multifunctionality of language lies at the level of meaning rather than form, and that a representation such as that in Figure 10 in Section 7.8 reflects this fact more accurately than the *IFG*-style diagram in Figure 7.

### 7.3.6 The key question

So far in Section 7.3 we have so far been concerned with the question of whether a representation of a text by a single (though multifunctional) level of analysis is adequate. And the answer has been that we should, in principle, represent a text in terms of its systemic features, because, in Halliday's words, "the system has priority". And I have suggested that it is preferable to show the multifunctional nature of language at the level of meaning, since it is in fact the "strands of meaning" (*IFG* p.34) that we wish to model.

We turn now to Question 1c. This was:

1c. In the representation at the level of form, is the conflation that occurs between the realizations of the various strands of meaning a conflation of whole structures or a conflation of individual elements?

Since this question concerns an issue that is internal to the representation of structure at the level of form, it might appear less important than the ones that we have just been considering. But it is in fact the key question for our present purposes, because the answer to it shows why it is necessary to question the status of the representations of functional structure in *IFG*.

The reason for asking Question 1c is that we need a clear answer on the issue of precisely what the syntactic phenomenon is that actually gets conflated — i.e., is it whole, clause-length structures, or is it single elements of the clause? As we shall see, the theoretical status of the 'multi-strand' representations in *IFG* depends upon the answer.

To discover this answer we must look not in *IFG* but in the accounts by Halliday and others of work in the theoretical-generative strand of the theory.

And we shall discover that, within the Sydney Grammar version of a SF grammar, there are two conflicting pictures of how the grammar works — and that only one of these has a sound theoretical base, so making it implementable in the computer. In what follows, therefore, I shall refer to the 'supposed' and the 'implemented' versions of the Sydney Grammar.

## 7.4 How the Sydney Grammar works: the two models and their implications

7.4.1 The supposed version: the 'structure conflation' model of *IFG*

We shall begin by asking how the representations of structure found in an *IFG*-style analysis fit into the theoretical-generative model of language that is used by Halliday and others. Specifically, we shall make explicit the implications of taking the position that the several strands of functional structure found in such representations are part of the generative grammar. In other words, we shall make a leap of faith (but only for a couple of pages) and assume that somewhere there is (or will be in the future) a systemic functional grammar that is capable of generating structures such as those in Figure 7 of Section 7.2.[7]

Adopting such an approach requires, as we shall see, the addition of a new component to the overall model of language and a new 'level' — or perhaps we should say 'stage' — in the representation of instances. The three stages of representation in such a model would be as follows:

1. the selection expressions for each unit (such as a clause), i.e., the features that display the unit's meaning potential (which could if we wished be displayed according to the clause's strands of meaning, as in the lower half of Figure 10 in Section 7.8),
2a. a set of several different structures, each corresponding to a major strand of meaning, and each consisting of a number of 'functions' (e.g., as in Figure 7 of Section 7.2, and as currently in *IFG*),
2b. the single structure into which these must finally be integrated (e.g., as in the last line of Figure 6 in Section 4.9 of Chapter 4, or in the upper half of Figure 10 of Section 7.8).

---

7. It may surprise some readers that it takes a "leap of faith" to adopt this position, but I shall show why this is precisely what is needed.

Thus the first type of representation corresponds to the 'selection expression' of features chosen in the system network, i.e., to the instance at the level of **meaning** in Figure 4 in Section 3.2 of Chapter 3. However, each of the second and third types can be seen as corresponding, in their way, to the instance at the level of **form** in terms of Figure 4 in Chapter 3 (which is why they are labelled "2a" and "2b", rather than "2" and "3").

But what is the relationship of the last two to each other? Does the Sydney Grammar first generate a set of several different structures for each clause, one for each line of analysis in Figure 7 of Section 7.2, and does it then bring into operation a set of 'mapping rules' which match up all of these structures and then integrate them into a single structure? This is the clear implication of Halliday's statement (cited earlier in Section 4.9 of Chapter 4) that

> it is the function of the lexicogrammar to map the structures onto one another so as to form a single integrated structure that represents all components [= 'components of the grammar, in the sense of 'metafunctions'] simultaneously. (1977/78:128)

If this was indeed how the Sydney Grammar worked, it would require another major component in the grammar itself to perform this complex task of 'mapping'. But is it?

The first part of the answer is that there appear to be **two versions of the Sydney Grammar** that differ from each other on this matter. Roughly speaking, the two seem to correspond to each of the two 'strands' of the theory that I characterized in Section 5.2 of Chapter 5 as the 'text-descriptive' and the 'theoretical-generative'. When Halliday or Matthiessen are writing from a 'text-descriptive' viewpoint, they typically write in terms of what we shall call the **structure conflation** model, but when they are writing from the 'theoretical-generative' perspective they tend to write in terms of what we shall call the **element conflation** model.

In the 'structure conflation' model several sets of structures, one corresponding to each metafunction (or more accurately each 'strand of meaning') are **first** generated as separate structures, and **then**, by an additional stage in the process of generation which has not so far been described by any SF linguist — they are mapped onto each other to form a single, integrated structure. Halliday is clearly assuming some such model as this when he writes, as in the passage cited above, that "it is the function of the lexicogrammar to map the structures onto each other". And Matthiessen strikes a similar note when he talks of "the structural unification of the metafunctional strands" (1995:613). Indeed, the use of 'multiple structure' diagrams throughout *IFG* can be said to presuppose the 'structure conflation' model.

Thus a model of language that posits a set of several different structures for a single clause must also provide a way to integrate them into a single output. As Halliday says in his introduction to *IFG*, "although each strand of meaning in the clause will be described independently in its own terms, [...] a clause is still one clause — it is not three" (1994:36). It is clear, then, that the next stage for the representations in *IFG* is that they should be 'conflated'.

However, the fact is that there is no description in the literature of the Sydney Grammar of the way in which the conflation of the various structures would actually be achieved. Let us therefore now try to fill this gap.

Clearly, the first requirement is that the architecture of the model described in Figure 4 of Chapter 3 should be considerably extended. It would need to generate a new type of output that integrated the various structures, and for this it would require a new component that would transform the second 'multiple structure' output into the third 'integrated' one. Thus the relatively simple model in Figure 4 in Section 3.2 of Chapter 3 would have to be modified in the way shown in Figure 8, i.e., to give it two 'levels' within 'form'.

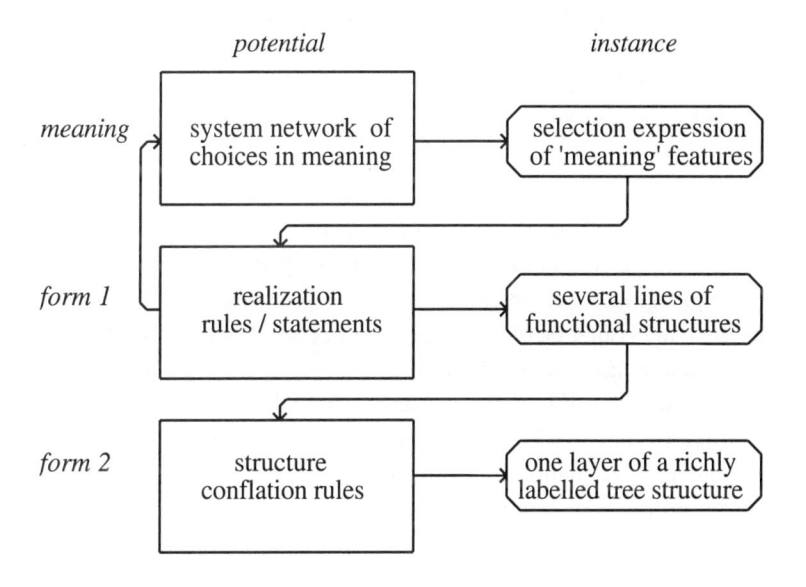

*Figure 8: The main components required in a systemic functional grammar that provides for 'structure conflation'*

The next question is that of what the rules in the "structure conflation rules" component in Figure 8 might be like. (Again, there is no guidance on this matter in the writings of those who work in the framework of the Sydney Grammar.) Let us therefore consider for a moment the nature of the task that such a component would be required to perform.

Many problems would need to be overcome. In fact, there are points in Halliday's writings when he shows that he is aware of some aspects of them. He hints at one problem when he writes in "Options and functions in the English clause" that "not every clause constituent occupies a role in respect of all three [of TRANSITIVITY, MOOD and THEME] — a Modal Adjunct, for example, has no TRANSITIVITY role" (1969/81:143). In other words, the structures that are to be conflated with each other are not necessarily coterminous, in that they may contain gaps at either end (or indeed in the middle). This raises problems for making explicit statements in the putative 'structure conflation rules'. It seems probable that such rules would need to include many conditional operations, if they are to provide for all possible eventualities, since the conflation rules cannot simply refer to the boundaries of the clause.

Halliday then goes on to make a second point about the nature of such conflations — and it is one that raises horrendous problems for the theoretical-generative strand of the theory. This is the fact that, in the approach to structure that it entails, "a role may extend over more than one element, for example Rheme over Process and Goal" (1969/81:143). Thus the model that is being proposed in the Sydney Grammar does not simply involve the conflation of non-coterminous structures. In addition, many of the elements of which those structures are composed are also non-coterminous.

These, then, are two serious, practical problems that arise in the 'structure conflation' model that is presented in *IFG*. It is interesting that Halliday himself identifies them in his first theoretical-generative paper about the then new model of systemic functional grammar. Yet this is as far as he goes, and there is no hint in his later writings of how the problem of formalizing this general proposal is to be solved. Thus, while he identifies the phenomena that cause the problems, he does not identfy them specifically as problems, and he does not show how he proposes to resolve them.

The more serious of the two types is that of how to 'conflate' the non-coterminous elements, such as 'Rheme' with 'Process + Goal'.

Let me now try to state precisely why this is a problem. The theory of generative Systemic Functional Grammar has always, since the mid-1960s, included conflation rules that 'fuse' two or more 'elements' into a single element, e.g., Halliday (1969/81) and Halliday (1970/76b). This is the core of the well-established 'element conflation' model, and we know how to implement computer models of language which incorporate such relationships. But **there is no published description of how to map an element onto another element that is not coterminous with it.** For example, there is no description of how the supposed 'element' of the 'Rheme' in the thematic structure comes to be mapped onto two or more elements in another structure, such as the Process, Goal and Circumstance in the experiential structure of Figure 7. And the total number of permutations of mappings of all such configurations of elements would be absolutely enormous.

Indeed, it is not even clear what it would mean to perform such a 'conflation'. For example, does it mean slicing the Rheme up into a number of pieces, and then conflating each of these with each of the Process, the Goal, and the Circumstance, thus: "Rheme/Process + Rheme/Goal + Rheme/Circumstance"? It is hard to imagine what other action could be performed that could conceivably be termed a 'conflation', but when this is done the effect is that the 'Rheme' is broken up into two or more bits, each of which matches the other 'functions' with which it is supposedly being 'conflated'. It would be a dismemberment of the 'Rheme' rather than its 'conflation' with something.

If this type of dismemberment really is what is intended, we have to ask if any insights follow from it. I can see none. Moreover, even if some insight could be identified, there remains the problem that any such rules would increase in complexity exponentially, once they were expanded beyond the needs of a 'toy' grammar.[8] In other words, the rules in such a 'mapping' component would need to be able to map all possible sequences of all possible 'functions' in each of six (and sometimes more) lines of structure onto each of the other five (or more) such lines of 'functions'. They would be incredibly complicated.[9]

---

8. For example, it is not the case that there is just one 'function' of 'Circumstance'; there are many different types (possibly around forty in all in English), each of which would have to be provided for separately in the grammar, in each of its various possible positions in the clause.

9. Trying to solve this problem would in fact bring grammar-modelling back to the basic question of how to handle economically the great variation in the sequence of elements in English clauses. This was the problem that defeated the early 'phrase structure' grammars of the formalist type, and which led directly to the introduction of the concept of the syntactic

In other words, the representations of structure used in *IFG*, which show many non-coterminous elements in different lines of structure, are easy to draw but probably impossible to implement in a theoretical-generative model.

Some of Halliday's analyses in *IFG* introduce a yet more serious problem. This is the fact that they involve presenting the same clause **at two different layers of structure** in the THEME and MOOD analyses. This occurs in his analyses of clauses with an **experiential enhanced theme** (also known as 'predicated theme' and the '*it*-cleft construction'), e.g., *It was his teacher who persuaded him to continue*. Halliday's analyses of the THEME and MOOD structures of such examples have very little in common. His THEME structure (*IFG* p. 60) presents *who persuaded him to continue* as a direct element of the thematic structure, while the equivalent clause in his MOOD analysis (p. 98) is two layers lower in the structure. This is because Halliday claims (wrongly in my view) that the Subject in the MOOD structure in the above text-sentence is *it* [...] *who persuaded him to continue* (where *who persuaded him to continue* must function as a qualifier in a nominal group whose head is *it*).[10] The problem is that the clause *who persuaded him to continue* is at a different layer of structure in each of these two analyses — so running counter to one of the basic assumptions of theoretical-generative SFL, i.e., that each traversal of the system network gener-\ates **one layer of structure**. I can think of no way in which 'structure conflation statements' could cover such cases.

Moreover, similar problems would arise for Halliday's analysis of what are termed in the Cardiff Grammar **evaluative enhanced theme** constructions (i.e., 'extraposition' in the terms of formal grammar) such as *It's marvellous to see you again*).

In my view the component of the grammar that would handle Halliday's analyses of such structures will never be built — if only because there are vastly

---

transformation. It is also the problem to which the combination of the system network and its associated realization rules has proved a more enduring response. But the new problem would be far more difficult than the old one, because there is not just one string of symbols with a variable sequence of elements, but six or more lines of analysis. If there were six, this would multiply the problem by a factor of 720 (i.e., 6 X 5 X 4 X 3 X 2). As if this was not enough, an additional problem for any such structure conflation rules would be the relative frequency (compared with other analyses) of discontinuity which Halliday's type of analysis engenders (especially in MOOD structures, e.g., Halliday 1994:81, 83, 86).

10. The elements of the TRANSITIVITY analysis that Halliday would give to such examples would be the same as the MOOD elements, judging by his analyses in Halliday (1967-8:236).

preferable approaches to the problem of modelling such structures.[11]

At this point in the development of the argument, the only possible conclusion is that it would only be desirable to try to construct a component of the grammar for integrating the various structures that correspond to strands of meaning if it could be shown that it is needed on independent grounds. In other words, we should not go down the road of turning the 'two-component' model of Figure 4 into the 'three-component' model of Figure 8 unless it is really necessary. In the next sub-section we shall see that it is not.

7.4.2 The 'implemented version: the 'element conflation' model of "Systemic theory" and Matthiessen & Bateman (1991)

What, then is the position on this matter of those who have sought to implement Halliday's model? The fact is that all of the theoretical-generative publications in the framework of the Sydney Grammar show that **no systemic functional grammarian has even considered building a generative grammar that works on the principle of 'structure conflation'.** The importance of this fact for the main argument that is made in this book cannot be overstated, because it shows that the multiple structure representations used in *IFG* have no real position in the theory. (It is of course still possible that they may have some other value — a topic to which we shall return shortly.)

Surprisingly, perhaps, Halliday's own published fragments of generative grammars all take the same position as that to described now, as we consider the procedure for generating the element *we* in *We would visit Mrs Skinner every Sunday* (i.e., the clause analyzed in the *IFG*-style in Figure 7). Drawing on Halliday (1969/81:142) and 1970/76b), we can say that Halliday would generate this composite element in the following manner:

---

11. For a fairly full account of the Cardiff Grammar analysis of such constructions in English developed by Huang and myself, see Fawcett & Huang (1995) and, for a comparison with the nearest equivalent Chinese construction, see Huang & Fawcett (1996). Huang (1996) provides a detailed critique of Halliday's proposals, and for another recent publication that illustrates our analysis, see Fawcett (1999). There are partial similarities to Halliday's approach to the 'experiential' structure of the main clause in such constructions in Halliday (1967-8:236), in that he sees them as having the Participant Roles of 'Identified' and 'Identifier', but otherwise our analysis is different from any of his. For the way in which 'higher components' in the full process of planning and generating a text-sentence are involved in the explanation of the relationship between, for example, *his teacher persuaded him* and *it was his teacher who persuaded him*, see Fawcett (1992) and Fawcett & Huang (in preparation).

1. At some early stage, the 'function' of 'Theme' is inserted in the structure.
2. At a later stage of generation the 'function' of 'Subject' is inserted, and either then or by a later rule it is conflated with the 'Theme'.
3. Later still, a Participant Role is inserted, e.g., 'Actor,' and this is conflated with the 'Theme/Subject' to create a composite element 'Theme/Subject/Actor'.

This is also essentially what happens in Matthiessen and Bateman's computer implementation of Halliday's Nigel grammar in Penman, according to their description of the process in Matthiessen & Bateman (1991:88-109). There are differences in the sequence in which 'functions' are inserted in various versions of SF grammars, but what is constant across all such grammars — whether they are produced in the Sydney or the Cardiff frameworks — is that the phenomena that gets conflated are coterminous 'functional elements' (or 'functions' or 'elements') — and **not structures**.

Moreover, there is no generative systemic functional grammar in existence that includes a rule which conflates 'chunks' of the clause such as 'Residue', 'Rheme' and 'Given' with the various 'functions' in other 'strands'.

The fact is that Halliday, in his immensely influential but still exploratory work 'Options and functions in the English clause' (1969/81) appears to adopt an anomolous position. On page 143 he emphasizes the concept that "the clause has a number of different but simultaneous structures" (while pointing out certain caveats, as indicated in the last subsection). But on the facing page he sets out a table of realization statements that demonstrates clearly that the model is in fact one that simply conflates 'functions' — and not structures. In other words, his rules show how to generate the 'function' of 'Theme', but not the 'function' of 'Rheme'; they show how to give a Participant Role the 'function' of being 'New', but not how to assign the supposed function of 'Given' to whatever experiential element or elements it is relevant to — and similarly for the 'Residue'.

This pattern — i .e. one in which certain parts of the structure illustrated in diagrams such as Figure 7 are provided for by the generative apparatus of the grammar and some are not — is reflected in all of the grammars that followed the publication of Halliday (1969/81). This stateement includes both the only published grammar with a genuinely wide coverage (Hudson's 1971 book

*English Complex Sentences*) and my own early work (Fawcett 1973/81).

Let us now ask: "What light do attempts by others to implement Halliday's model in the computer shed on the question?"

### 7.4.3 The evidence from the computer implementation of the model

It is highly illuminating to compare a recent description of the version of Halliday's Nigel grammmar that was implemented in the computer with the original account of a generative systemic functional grammar in Halliday (1969/81). Mann & Matthiessen (1983/85), Matthiessen & Bateman (1991), Patten (1994), Steiner *et al.* (1988), Teich (1999) and others have all sought to implement computer versions of Halliday's model, and here we shall take our evidence from the definitive account of the Penman project given in Matthiessen & Bateman (1991).

Consider the diagram shown in Figure 9, which is taken directly from Matthiessen & Bateman (1991:109).

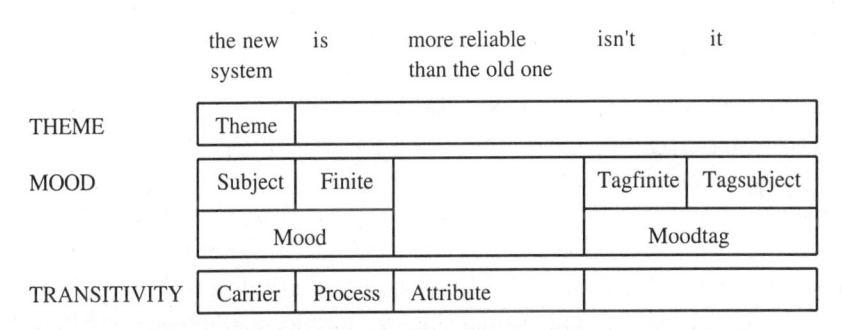

|  | the new system | is | more reliable than the old one | isn't | it |
|---|---|---|---|---|---|
| THEME | Theme | | | | |
| MOOD | Subject | Finite | | Tagfinite | Tagsubject |
| | Mood | | | Moodtag | |
| TRANSITIVITY | Carrier | Process | Attribute | | |

*Figure 9: Matthiessen & Bateman's "output structure of an example"*

Here Matthiessen and Bateman provide a visual representation of the output from their generator, following as far as they can the *IFG* layout. It looks, at first sight, very like Figure 7 in Section 7.2, and so also like one of the many representations of clauses given in *IFG*.

It is also a remarkably honest diagram, in the sense that it has not been adapted to make it more like the standard *IFG* analysis than the output from the computer really is (with one vital proviso, which we shall come to shortly). Yet the fact is, as we shall now see, that it is unlike the *IFG* diagrams in one vital respect. So let us compare Figure 9 with the *IFG*-style analysis of a clause in Figure 7.

Two differences that are not important for our present purposes are (1) that Figure 9 includes the 'tag' *isn't it*, and (2) that it contains no line for the INFORMATION structure shown in Figure 7 as "Given" and "New". (The reason for this omission is probably that their version of the Penman generator does not generate intonation.)

From our present perspective, the first important difference about Figure 9 is the blank boxes in the THEME and MOOD lines of the representation. Most of the THEME line of analysis is a long blank box, covering several elements, in which the label "Rheme" would be written if this was an *IFG* analysis. And there is similar blank box in the MOOD line of Figure 9, where "Residue" would be written in an *IFG* analysis (between "Mood" and "Moodtag"). This is not the trivial difference that it might at first appear, because when the blank boxes are labelled this suggests that there are 'functions' in these lines of analysis that correspond to them — and it is this fact that in turn allows one to read into such diagrams the idea that they represent a 'structure'. In other words, I suggest that there is not in fact a single 'functional element' called a "Rheme" that corresponds to several other clause elements; that there is no 'functional element' of 'Residue' that similarly covers one or more elements; and, in cases where there is an INFORMATION line of analysis, that there is no 'functional element' of 'Given' that covers one or more elements.[12]

The second important difference in Figure 9 from the standard *IFG*-style analysis follows from the first. It is that the potential for 'conflation' among the 'functions' in Matthiessen and Bateman's "output" diagram (and in fact in all other published accounts of SF generation) is very limited indeed. In the generation of their worked example (shown in Figure 9) the only conflations that occur are (1) the conflation of the elements "Theme", "Subject" and "Carrier", and (2) the conflation of the elements "Finite" and "Process". More specifically, notice that the only 'functions' that Figure 9 shows to be conflated are ones that are **coterminous** with each other.

The importance of establishing these facts is as follows. Despite the

---

12. As you may have noticed, the right hand box in the TRANSITIVITY line of analysis is also blank, but in this case an *IFG*-style analysis would not label it. This is because this element only has 'interpersonal' meaning. Since the tag *isn't it* is automatically derived from the main clause it has no 'experiential' meaning, so that there is nothing to say about it in terms of the TRANSITIVITY line of analysis.

similarity in appeararance of the representation in Figure 9 to those in *IFG*, it is clear from both the verbal description in Matthiessen & Bateman (1991) and from the diagram showing "successive states of the blackboard" (their Figure 9.15 on their page 108) that in their account of the generation of a clause (or any other unit) **there is no stage at which there are co-existing sets of different functional structures which must later be integrated**. And this is the case with all SF generators.[13]

However, there is a third point of interest in Matthiessen and Bateman's diagram. It is the fact that they have felt obliged to make some show of generating what for Halliday is the 'primary structure' in the analysis of MOOD. This is the 'function' 'Mood', which in an *IFG*-style description must be represented in addition to the 'Subject' and the 'Finite', which are shown as its two 'subcomponents". But the fact is that it is **only the 'Subject' and the 'Finite'** that are needed for (1) conflation with other 'functions' from other lines of the analysis, and (2) the next stage of the process of generation. In other words, the 'function' of 'Mood' plays no part in the generation of the clause. Clearly, it would be far simpler to generate the Finite and the Subject as direct 'functions' of the clause, so that they can be directly conflated with the appropriate other 'functions'.

The procedure described in Matthiessen & Bateman (1991) is first to generate the 'function' of 'Mood' in the 'primary' structure of the interpersonal line of structure, and then, apparently straight away (judging by the 'blackboard' representation in their Figure 7.15 on page 108), they insert the 'function' of 'Finite' by the use of what they term the "Expand" operator. The effect of this is to build the Finite into the secondary structure as what they term a "subconstituent" of the higher 'function' of 'Mood'.[14] A later realization

---

13. For our present purposes, we shall ignore the "Moodtag" in the Matthiessen and Bateman analysis, because it raises additional theoretical and descriptive problems. These arise because their analysis suggests that the elements labelled "Moodfinite" and "Moodsubject" function directly as elements of the clause, rather than being elements of a clause that is embedded within the 'Tag', as it would be in the Cardiff Grammar analysis. See Fawcett (1999) and (in press) for the Cardiff Grammar's analysis of such 'tags', and for the evidence that they should be modelled as embedded clause of a 'truncated' type.

14. The Finite is therefore in effect a 'function', while not being, oddly, a direct 'function' in a 'unit', in the usual manner. However, it seems that in some unspecified way it must still count as a direct 'function' of the clause, because it later gets conflated with the direct clause 'function' of Process. (This is necessary because the word *is* in the text is both the Finite and the Process, as Figure 9 shows.)

statement then adds the 'Subject' as a second 'subconstituent' of the 'Mood' 'function' in the same way, and then another finally orders them with respect to each other.

Unfortunately, Matthiessen and Bateman give no explanation as to why they find it desirable to generate the Finite and the Subject as "subcomponents" of the 'Mood', even though the same effect could have been obtained by simply inserting the Finite and the Subject as direct 'functions' of the clause. The only 'advantage' (if it is one) is that the final structure that is generated resembles slightly more closely the representations shown in *IFG* than it would otherwise. But there seems to be little point in going to all of this extra work when the 'sister' element to the 'Mood' (i.e., the 'Residue') does not get generated — and when, even if it did, it would serve no useful purpose.[15]

Thus, after the conflation rules have been applied, the structure of the clause *the new system is more reliable than the old one* (omitting the 'Moodtag *isn't it*), as generated by Matthiessen and Bateman, can be represented very simply as follows:

Theme/Subject/Carrier + Finite/Process + Attribute.

Thus two of the three elements are formed from conflated 'functions' and the third consists of a single 'function'. If you compare this economical representation with the corresponding part of the representation in Figure 9 above, you will see that, from the generative viewpoint, it contains all the necessary information. The key point is that Matthiiessen and Bateman's generator operates in essentially the same way as the one described in Halliday (1969/81) — and that **there is no conflation of non-coterminous elements**.

Indeed, Matthiessen and Bateman do not make clear precisely what role the *IFG*-like diagram given in Figure 9 plays in the process of generation. It may well be that their main reason for generating it was to provide a satisfactory visual representation of the structure for those who are expecting something that resembles an *IFG*-style analysis, rather than because it is necessary for the process of generation.

The reason why it is important to generate the Subject and Finite as direct elements of the clause (rather than the 'Mood' element') is that it is the Subject and the Finite on which further work must be done. This further work will

---

15. Incidentally, this criticism of the introduction of two layers of structure to model 'interactional' meaning is as valid for text-descriptive work as for theoretical-generative work.

generate (1) the nominal group *the new system* to fill the Theme/Subject/Actor and (2) the item *is* to expound the Finite/Process.[16] Interestingly, however, Matthiessen and Bateman do not explain why — or even how — these are generated as "subcomponents' of 'Mood'. (However it is done, the same principle presumably applies to the division of the "Moodtag" into its two elements.)

To summarize: it seems clear that that Matthiessen and Bateman's only purpose in generating the Mood elements is to generate a second line of interpersonal structure, and so to make available a visual representation that looks a little more like an *IFG* analysis. In other words, the generation of the 'Mood' element is simply a cosmetic exercise. Essentially, then, the Nigel generator that Matthiessen and Bateman describe here is one that generates single structures, just as Halliday's earlier models do (e.g., Halliday (1969/81). In other words, their generator conflates 'functions to generate **multiple elements**, as shown above, but it does not generate **multiple structures**.

I should add at this point that GENESYS (the computer version of the Cardiff Grammar, as described in Fawcett, Tucker & Lin 1993) uses a similar 'element conflation' procedure to the one described in Matthiessen & Bateman (1991) — except, of course, that it generates the Subject and Operator (the Cardiff Grammar term for Halliday's 'Finite') as direct elements of the clause.[17]

7.4.4 A summary so far

Let me summarize the stages of the argument that I have presented up to this point. We have established that the theoretical-generative model of a

16. Strictly speaking, in the Sydney Grammar it is the element 'Event' within the 'verbal group' (the unit that fills the clause element 'Predicator') with which the 'Finite' should be conflated, and not the 'Process', as an example with auxiliary verbs such as *the new system may be going to be more reliable than the old one* demonstrates. See Fawcett (2000 and forthcoming b) for a full critique of Halliday's approach to the 'verbal group' and Appendix C for a summary.

17. In developing the early versions of the grammar that was to lead to the GENESYS generator in COMMUNAL, I drew on the same early published sources, such as Halliday (1969/81) and Hudson (1971), as did the builders of Penman (Mann and Matthiessen), and not on Penman. I was therefore open to the possibility of being led in a different direction from that of Penman, so that the fact that the two SF grammars independently build structures by conflating coterminous elements is highly significant.

systemic functional grammar is always one of 'element conflation' and never one of 'structure conflation'. In other words, the 'mapping' between lines of analysis is performed on individual pairs and trios of 'functions' or 'elements', which from then on function as a single element of the clause. I would therefore say that those systemic functional grammars which suggest that the representation of a clause should include 'functions' such as 'Residue', 'Rheme' and 'Given' are in fact introducing what we might term 'pseudo-elements', i.e., chunks of text that do not contribute in any way to the functional structure of the clause. Their chief effect is to give the misleading impression that there is a 'structure' of roughly the length of a clause that corresponds to each of the strands of meaning. In other words, the only type of conflation that occurs in such a grammar — as it generates its single, 'flat-tree' structures — is the conflation of single, coterminous elements.

Thus, while the representation of the structure of a clause in Matthiessen & Bateman (1991:109) may look roughly like the representations of clauses in *IFG* in terms of the number of boxes and in its use of some of the same labels as in an *IFG* representation, the structures that it generates are in reality more like the representations in the Cardiff Grammar (e.g., the example that we shall meet in Figure 10 in Section 7.8). In other words, the two have in common that (1) the only type of conflation that they have is 'element conflation', and (2) they both leave empty the quite sizeable boxes where an *IFG* analysis would write in labels such as "Rheme" and "Residue".[18]

Note that the structure that is generated in Matthiessen and Batemen's generator is indeed a **single integrated structure**. Indeed, none of the grammars referred to in this section generate first a set of different structures (as is implied by representations such as those in Figure 7 of Section 7.2) and then conflate them. As the decriptions in all of the publications from Halliday (1969/91) to Matthiessen & Bateman (1991) and Fawcett, Tucker & Lin (1993) show, it is a single structure that the grammar builds — and not a multiple one.

If this is so — and there can be no doubt that it is — any grammarian who wishes to claim that the 'structure conflation' model has a theoretical status (rather than some other value) has a number of problems to solve. Consider again the nature of the representations in Figure 7, which is a typical *IFG*-style

---

18. The same principle would apply to "Given", if Matthiessen and Bateman's generator generated intonation too (as the Cardiff generator does). This is because, like "Rheme" and "Residue", "Given" is essentially 'that which is not New'.

analysis. The main problem with it is that so few 'functions' in one strand are coterminous with 'functions' in another strand. What, precisely, would the rule be like that 'conflated' all four of the Finite, the Predicator, the Process and the Goal with the Rheme? How would it be formulated in such a way that it could be generalized across many cases? The answer is that we do not know — and I for one do not think that it would be worth spending a lot of time in exploring this route, since we know that there is already in existence a simpler and more insightful alternative.[19]

In other words, the fact is that the work of all of those who have worked on building generative versions of SFL — including Halliday himself — has been done in the 'element conflation' model rather than in the 'structure conflation' model. Indeed, there is no discussion in the 'theoretical-generative' strand of work in SFL as to how the 'structure conflation' model of language might work, and nor is there any discussion (other than that in Section 7.4.1 of this chapter) of what might be involved if it was to be attempted.

Where, then, does this leave the representations in *IFG*?

### 7.4.5 Implications for the theoretical status of the *IFG* representations

The clear implication of these facts is that the representations in *IFG* do not have the solid basis in the theory that they surely should, if they are to be used as the standard method of describing texts in systemic functional terms. In other words, if generative systemic functional grammars do not build structures like this, *IFG*-style representations give a misleading picture of the systemic functional view of the structure of language. As a specific example, we may say that it is positively misleading to label the portion of the clause that is not a Theme as the "Rheme", because the label "Rheme" simply means 'that which is not Theme' — or, more fully, 'the elements corresponding to this block are not one of the Themes'. Similarly, "Residue" simply means 'those elements that

---

19. It would be quite a simple matter, of course, to add to a computer implementation such as Matthiessen and Bateman's a small program that inserted the label "Rheme" in any box in the line of thematic meaning that was not already labelled, and to do the same for "Given" and "Residue". But this would be simply a cosmetic adjustment to make the output appear even more like that in a typical *IFG* representation, rather than the positive conflation of elements, such as happens in the 'element conflation' model. Matthiessen and Bateman are to be congratulated for resisting the temptation to make their computer output more like the *IFG* representations than they really are (e.g., as illustrated in Figure 9).

are not the Subject or the Finite' (or any other marker of interpersonal meaning). And essentially the same position holds for "Given".[20] To place the names of such supposed 'functions' in the long boxes in diagrams such as Figure 7 that would otherwise be empty is to sustain — on what we now see to be theoretically inadequate grounds — the initially attractive metaphor that each clause has several different structures, and so several different strands of meaning that run (virtually) all the way through (virtually) all of them.

We can now see that, in terms of the metaphor of a text as a 'rope' of interwoven strands, the 'rope' often consists of just one strand — though it also often has two or three very short multiple 'strands of meaning' which extend over one or two elements. Matthiessen and Bateman's diagram in Figure 9 exemplifies this point in terms of the Sydney Grammar, and Figure 10 of Section 7.8 does so in terms of a Cardiff Grammar representation.

Can it really be the case, you may be asking, that all of the representations throughout *IFG* and all the representations in all of the derived works have no status in the theory? Perhaps, you might think, the cumulative effect of the conflation of several individual elements would be to provide a conflation of structures? The answer is that while this is theoretically possible, in practice it does not do so. This is because the supposed 'functions' of 'Rheme', 'Given', 'Residue' and others do not correspond to single 'functions' and they do not play any role in generative systemic functional grammar, for the reasons given in recent sections of this chapter. And nor, as I have suggested above, has anyone yet made any viable proposal as to how such a model could be made to work. Conflation is, by all current SF definitions, an operation that applies only to individual, coterminous elements.

If this is so — and the theoretical writings of both the chief architect of SFL and the major implementers of both the Sydney and the Cardiff Grammars leave no room for doubt that it is — we are left with the following question: "What is the role of the representations of functional structure in *IFG*?"

To ask this is to question one of the basic assumptions about the representation of language that Halliday has been making since the late sixties. Yet it is

---

20. As stated erlier, "Given" is essentially 'that which is not marked as New' — but only so long as it precedes the element marked as "New". It is in fact only possible for the text analyst to make a guess at which portion of the text is 'Given' and which is 'New' by drawing on other evidence than intonation, such as the meaning of pronouns, so that we cannot automatically treat every element that is not marked as "New" as "Given". However, what comes after the New in the same information unit is indeed always 'Given'.

not, I shall argue, one of those assumptions that is fundamental to the theory, because the concept that such representations are designed to display (i.e., the multifunctional nature of language) can be displayed equally well — and in fact more appropriately — in a representation of the level of meaning (as we shall see in Section 7.8). It is the multifunctional nature of language — and not its representation in a particular manner — that is to be placed among the fundamental concepts of SFL.

## 7.5 The status of *IFG*-style representations

### 7.5.1 The current value of IFG-style representations

Even though Halliday himself defines 'conflation' as a relationship that operates on individual elements, as we saw in Chapter 5 (Halliday 1993:4505), he also writes regularly about the structure of clauses in a way that appears to give *IFG*-style representations some status in the theory (e.g., 1993:4506) — so implying that conflation also occurs between structures with many elements.

Matthiessen similarly defines the term "conflation" as an operation that relates individual "functions" (1995:778), and then goes on to write about "the structural unification of the metafunctional strands — the conflations of the textual, interpersonal and experiential clause functions" (Matthiessen 1995:613-17).

Are Halliday and Matthiessen being inconsistent in such passages? Or is it possible that they do not in fact take the absolute position on this issue that one might assume?[21]

The proposal that there are complete (or nearly complete) clause-length structures for every strand of meaning was stated quite explicitly in Halliday's early and twice-reprinted paper "Options and functions in the English clause" (1969/81) — and I shall discuss the effect of this paper on the development of the theory in the next sub-section. But it is not until Halliday (1979) that we find a full statement of the more specific proposal that a completely different type of structure is involved in the realization of each of the major

---

21. In the above quotation from Matthiessen, it would just be possible to interpret the plural form "conflations" as being intended to suggest that the 'unification' of the various metafunctional strands in fact comes about — to the extent that it does — through many individual 'conflations'. But I do not think that this was in fact his intended meaning.

'metafunctions' — i.e., to use Halliday's own terms, that 'experiential' meanings are realized in 'constituency' structure, 'interpersonal' meanings in 'prosodic' structures, 'textual' meanings in 'culminative' structures and 'logical' meanings in 'iterative' structures'. This suggestion has been repeated in various later writings (e.g., p. 4506 of "Systemic theory" and pp. 35-6 of *IFG*). However, it is undoubtedly Halliday's use of the concept that each metafunction has a corresponding structure in all of the representations of clauses in *IFG* that has provided the main momentum behind the spread of the concept. Indeed, it is almost as if the whole description of English in *IFG* hangs on the assumption that there is a separate clause-length structure for each metafunction. But is this really what Halliday is saying?

A careful reading of the relevant recent texts shows that Halliday is in fact making a less extreme statement than the above summary implies. In a table on p. 36 of *IFG*, for example, one column lists words ('constituency', 'prosodic', etc) that describe the "**favoured** type of structure" [my emphasis]. And in "Systemic theory" (1993:4506) his wording is that "the different metafunctions [...] **tend** to be realized by different structural resources" [my emphasis]. In other words, from the theoretical viewpoint it can be said that he is simply pointing out interesting **tendencies** in the structural patterns in which each type of meaning gets realized. This falls a long way short of saying that each strand of meaning must obligatorily be realized in that type of structure. Indeed, the emphasis in his general descriptions is on the fact that, in his words, "constituent structure is the prototype to which all three [in fact four] metafunctions can be referred" (1994:35), and the box diagram representations that he provides in *IFG* are, of course, simply one way of representing the 'flat tree' type of constituency. But the fact remains, as I pointed out in the last subsection, that Halliday gives 'function' labels to many of the 'long boxes' in his diagrams that it would be more accurate to leave unlabelled. In practical terms, however, the simple fact that Halliday always represents the structure of clauses as a set of parallel structures sends a powerful message to his readers that the structure of language combines several 'strands of meaning'.

It is just possible, of course, that Halliday simply regards the 'multiple structure' model of structure as convenient reification of 'how language really is', and that he considers it worth sacrificing the purity of the theory to provide a strong visual image of the clause as the realization of the several different 'strands' of meaning.

To summarize so far: we have seen that when Halliday suggests that different patterns of elements in the clause tend to be associated with different strands of meaning, he is simply pointing out a tendency rather than issuing a prescriptive statement. And yet the proliferation of multi-strand analyses of functional structure in *IFG* and in the many 'spin-off' works has established and re-enforced a firm belief in many users of the theory that this is an accurate model of the structure of language. Indeed, many of those who use Halliday's theory would be surprised that there could be any other way of representing the structure of language in a SF framework.

What status, then, should we give to a representation of the structure of a clause-length text-sentence that shows it as consisting of several lines of structure, as found in *IFG* and the many derived works? The answer, I suggest, is that **it is a mental construct whose purpose is to make it easier for the text analyst to think about the multifunctional nature of language in structural terms**.

From the theoretical viewpoint, such constructs are a representation of what one stage in the generation of a text-sentence might be like — **if** it were the case that the grammar worked by first generating several functional structures and then conflating them. From the practical viewpoint of the text analyst, they may be a helpful 'reification' of the abstract semantic features that they represent. In other words, we might wish to say that, in this type of representation, the abstract features are made visible as 'objects' on the page, through the device of viewing them as 'elements' of clause-length structures, and by labelling each element of each supposed 'structure'. The only problem with representing the structure of language in this manner — i.e., in the *IFG* manner — is, as we have seen, that no systemic functional grammar actually generates such structures.

To describe such representations as "mental constructs" does not imply that they have no role to play in establishing an understanding of the nature of language. Indeed, many scholars would take the view that *IFG* provides the best available broad-coverage functional description of English that we have today. However, the recognition of their current value does not exclude the possibility that there may be other and better systemic functional representations of texts — and specifically ones that focus on the direct use in the representation of a clause of the features that have been selected in the system networks. Section 7.8 will outline one such alternative that is currently being prepared for publication.

### 7.5.2 How the *IFG*-style representations have acquired their current status in the theory

Given that systemic functional grammars do not generate *IFG*-style multiple structures, how it is that such structures have become so widely assumed to be a central part of the theory? There are at least the following three reasons.

The first, of course, is that Halliday himself seems to have assumed the insightfulness of this approach from the earliest days of the metafunctional hypothesis. Notice, however, that historically it emerged as an extension of the 'element conflation' approach, and not as a replacement for it. In Halliday (1969/81:138f.) he introduces **both** the 'element conflation model' **and** the 'structure conflation model'. Having shown in detail how 'element conflation' works (as described in Section 7.2), Halliday then writes that "the clause has a number of different but simultaneous structures" (as already cited in Section 7.2 above). It seems that in the few lines between these two quotations Halliday has switched from thinking in terms of the rigorous demands of building a generative grammar to the more open-ended task of trying to provide an insightful diagrammatic representation on paper. In other words, the two diagrams of the different structures given on pages 143 and 144 of Halliday (1969/81) give a significantly different picture of conflation from that given in the generative part of the paper. As I have already pointed out, the generative grammar does not generate the elements "Rheme", "Given" and "Residue", so that the two positions are only compatible if we interpret the 'multiple structures' of *IFG* as visual aids to help us to a better understanding of the view that the various 'strands of meaning' occur simultaneously in the clause, rather than as parts of the generative systemic functional grammar of the first part of the paper.

A second reason for the current status of the *IFG* style representations is the great disparity between the numbers of publications in each of the two major 'strands' of the theory — these being what I described in Section 5.2 of Chapter 5 as the 'theoretical-generative' and the 'text-descriptive' strands. The fact is that most of those who read Halliday's work read it for its applicability in the description of texts, so that the readership of a theoretical paper such as "Systemic theory" will be a small fraction of the readership of *IFG*. Indeed, many of Halliday's other publications are also addressed to readers who wish to use his theory for one of various fields of 'applied linguistics' or to interdisciplinary audiences. Typically the intended reader is someone who wishes to use the theory to describe texts, for any of a wide variety of possible purposes. Indeed, Halliday describes *IFG* as "a grammar for [...] text analysis" (1994:xv). For such purposes there is an undeniable initial attractiveness about a model in which (1) a text requires analysis at one level rather than two (even if it turns out that there are several structures at the one level) and (2) the 'multifunctionality' of language is 'reified' in those structures.

The third reason why the representations used in *IFG* have become so widely accepted as an integral part of the theory is that *IFG* does not invite its readers to consider the problems of how these very different structures are to be conflated into a single, unified structure. There is no reason, of course, why Halliday should have addressed this question in *IFG*, since its aim is to provide an insightful model for describing texts, rather than to show how a SF grammar works. But the result is that vital questions about this important aspect of the theory have long remained both unasked and unanswered — and it is upon the validity of the theory that the validity of the description ultimately rests.

In summary, we can say that the main focus of interest among most systemic functional linguists is the description of texts. When one is working on text analysis, what matters most is that one has as one's working tool the most insightful method of analysis that one can find. The approach to representing structure in *IFG* has one great advantage over others (such as an updated Scale and Category analysis, e.g., as advocated in Morley 2000). This is, of course, that it provides a clear visual image of the **multifunctional** nature of language.— and so a clear mental construct. Moreover, it is currently the only SF framework for describing language that is available in published form (i.e., in *IFG* and the various derived publications). This fact has led to the widespread acceptance of *IFG*-style analyses as the only 'correct' SF analyses — and so, coincidentally, to the widespread acceptance of the 'structure conflation' model.

Furthermore, it seems probable that most inquirers into the nature of SFL have ignored works such as Halliday's "Systemic theory" (1993) and Matthiessen & Bateman's *Text Generation and Systemic Functional Linguistics.* (1991) — and yet it is in such works that we find the statements that define the Sydney version of the theory. On the other hand, even these works fail to bring out the fact (as we have seen it to be) that there is no theoretical-generative SF grammar that is capable of either (1) generating multiple structures of the type illustrated in *IFG* and (2) integrating them into a single structure.

## 7.6 The availability of Sydney Grammar descriptions of English

In our survey of the Sydney Grammar, we come now to Question 2 (from Section 7.1), i.e., "Does the Sydney Grammar make available theoretically motivated descriptions of English that are at the levels of language that Halliday's theoretical statements suggest to be desirable?"

Given Halliday's statement that "in systemic theory the system takes priority" (1993:4505), systemic functional linguists should be describing texts in terms of the features that have been chosen in generating them. We are entitled to ask, therefore, "Where are the networks?" and "How can they be used in the analysis of texts?"

As we have seen, the only publication that provides anything approaching an adequate coverage of the Sydney Grammar's current system networks for English is Matthiessen's *Lexicogrammatical Cartography* (1995). This major work (with almost 1000 pages) is intended as a "reference source" (Matthiessen (1995:iii). However, it gives the reader no guidelines on how to use the various system networks for analyzing texts, and barely any examples of what such analyses might be like. Indeed, there are, so far as I know, still no published analyses of texts whatsoever that are truly systemic, other than the few that use the Cardiff Grammar, such as the example in Figure 10 in Section 7.8.[22]

The implicit assumption of most writings in the framework of the Sydney Grammar is that an *IFG*-style analysis of what we might call 'the implied functional structures' is sufficient — and, presumably, that an analysis in terms of the features would add relatively little. Yet this situation is strikingly at odds with Halliday's claim — a claim that expresses the core concept of systemic functional theory — that "the system takes priority". The *IFG*-style method of

---

22. The one exception to this generalization that I know of in a published work is where Matthiessen shows the features for his examples of the analysis of 'modality' in texts (1995: 507f.). But his analyses of all other types of meaning simply shows structural analyses of the *IFG* type. However, he has used features for the analysis of text in public lectures, e.g., at the 25th International Systemic Functional Congress. Cardiff 1998. There he showed a simplified version of the relevant system networks, and then placed figures on the features that had been chosen in the text being analyzed to indicate the frequency with which they had been chosen. This interesting technique can be used to show how the probabilities have been skewed under the influence of a register variable (or some other variable) in the text. Interestingly, however, an analysis of that type skips over the logically necessary intermediate stage, i.e., the systemic representation of the features chosen **in each clause**, e.g., as illustrated in Figure 10 of Section 7.8. (Compare the interesting study in Matthiessen 1999, which offers TRANSITIVITY probabilities for English as a whole, based on a study of 2,000 clauses).

analysis is therefore simply the only currently available way to show 'strands of meaning' — though it is one that is now seen to lack a base in the theory.[23]

Thus th position is that there is a considerable gap in the Sydney Grammar framework between, on the one hand, Halliday's theoretical statements about the centrality of system networks in the theory and, on the other, the provision of publications that show the text analyst how to go about the task of describing the meaning potential of texts in terms of their systemic features.

## 7.7 Summary of the answers to the two questions

Let us now summarize where the Sydney Grammar stands in relation to the searching questions asked in this chapter. In answer to Question 1a, it is clearly desirable to have representations of a text at the levels of both form and meaning. In answer to Question 1b, it is natural for the semantic representation to show the different 'strands of meaning' (which do not necessarily run all the way through a clause), but the whole purpose of the representation at the level of form is to integrate the various types of meaning into a single structure, so that it is not appropriate to show the various strands of meaning at this level too. (The only reason for doing so would be if we did not have the descriptive apparatus at the level of meaning, which appears to be the case in the framework of current Sydney Grammar publications.) The answer to Question 1c is that 'conflation' is an operation that relates two elements (or 'functions') in a clause rather than clause-length representations. The 'multi-strand' representations of the functional structure of clauses in *IFG* may be a helpful aid to some when thinking about the strands of meaning that are found in a text — if no better means is available — but they play no part in a generative systemic functional grammar. Indeed, it would be helpful if this could be made clear in future writings in the Sydney Grammar framework, e.g., in the next edition of *IFG*.

In Section 7.8 we shall meet an alternative way of representing the multifunctional nature of language in diagram form. It is an exploration of a

---

23. There is a further problem about trying to use *IFG* for text analysis. This is that it is not in fact easy to use (even with the addition of an index in the 1994 edition). Analyzing language is of course inherently problematical, so it is hard to judge how far the difficulties in using *IFG* are inherent in the nature of language, and how far they are the result of (1) the theory and description used in *IFG* and/or (2) how it is presented. Certainly, many students have been helped to understand it better by reading introductory works such as Eggins (1994), Bloor & Bloor (1995) Thompson (1996) and Martin, Matthiessen & Painter (1997).

method suggested by Halliday himself in the passages cited in Section 7.3, and it has the advantage that it suffers from none of the problems that we have encountered in our examination of the type of representations used in *IFG* — except that there is no published account of it with the breadth of coverage of *IFG* and Matthiessen (1995) — not as yet, that is.

## 7.8 An alternative approach: the two levels of representation in the Cardiff Grammar

The purpose of this section is to provide a brief sketch of the approach to analyzing a text that is advocated here as an alternative to the *IFG* approach. It involves representations at the two levels of language and form. Since the 'text-descriptive' and the 'theoretical-generative' aspects of the model are two sides of the same coin, it can also function as an informal introduction to the way in which the Cardiff Grammar works. Let us now ask the same difficult questions in relation to the Cardiff Grammar that we asked about the Sydney Grammar.

The first was 'Is it desirable — or indeed necessary — to have representations of a text at the levels of both form and meaning?" The answer is clear: In this model of language it is both necessary and desirable, and the model operates with the two representations of texts implied by the model of language summarized in Figure 4 in Section 3.2 of Chapter 3 — both in the description of texts and in text generation. Thus, if our goal is the full analysis of a text, it is necessary to provide representations of a text in terms of (1) the features that define its meaning potential and (2) the single functional structure that integrates the various different types of meaning (as in Figure 10).

The second question was "In a model with representations at the level of both form and meaning, is it desirable — or indeed necessary — to show explicitly the multifunctional nature of language at both levels?" In the framework of the Cardiff Grammar, where the representation at the level of form is the final, integrated output, it is clear that the level of representation at which the multifunctional nature of language shouild be displayed is in the representation of the meanings — because at the lower level the various strands of meaning have already been integrated into a single structure. The effects on the structure of the various strads of meaning can be discerned, of course, but it is the division of the selection expression of features chosen in the system networks into their various types of meaning that displays in the most straightforward manner the multifunctional nature of language. It is therefore the role of the semantic representation to display the contribution of the various types of meaning to the text, and it is the role of syntax to show the integration of these intermittent 'strands of meaning' in a single structure. The third question was "In the representation at the level of form, is the conflation that occurs between the realizations of the various strands of meaning a conflation of whole structures or of individual elements?" Here the answer will be clear from the previous sections, and it is that the conflations occur between specific coterminous elements, as complex nodes in the single integrated syntactic representation.

It follows from this that the approach to analyzing texts when using the Cardiff Grammar has certain significant differences from that of the current Sydney Grammar. The first stage is to analyze its **functional syntax**. This is shown in a single but richly labelled functional structure, as in the upper half of Figure 10. Thus the analyst does not go looking for a set of structures that correspond to each strand of meaning, as an *IFG*-style analysis of a clause. For the reader who is familiar with Halliday's work, it may be helpful to think of the structure of a clause as being represented in the present approach rather as a group is represented in *IFG*. In other words, the 'metafunctions' "are not represented in the form of separate whole structures, but rather as partial contributions to a single structural line" (Halliday (1994:179). This does not deny the fact that many elements of the clause constitute the simultaneous realization of several different types of meaning. In Figure 10, for example, the word *We* simultaneously realizes the Subject and the Agent — and, as we shall see in a moment, the Subject itself is the realization of two meanings.

Then, at a second stage of analysis, the text is described in terms of its key **semantic features**, i.e., the most significant of the many features that have been chosen in generating it. An example of this type of analysis is shown in the lower half of Figure 10. This displays the key semantic features, arranged in a number of **strands of meaning**. But note that there is no expectation that all or even most of a 'strand' will be used. Each feature is placed below the element (or elements) of the clause to whose generation it has contributed. There is no space here, of course, to show the system networks from which these features are derived, nor to comment on each feature. Notice, though, that the Subject contributes to two types of meaning: that of 'information giver' and that of 'subject theme'— as well as being conflated with the Agent. I hope that the labels used for the features are sufficiently transparent to give a flavour of this type of multi-strand analysis, and so of its value in analyzing texts.

148                    REPRESENTATIONS IN *IFG*

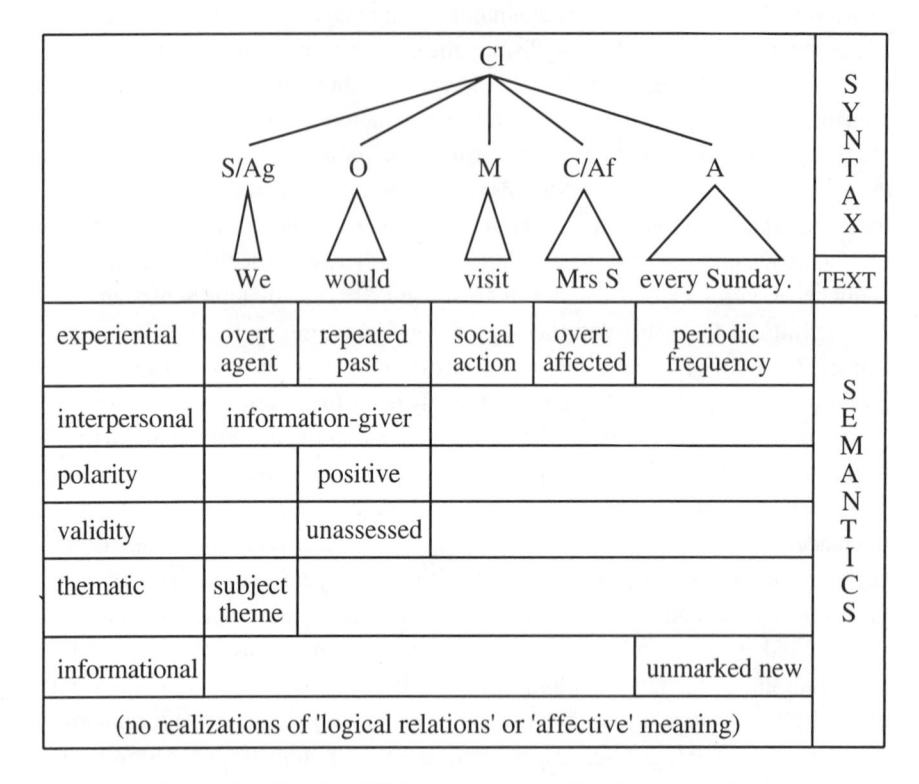

| | | | | | | |
|---|---|---|---|---|---|---|
| | | | Cl | | | S Y N T A X |
| | S/Ag | O | M | C/Af | A | |
| | We | would | visit | Mrs S | every Sunday. | TEXT |
| experiential | overt agent | repeated past | social action | overt affected | periodic frequency | S E M A N T I C S |
| interpersonal | information-giver | | | | | |
| polarity | | positive | | | | |
| validity | | unassessed | | | | |
| thematic | subject theme | | | | | |
| informational | | | | | unmarked new | |
| (no realizations of 'logical relations' or 'affective' meaning) | | | | | | |

*Figure 10: The Cardiff Grammar analysis of a simple clause*

Perhaps the most important characteristic of the diagram is that it shows how an analyst can first determine the **functional syntax** of a one-clause text such as this example, and then go on to derive from it, in a relatively direct and natural manner, the **semantic analysis**, showing these features in terms of the major strands of meaning.

It is an important feature of the analysis that there is no expectation that each vertical column should be filled by a label for each strand of meaning. In other words, the analysis does **not** reflect the view embodied in *IFG* that a clause consists of a conflation of several different structures. Instead, a clause is regarded as the realization, in a single, integrated structure, of the various types of meaning that are modelled in the system networks of TRANSITIVITY, MOOD, THEME and so on. This view of the nature of language is no less 'systemic' and no less 'functional' than that expressed in Halliday's "Systemic theory" and in *IFG,* because the sentence is still derived from system networks of choices between meanings, and the representation still shows the contribution to the integrated structure of the various strands of meaning for which the system networks provide. There is some conflation of individual elements (as opposed to structures), as Figure 10 shows, but the emphasis is now squarely on the representation of 'meaning' through the use of the features from the networks that model the 'meaning potential' of the language. And this is surely as it should be in a systemic functional representation, if Halliday is right that, in this theory, "the system takes priority" (Halliday 1993:4505). Moreover, the Cardiff representation adds an important element that is missing from the *IFG* representation, namely the representation of the integrated structure.

Let us now look for a moment at how the Cardiff Grammar operates in its full, generative version. The first stage is the selection of the features in the system network, i.e., the creation of a **selection expression**. The 'key' features that have been selected in the present example are displayed in the lower half of Figure 10. The realization rules then integrate the various partial 'strands of meaning' that are represented by these features into a single functional structure (e.g., as shown in the top half of Figure 10). This involves the **conflation** of some elements with each other and with participant roles, such as the conflation of the Agent ("Ag") with the Subject ("S"). Notice that, in contrast with the 'structure conflation' version of the Sydney Grammar, there is no expectation that every element — or almost every element — will be conflated with an element in another strand of meaning.

The representation of the syntax is sufficiently rich for all aspects of its multifunctional meaning to be shown in it — or to be directly inferable from it. Thus a text analyst who is equipped with an appropriate handbook can work out, from the evidence of the items and the functional structure, what the associated semantic features are. For example, even though the structure does not show that there is a 'Theme' that is conflated with the Subject and Agent, we can infer directly from the structural analysis that the item *We* is the type of Theme called here a "Subject Theme". (If it had been an 'empty Subject', as in *It's nice to see you*, it would not have a Participant Role conflated with it.)

In a computer model of text analysis there is a broadly equivalent component (calledthe 'semantic interpreter'). In a similar way this reconstructs, on the evidence of the analysis of the functional syntax, the features that must have been chosen in generating that particular structure.[24]

We can summarize this section by answering Questions 1a to 1c with respect to the Cardiff Grammar. Firstly, in a full account of the analysis or generation of a text, we need to show representations at the levels of both **meaning** and **form**. Secondly, the multifunctional nature of language is most appropriately shown at the level of meaning. Thirdly, conflation occurs between individual elements, as exemplified in the relations between the Subject and Agent in Figure 10, and not between clause-length structures.

But what about Question 2? How complete are the Cardiff Grammar's descriptions of English (or any other language) at each of these two levels? And how available are they for general use in analyzing texts? The first part of the answer is that the description and computer implementation of the lexicogrammar of English is very large indeed. Moreover, it has the advantage over other SF models that its system networks have been developed to function explicitly at the level of semantics, so that there is no need for a further level of analysis. e.g., as suggested in Halliday & Matthiessen (1999).[25]

Very large quantities of text analysis in terms of the Cardiff Grammar have been undertaken over the last twenty-five years as part of its development — most at the level of functional syntax (e.g., in the major text-analysis project described in Fawcett & Perkins 1980), but also in the last decade at the level of meaning (a good example of the latter being Ball 1995). Tucker (1998) provides a very fine introduction to the treatment of adjectives and of all of the structures into which they may enter in Cardiff Grammar terms, but since Fawcett (1974-6 /81) there has unfortunately not been a publication that offers

---

24. See O'Donoghue (1994) for a description of the semantic interpreter that has been developed for the Cardiff Grammar, its task being to turn a syntactically analyzed clause into its set of selection expressions.

25. One great advantage of a model in which the system network is explicitly semantic is that it often avoids the need to introduce the 'double analysis' of a single 'strand of meaning', which involves what Halliday calls 'grammatical metaphor'. (For an introduction to this set of concepts see Halliday 1994:340-67.) Consider the case of *Could you read that again?* In the Cardiff Grammar this is analyzed as directly expressing the meaning of 'request' (a choice in the semantic network for MOOD), but in *IFG* there is no such feature at this level of analysis and it would be analyzed as a 'polar interrogative' — but one which the Addressee is expected to re-interpret as the 'imperative' *Read than again!*. A similar example of "interpersonal metaphor" occurs in *IFG* (p. 378), where Halliday first analyses *you have to be beautiful with it* as a 'declarative', and then re-expresses it as *be beautiful with it* and analyzes it as an 'imperative'. In the Cardiff Grammar, it is treated as a **direct realization** of an option in the semantic MOOD network (specifically, as a sub-type of 'directive' with the feature 'requirement').

overall coverage of either level of description.

However the publication of Fawcett (in press) will make publicly available both a broad coverage grammar of functional syntax and full guidelines for analyzing texts in these terms. Then Fawcett (forthcoming a) will make available, in a form that is usable for text analysis, the major system networks for English, in a systemic functional grammar in which the networks constitute the level of semantics. This volume will also provide guidelines for using the system networks for the semantic description of texts.

## 7.9 The alternative ways of representing functional structure in the analysis of a text

The problem for the text analyst who is using SF grammar is that of how best to represent all three of (1) its functional syntax, (2) its meanings and (3) the multifunctional nature of language.

As we have seen, the Sydney Grammar's approach is to present each clause as having several different functional structures, one for each of the five to eight lines of analysis that are recognized in that approach. (There are not just three or four, as many of the writings of Halliday and others imply). In this view every clause is a conflation of several different structures, each roughly of clause length (give or take an element or two). Any one element in such a structure is said to be capable of being conflated with other elements in other structures — including ones that are not coterminous. This approach produces attractive diagrams that illustrate the 'strands of meaning' metaphor of language. However, such diagrams are essentially a misrepresentation of the real position, because it is only **some** functional elements in **some** of the functional structures that are recognized in this version of the theory that can be conflated in this manner, and there are long stretches in several of the strands of meaning in which there is nothing to be said about the meaning (i.e., the boxes labelled 'Rheme', 'Given' and 'Residue', in Sydney Grammar analyses).

Two further problems with Halliday's current approach to modelling structure are that we are not shown (1) what the final, integrated structure would be like, or (2) what the component that performs this integration on structures with non-coterminous elements would be like. It seems likely that the final structure would have to be something like the structure shown in the upper half of Figure 10, but after Halliday (1970/76b) and (1977/78), Halliday appears to have abandoned that position, as we saw in Section 4.9 of Chapter 4.

So far as I am aware, the present book is the first publication in which the point is made that *IFG*-style representations do not play a role in the theoretical-generative version of the theory — and indeed that they are incapable of doing so, because of the inherent problem that it is only possible to conflate elements (or indeed units) when they are coterminous.

However, Halliday also occasionally states that it is desirable to represent the clause in terms of the features selected in the system networks that show the language's 'meaning potential', i.e., the features from which it has been generated. The problem is that he provides no examples of descriptions of this sort. It is hard to understand why this should be so. It may be that the need to provide a systemic representation seems less urgent to those working in the Sydney Grammar, because an *IFG*-style analysis already expresses (though in a misleading way, I would of course say) the multifunctional nature of language.

In the Cardiff Grammar, on the other hand, a systemic representation in terms of the features that have been chosen in generating the text is regarded as a vital second level of representation in any attempt to represent the meanings as well as the forms of language. As the lower half of Figure 10 shows, the systemic representation takes the form of a display of the key features from the selection expression, arranged in separate lines, such that each feature is entered in a column below the element to whose generation it contributes. Since it is at this level that meanings are modelled, it is natural to show the strands of meaning at this level too — and there is therefore no need to show them at the level of form as well. The representation of functional structure in the Cardiff framework is therefore much simpler than its equivalent in *IFG*, in that there is only a single structure at this level — not the five to seven (or even sometimes eight or more) structures that are shown in the analyses in *IFG*. To see the difference, compare the structural analysis in Figure 10 with that in Figure 7.

## 7.10 The need for a theory of syntax for SFL: the argument summarized

We are now in a position to bring together the main steps of the argument that is presented this book.

1. Scale and Category Grammar (S&C) was essentially a theory of syntax, and so an account of the structure of language at the level of form (as we

saw in Chapter 2).
2. A modern, computer-implementable theory of language must have levels of **form** and **meaning**, providing for both a 'potential' and 'instances' of the potential at both levels (as described in Chapter 3).
3. Halliday's development of the theory into Systemic Functional Grammar involved (1) placing the concept of 'system' at the centre of the theory, (2) presenting the resulting system networks as choices between meanings, and (3) seeing each clause as the realization of several different 'strands of meaning' (as outlined in the first half of Chapter 4).
4. However, Halliday's writings in the 1970s and 1980s have explored **two** approaches to modelling meaning in language. One of these involves treating the system networks for TRANSITIVITY, MOOD, THEME and so on as the level of semantics. In the second model these networks are considered to be, in some sense, at the level of form — though it is a 'form' that has been 'pushed in the direction of the semantics' (Halliday 1994:xix) — and there is (in principle) a higher stratum of even more 'semantic' system networks that correspond to each of the networks of TRANSITIVITY, MOOD, THEME, etc. I prefer the first (and simpler) of these two positions, and I consider that the phenomena for which Halliday sets up the second level of 'meaning' can be more appropriately accounted for in other ways (as argued in Sections 4.6 to 4.8 of Chapter 4).
5. In two of the papers in which Halliday takes the position that the system networks of TRANSITIVITY, MOOD and THEME are at the level of semantics (1970/76b and 1977/78) he includes diagrams that show (1) several lines of analysis, each of which clearly corresponds to a major strand of meaning, and (2), below these, a single line of analysis that shows the 'Scale and Category' elements of the clause, such that this line represents the **integration** of the metafunctional representations above it. It is from this stage of Halliday's thinking that the Cardiff Grammar version of SFL has developed (as shown in Section 4.9 of Chapter 4).
6. However, these two papers represent just a brief period in the development of Halliday's concept of how structure should be represented, and almost immediately he dropped the integrative representation in his diagrams in favour of the type of representation shown throughout *IFG* and his subsequent descriptive works to date. Here the original S&C elements of Subject, Predicator, Complement and Adjunct are no longer shown as elements of the structure that integrates the various strands of meaning, but

instead they are introduced as a structure within the representation of 'interpersonal' meaning (with the addition of the Finite). Indeed, Halliday presents them as merely the 'secondary' structure of 'interpersonal' meaning, the 'primary' structure being that of "Mood + Residue" (also called "Modal + Propositional", in earlier works). Halliday's reasons for including the elements of 'Predicator', 'Complement' and 'Adjunct' in the 'interpersonal' line of analysis (which were summarized in Section 7.2) are considered here to be unpersuasive — especially in comparison with the much more persuasive reason for assigning them the role described in Point 5 above, namely their role as elements of the structure that integrates the various strands of meaning (with others, as illustrated in Appendix B).

7. Thus Halliday now presents the structure of a clause (and in principle other units) as **multiple structures**. In any such representation of a clause there is, in principle, a line of structure that corresponds to each 'metafunction' (but in practice several more, with seven for many text-sentences as analyzed in *IFG*). Each line consists of a string of 'functional elements', or 'functions'. The problem is that the elements of these 'structures' are not necessarily coterminous (and nor are the structures themselves coterminous). In other words, if two or more elements in two or more strands of meaning **are** coterminous, they can be conflated with each other to form a compound element, but when they are not coterminous it is not logically possible to conflate them (as described in Section 7.4 of this chapter). Despite these serious theoretical-generative problems, it appears that Halliday may regard the notion that there are many different structures (and so many non-coterminous elements) in a single clause as one of the riches of language — at least from the text-descriptive viewpoint, as exemplified in the analyses in *IFG*.

8. Halliday recognizes that the 'multiple structures' of *IFG* — which we shall assume for the moment to be capable of being generated by the grammar — must ultimately be merged into a single structure at the level of form.

9. However, there are several serious problems in reconciling Halliday's multiple structure representations with this position. No advocate of it has yet stated what it actually means when one says that the various structures get conflated with each other — other than treating all such 'functions' as elements of a 'flat tree' representation of constituency, which would be the dismemberment of those structures rather than a 'conflation of them. Such a conflation has not even been achieved with simple clauses, either in the

framework of a computer implementation or as a theoretical exercise (as I have shown in Section 7.4). On the basis of this evidence and my own failure to find a way to make this approach work, I make two proposals:

(1) 'multiple structures' with non-coterminous elements cannot be integrated in the manner proposed by Halliday, so that another solution to the problem of generating a single structural output must be sought; and
(2) even if such structures could be integrated, something like an updated version of S&C-type syntax would be required to achieve this — i.e., a syntax such as that to be described in Part 2.

This is the point that the argument has reached so far. Let us now follow it through to its logical conclusion:

10. Since it is agreed that, within Halliday's approach, the multiple structures must be integrated into a single structure as the final stage in generation, the next logical step is to ask whether it is in fact possible to **first** generate the type of multiple structure representation found in *IFG* as an intermediate stage between the systemic features and the single representation, and **then** to generate from the multiple structures the single integrating structure (which would require the architecture illustrated in Figure 8 in Section 7.4.1). If the answer were to be that it **is** possible (which I doubt), we would then need to ask whether this way of generating the final integrated structure is either necessary or desirable. The alternative that should be considered is to generate it directly by realization rules that take as their input the semantic features chosen in the system network.
11. This is precisely what is done in the very large computer-implemented Cardiff Grammar (as we saw in Section 7.8). The fact that it is possible to generate text-sentences directly from systemic features demonstrates that there is no need first to generate multiple structures of the type illustrated in *IFG* and then to integrate them into a single structure.
12. We therefore know that it is **not** necessary to generate multiple structures of functions as an intermediate stage. This fact is particularly welcome, given that it is not possible to build a component that will convert seven or more different non-coterminous structures into a single structure (for the reasons given in Section 7.4.1).
13. The 'multiple structures' showing strings of 'functions' for each strand of

meaning are therefore redundant.
14. However, while they are not **necessary**, there might still be some reason why they are **desirable**. The reason that seems most likely to be justifiable is that they may help the student of language to picture some central aspect of language, such as the fact that clauses — or, more accurately, several elements of structure in a typical clause — express several different meanings at the same time.
15. However, the concept of 'strands of meaning' in a clause can be modelled in an equally insightful (and more accurate) way as part of the representation of the semantics of the clause (as exemplified in Figure 10 of Section 7.8). When guidelines for analyzing clauses in these terms (and also in setting out such representations) are available, there will be no logical reason to continue using 'multiple structures' for this task — especially if it is agreed, as proposed here, that the concept that a clause consists of a set of several different 'functional structures' should no longer be a part of the theory.
16. As a final point, we might note that the Cardiff Grammar has a simpler architecture than the Sydney Grammar with respect to the relationship between the system networks of TRANSITIVITY, MOOD, THEME etc. and their realizations in form. The former is summarized in Figure 4 of Chapter 3 and the latter in Figure 8 of Section 7.4 3. The Cardiff model is also simpler in that its system networks have been semanticized to the point where there is no need to have a higher layer of networks, as there seems to be in the model described in Halliday (1994) and Matthiessen (1995).

As an addendum to the line of argument set out here, we should note that there are important theoretical differences between the Cardiff Grammar and the Sydney Grammar (within the general framework summarized in Figure 6 in Section 4.9 of Chapter 4). The most important difference is in way in which the various 'strands of meaning' are represented. While the Cardiff Grammar represents the meanings **systemically** — i.e., in terms of the features that have been chosen in the system networks that constitute the 'meaning potential' of the language — Halliday represents the meaning by 'functions'. His use of this concept for representing meanings can be traced back to the stage in the development of the theory in which it was believed that the **realization** of the features in the system networks necessarily took place in two stages: in the first the grammar would use the 'selection expression' of features that were chosen on a traversal of the system network to create an unordered string of 'functions' (and of conflated functions), and in the second these 'functions' would be ordered in sequence.[26]

## 7.11 The implications of the argument

The main purpose of this chapter has been to clarify the status of the representations of clauses given in *IFG* and the derived works. We have also seen, in Section 7.9, that there is an alternative and more truly systemic means of representing the multifunctional nature of language, i.e., a representarion of the systemic features. In systemic functional grammar such a representation is inherently more revealing than any structural representation. As Halliday himself says, "the system takes priority; the most abstract representation [...] is in paradigmatic terms. Syntagmatic organization is interpreted as the 'realization' of paradigmatic features" (Halliday 1993:4505).

The consequence of having both a representation at the level of meaning and a representation of the single integrated structure — something that is required, as we have seen, in the Sydney model as well as the Cardiff model — is that the many lines of structure in an *IFG* analysis are, from both the theoretical-generative and the text-descriptive viewpoints, redundant. They are redundant because the analysis in terms of the features chosen in the system networks already displays clearly the different strands of meaning, as in the example of such an analysis in Figure 10.

However, since the current situation is that there is not yet a published work in any version of SFL that demonstrates how to use the features in system networks for the systemic analysis of texts, *IFG*-style analyses may still have a role to play for a while. The system networks for the Sydney Grammar have of course now been published (in Matthiessen 1995), but these networks are not in fact designed for use in text analysis, and they are often hard for the reader to interpret. Moreover there are no published guidelines as to how to use system

---

26. See Berry (1977:29-31) for an introductory account of this version of the model. The fullest implementation by far of the concept of realization in two stages is that described in Hudson (1971), which had 76 such 'functions' (these being explicitly at the level of form, however). In a later work Hudson reduced them to just three (Hudson 1976), and this constitutes a little subsidiary evidence for the position taken here, i.e., that it is unnecessary for a systemic grammar first to generate 'functions' and then to order them.

networks for the task of making analyses of real-life texts, and no published examples of such analyses, other than those in Fawcett (1999) and in Figure 10 of Section 7.9. The publication of Fawcett (in press) and Fawcett (forthcoming a), as described at the end of Section 7.8, make available the Cardiff Grammar versions of (a) the functional structure of text-sentences and (b) system networks that are equivalent in their coverage (but more explicitly semantic) to the Sydney Grammar networks found in Matthiessen (1995). Moreover Fawcett (forthcoming a) contains guidelines that show the analyst how to go about making such analyses, and it contains many such examples.

However, the focus in the present book is not on text analysis, but on establishing the concepts that are required in a theory of syntax for SFL. We shall therefore not discuss such representations further, except in so far as they affect the theory of syntax that is required in a modern SFL. Clearly, the focus from now on must be on the nature of such a theory — and this is, of course, the topic of Part 2.

Up to this point, Part 1 has been principally concerned with establishing the antecedents to a modern theory of SF syntax in terms of the Sydney Grammar, principally through the writings of Halliday himself. However, there is a third set of post-"Categories" concepts that has had some influence on a number of current descriptions of systemic syntax, and it is this body of work that is the direct antecedent of the framework of concepts to be set out in Part 2. It is to this work that we turn in Chapter 8.

Its genesis is significantly different from that of either "Systemic theory" or *IFG*, in that it was formulated as a theory of syntax in the 1970s as an explicit response to Halliday's still recent proposal that the system networks should regarded as modelling the meaning potential of a language. It is not impossible that Halliday might have produced a theory of syntax that would have been something like the one to be considered in the next chapter, if in the 1970s he had chosen to develop SFL in the way indicated in Sections 4.3 and 4.9 of Chapter 4, i.e., with the system networks of TRANSITIVITY, MOOD, THEME and so on treated as explicitly modelling semantics.

# 8
# "Some proposals for systemic syntax"

## 8.1 The situation in Systemic Functional Linguistics at the time of Fawcett's "Some proposals" (1974-6 and 1981)

As its dates of its first publication indicate, the three-part paper by myself that is to be reviewed here first appeared about fifteen years after "Categories", and it was later republished informally in a lightly revised edition in 1981.[1] By the mid-1970s the new set of concepts associated with Systemic Functional Grammar (described in Chapter 4) were beginning to make themselves felt, but the original concepts presented in "Categories" were still widely accepted among systemic functional linguists (as we were beginning to call ourselves) as fully relevant to the description of the level of syntax or "grammar", as Halliday terms it. I would claim that "Some proposals" reflects the position of syntax in the model much as Halliday presents it in Halliday (1970/76) and (1977/78).

I gave "Some proposals" the subtitle of "an iconoclastic approach to Scale and Category Grammar" — a subtitle that was, I have to admit, a little provocative. But I did so for what I thought at the time (and still think) to be a good reason — namely, that too many of those who were working in SFL seemed to look upon "Categories" as a set of concepts whose authority fell not far short of the tablets brought down from Mount Sinai by Moses. And yet there were serious questions, I felt, that needed to be asked.

If, for example, the meaning of the term "system" had changed by becoming a choice between meanings rather than forms, where did that leave the concept of "class"? After all, 'class' was a term which had been interpreted in "Categories", like 'system', as a paradigmatic relationship, such that one might set up 'systems' of 'classes'. So what did it mean, in a model in which the system networks were semantic, to say that a nominal group was a 'class of

---

1. In the "Preface" to the limited re-issue published in book form in 1981, I wrote "I have been agreeably surprised that 'Some proposals' has been used as a teaching text in a number of universities, polytechnics and colleges, and the fact that others have found this a helpful descriptive framework has encouraged me to work on a revised edition" (Fawcett 1974-6/81:i). For many reasons, including over a decade of work on the COMMUNAL Project, it is only in the present work and in Fawcett (in press) that this intention is finally being fulfilled.

group'? Since the concept of a 'nominal group' was used to refer to a syntactic unit, it belonged, surely, at the level of form rather than meaning — so at what level of language did the concept of 'class' now belong? Indeed, did **any** of the original four categories remain as concepts that could be used for the task of modelling what we might term 'pure form'?

In other words, it seemed to me that the elevation of the concept of 'system' to the level of meaning meant that the whole framework for describing language needed to be re-examined. Moreover, if we did retain concepts such as 'class of unit' at the level of form, we needed new terms for the equivalent concept at the level of meaning.[2] (See Figure 12 in Section 10.2.10 of Chapter 10 for the equivalent terms that I use.)

At the end of the 1960s and the start of the 1970s there was a spate of text books that functioned as introductions to Scale and Category syntax — rather as there was to be a second spate of introductory grammars in the theory in the 1990s, this time based on Halliday's *IFG*. Each of those early textbooks had its stong points, but two stood out because of their clear vision of a model of language in which one component was **systemic** and presented the system networks that constituted the 'meaning potential' of the language, and another component which provided for the **structures** — using the familiar Scale and Category concepts (minus 'system'). The first was Muir's two-part text book, with one part on structures and one on systems, and the other was the two-volume work that became the standard introduction to the theory (Berry 1975 and 1977). Berry (1977) is particularly noteworthy for providing, in a book that was essentially designed to enable its readers to analyze texts, a sketch of how a generative version of the model would operate.[3] But the key point here is that in both Muir's and Berry's books the picture of syntax that was presented was that of "Categories".

---

2. The entry conditions for Halliday's system networks for 'meaning potential' have always had labels such as "clause", "nominal group", etc. It is odd to find these terms being used at the level of meaning, because they are the names of syntactic units at the level of form — the outputs from the grammar. This is why, in the Cardiff Grammar, the equivalent features have explicitly semantic labels, such as "situation" and "thing".

3. This set of books also included Strang (1962/69), Leech (1966), Scott, Bowley *et al.* 1968 (where Bowley was the principal contributor), Turner & Mohan (1970) and Sinclair (1972). One reason why Berry (1975 and 1977) quickly became established as the standard introduction to the theory was that she introduces more of the theory that underpins the description than Muir (1972), including an early picture of how 'realization' works.

As will by now be clear, my view at the time was that the elevation of the concept of 'system' to the semantics was so revolutionary a change that it should be expected to affect every part of the theory. In a sense, the strongest possible support for this position came when Halliday introduced an entirely new way of representing the structure of clauses. You can see this difference very clearly if you compare Figure 1 in Chapter 2 and Figure 7 in Chapter 7.

It is ironic, therefore, that I should have been admonished in the mid-1970s by two senior systemic linguists at the time (though not by Halliday himself) for the changes that I suggested in "Some proposals". The irony lies in the fact that my proposals were for a syntax whose representations were far more like those of the Scale and Category model than the proposals for representing structure that Halliday himself developed during the very late 1960s and the early 1970s. As we saw in Chapter 7, it was during this period that he shifted his representations of structure away from the model presented in "Categories" (in which the major clause elements were 'Subject', 'Predicator', 'Complement' and 'Adjunct') to the multiple structures used in *IFG* and widely elsewhere, in which an analysis in terms of such elements plays little or no role. The changes made by Halliday were far greater than the changes that I was suggesting in "Some proposals", and yet the position of my critics at the time seemed to be that I should not be suggesting any changes to "Categories" at all! The fact is that, even though Halliday's changes were already well under way by the mid-1970s, the key role of "Categories" as the founding document of the new theory seems to have placed it beyond criticism for many. On the whole, then, I think that my critics' response shows that the admittedly provocative use of the term "iconoclastic" in the subtitle of "Some proposals" was justified.

However, "Some proposals" was really not as revolutionary as its critics felt it to be. With the benefit of a further twenty-five years of hindsight, I see now that, far from being too critical of "Categories", "Some proposals" did not go as far as it should in proposing changes, as we shall see in due course.

## 8.2 The purpose of "Some proposals"

The purpose of "Some proposals" was to present the set of revisions to the concepts of "Categories" that I considered at the time (1974) to be required, in order to constitute a 'systemic syntax' that would complement Halliday's revolutionary proposal that the system networks of TRANSITIVITY, MOOD and THEME should be regarded as choices between meanings (as described in Section 4.3 of Chapter 4). As Butler wrote in 1985:

> Halliday's most recent proposals [...] make it clear that the functional component networks are to be regarded as semantic, but **we are given very little idea of what the lexicogrammar** [i.e., the level of form] **might now consist of** [my emphasis] (Butler 1985:94).

"Some proposals" was a first attempt to fill this gap, and it probably reached its widest readership through Butler's generally approving summaries of its contents — first in Butler (1979), and then in Butler (1985:94-102). He makes the key point when he states, "[Fawcett's] approach to the recognition of syntactic categories is dictated by his commitment to the centrality of semantics" (Butler 1985:94). In this approach, then, a large part of the description of a text should be in terms of the semantic features that have been chosen in generating it (e.g., in the way described in Section 7.8 of Chapter 7). There was a second motivation, however. This was that my attempts to apply Halliday's categories in the analysis of text at the level of form had led me to modify his description in a number of ways — and so in due course to think about the consequences of these descriptive changes for the theory upon which the description rested.

The following words provide the key to understanding my original motivation for developing a framework for representing structure — a framework that was very different from the 'multiple structure' model that Halliday was developing at about the same time:

> the syntactic categories [...] are those [...] needed to state with the greatest economy the realization rules that express the options in the semantics (Fawcett 1974:4-5).

Over twenty-five years later, my theory of syntax and the consequent description of English syntax have both developed in various ways, but those words still express exactly what I wish to say on this matter. It is because the description of the functional structure is necessarily complemented, in my approach, by a description in terms of a functional semantics that the syntax can — and should — be less "extravagant" (Halliday 1994:xix) than it is in Halliday's *IFG*. Moreover, I have discovered in the intervening time that this general principle holds just as strongly for the version of the grammar that is used for the computer model of natural language generation as it does for the version used for text analysis. The clear implication of all of this work is that we cannot provide a complete description of a text without providing both an analysis of its functional syntax and an account of the semantic features that have been chosen in generating it.

The rest of this chapter introduces the main concepts in "Some proposals". This will be done only very briefly, because many of them reappear in Part 2.

"Some proposals" was written as a short description of the syntax of English, and it concludes with a summary of the theory that the description presupposed. The structure of the paper therefore reflects the view that theory should grow out of description — or, more accurately, out of the attempt to apply the concepts of an earlier theory (here "Categories") in a description. In my view, this interleaving of theory and description is one of the more effective ways to improve one's theory — as well as through the use of corpora and, as suggested in Section 1.2 of Chapter 1, large scale computer implementations. (See also the discussion of the relationships between theory, description and application in Halliday & Fawcett 1987b:1f.).

We must begin by relating the model of **syntax** to the model of language as a whole. Within a model of the sort presented in Figure 4 in Section 3.2 of Chapter 3, "Some proposals" sees syntax as one of three ways in which **meanings** are realized as **forms** — the other types of 'form' being **items** and **intonation** or **punctuation** (depending on the channel of discourse).

I shall structure what follows by presenting first the **categories** of the theory (which correspond roughly to the categories in Halliday's "Categories"), and then the **relationships** through which those categories are connected to each other.

## 8.3 The 'categories' of "Some proposals"

"Some proposals" recognizes a number of **units** (in precisely the same sense of "unit" as in "Categories"). These units are related to each other on a **'rank scale'**, and for English they are: **clause, group** and **cluster.** The unit 'cluster' is a new unit that is lower on the 'rank scale' than the group; see below for examples. (The concept of 'unit', which is mutually defining with that of the 'rank scale', is not used in the framework to be proposed in Part 2.)

"Some proposals" uses the concept of **class of unit** in a way that is loosely similar to its use in "Categories". It relates the concept of 'class of unit' to 'unit' essentially as in "Categories", except that the criteria for recognizing a given class of unit are the elements of its internal structure, rather than its potential for operation in the unit above, as in "Categories". (For a full discussion of the criteria for recognizing classes of unit, see Section 10.2.2 of Chapter 10.) On this criterion, "Some proposals" recognizes only classes of groups and clusters (and not clauses or words). Thus it recognizes that, at the 'rank' of clause rank in English, there is only one 'class' of clause, so that the concept of 'class of unit' is not applicable to this unit. At **group** rank "Some proposals" initially recognized four classes. These were the **nominal group** (e.g., *she, Ivy* and *the man in black*), the **prepend group** (e.g., *in black*), the **adjectival group** (e.g., *very quick*) and the **adverbial group** (e.g., *very quickly*). In the 1974-6 edition I further suggested (1974-6/81:31) that "in an introductory analysis it is probably helpful to make use of the traditional S&C concept of the **'verbal group'**"(e.g., *might have seen*).

However, by the 1981 edition I had made several changes to the model. Firstly, I had strengthened my position on the supposed 'verbal group', writing that even for text analysis the elements of the supposed 'verbal group' "would in my view be best shown as **clause** elements" (Fawcett 1974-6/81:31) (See Fawcett (2000) and (forthcoming b) for the full set of reasons and Appendix C for a summary of them.) Secondly the 'adjectival' and 'adverbial' groups, which were already shown in the 1974-6 edition as sharing a common structure, were brought together as the 'quantity-quality group' (since they typically express the meaning of a 'quantity' of a 'quality'). And thirdly the 'prepend group' had been re-named the "prepositional group". Later still, as Part 2 shows, I realized that, in order to provide an adequate description of English and other languages, we need to recognize both a **quality group** and a **quantity group**. See Tucker (1998) for the fullest explanation of the quality group in English and Fawcett (in press) for an introduction to both classes of group.

Three classes of the new unit of the **cluster** were tentatively recognized in the 1974-6 edition: the **genitive** cluster (e.g., *her boyfriend's*); the **proper name** cluster (e.g., *Dr Ivy Idle*) and the **tempering** cluster (e.g., *much less* in *much less painful*). By 1981 the 'tempering cluster' had been absorbed into the 'quantity-quality group', and later still the data that it covers became part of the evidence for the need to introduce the 'quantity group'. Further classes of 'cluster' are added in the current version of the grammar, as described in Part 2.

There was no discussion in "Some proposals" of the concept of 'class of word', because 'words' are treated there as **items** rather than as syntactic units (1974-6/81:67). (See Part 2 for a fuller justification for taking the position that the relationship of morphemes to a word is not the same as that between, let us say, groups and clauses.)

The last of the three theoretical categories recognized in "Some proposals" (along with 'unit' and 'class of unit') was **element of structure**. Like 'unit', this term was used in essentially the same sense as in "Categories". However, the concept plays a far stronger part in the theory as a whole than it does in "Categories" because of the mutual dependency, in the present framework, of the definitions of a class of unit and its elements of structure. In "Categories", in contrast, a class of unit is defined by its potential for "operation in the structure of the unit next above" (1961/76:64).

In two of its 'categories', then, "Some proposals" is similar to Halliday (1961/76). While the concept of 'class of unit' is broadly similar, the criteria for recognizing the 'class' of a 'unit' are very different, and the concept of 'system' does not appear at this level of description at all. However, there are even greater differences between the 'scales' of "Categories" and the 'relationships' of "Some proposals", as the next section shows.

## 8.4 The 'relationships' of "Some proposals"

The first difference is that "Some proposals" recognizes many more 'relationships' than the three 'scales' in "Categories". There are ten of them.

One of its major innovations is to split Halliday's 'scale' of 'exponence' into three: **componence, filling** and **exponence** proper. To cite Butler's excellent summary of these concepts:

> Componence is the relation between a unit and the elements of structure of which it is composed. For example, a clause may be composed of the elements S, P, C and A. Each of these elements of structure may be (but need not be) filled by groups. In the specification of a syntactic structure, componence and filling alternate until, at the bottom of the structural tree, the smallest elements of structure are not filled by other units. It is at this point that we need the concept of exponence, as used by Fawcett: the lowest elements of structure are expounded by 'items', which are [...] more or less equivalent to 'words' and 'morphemes' in Halliday's model. (Butler 1985:95)

These three concepts, which today still form the basis of the Cardiff Grammar's model of syntax, are clearly exemplified in the top half of Figure 10. These concepts are necessary, in one form or another, in any adequate systemic functional model of syntax, and they will be illustrated, discussed and compared with their antecedents in the relevant sections of Chapter 11.

The concept of **rank** from "Categories" is retained in "Some proposals"

— at least in relation to the clause and the group, which form the core of the model of syntax in all SFL descriptions (with far less work on the proposed 'morpheme-word' relationship). However, this small syntactic 'rank scale' is interpreted in a very different way from "Categories", because it is seen as the **realization** of an equivalent **semantic** relationship between a 'situation' and the 'things' and 'qualities' that are its 'elements' at that higher level. And, as we shall see in Part 2, later work in this version of the theory was to reduce the role of the concept of a 'rank scale' to the point where it no longer has any status in the theory at all. (It is of course still possible to see 'traces' of the concept of a 'rank scale' in a description that is based on the present theory, since the phenomena that originally suggested it are still present in the language, and these will be pointed out in Section 10.1.2 of Chapter 10.) In the theory of syntax to be presented in Part 2 the concept of the 'rank scale' is replaced by the concept of probabilities in the relations between elements and units.

Two types of sequential relationship between sister elements of structure are recognized in "Some proposals": the **segmental** relationship of adjacency and the **discontinuous** relationship that occurs when elements are non-adjacent. These are not explicitly mentioned in "Categories", but every theory of syntax must have adequate ways of handling the various types of discontinuity found in language. Part 2 will introduce these concepts in Section 11.7 of Chapter 11.

Finally, two types of **recursion** are recognized. The first is **embedding**, in which a unit is 'rankshifted' (to use Halliday's original term) to fill an element of structure in a unit of the same or a lower rank. The second is **co-ordination**, in which two or more units fill a single element of structure.

With the exception of the concept of 'rank' — and so the derived concept of 'rank shift' — all of these 'relationships' are retained in the model of syntax to be presented in Part 2, and a small number of additional concepts that are not included in "Some proposals" are added to them. There is no need, therefore, to discuss the concepts of "Some proposals" any further at this point.

## 8.5 The role of "Some proposals" in developing a modern SF theory of syntax

Let me now summarize this short chapter. "Some proposals" began the work of overhauling the concepts first presented in "Categories" in the light of the requirements of a modern theory of SF syntax — a theory in which the system networks of TRANSITIVITY, MOOD, THEME and the rest are regarded as modelling the level of meaning. As I wrote at the time, "the syntactic categories [...] are those [...] needed to state with the greatest economy the realization rules that express the options in the semantics" (Fawcett 1974:4-5). The new ideas that it introduced have all proved their value, both in the construction of computer parsing systems (Weerasinghe & Fawcett 1993, Weerasinghe 1994 and Souter 1996) and in the hand analysis of texts by myself, my teaching colleagues, members of a large team of researchers in a study of the language of children aged 6-12, and many generations of students.

However, later work has shown that in some cases the revisions were not drastic enough (e.g., the retention of the concept of the 'rank scale'). Yet in most cases the concepts established in "Some proposals" have passed the test of twenty-five years of use in various fields of application as a descrpition of English, as well as in describing various other languages, and they are the central concepts in the theory of syntax for a modern systemic functional grammar that I shall present in Part 2.

# Part 2

# The New Theory

# 9
# A theory of syntax potential

## 9.1 Towards a new theory of syntax for systemic functional grammar

### 9.1.1 How "new" is the new theory?

Since the title of Part 2 is "The new theory", I should perhaps begin by saying a little about the claim that is implied by the use of the word "new" — and also about the two major parts to the theory of syntax to be described here, and the sources and evidence that have most strongly influenced the new theory.

There is, of course, no such thing as a completely new theory of syntax. Any 'new' theory is built upon earlier work — as indeed the division of this book into a prolegomenon and a presentation of the theory suggests. However, when the concepts that are placed at the core of the theory are fundamentally different from those of any preceding version of the theory, so that the old core concepts are dropped and important new concepts are introduced — then it is not unreasonable to describe the revised theory as "new". And by these criteria the proposals that follow are new.

However, it is important to issue a warning against expecting too much from the new theory. As we saw in Section 3.4 of Chapter 3, it would be wrong to expect to have an 'autonomous' theory of syntax within a systemic functional model of language. In this theory the explanation of why syntax is as it is and the nature of its potential — and so of its constraints — are to be sought in the interplay between the system networks and the realization rules through which they are expressed in structures. This is the mutual dependency of levels that is described in Chapter 3 and exemplified in Fawcett, Tucker & Lin (1993) — and also in a simple way in Appendix A.[1] The theory to be presented here

---

1. There are certain characteristics of text-sentences that arise from the limitations of human cognitive processing — and in particular from human memory. Some linguists and psycholinguists would consider these to be purely syntactic. In the present approach to modelling language, however, syntactic units are assumed to realize semantic units, so that the level of meaning is involved here too. See Sections 11.7 and 11.8.4 of Chapter 11 for some comments on the possible cognitive limits when processing syntactic structures, and for

therefore does not constitute an "explanation" of syntax; it is simply the syntactic part of a full systemic functional theory of language.

9.1.2 The need for a theory of both 'syntax potential' and 'instances of syntax'

As we saw in Chapter 3 — and most clearly in Figure 4 in Section 3.2 of that chapter — any adequate theory of language must provide, for each level of language, for both the **potential** and the **instances** of that potential. In some theories of language, of course, it is assumed that it is precisely the task of the theory of the potential (the grammar) to specify the instances that can be generated from the potential (the sentences of the language). But I have argued — both in Section 6.5 of Chapter 6 and more fully in Fawcett (1994a) — that, if we want a theory that can be used for modelling both the understanding and the generation of language texts, we need to recognize that we require a different set of concepts when faced with the task of analyzing an incoming string of words (i.e., parsing) from those that are needed when we are trying to model the grammar in use for generation. In the process of generation there is no equivalent of the problematical task of parsing, as is demonstrated in Fawcett (1994a).

The main topic of this chapter will be the theory of **syntax potential** that is required in a modern SF grammar. I first used this term in Section 3.3 of Chapter 3 and it is modelled, as will be clear, on Halliday's characterization of the system networks of TRANSITIVITY, MOOD, THEME and the rest as **meaning potential**. In Figure 4 we contrasted the 'meaning potential' of the grammar with its 'form potential', and 'syntax potential' is simply one part of the form potential.

First, however, there are certain general issues to clarify. The first is: "Which of the works summarized in Part 1 should be taken as potential sources of concepts for the new theory?"

---

examples of certain principles that are derived from these that affect syntax. See Fawcett (in press) for a fuller account of the 'pragmatic' principles that it is useful to recognize. It may be relevant — or it may not — that the number of types of meaning found woven together in a clause seems to be about seven or so; see Section 11.8.4 of Chapter 11 for other contexts in which the number seven appears to be some sort of cognitive limit. (There are probably also cognitive limitations on the operation of system networks, though these have not so far been investigated, and any attempt to do so would have to face the problem that they are even more abstract than syntactic structures.)

## 9.1.3 Relevant sources

In Part 1, we have examined four accounts of syntax in SFL. In Chapter 2 we looked at Halliday's "Categories of the theory of grammar" (1961/76), and in Chapters 5 and 6 we noted the considerable changes between the set of concepts presented in "Categories" and the concepts found in his "Systemic theory" (1993) and his *An Introduction to Functional Grammar* (1994). Then in Chapter 8 of Part 1 I described the framework of concepts set out in my "Some proposals for systemic syntax" (Fawcett 1974-7/81) — this being a revision of the concepts of "Categories" that was made as an explicit response to two factors: the exciting changes which Halliday made to the theory in the 1960s (described in Chapter 4), and very large quantities of work in text analysis.

We therefore have three 'post-Categories' accounts of SFL syntax. The question now arises as to which of the three should be drawn upon — and to what extent — in the task of establishing a modern theory of SF syntax.

Clearly, Halliday's important summary of current SFL in "Systemic theory" must be given due weight — especially because so many of the concepts that are new since "Categories" are present in the equivalent Cardiff Grammar work of Fawcett, Tucker & Lin (1993), as we noted in Section 5.5 of Chapter 5. Yet we must also take into account the evidence from Halliday's actual descriptive practice in *IFG*, even though it is harder to establish what the concepts are in this work. As we have noted, the concepts behind the representations of structure in *IFG* have more in common with the concepts of "Categories" than they have with "Systemic theory" — despite the great differences between the 'single structure' representation used in "Categories"-style analyses (as exemplified in Figure 1 in Chapter 2) and in the *IFG*-style analyses (as in Figure 7 in Chapter 7).

In addition, we must also draw on the evidence from work in the framework of the Cardiff Grammar, both from the 'text-descriptive' work that is roughly equivalent to *IFG* from Fawcett (in press) and from the 'theoretical-generative' work such as that in Fawcett, Tucker & Lin (1993) that is the equivalent to Halliday's "Systemic theory".

Finally, we have noted at various points that work on the formalization of systemic functional grammars in computers has had an important influence on the theory, and in both the Sydney and the Cardiff Grammars this has led to the further refinement of the categories and relationships that need to be recognized in the theory.

### 9.1.4 The original questions revisited

In Part 1 we considered a number of different approaches to syntax in SFL, and we made some surprising discoveries about the status of the 'multiple structure' representations in *IFG*. That prolegomenon to the new theory will, I hope, have changed your perspective on the two original questions that were asked in Section 1.2 of Chapter 1. Most importantly, we are now aware that the theory of syntax must contain both a theory of 'syntax potential' and a theory of 'instances of syntax'. The main question was:

(1) What theoretical concepts are required for the description of syntax in a modern, large-scale systemic functional grammar?

And, as a supplementary question of historical interest, we asked:

(2) How far are the founding concepts introduced by Halliday in "Categories" (1961/76) still valid in such a model?

It is the goal of the rest of Part 2 to answer the first of these two questions — with the second being attended to in Section 12.7 of the final chapter. In the rest of the present chapter I shall specify the **theory of syntax potential** that is required in a modern, large-scale systemic functional grammar — i.e., the concepts that are required in the grammar itself. Then Chapters 10 and 11 will provide an account of the theory of **instances of syntax** — i.e., the part of the theory that underlies the description of text-sentences. Finally, Chapter 12 will summarize the current theory in relation to its antecedents, including "Categories", offering an evaluation of its importance today.

Thus most of this chapter will be wholly oriented to the **theoretical-generative** strand of work in SFL. It might at first appear that Chapters 10 and 11 are oriented to the **text-descriptive** strand. However, they are only 'text-descriptive' in the sense that the emphasis is on the text-sentences that are the output from the operation of the grammar, and it is these that constitute the texts that are analyzed in 'text-descriptive' work. These two chapters are also in fact primarily theoretical, in that the concepts covered there are the theoretical concepts that are required in the description of the structure of English that is needed by a computer for parsing a text — and, indeed, by a human text analyst. The concepts that characterize instances are therefore as much a part of the overall theory as the concepts required in the grammar itself to generate those outputs.

## 9.2 Syntax potential as both realization operations and potential structures

9.2.1 The major types of realization operation

We saw in Chapter 5 that one of the major changes between the Scale and Category Grammar described in "Categories" (1961/76) and the Systemic Functional Grammar of "Systemic theory" (1993) was Halliday's introduction of "realization statements". These are essentially structure-building rules, and they correspond to what are termed in the Cardiff Grammar, following Hudson (1971 and 1974/81), "realization rules". At the core of each "realization rule" or "realization statement" lies a **realization operator** such as "Insert X", and each such operational procedure constitutes a complete **realization operation**. In the Cardiff Grammar a "realization rule" may contain more than one "realization operation" (though not in the Sydney Grammar, according to Matthiessen & Bateman (1991:95). To avoid confusion we shall here use the term "realization operation" rather than "realization rule" of "realization statement".

In this chapter I shall briefly introduce each of the six major types of realization operator that are used in the Cardiff Grammar, and I shall then compare them with their equivalents in the Sydney Grammar. For the former I shall draw on Fawcett, Tucker & Lin (1993:129-34), and for the latter I shall draw mainly on Halliday's "Systemic theory" (1993:4505), with supplementary clarifications from Matthiessen & Bateman (1991:95f.).

Each realization operation has a direct correlate with one of the "relationships" to be discussed in the rest of this chapter. This will be indicated in the following summary, but we shall defer any further comments until the relevant section.

The major realization operations are listed below in their typical order of application:

1 **Insert a unit** (e.g., "ngp") into the structure to 'fill' (or 'function at') an **element or Participant Role** (e.g., "cv") — so introducing to the structure the relationship of **filling**. (The topmost clause in a text-sentence fills the 'placeholder' element of 'Sentence'; see below for a fuller explanation.)
2 **Locate** an **element** (e.g., "S") at a given **place** in a **unit** — so introducing the relationship of **componence**.

3  Insert an element or Participant Role into the structure in such a way that it immediately follows and is **conflated** (or 'fused') with an existing element — so introducing the relationship of **conflation** (e.g., "S/Ag").

4  **Expound** an **element** by an **item** — so introducing the relationship of **exponence**. A variant of "Expound", i.e., the operation "Fetch", is used when the exponent is a name; see the description of this operation below.

5  **Re-set** the **preferences** (i.e., the percentage probabilities on features in systems specified in the rule), including **preselection** of **features** by the use of 100% and 0% probabilities — these probabilities being reset to their original percentages after the next traversal of the network.

6  **Re-enter** the **system network** at a stated feature, typically the initial entry condition of [entity] — so possibly also introducing the recursion of **co-ordination**, **embedding** or **reiteration**.

It may be helpful to add the following three notes on the above operations:

a  Operations 1 and 4 both assume that the element referred to has already been located at a place by Operation 2 (as typically happens in the clause). If it has not (as typically happens in a group or cluster), a **potential structure** for the unit is consulted, which shows the fixed place at which the element occurs.

b  The result of applying Operation 6 (and so in turn Operation 1) is to introduce to the structure either a **single unit** or two or more **co-ordinated units**. In either case the resulting structure may additionally involve the **embedding** of a unit inside another unit of the same class — depending on what choices have been made in the system network.

c  In the case of any unit other than the clause, Operation (2) is not used. This is because the realization rule will consult the **potential structure** of the unit, which identifies the fixed **place** in the unit at which the element identified in Operation (1) or (4) occurs — so making Operation (2) unnecessary.

While the system network models choices between meanings, the early choices are between the generalized meanings such as 'situation', 'thing' and 'quality', which are realized as the major syntactic units of the language. Thus each traversal of the network generates first a unit, then its elements, and then the units that fill those elements or the items that expound them. Operation 1 is therefore the essential prerequisite for building any structure at all, because without the insertion of the unit there can be no elements and so no lower structure. Operation 1 must be followed by at least one of Operations 2 or 4, in order to generate the unit's elements.

In generation, the first unit to be generated is always a **clause**. The 'element' that it fills is an element of an unusual sort, because it is not an element in a unit that is recognized in the model of syntax presented here. The element is the 'Sentence', and this term is interpreted as a placeholder for the 'element' of discourse structure (whichever it is) for which the text-sentence is being generated. (See Fawcett 1993 for a simple example of how to model this interface between discourse and the lexicogrammar.)

All subsequent insertions of units in the sentence involve locating the unit so that it **fills** (or "functions at") an element of a unit that is higher than it in the tree structure. When another clause is co-ordinated with the current one this co-ordination is expressed by having it fill the same element.

Let us turn now to Operation 2. Whenever the unit that is being inserted into the structure is the clause, Operation 2 is essential. However, if the unit is not a clause it is only used very rarely. This is because Operation 4 provides that, if the element has not already been located at a place in structure by Operation 2, a **potential structure** will be consulted in order to ascertain the sequential relationship of the new element to the other elements in the unit — so making Operation 2 unnecessary.

Operation 3 presupposes that Operation 2 has already been applied. **Conflation** is the implementation in the generative version of the grammar of the concept that language is multifunctional. Conflation occurs only between coterminous elements (including Participant Roles); see the discussion of this issue in Chapter 7.

Operation 4 illustrates the fact that the very general sense that the term **exponence** had in "Categories" has been narrowed down to roughly the sense in which it was originally used by Firth (1957:183). In the Cardiff Grammar, there is a variant of Operation 4, which we shall call Operation 4a. This is the **Fetch** operation, and it is used to expound items when the item is not an ordinary word in the language that has a 'meaning', but a 'name'. Thus the 'meaning' of *Mr White* is nothing to do with the colour quality of 'white'.

Rather it is something like 'formal', in contrast with *Peter*, which may be 'informal'. In order to expound such meanings, e.g., in a computer model of generation, the generation system must consult its 'knowledge' (or, to use a preferable term, its 'beliefs') in order to discover the specific title (realized as *Mr, Mrs, Ms, Dr*, etc) and family name of the referent, and then 'fetch' the relevant forms for use in the sentence generator. Hence the need to use a different type of operation in the generation of names.

Just as Operation 1 must be followed by Operations 2 or 4, Operation 5 must be followed by Operation 6. If it was not, there would be no point in resetting the probabilities. In principle Operation 6 could occur without being preceded by Operation 5, but in practice this does not happen. Whenever the operation of **re-entry** to the network is performed, it is always for the purpose of filling a specific element, so that a re-entry rule has the form "For element X re-enter at feature Q". Thus two of the central concepts in the theory are (1) that there are probabilities on features in systems and (2) that the generator has the ability to change those probabilities (see Fawcett, Tucker & Lin 1993:127-9).

There is also a special type of re-entry operation that is used for generating **co-ordinated** units, and this ensures that the network is re-entered again for the same element. The result of applying Operation 6 may therefore be either (a) the introduction of a **single unit**, or (b) the introduction of the second or third, etc., of two or more **co-ordinated units**.

And in either case it may additionally involve the **embedding** of a unit, i.e., the generation of a unit inside another unit of the same class (or, much less frequently, the **reiteration** of an item at an element). See below for a fuller account of these concepts.

9.2.2 Potential structures

There is a second concept, besides that of the realization operators, that is a part of the syntax potential — and it is one that we have necessarily already had to invoke in order to characterize the realization operations. Indeed, the name of the concept shows that it is part of the 'potential'. This is the concept of **potential structures**.

In most (and perhaps all languages) the elements of certain classes of units occur **in a fixed sequence** (or in an almost fixed sequence). In English, for example, this is true of practically all of the elements of all classes of **groups** and **clusters**. The rare cases that do not can be handled in the same way as clause elements.[2]

There is an important consequence of the fact that groups and clusters have little or no variation in the sequence of their elements. This is that the grammar does not need to introduce an operation that will locate an element of structure at its place in sequence every time it is introduced. Instead, the grammar contains, for each unit with a fixed sequence of elements, a list of elements and their places (these being numbered as "Place 1", "Place 2", etc. These lists of **elements** located at numbered **places** are called **potential structures**. (For the concept of 'element' see Section 10.4.3 of Chapter 10, and for the concept of 'place' see Section 10.4 of that chapter). The great advantage that the concept of potential structures brings to the grammar is that they make the operation of the realization operations much simpler. This is because the grammar does not need to check what place to locate an element at every time an element is inserted. It knows, for example, that the head of a nominal group is always located at Place 64 (in the current large computer version of the Cardiff Grammar). It appears that this device is not used in the Penman project, and that all units are treated in the same way as the clause, i.e., every element is inserted individually. (See Section 10.4.3 of Chapter 10 for some further comments on potential structures.)

### 9.2.3 A comparison of the realization operations in the two frameworks

Since the realization operations are such a central part of systemic functional theory, it is important to ask: "How closely do the realization operations set out above match those in the current 'theoretical-generative' accounts of the Sydney Grammar (i.e., Matthiessen & Bateman 1991, Halliday 1993 and Matthiessen 1995)?"

Figure 11 gives the answer in general terms — i.e., there is in most cases a fairly close correspondence. The exceptions are the apparent lack in the Sydney Grammar framework of an operation that corresponds to the Cardiff Grammar's Operation 1 (a matter to which we shall return shortly) and the lack

---

2. The description of the quality group in Appendix B provides two examples of variation in sequence of an element of a group; for a further discussion of these and other such cases, see Fawcett (in press).

in the Cardiff framework of an equivalent to the Sydney Grammar's Operation (e). I have based the summary of the Sydney Grammar operations on Halliday's "Systemic theory" (1993), but supplemented by Matthiessen & Bateman (1991), which is shown as "M&B").

| Fawcett, Tucker & Lin (1993) | Halliday (1993) and M&B (1991) |
|---|---|
| 1. Insert a unit (to fill an element). | (no equivalent listed) |
| 2. Locate an element at a place in a unit. | (a) 'Insert' an element.<br>(c) 'Order' an element with respect to another, or to some defined location. |
| 3. Conflate an element or Participant Role with an existing element. | (b) 'Conflate' one element with another. |
| 4. Expound an element by an item.<br>(NB: if the element has not been located by 2, a 'potential structure' locates it.) | (g) 'Lexify' an element. |
| 4a. Fetch a name to expound an element. | |
| 5. Prefer certain features on re-entry to the system network, including preselection (= 100% preference). | (f) 'Preselect' some feature at a lower rank (= unit).<br>(d) 'Classify' an element. (absent in M&B) |
| 6. For an element, re-enter the system network. | (included in 'Preselect' in M&B) |
| (no need for an equivalent) | (e) 'Split' an element into a further configuration. ('Expand' in M&B) |

*Figure 11:*
*The realization operations in the Cardiff and Sydney Grammars*

As Figure 11 shows, Halliday's Operation (a) 'Insert an element' is roughly equivalent to our Operation 2, with the important proviso that Halliday's operation is simply an 'insertion in the unit'. In other words, it does not identify the specific location within that unit at which the element is to be located. The reason why we treat 'insertion' and 'location' as parts of the same operation in the Cardiff Grammar is that there is little point in inserting an element in a unit without at the same time locating it. Indeed, it is not possible, strictly speaking, to insert an element into a unit without at the same time specifying the location at which it is to be inserted — as the implementation of the grammar in a computer model quickly demonstrates.[3] Since this is so, the Cardiff Grammar's rules for the 'insertion' of an element tend to be attached to more delicate features in the system network than in the published versions of the Sydney Grammar. In other words, the realization rule that inserts an element in a unit is attached to a feature that occurs at the point in the system network by which we know not only that the element will be present in the unit but also the precise place at which it will occur. Thus Halliday's nearest equivalent to our Operation 2 is the combination of his (a) and (c), as the table suggests. Interestingly, Halliday's original version of his Operation (c) specifies that the task of locating elements in the appropriate sequence in a unit should be achieved by 'ordering' elements in relation to each other — but in "Systemic theory" he adds, after the words "order an element with respect to another", the further words "or to some defined location". This wording seems to suggest that Halliday may wish to extend his original approach to 'ordering' to include the Cardiff Grammar concept of a '(numbered) place in a unit' — and perhaps even to embrace the concept of a 'potential structure' (i.e., an 'ordered list of elements at places in a unit') — as introduced in Fawcett (1973/81). Since this concept has actually been used in the Penman implementation of the Sydney Grammar (as noted in Section 10.4.2 of Chapter 10), it is possible that Halliday's wording here may be intended to reflect the adoption in the Penman implementation of my concept of 'places'.

The "Conflate" operation is clearly the same in both models, and Halliday's "Lexify" is equivalent to our "Expound". However, it is important to note that the example of 'lexification' is the exponence of the Subject by the item *it* (presumably for cases of 'empty Subjects' such as *It's raining*). In other words, it seems that the "Lexify" operation is not limited, as one might at first suppose, to lexical items, in the usual sense of that term, and that it can also introduce grammatical items to the structure. It therefore covers all types of

---

3. Separating the operation of 'insertion' into the two stages of 'insertion' and 'location' ('ordering' being one way of 'locating') risks inviting misleading questions such as the following: "Where, in the unit, does the element wait between the time when it is first inserted and the assignment of its final position?", and "When it is moved from that place to its final place, isn't that some kind of syntactic transformational rule?" Halliday might dismiss such questions as failing to recognize that any such 'insertion' of an element is at an abstract level, but the fact is that in a computer implementation of the concept of 'insertion' a location must be stated.

'item' — just as the operation "Expound" does in the Cardiff Grammar.[4]

One relatively minor difference is that there is no statement in the accounts of the Sydney Grammar as to how to handle the generation of **names** (for which the operation "Fetch" is used in the Cardiff Grammar, as we saw in Section 9.2.1).

Halliday's Operation (f) is roughly equivalent to our Operation 5, with the important difference that ours is expressed in terms of **preferences** — and preferences can set the probability of a feature being selected on re-entering the system network to any point on a scale from 0% to 100%. In contrast, the more limited concept of **preselection** implies an absolute probability (i.e., 100%) that the specified feature will be selected. Interestingly, it appears from Halliday's examples that his "Classify" operation is essentially the same as his "Preselect" operation, and both Matthiessen & Bateman (1991) and Matthiessen (1995) simply omit "Classify" from their lists. The two are therefore treated as equivalent in Figure 11.

However, the most striking difference between the two sets of realization operations is the omission from all three of the Sydney Grammar lists of our Operations 1 and 6. Operations 1 and 2 are in a sense the two fundamental operations, in that each adds one of the two major categories to the structure: Operation 1 adds a unit and Operation 2 an element. For example, the choice of the feature [situation] is realized by inserting the unit 'Cl' (for 'Clause'), and the choice of the feature [thing] is realized by inserting 'ngp' (for 'nominal group'). If there is no unit, there can logically be no elements, and so no structure. Thus the computer implementation of the Sydney Grammar must have such an operation, or it could not work. The odd thing is that it is not listed here. Operation 6 equally is crucial, because if the network is **not** re-entered only one layer of structure can be generated.

The clue to the answer comes in Matthiessen and Bateman's description of what is covered by their term "preselection". For them, "preselections are instructions to re-enter the grammar to develop the function constituents of the clause as nominal groups, [...] and so on" (1991:108), so that their "Preselect"

---

4. It is surprising to find Halliday using this example, because it goes against the principle of 'total accountability at all ranks'. This requires, of course, that the Subject should be filled by a nominal group (or some other unit of that 'rank' or above). In the Cardiff Grammar the item *it* functions as the direct exponent of the Subject only in cases with an "empty Subject", such as *It's raining* and *It's nice to see you*, so perhaps this is the case in Halliday's example? But, if this is so, it breeches his 'rank scale' principle.

operation includes all three of (1) 'preselection' (in the strict sense of the term). (2) 're-entry' and (3) the insertion of a new unit. No doubt we can infer from this that Halliday's "preselect' operation includes the same three steps.

It is hard to understand why the Sydney Grammar lists of realization operations should not give Operation 1 at least the status of being a separate operation from 'preselection'. For a start, this operation will only generate units for the lower layers of a structure, so their realization operations appear not to have any means of generating the initial unit of the clause. Moreover, even when we limit ourselves to lower units in the structure (such as how a nominal group comes to fill an element such as Subject, we should note that it is perfectly possible for the grammar to need to select a given feature on the next pass through the network without thereby also inserting a new unit, so that preselection must in any case be treated as a separate operation from the insertion of a new unit.

It is therefore hard to understand why Halliday, Matthiessen and Bateman have no equivalent of Operation 1. The reason may possibly be connected with the fact that the emphasis in the Sydney Grammar is strongly on the generation of clauses. Perhaps this leads those working in that framework to take it for granted that all the choices being made in the system network are for the clause unless the rules state otherwise, so that the insertion of the initial clause does not get stated explicitly. Indeed, one surprising fact about the literature of the Sydney Grammar is that it contains no examples of generations of texts that involve a further layer of structure beyond that of a single clause — even in the fairly full description of the Penman Project given in Matthiessen & Bateman (1991). So there is no account of how the process of re-entry operates in the Sydney Grammar, whether for a clause or even for a simple nominal group. In practice, however, the computer implementation of the Penman model must have some equivalent operation to our Operation 1, or it would be unable to generate structures with more than a single layer (as it does when used in computer implementations). Indeed, the existing realization operations refer to the generation of lower units (e.g., "Preselect nominal group" in Halliday (1993:4505) — though there are no worked examples.

In contrast, consider the account of how the Cardiff Grammar works, e.g., as given in Fawcett, Tucker & Lin (1993). Here Operation 1 is the foundation of the whole process of generation. The grammar first generates the functional structure of a clause, and then, after re-entering system network, it generates the groups and embedded clauses that fill its elements. This is still, so far as I know, the only published account of the complete generation of a clause-length sentence in a SF grammar, including not only the clause structure but also all the groups, words, morphemes, and intonation or punctuation.

The last realization operation that requires a comment is Halliday's Operation (e) of "Split". This has no equivalent in the Cardiff Grammar. A "Split" operation is only needed in a grammar which represents both 'primary' and 'secondary' structures (as introduced in "Categories" and still used regularly for some aspects of structure in *IFG*). Halliday introduces it to enable the grammar **first** to generate what he would term a 'primary structure' (such as "Mood + Residue" in Figure 7 in Chapter 7), and **then** to 'split' the 'Mood' element into the two elements of its supposedly 'secondary' structure, i.e., into "Subject + Finite". Halliday does not explain why he thinks it desirable to generate the "Mood" element first and then to split it into two, but we can presume that the intention is to give expression to the idea that the "Mood + Residue" structure is 'primary' and the "Subject + Finite" structure is "secondary'. Nor does Halliday explain what would actually happen in practice when a "Split" operation is carried out.

The reason why the Cardiff Grammar has no such realization operation is, of course, that we recognize only one degree of 'delicacy' in the structures of the clause, so that there is no need for an operation whose function is to add another line of analysis to the representation. Instead, we treat the Subject and the Operator (Halliday's "Finite") as direct elements of the clause.

The other line of structure where Halliday frequently shows more than one line of structural analysis is in THEME, and this happens whenever there is a case of 'multiple theme'. For example, on page 55 of *IFG* there are three lines of structure for THEME in the analysis of *Well but then Ann surely wouldn't the best idea be to join the group*. On the pattern of the *IFG* approach to the structure of MOOD (as in Figure 7 of Chapter 7), Halliday's grammar would operate by first generating the 'multiple theme' of *Well but then Ann surely wouldn't the best idea,* since he analyses all of these items as different 'subcomponents' of the 'Theme', and it would then "split" it into its separate parts. It seems most unlikely that Halliday (or anyone else) would wish to treat all of these as parts of a single element, but that is the clear implication of the introduction of his "Split" operation. (See Section 10.3.4 of Chapter 10 for a discussion of 'primary' and 'secondary' structures.)

Matthiessen & Bateman (1991) and Matthiessen (1995) call Halliday's "Split" operation "Expand", but otherwise there is, in principle, no difference between them and Halliday. In practice, however, they do not fully implement Halliday's concept that the MOOD structure consists primarily of "Mood + Residue" and only secondarily of "Subject + Finite + Complement" (or whatever it happens to be). See the examination of their account of generation in Section 7.4.2 of Chapter 7, which showed that their model is not a 'structure conflation' model, as the *IFG* model is, but an 'element conflation' model. As I argued there, this fact demonstrates that in the theoretical-generative strand of work in the Sydney Grammar the concept of 'structure conflation' is unnecessary, undesirable, and ultimately unworkable.

Let me summarize. Leaving aside the "Split" and "Expand" operations of the Sydney Grammar, which are either unworkable or unnecessary, the Sydney Grammar has an equivalent for every realization operation in the Cardiff Grammar except the first (though these are not always in a one-to-one relationship, as we have seen). These realization operations are important concepts in the theory, as their treatment in both Halliday (1993) and Fawcett, Tucker & Lin (1993) clearly demonstrates.

However, these 'operation' concepts are a part of the grammar itself, so that they are relevant **only indirectly** to the outputs from the grammar — i.e., to a description of the structure of the text-sentences that are the instances of the potential specified in the grammar. Essentially, their function is to generate the **relationships** between the **categories** that we shall establish in Chapter 10. It is in Chapter 11 that we shall meet the relationships again. And it is perhaps significant that the first concept to be discussed there — that of 'rank' — has no equivalent among the realization operations and will be rejected, while all of those to be considered in Sections 11.2 to 11.8 do have such a relationship.

## 9.3 A theory of instances of syntax: the plan of the rest of Part 2

In Chapters 10 and 11 we turn to the concepts that are required for the specification of 'instances of syntax'. As we have seen, these concepts are drawn on in a computer model of parsing such as that described in Weerasinghe & Fawcett (1993), Weerasinghe (1994) and Souter (1996). However, these concepts are also referred to in the realization rules, and are in that sense presupposed by them.

As will be now clear, we shall be using the Cardiff Grammar rather than the Sydney Grammar as the baseline for constructing a modern theory of SF syntax.[5]

There are two parts to a theory of instances of syntax: the **categories** and the **relationships** by which these are related. We shall begin in Chapter 10 with the more 'object-like' concepts of the theory, i.e., the **categories**. Then in Chapter 11 we shall examine the **relationships**. There is a fairly close parallel between this pair of concepts and the "categories" and "scales" of Halliday (1961/76). But it is important to emphasize that my term "relationships" includes a wider range of concepts than Halliday's term "scales".

The structure of what follows therefore broadly reflects that of both Halliday (1961/76) and Fawcett (1974-6/81).

For each concept that is discussed, I shall also present and evaluate the Sydney Grammar's position (where this is stated), referring to both the 'theoretical-generative' writings summarized in Halliday's "Systemic theory" (1993) — when there is a relevant comparison — and the 'text-descriptive' framework set out in the second edition of *IFG* (1994). And I shall also compare each concept with its equivalent — when there is one — in "Categories".

By the beginning of Chapter 12, therefore, we shall be in a position to summarize the concepts that are required for a modern systemic functional theory of syntax, and also to evaluate how far the seven "fundamental concepts" established in "Categories" are still valid today. That chapter will therefore begin by addressing these two topics, and it will also evaluate the wider significance of Halliday's "Categories" in the development of linguistic theory in general, and systemic functional theory in particular. It will then conclude with a summary of the prospects for making publicly available descriptions of English which 'instantiate', as it were, the theoretical position set out here.

---

5. Apart from the reasons that follow from our findings in Chapter 7, there are two more reasons for this. Firstly, the Cardiff Grammar has taken the revolutionary proposals for changes to the theory made by Halliday in the 1960s (as summarized in Chapter 4) significantly further than the Sydney Grammar has. It has full implementations of (1) explicitly semantic system networks, (2) the concept of lexis as "most delicate grammar", (3) the integration into the system networks of the meanings realized in intonation and (4) the integration of meanings realized in punctuation. Secondly, the Cardiff Grammar provides a much fuller specification than the Sydney Grammar does of the syntactic concepts that are required, both for language in general and for the description of English in particular — especially in its recognition of classes of group and cluster that are not provided for in the Sydney Grammar.

# 10
# A theory of instances of syntax: (1) the categories of syntax

## 10.1 A model without a 'rank scale' of 'units'

10.1.1 The concepts of 'unit' and 'rank'

The concept of 'unit', in the sense defined in Halliday's "Categories", is inextricably bound up with the concept of 'rank' (as we saw in Section 2.3 of Chapter 2). In other words, there can be no concept of 'unit', in the "Categories" sense of the term, without the concept of a 'scale' of units that relates such units to each other in terms of their 'rank' on that scale — together with the accompanying set of 'rank shift' restrictions as to what 'rank' of unit may occur as an element of what other 'rank' of unit. Thus the concepts of 'unit' and 'rank' are inextricably intertwined in Halliday's theory of language, and together they make up the composite notion of the 'rank scale' that provides the backbone of Scale and Category (S&C) Grammar.

It is a tribute to the continuing influence of Halliday's founding paper "Categories of the theory of grammar" (1961/76) that the most helpful first step in explaining the new theory of syntax to be set out here to state the two basic Hallidayan concepts that it does **not** have. These are the precisely two concepts of 'unit' and 'rank'.

Thus, while the concept of the 'rank scale' has survived into the reincarnation of S&C as Systemic Functional Grammar in the Sydney version, it has not in the Cardiff version. Its centrality in the Sydney version is given a visual manifestation in the well-known summary diagram of the lexicogrammar in which the two dimensions of organization are (1) the 'rank scale' of units and (2) the four major 'metafunctions' (e.g., Halliday (1971/73b:141), Halliday (1977/78:132) and Martin (1992:18). A similar diagram with eight 'strands of meaning' can be found in Fawcett (1980:95). However, the crucial requirement of the 'units' dimension in such diagrams is not that the units should be arranged on a 'rank scale', but that the set of units should be complete. This may sound a small difference, but it is not, as we shall see.

However, while the "Categories" concept of the 'rank scale' is clearly still present in the Sydney Grammar, we have noted (in Section 5.3 of Chapter 5) that in "Systemic theory" Halliday defines 'rank' in a curious way that avoids mentioning the concept of a 'rank scale of units'. And we have also noted (in Section 6.2 of Chapter 6) that 'rank' has an apparently diminished role in *IFG*.

One reason for approaching the 'new' theory in the way that we now are is that it establishes from the start that there is a major change in this basic aspect of the theory. The precise nature of the concept that replaces the 'rank scale of units' will become clearer in the next section, and clearer still in Section 11.2 of Chapter 11. We shall find that the framework of syntax proposed here retains only a few incidental traces of the concept of 'rank'. There is consequently no role in the present theory for the concept of 'unit' in Halliday's original sense of 'unit on the rank scale'.

The major critical evaluation of the concept of the 'rank scale' will come in Section 11.1 of Chapter 11, under the more general heading of "constituency", and Appendix 4 provides some further notes on 'the rank scale debate'.

Even though the concept of 'unit' is not used here, a concept that was originally derived from it plays a central role in all modern SF grammars. This is **class of unit**, which we shall come to in Section 10.2. However, while all systemic functional grammars use the concept of 'class of unit', there is an important difference between Halliday's criteria for defining a class of unit and the criteria used by most other systemic functional grammarians who have written on the subject, as we shall see.

We should therefore ask how far the concepts of 'unit' and 'rank' are still actually used in Halliday's current framework. As we noted in Sections 5.3 and 5.4 of Chapter 5, the concept of a 'rank scale of units' is surprisingly absent from the list of "basic concepts" of Halliday's authoritative "Systemic theory" (1993), where the focus is mainly on the grammar as a generative device. However, we also noted that in *IFG* it continues to be used in virtually the same way as in "Categories". Thus Halliday writes, as part of the opening sentence of Chapter 1 of *IFG* (Halliday 1994:3), that "a passage of English [...] consists of larger units made up out of smaller units, [and] these smaller units, in their turn, are made up out of units that are smaller still." On the other hand, the index of *IFG* shows that the term "unit" is not used after the introductory chapters (as we saw in Section 6.2.2 of Chapter 6), and nor is "rank", except in the two brief discussions of 'rank shift'. Matthiessen (1995) goes even further, only mentioning the concept of 'unit' twice in his work of almost a thousand pages (though he has rather more to say about 'rank' and 'rank shift'). Furthermore, in the brief section in *IFG* on 'rank shift', Halliday quickly introduces the terms **embedding** and **embedded** as alternatives to "rank" and "rankshifted", and he then drops the original two terms completely. So it seems that Halliday himself appears to prefer the terms "embedding" and "embedded". (This is my preference too — but Halliday would not share the reason for my preference, which is that the term "embedding" expresses the key concept in the new theory that a unit frequently occurs within a unit of the same class without invoking the notion of the 'rank scale'. Again, see Section 11.1 of Chapter 11).

Taken together, the above facts suggest (1) that those who work in the framework of the Sydney Grammar do not in fact find the concepts of 'unit' and 'rank' useful when they are engaged in the nitty gritty work of describing a language or of describing a text; (2) that they only find the concept of 'rank' useful when embedding occurs, and (3) that in any case the term "embedding" is to be preferred to "rank shift". However, this apparent down-grading of the theoretical importance of the 'rank scale' and 'rank shift' is accompanied by a far stronger claim about the limitations on when 'rank shift' can occur than the claim made in "Categories", as we shall see in Section 11.8.5 of Chapter 11.

Finally, I should perhaps point out that, while the term "unit" is used frequently in the writings of Cardiff grammarians, it is always with the meaning of 'class of unit' (this being the topic of Section 10.2).

10.1.2 The remaining traces of the concept of a 'rank scale' of 'units'

It would be surprising if the concept that was the backbone of Halliday's original theory of syntax were to disappear without trace from the theory proposed here. After all, the phenomena in language that led Halliday to recognize the concept in the first place are still there. We should ask, therefore, whether the concepts of 'unit' and 'rank', in Halliday's original senses of the terms, have any correlates in the framework of concepts proposed here. Let us examine this question for a moment.

One way in which a clause may be said to be a 'higher' unit than the others — as the 'rank scale' concept predicts it to be — is the fact that the unit that is shown as the 'highest' on the page in any tree diagram representation of a text-sentence is always the clause.[1] In a generative SF grammar, provision for this fact is built into the probabilities on the features in an early system in the overall network, so ensuring that a clause is always generated first. However, we may note that the informal summary of clause syntax for text analysis purposes shown in Appendix B shows that a clause is the only unit that can fill the "element" of "sentence", and this fact is given to the computer parser of texts as a relevant part of its knowledge of syntax. However, this is a fact about clauses in relation to all other units, and on its own it does not constitute evidence that there is a 'rank scale' of units in the "Categories" sense of the term.

The closest that it is possible to come to the 'rank scale' concept in the theory to be described here is to extract from a wider, probabilistic set of statements (which we shall come to in Section 11.2 of Chapter 11) a statement that the various classes of **cluster** always fill elements of **groups** (though they are in fact virtually limited to one class of group, i.e., the nominal group), and that groups quite frequently fill elements of **clauses** (though they also frequently fill elements of every class of group and cluster, and there is one class of group — the quantity group — which fills elements of groups very much more frequently than it fills an element of the clause). Or we might take a different approach and, ignoring the cluster, we might say that, for each word in a text that is being analyzed, there is a fairly good possibility that it will be functioning as an element in a group (though many high frequency words such as forms of *be* function directly as elements of clauses), and also that, if one has identified a group, there is a fairly good possibility that it is functioning as an element of a

---

1. In other words, the topmost unit in a representation of syntax is always a clause — even though the topmost unit in a given text-sentence may appear to be a nominal group because of **ellipsis**. (Ellipsis is defined as 'recoverability at the level of form'.) Consider, for example, the first of B's possible responses in the following simple exchange: A: *What's your name?* B: *Ivy* or *It's Ivy*. Here the second possible response shows the unellipted form of the first. Consider too the label on a jar of home-made marmalade, which simply says *Granny's marmalade* (so by the long-established labelling convention ellipting *This is*). A partially similar problem arises with utterances which include a **formula** such as *Yes* or *Hi!* These too are modelled as clauses (though in this case the item is a 'Formula' element) because they can co-occur with aspects of clause syntax, e.g., *Yes, with pleasure*. Here we shall not go into the arguments for and against the proposal that utterances that appear to consist solely of a group and/or formulas can stand on their own. All I shall say is that whenever I have found counter-examples that were initially persuasive, it has always been possible to handle them satisfactorily as occurring within a clause — even though it would sometimes need to be one in which "F" (for "Formula") is an element, e.g., *Thankyou* can be extended to *Thankyou for all your help over the last two years*. And so on, for *Hello on this wonderful morning*, etc. (See Appendix B for further examples of a Formula as an element of a clause.)

clause (though many groups do not).

However, these heavily hedged statements are as far as one can go, in the present theory, in trying to state generalizations about the syntax of English in 'rank-like' terms. Notice, moreover, that we cannot turn such statements on their head and say, in the manner of "Categories", that clauses "consist of" groups and groups "consist of" clusters or words, because in the present model it is only some elements of clauses that can be filled by groups; it is only a very few elements of groups that are filled by a cluster (see Section 10.2.12); and it is only some elements of groups that are always expounded by words. (In any case, in the present theory we would not wish to say that groups "consist of" words, because the phenomena typically described as "words" are treated as a type of 'item', and so not as 'units'. See the discussion of this point in Section 10.5.) Thus, while some of the phenomena that originally gave rise to the concepts of a 'rank scale' of 'units' have their place in the new theory, the concept of the 'rank scale' itself plays no part in it.

The unit of the **clause** and various classes of **group** (or "phrase", as the group is termed in traditional grammars) are well-established in all theories of syntax. However, so far as I am aware no linguists other than those who use the Cardiff Grammar have yet recognized the unit of the **cluster** (though Quirk *et al.* (1985:1276) come close to doing so in the case of the genitive cluster). For a brief discussion of this matter and an account of the various classes of cluster, see Sections 10.2.10 to 10.2.12.

Halliday's formalization of the concept of the 'rank scale' is, as with a number of his concepts, the formalization of concepts that are found in traditional grammar. We therefore find broad equivalences to his proposals in works such as Quirk *et al.* (1985), with the presentation of the concept that the units of the **sentence** (but often with reservations) **clause**, **group** or **phrase**, **word** and **morpheme** are typically related to each other in a 'constituency' relationship. Interestingly, however, Halliday later changed his view on the status of the "sentence", redefining it as a "clause complex", and limiting the use of the term "sentence" to clause complexes that occur in writing. Since his framework also allows for "group complexes" (and also, though very much less frequently, for "complexes" of "words" and "morphemes"), it is clear that a "sentence" is not a unit in the same sense that a clause or group is. For Halliday, then, the "sentence" is simply another type of "unit complex". The significance of this change of position is that it makes the clause the highest unit of English syntax.[2]

The present model takes broadly the same position as Halliday on this matter, i.e., the clause is taken to be the "highest" unit of English syntax. The term "sentence" is used here simply as a place-holder for the function served by the clause (or clause complex) in discourse. Thus it operates at the interface between the grammar and the 'higher grammar' that specifies the structure of discourse. Thus it is more like an "element" (see Section 10.5) than a "unit".[3]

Finally, I should comment briefly on the fact that the concepts of 'word' and 'morpheme' are not even considered as candidates for any possible 'rank scale'. The explanation is connected with the meanings of the terms **item** and **exponence**, as defined in this theory, and these will be explained in the sections dealing with those concepts (Section 10.5 of this chapter and Section 11.5 of Chapter 11). The present theory regards the relationship of words and morphemes to the 'higher' units on the supposed 'rank scale' as different from the relationship between, let us say, groups and clauses. Indeed, it is the relationship between clauses and the various classes of groups that lies at the heart of understanding English syntax, as Appendix B demonstrates.

To summarize: the two mutually defining concepts of 'unit' and 'rank' have no explicit role in the theory of SF syntax that is set out here. Moreover, although they are heralded as central concepts in most works that describe the Sydney Grammar, neither Halliday nor Matthiessen make much use of them in

---

2. It should be noted that, while the concept that a sentence is a "clause complex" underlies all of Halliday's analyses of texts in *IFG*, he nonetheless still includes "sentence" in the list of units in his discussion in Chapter 1 (1994:23) of the theoretical concepts use in *IFG* — while warning that this will be "re-interpreted" later in the book.

3. However, there is still the major difference between the two models in what types of relationship they permit between two (or more) clauses that make up a sentence. While the Sydney Grammar allows for "paratactic" and "hypotactic" relationships between clauses, the Cardiff Grammar recognizes only the first of these. The prototypical type of "paratactic" relationship is that of 'co-ordination', as in *My brother has arrived but his girlfriend will be a few minutes late*, and all grammars recognize this relationship. In contrast, Halliday's "hypotactic" relationship between two units is not recognized in most other grammars. It is said to be one of 'dependency' without 'embedding', an example being *He told us that he would be there*. In Halliday's model the unit *that he would be there* is said to be 'projected by' the superordinate clause *He told us*, **rather than being an element of it**. In the Cardiff Grammar it would be regarded as a 'Participant' in the Process of 'telling', and it would be treated as an embedded clause that fills a Phenomenon that is conflated with a Complement. Thus the Cardiff Grammar treats virtually all of Halliday's "hypotactic" relationships as types of **embedding**.

practice — either in their theoretical statements or in their descriptions of English (except in their accounts of 'rank shift', where Halliday's preference is now for the term "embedding"). The twin concepts of 'unit' and 'rank' play no part in the operation of the grammar, and the centrality of the concept of 'unit' in "Categories" is replaced by the centrality of the concept of **class of unit** (as described in Section 10.2 below). The concept of the 'rank scale' is replaced by a statement about the probabilities that a given class of unit fills a given element of the same or another class of unit, as discussed in Section 11.2 of Chapter 11 and as exemplified in Appendix B.

## 10.2   Classes of unit

10.2.1 The general concept of 'class of unit'

**Class of unit** (or **unit** for short) is the first of the three fundamental categories in the theory (together with **element of structure** and **item**).

As I have emphasized at various points in Part 1, the present theory of language assumes a model with the two levels of **meaning** and **form** (as described in Chapter 3 and as summarized in Figure 4 in Section 3.2 of that chapter). In such a model we need to be able to talk about both **semantic units** and **syntactic units** (where "unit" means, as stated above, 'class of unit'). Indeed, the **class** of a syntactic unit and of the semantic unit that it realises are mutually determined (as is the case for any **sign** in a Saussurean approach to language, as we saw in Chapter 3).

Thus the Cardiff Grammar's approach to the concept of 'class of unit' in syntax is to recognize that each such class exists to express the specific array of meanings that are associated with each one of the major classes of **entity** in the semantics. For English these are what we might term **situations, things, qualities** (of both situations and things) and **quantities** (typically of things, but also of situations and qualities). English also has a semantic unit that can be termed a **minor relationship with thing**.[4] Each of these semantic units corresponds directly to one of the five major classes of syntactic unit that are recognized in the present syntax of English. These are:

---

4.  It seems probable that all other natural human languages operate with 'situations' and 'things', but the other semantic units named here may well be less universally recognized.

clause,
nominal group,
prepositional group,
quality group, and
quantity group.

Each of these will be discussed in turn in the rest of this section, together with two minor classes of unit, i.e., the **genitive cluster** and the **human proper name cluster**. (For some other types of 'name' cluster, see Fawcett in press).

I have just stated that each semantic unit has an associated "array of meanings". Such arrays of meaning are in effect the 'elements' of the higher unit that is constructed in the **planner** and that corresponds to each syntactic unit. They are realized — though not in a one-to-one relationship — in the different **elements of structure** of which the syntactic unit is composed.[5] More precisely, these "arrays of meanings" are those with respect to which choices are made in the system network of semantic features from which each syntactic unit is generated — and it is these choices that trigger the introduction of each element of structure to a syntactic unit. Thus the concepts of **class of unit** and **element of structure** are closely interrelated. These general statements will be filled out a little when we consider each of the classes of unit for English (from Section 10.2.3 onwards). See Section 10.2.9 for a little more on the "higher units" that are the inputs to and outputs from the language system, and Section 10.3.1 for more on the key concept of 'element of structure'.

Once we recognize that each element of a syntactic unit makes a unique contribution to realizing the meaning of that unit, we can dispense with the traditional, over-narrow characterization of the internal structure of groups as a series of 'modification' relationships. In its extreme form, this model presents groups as simply the 'hypotactic expansion' of the word class that functions as the 'head', in a series of 'modifier-head' relationships. This concept is central to 'sister dependency' grammars such as that of Hudson (1976), and it is reflected in Halliday's suggestion that there should be a 'logical' as well as an 'experiential' structure in the nominal group and the supposed 'verbal group'.

---

5. One example of the lack of a one-to-one relationship between the higher units in the planner and syntactic units of English is that a single element of the nominal group (the head) typically realizes the two semantic variables of (1) the 'cultural classification' of things (which are realized by the 'common nouns' of a language) and (2) 'number' (i.e., 'mass' or 'count' and, if 'count', 'singular ' or 'plural', to slightly oversimplify).

(For a critique of the concept of a 'logical structure' in the 'verbal group' see Fawcett 2000.) However, to see groups as little more than the 'hypotactic expansion' of a word is to lose the important insights that come from approaching each group on its own terms, as a unit whose elements function to express meanings. Yet this is what Halliday is at times inclined to do. (See *IFG* pp. 180-1 and 196, and for a specific case where he treats the group *very small* as a 'word complex', see *IFG* p. 184.)

The nearest that the present grammar comes to a generalized concept of a 'modifier + head' relationship is its recognition of the fact that other elements of a group typically depend on the presence of the 'pivotal element'. Thus when the grammar generates a "common nouns" as the head of a nominal group, other elements realizing other types of meaning typically get brought into play as well. Thus it is preferable to characterize the nominal group as a unit for expressing the wide range of types of meaning associated with a 'thing', rather than in terms of an over-simple series of 'modifier + head' relationships.

So far I have been explaining the concept of 'class of unit' in terms of the concepts of the Cardiff Grammar. In very broad terms, the concept is the same in *IFG* — except that the account of 'class of unit' given above is more directly connected to the level of meaning here than it is in *IFG*. However, the criteria used in the present theory for setting up different classes of unit are completely different from Halliday's, and the concept of 'class of unit' is therefore also significantly different. Indeed, the result is the recognition of a different set of classes of unit for English, as we shall see in the rest of Section 10.2.

### 10.2.2 Criteria for recognizing classes of unit

Since our topic in this book is syntax, I shall now re-express the semantic view taken in Section 10.2.1 in terms of concepts that are at the level of form. Then, since 'class of unit' is a key category in the present theory, I shall examine the extent to which the criterion for recognizing 'classes' of unit proposed in "Categories" has been supported by other scholars.

In terms of criteria at the level of form, then, the different classes of syntactic unit that are recognized in the description of a language are to be identified **by their internal structure**, i.e., by the **elements of structure** of those units. This concept will be exemplified in the classes of unit in English described in Sections 10.2.3 to 10.2.12. For a fuller discussion of the concept of 'element of structure', see Section 10.5.6

In many theories of syntax there is an assumption that each unit has an element that is obligatorily present (often called the 'head'). This reflects the traditional assumption that a unit is essentially the 'expansion' of a word — a concept which is replaced here by recognizing the fact that each element realizes one aspect of the unit's meaning, as explained in Section 10.2.1. But among formal grammarians — i.e., those who are influenced by formal language theory (i.e., the theory of 'formal' languages) — there is a tendency to transfer the characteristics of formal languages to natural languages, and so to construct theories for parsing natural languages on the basis of such assumptions (e.g., 'head-driven parsers'). However, the data of natural language texts suggest that such concepts express strong tendencies rather than absolute rules.

On the other hand, the concept of an element that is **typically** present in a given class of unit is useful (e.g., when the theory of syntax is to be used by a parser), and on those occasions when we need to refer to such an element we shall call it, informally, the **pivotal element** of the unit. Examples of nominal groups that have no heads include *the very rich* and *five* in *Give me five* (see Fawcett in press for the reasons for these analyses). And for a discussion of the Main Verb as the pivotal element of the clause, see Section 10.4.2.

In the present theory, then, the decision to recognize a possible class of unit is dependent on the recognition of the semantic similarities between configurations of functionally motivated elements, based on the comparison of large numbers of instances in texts of potential members of that unit. However, we

---

6. Let me give an example of the use of these criteria when introducing a new class of unit. The quantity group was only introduced to the present description of English syntax when detailed studies of this area of the grammar showed that it could not reasonably be handled in terms of an existing unit, such as the quality group. In other words, it became clear that there are units with 'quantities' as their pivotal element (e.g., *over sixty*) as well as groups with 'qualities' as their pivotal element (e.g., *quite clever*) — and that the elements of structure in the two classes of unit serve different functions. However, there is also a different type of principle to take into account when setting up classes of unit. This derives from the need to keep the model within the bounds of what the human user of it can handle (and so within the natural limits of human memory). This principle warns against the proliferation of classes of syntactic units. Thus we decided to avoid introducing an additional class of unit to the present description of English syntax by 'borrowing', as it were, the quantity group to enable us to represent the internal structures that are occasionally found within (1) Binders ("subordinating conjunctions" in traditional terms), and (2) prepositions, e.g., *immediately before (he came in)* and *some time after (his visit)*. Model-building sometimes requires a compromise between the demands of these two types of criterion. (Note that prepositions are also occasionally filled by quality groups, i.e., when the pivotal element is *near* or *like*.)

should also note that it is not the case that a syntactic unit always corresponds in a one-to-one manner to the event or object etc. to which it refers, i.e., to its equivalent 'conceptual' representation in the **belief system**. In a slowly evolving construct such as a natural human language (as opposed to an artificial language such as a logic) we should expect to find quite frequent cases of the lack of a one-to-one fit of this type. (For some typical cases such as that of 'nominalization', see Section 10.2.10.)

Halliday takes a very different approach to the criteria for recognizing a 'class of unit'. While the criterion used here is the unit's internal structure (together with semantic criteria, as described in Section 10.2.1), for Halliday the criterion is the unit's ability to fill elements of units at the 'rank' next above it on the 'rank scale' (as we saw in Section 2.3 of Chapter 2). Thus Halliday's definition of 'class of unit' is dependent — like so much else in his theory — on the concept of the 'rank scale'.

It is interesting to note that Halliday later (1963/76) introduced to the theory a concept that he termed "type". It was introduced as a complement to 'class', in a sense that is exactly equivalent to the concept of 'class of unit' as it is used here. In other words, in Halliday (1963/76) a unit's 'type' is defined in terms of a unit's internal structure. Interestingly, while Berry's introduction to the theory gives a clear account of the difference between this concept and Halliday's "Categories" sense of 'class of unit' (1975:76-7, 124-6), Berry makes no further use of it, and the concept has not been used in most later accounts of the theory. Thus it is not mentioned by Halliday in either "Systemic theory" or *IFG*, nor by Matthiessen (1995). Moreover, in both *IFG* and Matthiessen (1995) units continue to be defined in the "Categories" manner. Halliday is clearly using this criterion when deciding to treat *very lucky* in *You're very lucky* as a nominal group (p. 194 of *IFG*), and Matthiessen emphasizes the correlation between "grammatical units of different classes" and their "functional potential [in the unit above]" (Matthiessen 1995:22).

There is a crucial difference, therefore, between the theoretical positions taken on this matter in the Sydney and the Cardiff Grammars. Moreover, there are many other systemic linguists who have differed from Halliday on this key matter, as we shall now see.

Butler (1985:33-5) provides a valuable discussion of several of the problems with Halliday's concept of 'class', referring to some of the key contributions to the literature that it has generated. He points out that "certain other systemicists" — including Huddleston (1966/81), Hudson (1967/81) and myself (Fawcett 1974-6/81) — had by then abandoned Halliday's criterion of the potential for operation in the unit above it on the 'rank scale', in favour of the criterion of "the internal structure of units".

This leads to the question of why I and others should have abandoned this central tenet of Halliday's theory. My own answer — and I cannot speak for Huddleston and Hudson — is that my experience of building models of English syntax (for use in both generating and describing text) has taught me that the model become far more insightful, when I treat the **internal** structural patterns of a unit as the defining ones (for the reasons given in Section 10.2.1). One must operate with either internal criteria or external criteria (the latter being operation in the unit next above on the 'rank scale'), because the two are often in conflict. I find that the descriptive facts of natural texts in English and other languages provide just too many clear examples where it distorts the facts to categorize them in terms of their operation in a higher unit, and where it is insightful to categorize them in terms of their internal syntactic-semantic structure.

What reasons could Halliday have had for setting up classes of unit on the basis of their potential for operation in the unit above? The most likely is the generalization that nominal groups tend to occur as the Subjects and Complements of clauses. The first problem for his criterion is the fact that nominal groups also occur very frequently as elements of other units — particularly in prepositional groups. Such cases challenge his criterion, because it requires the higher unit to be 'above' the current unit on the 'rank scale', and in such cases it is at the same 'rank'. A second problem for Halliday's criterion, as Butler points out (1985:33), is the fact that an expression such as *very clever* is classified by Halliday as a type of "nominal group". The problem is that, although it occurs naturally as a Complement, it does not occur (except in quotation marks) as a Subject. It is therefore a counter-example to the claim that nominal groups are defined by their potential to operate as both Subject and Complement. While Halliday himself points out this inconsistency (*IFG* p. 80), the fact that he does so does not weaken its force as an argument against his general claim. And the problems for his claim increase when we also take into account the fact that a unit such as *very clever* can also function as the modifier in a nominal group (e.g., *a very clever cat*). Is it still a nominal group in such a case, in *IFG* terms? It appears not, since on p. 192 it is analyzed as a case of "submodification". But there is no explanation of this inconsistency. These facts present no problem for the model outlined here, because it assumes that it is a natural characteristic of language that two units with the same internal structure should be able to fill two or more elements of other units (as is demonstrated in the summary of what units can fill what elements in Appendix B).

So far as I am aware, Halliday has never shown why facts such as those described above are not counter-examples to his claim. However, he has commented in an interesting manner on a partly similar set of examples in Halliday (1963/76). Here he addresses the fact that a nominal group such as *this morning* functions as an Adjunct just as naturally as it functions as a Subject or Complement (and far more frequently). Here he reaches the conclusion that

> *this morning* "clearly resembles other nominal groups (*the morning, this man,* etc.) rather than other adverbial groups (*quickly, on the floor,* etc.) **and this can be allowed to determine its primary syntactic assignment** [my emphasis]. (Halliday 1963:6)

How does this acknowledgement of the facts affect his view of the criteria for recognizing units? The answer is that it appears to remain unchanged, on the evidence of the criteria used for recognizing units in *IFG*. But if the criterion of the internal structure applies in the above case, one asks, why not in all cases?

Sinclair, who was one of Halliday's closest colleagues at the time, published in 1972 an introduction to systemic grammar in which he included all of the following as criteria for recognizing units:

a) the guidance given by similar or different meanings (i.e., semantic criteria);
b) the internal details or componence of structure;
c) the external details, or syntax of structures. (Sinclair 1972:23)

Since the second and third criteria are often in conflict, this list should perhaps be taken as an indication of the order of Sinclair's preferences — and we note that Halliday's standard criterion is relegated to third place. In the present theory we go one step further, as in Fawcett (1974-6/81:10), and exclude the last criterion altogether. Sinclair does not explain what he intends by "semantic criteria", but at the very least his wording allows for the possibility that semantics influences syntax in the way described at the start of Section 10.2.1.

Butler, in his useful discussion of this issue, is quite clear about what the answer should be. He points out that "if we are to account for the variety of structures available in a language, we shall have to elevate structural type to a more central position in the theory than Halliday suggests" (Butler 1985:34). And, referring to two papers by Halliday's two closest colleagues in the 1960s (Huddleston 1966/81 and Hudson 1967/81) he goes on to say that: "although neither [...] actually defines class, their discussion suggests that their criteria for classification are those of internal constituency".

It therefore seems that there is a basic difference here between, on the one hand, Halliday and those whose publications have been written with the goal of expounding and complementing *IFG*, and on the other hand almost all other grammarians who have worked on the analysis of English using SFL.

One notable fact about most published description of English using SFL is that the accounts given of the groups are very much less full than those of the clause. It therefore seems possible that in a future revision of *IFG* Halliday may take to its logical conclusion the change in criteria signalled in Halliday (1963). As one indication of the advantage of changing, consider the fact that, in Halliday's current approach there can be no equivalent of the useful summary of English syntax given in Appendix B, because generalizations based on the internal structure of units have little or no place in his theory of syntax.

We shall turn discuss briefly each of the major classes of unit in English.

10.2.3 The clause

The unit of the 'clause' is almost certainly central in every human language. It is the syntactic unit that corresponds to the semantic unit of the **situation** — and so typically, as we shall shortly see, to the unit of **event** in the belief system. A clause has the syntax potential that it does because of the particularly rich and complex array of meanings that we wish to express to each other about 'events'. However, a clause occasionally refers to an **object** that is identified by its **role in an event**, as in *what I ate*; see Section 10.2.9 below.

The most frequent elements of the English clause are the **Subject**, **Operator** and **Main Verb**, with one or more **Complements** and potentially many **Adjuncts**, selected from over forty functionally differentiated types. Typically, a **Participant Role** (such as Agent, Affected, Carrier or Attribute) is conflated with the Subject or Complement. **Auxiliary Verbs** and **Main Verb Extensions** also occur frequently, as do the **Binders** and **Linkers** that relate the clause out to another unit. See Appendix B and Fawcett (in press) for a fuller picture, including six other elements. It may be helpful to add that in this grammar the underlined portions of *My friend Ivy, you'd like her,* and *She's very clever, my friend Ivy* are handled as two different types of Adjunct (so not as 'left-dislocation' and 'right-dislocation', as in transformational grammars). To see why, compare *As for my friend Ivy, you'd like her* and *She's very* *clever, my friend Ivy is.*

We have noted that, in the "Categories" framework, there is a 'unit' on the 'rank scale' called the "clause". From the 'rank scale' viewpoint it is surely odd that, unlike the 'rank scale units' of 'group' and "word', there is only one class of the "clause", namely the clause. Yet this fact is never commented on.[7]

The most important syntactic fact about the English clause is the great variety in the positions in which its elements occur. However, this is not a matter of so-called 'free word order' (i.e., 'free element order'), since each positional difference realizes a different meaning, however fine the distinction.

There is no element of the clause that is obligatorily realized — not even the Main Verb. Moreover it varies in its position, so that there is no element that can be used as an 'anchor-point' from which to start building the structure of the unit in generation — a vital point to which we shall return in Section 10.4.2.[8] In text analysis, however, it is useful to begin with a working assumption that each unit has a 'pivotal element' that is typically realized, and in the case of the clause in English this 'pivotal element' is the Main Verb.

### 10.2.4 The four classes of 'group'

Following the principles set out in Sections 10.2.1 and 10.2.2, the present grammar takes a rather different approach to the groups found in English syntax

---

7. Clauses can of course be classified in terms of the features in the network that generates them, e.g., as 'independent' or 'dependent' clauses, and as 'action' or 'mental' or 'relational' clauses — but this should not lead one to set up "classes of clause". These differences are quite unlike the distinction between a nominal group and a prepositional group; rather, they are like the distinction between a nominal group that has a modifier and one without one — i.e., they are different from each other, but they are still the same 'class of unit'. If a grammar did set up 'classes of clause' along these lines, there would be as many different classes of clause as there are combinations of semantic features realized in the clause — i.e., millions of millions. Surprisingly, Matthiessen (1995:77) describes the following as "grammatical classes" of clause: 'major' and 'minor' clauses and, within 'major clauses', 'free' and 'bound' clauses. Yet these are simply early features in the sub-network for the clause.

8. In a SF grammar, however, the concept of 'syntactic dependence' (which is so dominant in X-bar syntax and other formal theories of syntax) belongs ultimately not in syntax but in the system networks. Any apparent 'dependence' in syntax is a reflection of dependence in the system network — in which every system is **dependent** on a feature (or features) in another system (or systems). Thus the obligatoriness (or near-obligatoriness) of the 'pivotal elements' in a syntactic unit is simply the realization of certain choices in the system network.

from that of *IFG*. In *IFG*, Halliday in fact recognizes only two major classes of group, to each of which he devotes quite substantial sections of his chapter on groups. Thus there are 18 pages on the nominal group (pp. 180-96) and 30 pages on the verbal group (pp. 180-210). However, the elements of his 'verbal group' are treated here as elements of the clause — the full reasons being set out in Fawcett (2000) and (forthcoming b). Halliday also gives a page and a half to each of the 'adverbial group' (pp. 210-1) and the 'prepositional phrase' (pp. 212-3). In addition, in order to model the structures that occasionally occur inside prepositions and conjunctions, he introduces two new groups: the 'preposition' and 'conjunction groups' (pp. 210-212). He is right that we need to have a unit to cover such phenomena, but here I offer a simpler solution to the problem (in Section 10.2.8 of Chapter 10). In contrast, Fawcett (in press) gives substantial chapters to each of the four main classes of group recognized here, i.e., the nominal, prepositional, quality and quantity groups. Thus only one of the four classes of group recognized here receives detailed treatment in *IFG*. (For further comments on Halliday's 'classes of group' see Sections 10.2.4 to 10.2.8.)

It is interesting that, despite the fact that the two grammars are based on the same systemic functional principles, they take such a different approach to the grammar of groups. As I have said, the Cardiff Grammar's approach is as it because of our commitment to relating the elements of the syntactic units to their meaning potential in the system networks — and so to the 'conceptual units' of logical form in the belief system. But it also provides a much fuller account of their functional structures, and this may be because the Cardiff Grammar focusses on the analysis of groups as well as clauses — whereas in *IFG* and the many derived works the emphasis is overwhelmingly on the clause.

Typically, a group is capable of functioning as a complete **referring expression** — in the sense that it can stand on its own, after ellipsis, as a natural-sounding answer to a question such as *Who's this?*, *Where did you put it?*, *What is she like?* and *How much do you love him?*, each of which can be responded to by one of the four classes of group. The main exception to this generalization is that quantity groups with certain items as their 'amount' occur only within quality groups and other quantity groups, and consequently cannot stand alone (e.g., *far too* is very unlikely as an answer to the question *How heavy was it?*) Thus the ability to function as a referring expression is a useful guideline when trying to identify a stretch of words in a text that constitutes a clause or group, and not an absolute test of one.

In the following four sub-sections I shall comment briefly on each of the four classes of group that are recognized in the Cardiff Grammar's description of English. No distinction is made here between a 'phrase' and a 'group', so that those who prefer the term "phrase" to "group" (e.g., Sinclair 1990) could rename them as classes of "phrase" without affecting the concept itself.

### 10.2.5 The nominal group

The **nominal group** has as its pivotal element either a **noun**, a **pronoun** or a **proper name**. The latter, however, is not in fact an **item** (as a noun and a pronoun are) but a **unit**. It is most frequently the unit of the **human proper name cluster,** which has its own internal structure. (For this see Section 10.2.12).[9]

Halliday's **nominal group** is the only class of group that comes at all close to sharing both the same name and the same coverage of phenomena as it does the Cardiff Grammar — but even here there are important differences.

The first is that Halliday treats the type of **quality group** that has an adjective as its apex (e.g., *more generous than most people*) is a type of "nominal group" in *IFG*. He does this in spite the fact that its internal structure is clearly very similar to that of his "adverbial group". Here, then, he is clearly applying the criterion for assigning an expression to a class of unit that what matters is the unit's ability to function at given elements in the unit above on the 'rank scale' (as discussed in Section 10.2.2). His reason is clearly that an 'adjectival group' such as *very bright* can function in the clause as an Attribute

---

9. The name "nominal group" is not a particularly good one for this unit, since in everyday usage the term **nominal** is the adjective corresponding to the noun **name**, e.g., *a nominal candidate* in an election is a candidate who stands in name only. The problem is that 'naming something' is only one of the three main ways in which nominal group refers to an object — and it is by far the least frequent. Thus every object can be referred to by either (1) a nominal group with a noun or *one(s)* at its head, or (2) a pronoun — but only certain classes of object can be referred to by a name. In other words the term **nominal group** is the legacy of an idea that has been accepted very widely for a very long time but which is fundamentally mistaken, i.e., that a common noun such as *table* or *water* 'names' something. Strictly speaking, a noun denotes the **cultural classification** of a class of referents, of which the present referent is an instance, e.g., as in the nominal group *this book*. So, while a noun may be used as the pivotal element of a nominal group that refers to an object, it does not 'name' that object. (Lyons (1977) has a useful discussion of these points.) Thus the 'nominal group' corresponds to the semantic unit of 'thing' — and so, typically, to the conceptual unit of 'object'. And only sometimes does a nominal group literally 'name' the object.

in the same way as a nominal group can, e.g., *She is very bright / a very bright student*. However, this decision appears to ignore the fact that such expressions also function very frequently as the modifier in a nominal group, e.g., the underlined portion of *three very bright students*. In both cases the unit realizes the meaning of a **quality** of a **thing** — and so not the meaning of a 'thing'. It is not clear why, since Halliday is willing to allow the internal structure of *this morning* "to determine its primary syntactic assignment" (as we saw in Section 10.2.2) the internal structure of *very bright* should not also be allowed to determine its class of unit. The solution to the problem is clear: we should use the internal syntax and semantics of a unit to determine its class.

The second major difference between the two models is that the coverage of the nominal group in the Cardiff Grammar is considerably fuller than that in *IFG*. This is especially true with respect to the many types of determiner that it introduces and the concept of 'selection' that holds between them, e.g., as in *five of the ripest of those mangoes*. It also includes a full treatment of **compound nouns** — a very important category that is the source of many problems in text analysis and text generation. Halliday simply omits these from *IFG* (presumably on the grounds that the primary focus in *IFG* in on the clause, with groups and words receiving a much lighter treatment). For a fuller picture of the nominal group, see Appendix B and Fawcett (in press).

### 10.2.6 The prepositional group

The **prepositional group** has as its pivotal element a **preposition**, and it corresponds to the meaning of 'minor relationship with thing' at the level of semantics. It is tempting to rename the group with an explicitly functional label (e.g., the 'relator group'), but the formal term "preposition" is so strongly established that we shall not do this. (However, one 'preposition' in English is in fact a 'postposition', i.e., *ago* in examples such as *a year ago*.)

The element 'preposition' is typically expounded by an item from the word class with the same name, i.e., by a preposition. But occasionally it is filled by a quality group, as in the underlined portions of *very near the wall* and *more like his mother than he used to be*. (In this last example the quality group is discontinuous; see Section 11.7 of Chapter 11 for 'discontinuity'.) And in other cases the unit of the quantity group is 'borrowed' to express the internal structure within the prepositional element, as in *right into the corner*. The second major element is the **completive**, and this is practically always filled by one or more nominal groups; see Appendix B and, for a more complete picture of this unit, Fawcett (in press).

The equivalent term in *IFG* is not "prepositional group" but "prepositional phrase". Halliday has maintained a distinction between 'group' and 'phrase' from the very start, stating in "Categories" that it is needed to express a difference between classes of unit that is "so fundamental that it is useful to have two names for this unit" (1961:253). Interestingly, Kress (or Halliday?) has chosen to omit this passage from the 1976 version, perhaps because Halliday, unsatisfactorily, gives no reason for this intriguing claim. The reason is finally stated in *IFG*, i.e., that, "whereas a group is an expansion of a word, a phrase is a contraction of a clause" (1994:180). This offers a potentially interesting perspective on the distinction — as Halliday's ideas often do — but it is no self-evidently worthy of the epithet "fundamental".

Indeed, we might well ask what evidence there is to support the claim that a phrase is "a contraction of a clause". Halliday gives none, so we must look for it ourselves. (As we do so, however, we shall also dig up evidence for taking the contrary view.) The strongest evidence that I can think of is the fact that, when a prepositional group is functioning as the qualifier in nominal group, it often seems possible to 'expand' it to a clause. For example, the last two words of the title of the popular British TV programme *Neighbours from Hell* are a prepositional group or phrase, and this can be "expanded" into a clause by adding *who come* so that it reads *Neighbours who come from Hell*. However, if we follow this line of argument to its logical conclusion, we shall find ourselves deriving all modifiers from a clause that fills the qualifier, e.g., *friendly neighbours* from *neighbours who are friendly* — and so on for many other types of modifier. In other words, if Halliday is going to relate prepositional groups functioning as qualifiers to clauses, why not do the same with quality groups that are functioning as modifiers? (This is the road down which the transformational grammarians went in the early 1960s, and up which they later retreated in view of examples such as *the late president*.) Moreover, even if we consider only prepositional groups functioning as qualifiers, there are examples such as *young men with long hair* that cannot be 'expanded' (i.e., we shall not find examples such as *young men who are with long hair*). Finally, consider the even more frequent use of prepositional groups when they function as clause elements. In such cases there is normally no possibility of 'expanding' the group or phrase to a clause. For example, we can say *I'll put it in the box*, but we cannot expand *in the box* in any natural way into a clause.[10]

The conclusion must be that, within the linguistic description of a text, we should treat prepositional groups as syntactic units in their own right. In other words, we should not try to capture at the level of syntax the fact that the referents of *young men with long hair* are (probably) the same as the referents of *young men who have long hair*.

### 10.2.7 The quality group

The **quality group** has as its pivotal element (the **apex**) an **adjective** or an **adverb** (typically a **manner adverb**). The quality group corresponds to the semantic unit of 'quality'. However we should note that the 'quality' may be a quality of either a 'thing' (e.g., *clever*) or a 'situation' (e.g., *cleverly* in *He cleverly opened it with a paper clip*). Thus quality groups that refer to the quality of an object have an **adjective** as their apex, and quality groups that refer to an event have, typically, a **manner adverb** at their apex — but sometimes other classes of adverb, such as the 'usuality' adverb *often*.[11]

The term 'quality' is borrowed directly from the term used in the system network for the meanings that are realized in this unit. But, in a model of language in which the syntax is seen as the reflection of meaning, it is natural to introduce an explicitly functional label in this way. (The reason why this approach is not followed for the 'nominal' and 'prepositional' groups is that the labels that reflect the 'word class' tradition are so well established.) There is, of course, a long tradition in linguistics of using functional labels for categories

---

10. It is true that we can **replace** a prepositional group such as *at five o'clock* by a clause in *I'll call round when it's five o'clock* — but that is a replacement rather than an expansion. The utterance *I'll call round when it's at five o'clock* sounds very odd, and *I'll put it where it's in the box* sounds if anything even odder.

11. In some earlier systemic grammars the concept of 'adjectival' and 'adverbial' groups was explored. But the fact is that the system network of meanings and the elements of structure in syntax that it is necessary to set up to handle the type of 'quality group' with an **adjective** at its apex includes essentially the same types of meaning and structure that are needed for the type with a **manner adverb** at its apex. It is therefore appropriate to capture this significant overlap by modelling the two phenomena in the same system network and the same syntactic unit. Compare *He is <u>less slow than he used to be</u>* and *He climbed the stairs <u>less slowly than he used to climb them</u>*. See Tucker (1998) for the fullest and most persuasive account yet published of this area of meaning and form in any theoretical framework.

that are in fact the realizations of meanings (as the term 'nominal" originally was), and there is certainly no reason to avoid using such labels — especially in an explicitly functional grammar such as the present one.[12] This discussion illustrates nicely the important fact — which is often overlooked — that it is not only the elements that are functional, but also the units.

As we saw in Section 10.2.5, Halliday treats the type of unit that has an adjective as its 'pivotal element' as a 'nominal group' — despite the fact that its internal structure is clearly similar to that of his 'adverbial group'. Thus Halliday describes the group *very lucky* as a nominal group that has the adjective *lucky* as its "head" — while also stating that such units are "sometimes referred to distinctively as adjectival groups" (1994:194). However, a few pages later in *IFG* he also recognizes that examples such as *more easily* (and so presumably *very cleverly* too) are what he terms "adverbial groups", saying that they have a "modifier-head" structure. He recognizes that this class of unit may have the "postmodification" of "comparison" (1994:210) — and yet he fails to mention that a group with an adjective at its "head" may also have this type of "postmodification" — and indeed that both types of "quality group" may also have other elements (a **finisher** and one or two **scopes**) also, as Appendix B shows. This area of *IFG* appears, frankly, to be internally inconsistent and to require considerably more work. Perhaps the next edition of *IFG* will draw on the major contribution within SFL to this area by Tucker (1997 and 1998).

See Appendix B, Fawcett (in press) and especially Tucker (1998) for a fuller picture of the quality group.

### 10.2.8 The quantity group

The fourth and last class of group is the **quantity group.** This has as its pivotal element an expression of 'quantity'. It takes its name from the semantic unit of 'quantity' that it realizes, and the "quantity" that it refers to may be a quantity of a 'thing', a 'situation', a 'quality' or, perhaps surprisingly, a 'quantity' (as in the underlined portion of *very many more*) — and so to

---

12. It has been suggested that we might call the group the "adjective-adverb group" to preserve the parallelism with the "nominal group", but it seems more natural, in the framework of an explicitly functional grammar, to use a label that directly expresses the type of meaning that this unit expresses.

equivalent conceptual units.[13] (See Section 10.5.3 for a discussion of the role of 'word class' labels such as 'noun' and 'adjective' in this theory of syntax.)

There is no equivalent in *IFG* — nor in any other grammar that I know of — for the concept of the 'quantity group'. Halliday would probably handle the type of meaning that occurs as a Degree Adjunct (e.g., the underlined portion of *He loves her very much indeed*) as an 'adverbial group', because of its potential for functioning as an Adjunct.[14] Quantity groups in fact occur more frequently within nominal groups, as in *She hasn't smoked very many cigarettes today*, and it is not at all clear how this and the other types of quantity group illustrated in Appendix B would be handled in an *IFG*-style analysis.

Finally, we should note that here we use the quantity group to analyze structures for which Halliday introduces the two units of the 'conjunction group' and the 'preposition group' (1994:211-2). The purpose of the first is to handle the relatively rare cases of internal structure within Binders ("subordinating conjunctions") such as *almost as soon as* (where *as soon as* is the "conjunction"), and the second is for the equally rare case of structure within a preposition. I know of no cases where a Linker ('co-ordinating conjunction') has internal structure (items such as *and so*, and *and then* being treated as single items that include a space, like the preposition *in spite of*). Logically, in view of the 'rank scale' principle, an *IFG*-style analysis should treat every case of a one-word conjunction or preposition as an element of one or other of these two classes of group — but there is no sign that Halliday would in fact do so.

Note that Halliday's "preposition group" is a unit that fills a preposition,

---

13. The points made in the previous footnote about the use of the word "quality" as part of the label for the quality group apply equally to the quantity group. The difference is that here there is no standard name for the class of word that typically occurs as the pivotal element of the unit (unless we give this status to 'quantifier'). It may be this that accounts for the fact that no grammarian, till now, has proposed that we should recognize the existence of the 'quantity group' (except in a partial way in Fawcett (1974-6/81), where it was dealt with in a unit that was shared with 'quality', called the "quantity-quality group"; see Section 8.3 of Chapter 8).

14. In such cases, Halliday's stated criterion of the unit's ability to fill the relevant element in the unit above on the 'rank scale' would lead him to label this unit as an "adverbial group", but in cases such as the present one this criterion might be thought to be supported by the fact that in traditional grammar items such as *much* in such contexts are called "adverbs". However, the category of "adverb" in English is a 'ragbag', with items such as *very* also being traditionally classed as "adverbs", so these grounds are flimsy. It seems to respect the data more properly to introduce a unit that gives an appropriate weight to the concept of 'quantity' — as we do here.

and not, like our 'prepositional group', a unit that has a preposition as its pivotal element. Thus the meaning of its name runs counter to the pattern set by his use of the terms "nominal group", "verbal group" and "adverbial group". One of his few examples of a 'preposition group' is *right behind (the door)*.

In the Cardiff Grammar we take the view that it is not worth setting up two new units for such relatively rare cases, and we therefore 'borrow' the quantity group for use in modelling the internal structures of prepositions, Linkers and Binders — but only when there is an internal structure. Notice that, if one gives weight to the criterion of the internal structure of such units (as we do here), it would be odd to treat *immediately after* in *immediately after their visit to us* as a 'prepositional group', and *immediately after* in *immediately after they had visited us* as a 'conjunction group'. By using the quantity group in both cases we avoid setting up two completely new and little-used units for each of the preposition and the Binder.

For a slightly fuller picture of the quantity group, see the examples in Appendix B, and for a full description of this unit in English see Fawcett (in press). For the important concept of 'variation in depth of exponence' see Section 11.6.2 of Chapter 11.

10.2.9 Relationships between two major classes of unit and their 'higher' equivalents

I have referred in previous sections to correspondences between 'syntactic', 'semantic' and 'conceptual' units. Let us now consider the relationship between the syntactic units and their 'higher' equivalents. We shall focus upon the two main classes of syntactic unit: the **clause** and the **nominal group**.

How do these come to be generated? The answer is that they originate (typically) at the level of **logical form**, in the **planner** (which draws in turn on the **belief system**). They are typically represented as **events** and the **objects** that occur in events. These are then processed in the semantics, where an event is typically expressed as a **situation** and an object as a **thing** — and these in turn are then realized as a **clause** and a **nominal group**. However, there is not necessarily a one-to-one relationship between logical form, which is extralinguistic) and the intra-linguistic level of semantics. Figure 12 gives an overview of the two possibilities for **incongruent** correspondences between these.

| | | | |
|---|---|---|---|
| BELIEF SYSTEM | | event | object |
| expression | | typically expressed as | typically expressed as |
| LANGUAGE | MEANING | situation | thing |
| | realization | realized by | realized by |
| | FORM syntax, items, & intonation or punctuation | clause | nominal group |

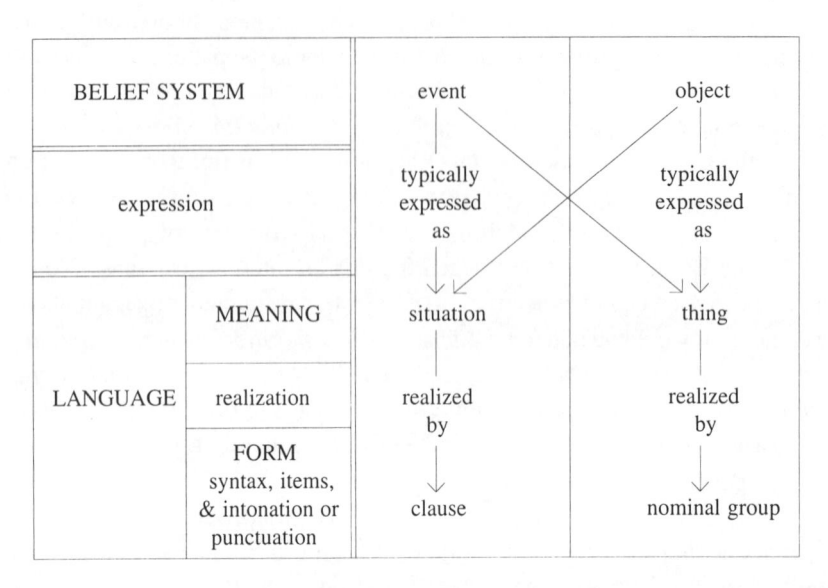

*Figure 12:*
*The relationships of logical form to semantics and syntax*

Figure 12 shows two of the main types of 'congruent' and 'incongruent' relationship, as they affect clauses and nominal groups. In the terminology of the Cardiff Grammar, the language **expresses** 'higher' beliefs (these being represented in logical form). Then, within language, forms **realize** meanings. Thus, if an **event** in the belief system is mapped onto a **situation** in the semantics (which will in turn be mapped onto a **clause** in the syntax at the level of form), then the relationship between the 'event' and the 'clause' is said to be **congruent** — a term introduced by Halliday (1970:149). However, an event can be incongruently realized as a nominal group, i.e., when 'nominalization' takes place, as in *his entering the room at that moment*. And an object can be incongruently realized as a clause, as in *what you gave me for my birthday*. While the nominalization of events is both the most frequent type of incongruence and the type with the most subtle variations, there are many others, such as the expression of a quality as a thing, e.g., *his great happiness*.

Halliday discusses such phenomena under the general heading of "grammatical metaphor" (e.g., Halliday 1994:340f.). However, the scope of the term has become very broad, and I find it more helpful to think in terms of specific types of phenomena. Thus, nominalization occurs within experiential meaning, so that it is a different matter from the **experientialization** of non-experiential meaning — e.g., saying *It's possible that he'll be there* rather than *He may be there*. See Fawcett (in press) for a rather fuller picture of these relationships.

## 10.2.10 The concept of 'cluster'

This unit of syntax is not found in any other grammatical framework. Yet the fact is that there are frequently occurring units in English syntax that have the characteristics of the classes of unit to be described below. Perhaps I may add, in support of the proposals put forward here, that most other grammarians simply do not say how they would handle, in a systematic manner, the syntax of the types of phenomena for which the various classes of cluster are used.[15]

Clusters are a special set of units whose function is to carry complex meanings associated with two elements of the **nominal group** in particular: the deictic determiner and the head. It seems that the semantics of referring to things is so complex that we regularly need to introduce units within the nominal group, and embedded groups of all classes therefore occur quite frequently within the nominal group. (For the concept of 'embedding' see Sections 11.8.3 to 11.8.5 of Chapter 11.) But certain classes of unit that occur within the nominal group can only occur within this unit (with one rare exception). We term these units **clusters**.

The reason why clusters occur within the nominal group is that the types of meaning that they express are inherently 'enrichments' of certain types of meaning that are inherently associated with things. Thus they do not realize meanings that can also be elements of situations, as groups do, so that they can never function as direct elements of the clause. They are therefore effectively sub-units of the nominal group. In this way, then, they are quite different from the four classes of group, all of which can fill various elements in various units.

As a consequence of the fact that they function within the nominal group, clusters can never function as referring expressions, as clauses and groups can.

---

15. In my experience, the need to recognize these units only becomes imperative (1) when one is working with a functional theory of syntax in which the criteria for recognizing a unit in are made fully explicit (as they are here) and (2) when there is a serious commitment to the full analysis of large quantities of naturally occurring text. The need to attend to individual orthographic words is also increased when one tries to build a computer model that parses a text consisting of a string of words into its functional syntax.

In other words, they can never be the answer to a question such as *Who's this?*, *Where do you live?* etc. (See Section 10.2.4 of Chapter 10.)

In the next two sub-sections I shall briefly describe two classes of cluster, and then, because these will be unfamiliar as syntactic units to most readers, I shall briefly present reasons for treating them as clusters rather than as groups.

10.2.11 The genitive cluster

The first of the two classes of cluster in English is the **genitive cluster** (genclr). This always fills either (1) the deictic determiner (dd) of a nominal group, (2) the head (h) or, less frequently, (3) a modifier (m), as in the underlined portion of *a girl's bike*, where the meaning is 'a bike that is suitable for a girl'), or (infrequently) (4) the type of deictic that occurs in a quality group (qld), as in *my sister's most precious doll*.[16] The two most frequent elements of a genitive cluster are the **possessor (po)** and the **genitive** element **(g)**. The possessor is typically filled by a nominal group (and occasionally by two or more co-ordinated nominal groups), and the possessor is always and only filled by the morpheme *'s* (or, after certain word endings, just an apostrophe, as in *the Jones' dog*).

Thus this cluster has the unusual characteristic that one of its two main elements is typically filled by a group and the other is always expounded by a morpheme.

Note however that, despite the small size of the item expounding the genitive element, it serves a function that is equivalent to a preposition, through its expression of the relationship of 'generalized possession' (i.e., 'part-whole' relationships, etc, as well as 'ownership'). Compare *the dog's back legs* and *the back legs of the dog*. It is the fact that (1) nominal groups such as *the dog* undeniably occur within the unit of that we are here calling the "genitive cluster" and (2) the genitive element *'s* functions as a 'relator' to the whole nominal group (and not just *dog*) that has led to the introduction to the grammar of the present unit. See Appendix B and, for a slightly fuller picture of this unit, Fawcett (in press).

---

16. It is not the case, of course, that **all** deictic determiners and heads are filled by genitive clusters; there are choices in the system network that lead to **either** the direct exponence of an element by an item (e.g., *the*) **or** to re-entry to the network, in order to generate a cluster (e.g., *this university's*). See Section 11.6.2 of Chapter 6 for 'variation in depth of exponence'.

10.2.12  The 'name' clusters

The **human proper name cluster** (hpnclr) always and only fills the head of a nominal group. Three of its most frequent elements are **title (t)**, one or more **forenames (f1, f2,** etc), and the **family name (fn)**. Other classes of cluster also name objects, e.g., the **address, date**, and **clock time clusters**. See Fawcett (in press) for more details of these.

Occasionally, when a cluster fills the head of a nominal group and there is no other element in it, the cluster may at first appear to function as a direct element of the clause. Examples of the two classes of cluster described here can be seen in the underlined portions of *This is my father's* or *She admired Sir Terence Conran*. But this is not evidence that they are functioning directly as elements of the clause, any more than is the occurrence of the items *his* in *This is his* and *him* in *She admired him*. These are all simply cases of what is termed "singularly branching". Compare examples such as *He's not the Terence Conran who I knew twenty years ago*.

## 10.3  Elements of structure

10.3.1  The basic principle

The concept of **element of structure** (or **element** for short) is the second of the three fundamental categories in syntax in the present framework (the others being **class of unit** and **item**). The term "element (of structure)" and the term "structure" are used here in broadly the same sense as in "Categories" — but with two important provisos that I shall mention below.

Elements of structure are the immediate components of classes of units. The main characteristic of an element is that it is defined functionally, rather than positionally. This should surely be a founding principle of a functional approach to syntax — and yet the tradition of using positional labels still lingers on in many functional grammars.[17] (The question of the 'position' of an

---

17. For example, terms such as 'pre-deictic' and 'pre-numerative' (as found in Halliday 1994:195-6) are simply positional labels. Rather similarly, the terms 'premodifier' and 'postmodifier' (Halliday 1994:194-5), signal a positional meaning more strongly than they signal a functional meaning. This is because, at Halliday's primary level of delicacy in the analysis of a nominal group, the term 'modifier' means little more than 'anything other than

element in a unit is attended to in Section 10.4, through the concept of 'place'.)

Appendix B summarizes the main elements that occur in each of the five major units of English (and also in the genitive cluster — a class of 'cluster' that may itself contain a nominal group). In the present section I shall state the general principles that underlie the concept of the 'element of structure' as the term is used here.

The basic principle is, as stated above, that an element is defined in terms of its function in expressing meaning. This has two important consequences for describing languages.

The first is the principle that **every element in a given class of unit serves a different function in that unit.** Sometimes, as in the case of the different types of modifier in an English nominal group, the differences between the functions of elements appear to be very slight — but they are always there.[18] Sometimes, when an element serves one of several functions (three at least in the case of the head of a nominal group), a more general — but still functional — label such as "head" must be used.

The second important consequence is that, since every syntactic unit realizes a different class of semantic entity, we should expect that, in principle, **every element in every class of unit will be different from every element in every other class of unit.** Thus we shall not use the terms "modifier" and "head" for more than one class of unit, as some form-centred grammars do (sometimes supplemented by other general, quasi-functional terms such as "complement", "adjunct" and "specifier"). Here the terms "head" and "modifier" are used only for nominal groups. So elements in the structure of other groups that may at first appear to be partially equivalent to the "modifier' and "head" of a nominal group are given different names, e.g., "temperer" and

the head'. So these terms give virtually no information about the element's function. However, I must admit to retaining one traditional 'positional' label in the Cardiff Grammar, i.e., 'preposition'. As said in Section 10.2.6, I would have preferred an explicitly functional label, but terms such as 'relator' are not specific enough, and we retain the traditional term "preposition" both because there is a lack of a clear alternative and because it is so strongly established. We define it as functioning to express a 'minor relationship with a thing'. Note that in the description of English one item that actually occurs 'postpositionally' is included as a 'preposition' — i.e *ago*, as in *five years ago*.

18. If there is no differences at all between the function served by two units, as with *scrumptious* and *delicious* in *(That was) a superbly scrumptious, dead delicious sweet*, they should be treated as two co-ordinated units that fill the same element.

"apex" in the quality group. The reason is simple: they express different meanings. Thus the head of a nominal group such as *large houses* tells us the 'cultural classification' of the object in terms of the culture associated with the language, and the modifier *large* tells us 'what sort' of thing it is (here, specifically 'what size' it is). But the apex in a quality group such as *very stupid* tells us that the 'quality' is 'stupid' and the temperer *very* tells us the 'quantity' of that 'quality'. The important generalization is that each element of structure appears — in principle — in one (and only one) class of unit, and this holds good both within each unit and across the different classes of unit.

The principle that each element in a unit realizes a different type of meaning brings with it the great advantage that it makes text analysis easier. This is because, once you have worked out what **element** an item expounds, you typically also know automatically what **class of unit** the element belongs to. This advantage applies both to human text analysts (perhaps consulting a summary of the syntax of English such as Appendix B) and to a computer parser of text-sentences, e.g., as built for the COMMUNAL Project (Weerasinghe & Fawcett 1993 and Weerasinghe 1994).

10.3.2 Some exceptions to the basic principle

However, there are a few exceptions to the basic principle, i.e., cases where an element occurs in several different classes of unit. But in all such cases this is because a higher principle is at work, as we shall see. The exception that is met most frequently is the element **Linker (&)** — or **linker** (with a lower case "l") in groups and clusters. This is expounded by *and, or,* etc, and such items occur at (or near) the start of any unit. (However, some of the items that expound them, such as *but* and *so,* only occur with some units.)

The second item of this type is the **inferer** element. This may occur in any class of **group**, and is expounded by *even, only* and *just*. (When these items occur in a clause with a similar meaning they expound the **Inferential Adjunct**.)

These two elements are always expounded by **items**, but the present model also includes punctuation (and intonation, which we shall not discuss further here). Two elements that are expounded by **punctuation marks** in written text are the **starter** and the **ender.** These can occur in any unit. The starter only occurs in an embedded unit, and it is expounded by a comma, a

216     A THEORY OF INSTANCES: CATEGORIES

dash or a bracket, while the ender occurs with both embedded and unembedded units, and it is expounded by a wide range of punctuation marks — but most frequently by a full stop at the end of a clause (as shown in Appendix B). And there are equivalent exponents of the starter and ender in spoken text.[19]

There is a good reason why, in all of these cases, the same element is permitted in more than one unit. It is that the same meaning is carried in relation to the entity being expressed, e.g., 'co-ordination' of one of several types in the case of the Linker. So, with the exception of these well-motivated cases, the principle that a unit and its elements of structure are mutually defining holds good.[20]


10.3.3  What is the relationship between elements in a unit?

What is the relationship between one element and its 'sister' elements in a unit? This has been a major focus of interest for some grammarians, leading to arguments about whether such relationships are those of 'daughter dependency' or 'sister dependency' (e.g., Hudson 1976). (For a brief comparison of the two, see Section 11.2 of Chapter 11.) Here I offer a new answer to the question asked above. It is one that follows directly from the adoption of the framework outlined in Chapter 2 and exemplified in Appendix A.

Let us take as an example the relationship between a modifier and the head in the English nominal group. In the framework of a systemic functional grammar the relationship is not, I suggest, the direct one that form-centred grammarians consider it to be. In formal and traditional grammars, it is simply assumed that what the modifier modifies is the head. Here, however, the general function of the modifiers in a nominal group is regarded as being **to describe the referent**. (See Fawcett (in press) for the sub-types of 'descrip-

---

19. The meanings of intonation are realized, like the meanings of punctuation, in items (in a broad sense of the term) including those that expound the starter and the ender. For a general account of the model of intonation in the Cardiff Grammar, see Tench (1996), and for a description of the first stage of its implementation in COMMUNAL, see Fawcett (1970).

20. To complete the picture, it should be said that there are two elements that occur in a quality group when it is being used to express a 'superlative' or 'ordinative' meaning, which have considerable similarities to the deictic determiner and the quantifying modifier in the nominal group, e.g., as in the use of *the* and *two* in the underlined portion of <u>*the most interesting two*</u> *of Shakespeare's plays* See Appendix B for the names of the elements.

tion' that the various sub-types of modifier express, e.g., 'colour modifiers', 'affective modifiers', 'general epithet modifiers' etc.) Similarly, the function of the head of the nominal group is (assuming that it is a noun) to state the 'cultural classification' of the referent. The referent is thus the object to which the **nominal group** refers, and it is the function of the noun at the head of the nominal group to express what Lyons (1977:206-7) terms the "denotation" (of some class of 'thing'). In other words, the head realizes one type of meaning that relates to the referent, while the modifier realizes another. So both the modifier and the head relate, via the meanings they express, to the referent — but **they are related only indirectly to each other**. Thus a modifier does not in fact 'modify' (or 'describe') the head; it modifies (or describes) the referent which the head denotes.

This general principle applies to all 'sister' relationships between elements, and it applies to all units. From this viewpoint, the question of whether an element is dependent on a 'sister' element such as the 'head' or on a 'mother' unit is beside the point; the 'dependency' is not in fact 'syntactic' at all, and what we observe in syntax is the realization of dependence in the system networks.

### 10.3.4 Are 'secondary structures' (a) necessary and/or (b) desirable?

Let us now address the question of how far we need, in a modern SF grammar, the "more delicate differentiations" in "structure" that Halliday introduces in "Categories" (1961/76:63). There the 'primary' structure of the nominal group was said to be "M H Q", i.e., "modifier + head + qualifier", and the distinctions within the "modifier" between "deictic", "numerative" and "epithet", etc., were said to be a matter of 'secondary' structure.

The first point to make is that these "secondary structures" do not — in principle at least — constitute another layer of structure in the representation. Halliday emphasizes that they are "still structures of the same unit, not of the unit next below" — the key point being that "they take account of finer distinctions recognizable at the same rank" (by which he means "in the same unit"). However, the fact is that when he introduces such "secondary structures" to the representation of a text-sentence alongside the "primary structures", he adds another line to the analysis — as the presence of two lines of analysis for MOOD in Figure 7 in Chapter 7 clearly illustrates. Indeed, every finite clause in *IFG* is analyzed terms of (1) its "Mood" and "Residue", and then within the "Mood" (2) its "Subject" and "Finite".

If the line showing the "Mood" and "Residue" is removed from such diagrams, the display of the analysis becomes simpler to read, while still preserving the essential insight that it is the relationship of the Subject and the Finite that is the primary expression of the meaning of MOOD. In other words, I am suggesting here that the additional layer of analysis into "Mood" and "Residue" detracts from the insightfulness of the diagram rather than adding to it. Figure 10 illustrates the way in which the semantic information can be extracted directly from the relationship of the Subject and Operator (or Finite). A similar argument applies to the *IFG* analysis of Theme, as in Halliday (1994:55). Here the analyses frequently show three layers of structure within one strand of meaning for the 'theme' meanings in a clause.[21] So, while Halliday may claim that the concept of "secondary structure" does not add another layer of structure, in constituency terms, it does add one or more additional lines of analysis to virtually every representation of a clause.

Thus Halliday continues to use the "Categories" concept of having a 'primary', 'secondary' and if necessary a 'tertiary' structure within each strand of text analysis. However, it is not clear how far this concept still has its former central role in Halliday's current theory. While it is not mentioned in the summary of "Systemic theory" given in Halliday (1993), it is there by implication in his realization operation "Split" (for a discussion of which see Section 9.2.3 of Chapter 9). And the concept that there is a 'primary' and a 'secondary' structure plays a fairly prominent role in the examples of clause analysis in *IFG*, often appearing twice in the analysis of a single clause (once for MOOD and once for THEME, whenever there is a case of 'multiple Theme'). Its main justification seems to be that it is thought to add insight to the description. (The theory does not require it, as I have shown in Section 9.2.3 of Chapter 9).

In my view, then, it is unhelpful to have 'primary' and 'secondary' struct-

---

21. The *IFG* example is *Well but then Ann surely wouldn't the best idea be to join the group?* It is hard to see why any analysis other than the third and most delicate is required in such cases of multiple Theme. It is unhelpful to imply that all of the thematized elements constitute "the theme" in any semantically unified sense. Similarly, there is little point in giving a line of analysis to showing where two or more happen to share a metafunction. The fact is that several different elements of the clause all happen to have been "thematized" at the same time, each for its own reason. (However, I should add that I do not consider all of the 'early' elements in the above example to be thematized, in that the items *well*, *but*, *then* and *wouldn't* are **not** early in the clause because of a systemic choice. But since there are also several genuinely 'thematized' elements, my point remains relevant to that example.)

ures in the representation of a clause. Firstly, it implies that elements form a 'multiple element', when the evidence from the syntactic distribution of the elements themselves shows that they do not. Secondly, they risk introducing misunderstandings about the number of 'strands of meaning' in a clause.

However, while the concept of 'more delicate structure' has no place in a modern theory of SF syntax, I have to admit that the Cardiff Grammar's description of English still contains a few historical remnants of the concept. One is found in the convention that the term "modifier" is used as the second part of the names of many different elements in the nominal group, e.g., the "affective modifier", the "epithet modifier", and so on. And the same goes for Adjuncts and, to a lesser extent, determiners in the nominal group and Auxiliaries in the clause. (See Appendix B for examples.) Moreover, at the introductory level of text description we simply use "m" for all the different types of 'modifier', "X" for the different types of 'Auxiliary Verb', and so on.

A more general reason why we should expect the use of the concept of 'secondary structure' to wither away in modern SF grammars is that we now have much fuller functional descriptions of languages than those that were available when Halliday was writing "Categories". The result is that it no longer feels adequate simply to label all the elements that precede the head in a nominal group as a single 'modifier', or to label all the thematized elements in a case of multiple Theme as a single Theme. In *IFG*, for example, we would not find a nominal group such as *that lovely porcelain vase from China that you broke last week me* being analyzed as if it had just three elements of structure at the 'primary' degree of delicacy (i.e., Modifier, Head and Qualifier, as these terms are used in "Categories"). Instead it would be analyzed immediately into its supposedly 'secondary' structure, i.e., as having (in *IFG* terms) a Deictic, an Epithet, a Classifier, a Head and two Qualifiers.


10.3.5 Summary of the discussion of 'element of structure'

In developing a SF grammar, both for very large computer implementations and for text analysis, priority must be given to the "most delicate" possible of structural descriptions, because a full account of the meaning potential of a unit (such as a clause) requires statements about each element **in its own right**. It is the individual elements of a unit that carry the different meanings that are the focus of interest for a functional grammarian. For example, the fact that the main mood meanings of a clause are realized by the configuration of the Subject and Operator is best shown by stating the semantic feature that generates this configuration in an analysis of the meaning potential of the clause, as in Figure 10 in Chapter 7 (rather than introducing an additional layer of structure as part of its syntax, as in the case of "Mood + Residue" in *IFG*). Moreover, the representation of any layers of structure other than the one that reflects directly the choices in the system networks is redundant. (It is not even useful for pedagogical purposes, since it is misleading to suggest that a string of elements of structure that function as the realizations of a set of individually chosen meanings are in some sense "a single element".)

An elements of structure should be defined in terms of the **function** it serves, i.e., by the aspect of the meaning of the unit that it expresses, rather than by its position in the unit. Since each element in each unit realizes a different type of meaning, it should have a different label. The position of an element in its unit is a matter that is handled separately, through the concept of 'place' — the concept that is to be discussed in the next section.

## 10.4 Places and potential structures

10.4.1 The need for the category of 'place'

Elements, as we have seen, are the 'components' of units. However, there is another category that intervenes between a unit and its elements. This is the concept of the **places** in a unit. In other words, **elements occur at places in units**.

In the analysis of texts the places are usually omitted (as in Figure 10 in Chapter 7). However, in the full, generative version of the grammar they play an essential role, as in Figure 13 in Section 10.4.4 below, and as illustrated in the generation of a text-sentence in Fawcett, Tucker & Lin (1993).

Like a number of other concepts that are central in a modern SF grammar (such as the concept of 'system' itself and 'lexis as most delicate grammar') the concept of 'place' can be found in "Categories" (as I pointed out in Section 2.3 of Chapter 2). The word is used rather than defined as a central concept, but its use there seems to be consistent with the sense in which it is used here.

## 10.4.2 Alternative ways to locate an element in its place

Systemic functional linguists have explored two ways of locating elements in an appropriate sequential relationship to each other in a unit. The first — which may at first sight appear to be the simplest — is to locate each element in its 'place' by relating it to some previously located element. This approach depends crucially on the existence of what we might term an 'anchor' element in each unit, i.e., the existence of a 'pivotal' element that is always present. It was this method that Halliday used in his seminal first description of a generative SF grammar (Halliday 1969/81). Surprisingly, references to this as a method of sequencing elements in a SF grammar are still found in current descriptions by Halliday (1993: 5405) and Matthiessen (1995: 23-4).

I say "surprisingly" because, when Mann and Matthiessen were working on the large-scale computer implementation of Halliday's SF grammar in the Penman Project in the late 1970s, this approach caused problems. When faced with the additional complexities of building an large, generative grammar, they found that in practice they had to turn to the second method — to which we shall come in a moment (Matthiessen, personal communication).

The problem with the first method is that if, in a given instance, the element that is used as the 'anchor' point for placing another element were to be either missing from the unit or located in an untypical position in it, then the statement for placing any 'dependent' element in the structure would become much longer. This is because it would have to include a set of conditional rules, whose role would be to specify what should be done under various possible scenarios if the 'anchor' element were **not** to be both (1) present and (2) in its typical place. And these conditional rules would become exponentially more complex as the grammar was extended to handle the great range of possible variations in the sequence of elements in the English clause that occurs in natural language texts — especially in the varying positions of the various types of Adjunct. Indeed, it is only practicable to use this first approach in a highly limited sub-set of cases — i.e., (1) where the grammar is small (e.g., one that has been developed for illustrative purposes such as that in Halliday 1969/81) and (2) where every unit recognized in the grammar has at least one element that is both (a) obligatorily present and (b) always occurs in the same position.

The crucial test case in English for this approach is the clause. The fact is that there is an enormous variety of sequences in which the elements of the English clause may come — both absolutely and in relation to each other. But the first question is whether there is any element that it always present and always in one position. The only candidate for this 'anchor' role is the Main Verb — but the places at which it occurs do in fact vary. The most frequent reason for this variation is that, when it is expounded by a form of the verb *be*, it is often conflated with the Operator. Consider the two positions of the Main Verb *is* in *Ivy is here* and *Is Ivy here?* Clearly, the Main Verb in the second example precedes the Subject *Ivy*. There is in fact no element in the English clause that is (1) always located at the same place and (2) always present. And the situation with respect to the groups in English is similar, e.g., the head of a nominal group and the apex of a quality group are not obligatory, as the relevant sections of Fawcett (in press) show.[22]

The second method of generating elements in their appropriate sequence is to use a simple 'list' of sequentially ordered places at which elements may be located, identified by numbers as "Place 1", "Place 2", etc. This concept was first introduced to SFL in Fawcett (1973/81), and it was adopted from the start in the COMMUNAL Project as the simplest and most elegant solution to the

---

22. As an illustration of the concept that there is merely a very strong probability that a clause will have a Main Verb, consider the underlined portions of the following: (1) *I wished that my tea had been hot*, (2) *I wanted my tea to be hot* and (3) *I wanted my tea hot*. It seems clear that we would wish to generate (3) in a way that shows that it is systemically close to (2), despite the fact that the dependent clause in (3) lacks a Main Verb. Rather similarly, while there is a very strong probability that a nominal group will have a head, some nominal groups do not. We could, if we wished, set up the grammar in such a way that every unit must have a 'head' (as is done in 'head-driven' models of syntax). But such grammars run into problems when they try to expand beyond canonical examples that clearly have such 'heads'. Consider the case of nominal groups such as *two* and *the very rich* in examples such as *Give me two* and *I don't envy the very rich*. In the Cardiff Grammar we generate *two* in the nominal group *Give me two* by the same rule that we generate *two* in *Give me two of them*, i.e., *two* is a quantifying determiner in both cases, and in the first the head is simply unrealized. But if we were to decide that we wished to say that *two* in *Give me two* was a head, we would need to have a realization statement of the form: 'If Feature A is selected the realization is X, but if Feature B is selected the realization is Y', in order to cover the cases where *of them* was and was not made overt. The realization rules for cardinals are already quite complicated (to accommodate cases such as *around fifty, five thousand two hundred, over five thousand two hundred* etc.), and it is therefore preferable to avoid the unnecessary additional complication of having *two* (and so every other cardinal) expound two different elements. And the same general principle applies to *the very rich, the poor, the old and infirm*, etc. (As is well-known, such examples do not lend themselves to an explanation in terms of ellipsis.) Similar principles apply to the clause. On these grounds (and others) it is greatly preferable to build into the grammar the possibility of having occasional nominal groups that have no head and clauses that have no Main Verb. Allowing for this avoids losing many useful generalizations such as those identified above. Note, however, that this is only possible when the grammar works by locating elements at places, rather than relying on the presence of some "anchor" element in relation to which all other elements are ordered.

problem. It was later also adopted by Mann and Matthiessen for the Penman Project, as we have seen. In this approach, the realization rule that inserts each element must also specify the place at which the element is to be located. (In the computer implementation, those places that are not used are simply stripped away before printing out the structure.)

The use of **places** therefore provides a mechanism for sequencing elements that is both simple and yet also capable of handling an immense amount of variation in the sequence of elements.[23] It is essentially an 'enabling' device, in the sense that the places do not have an explicitly functional significance in the theory — unlike all of the other concepts introduced here. Yet the concept of 'place' is an essential category in the theory, because without it the grammar would not work. In particular, it provides the vital concept, as we shall see in Section 10.4.4, in modelling the so-called 'raising' phenomena.

### 10.4.3 Potential structures

So far we have been focussing on the role of places in the clause. Now let us look at the way in which sequential relationships between elements are modelled in the other units. Strictly speaking, this takes us out of the theory of **instances of syntax** and back to the theory of **syntax potential**, and so to Section 9.2.2 of Chapter 9, but it will be useful to reconsider the concept here, in relation to the categories of 'element' and 'place'.

The fact is that in many languages the elements of certain classes of units occur in a fixed sequence (or in an almost fixed sequence). In English this is true of all classes of groups and clusters, but not the clause. We saw in Section 9.2.3 of Chapter 9 that there is an important consequence of the fact that groups and clusters have very little variation in the sequence of their elements. This is that the grammar can avoid introducing an operation to locate an element of structure at a given place in sequence whenever one is introduced by the use of **potential structures**.

There is a second use for the potential structures. In this case, however, it is not as a part of the theory, but as a contribution to the text-descriptive strand

---

[23]. It may be of interest to say that, because of the great variation in the places at which elements occur in the English clause, the number of such places is in the hundreds (about 250 in the current GENESYS grammar).

of work in SFL. In other words, it is the potential structures from the 'syntax potential' of the GENESYS generator that form the basis for the valuable summary descriptions of the syntax of the groups in English that are found in Appendix B.[24]

In English, every unit except the clause makes use of a potential structure of this type. The nearest equivalent to a 'potential structure' for the clause is its a numbered list of places, but since this list makes no claim about the nature of the clause, it does not provide the same insights into the structure of English as the potential structures for the groups and clusters.[25]

Thus potential structures are, from the theoretical perspective, simply an economical way of specifying places. They enable the grammar to avoid having to locate every element of a group at a place in a unit every time that an element is added to the structure. From the practical viewpoint of the text analyst, however, they enable us to make extremely useful summarizing statements of the type shown in Appendix B. Indeed, it is even possible to capture many of the more frequent variations in the clause by an informal application of the concept to this very different unit, as you will see if you inspect the structure of the clause shown in Appendix B.

10.4.4 The key role of 'place' in handling 'raising' phenomena

However, there is one aspect of syntax where the concept of 'place' assumes major theoretical importance. It is when a **place** in one unit — in practice, always a clause — is occupied by **an element from a lower unit**. This phenomenon occurs in cases such as *Who were you seen by?*, *Who did*

---

24. I first introduced the concept of what I now call a **potential structure** under the name of "starting structure" in Fawcett (1973/81). For the fullest explanation of the rationale for the concept of the 'potential structure', see Fawcett (1980:47-8 and 115f.)

25. It is important to emphasize (especially to those interested in building SF parsers) that it is not the task of the potential structures to specify what elements can co-occur with what other elements. In generation, this is achieved through the design of the system networks (supplemented at times by conditions in the realization rules). Potential structures simply specify the **sequence** in which the elements occur, **if those elements are activated by the realization rules**. Their sole purpose is to avoid the unnecessary use of the 'insertion' operation in the realization rules. For example, the potential structure for the nominal group specifies what place the head will occur at, this being unchanged, whatever item expounds it.

# A THEORY OF INSTANCES: CATEGORIES

*you give it to?*, *Where did you say you put it?* and so on.

Consider the first example, the analysis of which is shown in Figure 13. Here, the initial item *who* fills Place 28 in the clause. This is the place at which 'sought' elements (realized as *wh*-items) typically occur. However, the element *who* is not an element of the clause, but of the prepositional group that fills the Complement. In other words, in this example it has been made to occupy a place in the unit above the unit of which it is an element.

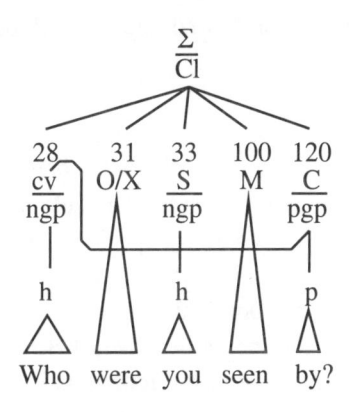

*Figure 13:*
*The use of the concept of 'place' to handle 'raising' phenomena*

Formal linguists use the transformational metaphor of 'raising' to describe such phenomena, and in their terms an element of the lower unit in the tree diagram is said to have been "raised" to occur in the structure of the higher unit of the clause. If we use that term here, it should not be interpreted as implying that a transformational 'movement rule' has been applied, (any more than it does when we said that an Adjunct is "thematized"). The meaning is simply that the element of the completive (cv) is made to occur in a position that is 'higher in the tree diagram' than its unmarked place in its own unit.

Essentially the same principles apply in the analysis of examples such as *Who did you say you saw there?* (See Section 11.7 of Chapter 11 for the concept of **discontinuity**, and see Fawcett (in press) for the analysis of these and other types of discontinuity.

It is important to emphasize that in such cases the "raised" element does not actually become an **element** of that higher unit; it simply occupies a **place** in that unit. As will now be clear, it is the fact that the theory contains the concept of 'place' as well as 'element' and 'class of unit' that makes it possible to handle this otherwise problematical phenomenon in a principled manner. It is not clear from the published works of Halliday, Matthiessen etc. how such problems would be handled in the Sydney Grammar, either descriptively or in a generative version of the grammar.

## 10.5 Items, the concept of 'word class' and morphology

### 10.5.1 Items

The third of the three major categories in the present theory of syntax (with 'unit' and 'element') is the **item**. This term includes both 'word' (in its traditional sense) and 'morpheme'. Strictly speaking, the concept of 'item' lies outside syntax, since items are a different manifestation of meanings at the level of **form** from syntax. The four manifestations are: (1) **items** (words or morphemes, their relationship being described below); (2) **syntax** (i.e., the concepts that define relations between items), and (3) either **intonation** or **punctuation** (depending on whether the text is spoken or written). However, we need to bring the concept of 'items' into the picture to complete the account of syntax, because syntax only ends when elements are expounded by items.

In the present theory of syntax, the lowest syntactic category on each branch of the tree in a tree diagram representation of a sentence is an **element** (e.g., the head of a nominal group). And each such lowest element is expounded by an **item** — or as we shall see shortly, by **items** (in the plural).

Notice, then, that an element such as the head of a nominal group is not 'filled' by the unit of the 'word', as it would be in "Categories" and, in principle, in *IFG*. (In practice, however, elements of groups are almost always shown in *IFG* as being expounded directly by words, roughly as advocated here — the reason being that the description in *IFG d*oes not go below the 'rank' of the 'group' (which of course includes its elements).

Items are quite different from the other categories that we have discussed so far, because they do not have an internal structure that it relevant to a generative grammar and so have, in spoken language, what Firth calls "phonetic and phonological 'shape'" (1957/68:183). (He also introduces the term "graphic exponents" for what he terms the "companion study" of written language.) It is precisely the fact that they have a phonological or graphological shape that differentiates them from the relatively more abstract categories of syntax that we have been considering in the earlier sections of this chapter.

### 10.5.2 Words and morphemes as elements of clauses

As we shall now see, languages vary quite considerably in how soon, as one moves down the layers of structure in the representation of a text-sentence, one escapes the abstract categories of syntax and reaches the first category that has the phonological or graphological "shape" of an item.

Halliday's concept of the 'rank scale' predicts, as we saw first in Chapter 2, that elements of clauses should be filled by groups. In the view of language taken here, however, elements of the clause are frequently expounded directly by items. In Fawcett (2000 and forthcoming b), I set out the many reasons why we should treat certain elements of the clause in English as being expounded directly by items. I suggest, for example, that modal verbs such as *may* and *might* directly expound the Operator (which is very broadly equivalent to Halliday's "Finite") and that lexical verbs such as *love* and *walk* directly expound the Main Verb. Thus in *Don't be caught!* all three items expound elements of the clause.

I should make it clear that the more complex grammatical morphologies of agglutinating languages — such as Japanese, Mohawk and Swahili — are also explicitly provided for in the theory, as also are inflectional languages. Indeed, in such languages morphemes function as direct elements of the clause. Consider the case of the Swahili expression *alimwona*. From the viewpoint of English *alimwona* appears to be a single word (and would probably be classed as a verb). Orthographically, of course, it is indeed a single word. Yet this 'word' expresses a rich series of meanings associated with an 'event', including the Process, the Participants in the Process, and the Time of the event. In a morpheme-by-morpheme translation, its meaning is roughly 'he/she + past + him/her + see', i.e., 'he/she saw him/her'. In other words, it contains elements that correspond roughly to the English clause elements of Subject, Auxiliary, Complement and Main Verb (though it should not be assumed that these would be appropriate names for the elements in Swahili). In a description of Swahili that uses the present theory of syntax, then, **morphemes** (here *a, li, mu* and *ona*) would be treated as expounding directly the elements of the **clause**.

Halliday originally proposed the concept of the 'rank scale' on the basis, one assumes, of his work on describing Chinese and English. In Section 4 of Appendix C I summarize the paper in which I show why the elements of the 'verbal group' proposed by Halliday for English should instead be treated as direct elements of the clause — and so, therefore, why words should be permitted to expound directly elements of the clause (Fawcett 2000 and forthcoming b). However, the example from Swahili suggests that a functional description of an agglutinating language requires a model in which the elements of clauses are allowed to be expounded by 'units' that are, in terms of the "Categories" concept of the 'rank scale', not two but three steps down the 'scale' — i.e., not by words, as I claim happens in English, but directly by morphemes.[26] Thus a general theory of syntax should provide that, when it is used for describing languages such as Japanese, Mohawk and Swahili, certain elements of clauses may be directly expounded by morphemes. See Tatsuki (1998) for a SF analysis of the Japanese clause in these terms.

There is one final point to be made about the representation of morphology — at least in English and other languages with little or no inflectional morphology. In English (and probably in all such languages) it is in fact possible to represent all of the structures that occur in such a way that there is no need to introduce the 'word' as a syntactic unit — i.e., as a unit with an internal structure of elements such as 'prefix', 'base' and 'suffix', each of which is in turn expounded by an item. And yet such a grammar is still able to show that, in a 'word-form' such as *eating*, the items *eat* and *ing* are the realizations of different choices in the system network, and that in the word *boys* the items *boy* and *s* are similarly the realizations of different meanings.

How is this achieved? The grammar's rules for generation simply show that each of the lowest elements in the tree diagram (e.g., the head of a nominal group) is **expounded** by an item (a 'free morpheme'). Then, whenever it is needed, another item (a 'bound morpheme') is simply added to the head as a further exponent of it. In this way we achieve the same effect that we would if we first generated an abstract unit (e.g., the word class 'noun'), and then gave it two elements (which we might call 'base' and 'suffix'), and then expounded each element by the items *boy* and *s*. The first approach has the great advantage

---

26. More precisely, the description of English in Fawcett, Tucker & Lin (1993) and Fawcett (2000 and forthcoming b) provides for certain clause elements to be expounded either by words (as in *be* and *reach*) or by the addition of a suffix (and so a morpheme), as in + *ing*.

of avoiding adding a whole new layer of structure to the tree. (See also Section 11.6 of Chapter 11, on the relationship of 'exponence'.)

It should be noted that items such as *unhappiness* are not analyzed as *un* + *happy* + *ness*; here *unhappiness* is regarded as a single 'fused' item, on a par with *sadness* and *sorrow*.[27]

To summarize: by allowing an element to be expounded by **two** items (one as its main exponent and one as an affix), we avoid the need to have an additional layer in the tree diagram, thus considerably simplifying the description. The full analysis of an English sentence using the Cardiff Grammar therefore has one layer of structure less than there would be in an analysis based on "Categories", since the latter's 'rank scale' model predicts that each element of a group is filled by a word and each element of a word by a morpheme. Thus in Berry (1975:85), the example *When the bus broke down the boys walked to school* is analyzed into thirteen elements at the 'rank' of the morpheme.[28]

In Cardiff we have successfully used essentially the same method of generation for modelling the morphemes of an agglutinating language (Japanese; for a brief description of which see Tatsuki 1998). This is one of the two ways in which morphemes may be added to the structure. The first is simply to generate morphemes as direct elements of the clause in the same way that we generate words as clause elements in English (ensuring at the same time that the printout leaves no spaces between elements). But it is also possible to add one or more affixes, as either prefixes or suffixes, to any item in the structure (with the order in which the realization rules are applied ensuring the correct sequence).

10.5.3 The concept of 'word class'

So far in this section, as you may have noticed, we have barely mentioned one of the most familiar concepts of traditional grammar: that of 'word class'.

---

27. The assumption made here is therefore that users of English treat items displaying **derivational morphology** as single items (an assumption that cannot be made for other languages, such as German), and that neologisms that exploit existing patterns are simply new coinages. See also the section on compound nouns in Fawcett (in press). The generative model from which the present descriptive framework is derived therefore provides only for **inflectional morphology**.

28. In practice, however, most SF grammars do not analyze the internal structure of words. Here I am making explicit the theoretical grounds for not doing so (for English).

This concept lies at the heart of many theories of language — perhaps because it is the easiest aspect of language to reify — and yet the fact is that it only plays a limited, informal role in the present theory. It is now time to establish why its role is so limited, and the status of the limited use that it has.

In the present theory, then, a term such as "noun" or "adjective" is used merely as a useful **label for the set of items that expound some element of structure** (strictly speaking, the element minus any possible affix), perhaps additionally of a semantically defined set. For example, a noun is an item which expounds the head of a nominal group, but only in those cases when the language's 'cultural classification' of 'things' is used to help specify the referent. The head of a nominal group may also be expounded by the 'proform' *one* or *ones*, or by a **pronoun** such as *she*, or by a **'proper name'**[29].

Similarly, when the performer wants to specify the 'quality' of a 'thing' (such as *slow*), an **adjective** expounds the apex of a quality group. And, when the 'quality' is a quality of a situation (such as *slowly*), it is typically expounded by a **manner adverb**. However, there is no generally agreed label for the items that expound the temperer in this group, such as *very, rather, too* and *enough*, except for the misleading use of the label "adverb".[30] The items that may expound the temperer in such groups is just one of the many sets of item which expound specific elements of structure and yet have no agreed name.

In the case of the **preposition**, the present model actually uses the name associated with the word class as the name of the element at which items in that word class occur. This is permitted because the 'preposition' class of words always and only occur at this element.[31]

---

29. More accurately — both because "proper names" have their own internal structure and because there are various types of "proper name", we should say that in such cases the head is filled by a **human proper name cluster** (as described briefly in Section 10.2.12) or by an **address, date,** or **telephone number cluster**, or by one of the adaptations of the nominal group that are also used for certain types of 'name'. See Fawcett (in press) for a full specification of the types of unit that are used to express the various types of 'proper name' in English.

30. Presumably this was originally introduced on the weak formal grounds that items such as *terribly* occur at this element, as in *He's terribly sad*, as well as at the apex of a quality group, as in *He played really terribly*.

31. However, some of the same items also occur as Binders, in which case their word class is "subordinating conjunction", and/or as Main Verb Extensions, in which case they are sometimes termed "particles". See Appendix B for examples.

The 'amount' element of most quantity groups is typically expounded by an item (or unit) that could be called a 'quantifier', though this term is more typically used in logic-based accounts of expressions that refer to objects. And there is no label at all for the 'adjustor' element in such groups.

There are several labels of convenience for the different types of 'verb', but there is little value in the term "verb" when used by itself. The most useful 'verb class' labels are **lexical verb** and **modal verb**. Simple lexical verbs expound the **Main Verb** and modal verbs expound the **Operator**. Each of the various **Auxiliary Verb** clause elements is typically expounded by a one-member class of items (i.e., by one or other forms of *be* or *have*), so that there is little point in referring to a class of "auxiliary verbs".[32]

The position is therefore that the traditional 'word class' labels are sometimes used when talking about the sets of items that expound certain elements of structure. However, it is an interesting fact that they simply have no role to play as a category that is required in the generative version of the grammar. In other words, the lowest element of structure in a tree diagram is not filled by a word class label, but is instead directly expounded by an item. For example, we say that the head of a given nominal group is expounded by the item *boy*, and not that it is filled by a noun and that this noun is then expounded the item *boy*. This has the two advantages of (1) making the analysis more economical and (2) avoiding the problem of having to invent names for all of the many sets of items that have no established label. In this way we also avoid the problem of having 'ragbag' categories of word classes such as "particle" and "adverb".

In summary, we can say that the names of word classes such as **noun**, **adjective**, etc, are only used here to refer informally to sets of items which expound the same elements of structure and which have a common source in the semantics. They are therefore not a part of the text-descriptive syntax that is used in the analysis of texts, nor are they a part of the generative grammar that underlies the text-descriptive syntax.

Classes of item are therefore not identified in the grammar by a 'word class' label, but in terms of the element that they expound, i.e., in terms of the semantic function that they serve. This does not mean that we should not use labels such as "noun", "lexical verb" and "adjective" as handy names to refer to classes of words, but that the definitions of the differences between "nouns",

---

32. Some grammarians treat all verbs that occur at O or X as members of the class of 'auxiliary verb', so also including the modal verbs and forms of *do*.

"pronouns" and "proper nouns" are ultimately made in terms of the semantic features in the networks from which these items are generated.[33]

## 10.6 Summary of the categories in a modern systemic functional grammar

We have considered a large number of concepts in this chapter. Of those derived from Halliday's "Categories", only the concept of **element of structure** is still used in essentially the same sense as in "Categories". However, the concept of **place** can also be found in "Categories", used in an apparently similar sense. The derived concept of a **potential structure** was then introduced, it serves to locate the elements in those units where the sequence of elements is fixed. The predominant "Categories" concept of 'unit' has disappeared, in its sense of 'unit on the rank scale' — though the term "unit" continues to be used in the new theory as a short form for **class of unit**. This concept is central in the new theory, but while 'class (of unit)' was also "fundamental" in "Categories" the concept of 'class of unit' is now based on new criteria in the new theory, and is therefore a different concept.

Finally, this chapter introduces the concept of **item**. This has no correlate in "Categories", where 'words' and 'morphemes' are treated as if they were like the clause and the groups, and so simply further 'units' on the 'rank scale'. Yet it is words and — where it is necessary to specify them — morphemes that have a phonological or graphological shape, and that therefore mark the point at which syntax ends and segmental phonology or graphology begins.

---

33. These points have serious repercussions for computer systems designed to 'tag' the items on large corpora with grammatical labels, or to 'parse' texts in the field of natural language understanding. One parser that combines these principles with probabilities is described in Weerasinghe & Fawcett (1993) and Weerasinghe (1994).

# 11
# A theory of instances of syntax: (2) the relationships between categories

## 11.1 Towards a 'non-rank' view of 'constituency'

We come now to the most fundamental of the revisions to "Categories". Halliday's original claim was that there is a 'consists of' relationship between the units on the 'rank scale': clauses were said to 'consist of' groups, groups to 'consist of' words, and words to 'consist of' morphemes — unless 'rank shift' occurred. This was said to happen when a unit occurred within a unit lower than itself on the 'rank scale'. As we saw in Chapter 8, I have realized increasingly clearly, in the period between writing "Some proposals" and the writing of the present book, that the concept of the 'rank scale' has no practical role to play in either the theoretical-generative version of the Cardiff Grammar or in the text-descriptive version that is used for analyzing texts. As I made various other changes to the model, the value of the concept of 'rank' quietly diminished to the point where it now has no status in the theory at all. Let us ask, then, what replaces the concept of 'rank' in the new theory.

We shall start by noting that there is a little evidence that 'rank' may have diminished in importance a little in Halliday's theory too. In Chapter 5 we saw that 'rank' is presented in Halliday's "Systemic theory" (1993) as a type of 'constituency', but with no hint of 'total accountability at all ranks'. Then in Chapter 6 we saw that, although it is present in the background in *IFG*, the concept of 'rank' is only actually used in the context of 'rank shift' in the descriptive part of the book. It is reasonable to ask, therefore, how far the concept of the 'rank scale' is still the foundation of Halliday's theory of syntax today, as it was in "Categories".

The answer is that it is hard to be sure. Let us look at what Halliday says in the one place in his recent writings when he gives time to the question of the 'rank scale', i.e., the last section of Chapter 1 of *IFG*. By p. 12 he has introduced the reader to the general concept of 'constituency', and he is illustrating the proposal that it can be "strengthened" by adding to it the concept of the 'rank scale'. As he then says, the "guiding principle [of the concept of the 'rank scale'] is that of exhaustiveness at each rank". (This is also known as the "total accountability at all ranks" principle.) This means, for example, that in *Most people love chocolate* the word *chocolate* is treated as the head of a nominal group that fills the Complement of a clause — rather than simply functioning as a direct element of the clause. Most linguists, of course, including those who are not adherents of the 'rank scale' concept, would agree with this analysis (or some broadly equivalent one).

Let us be clear from the start of this discussion that the general concept of 'rank' and the specific concept of 'total accountability at all ranks' are interdependent. In other words, the concept of a 'rank scale of units' makes no theoretical claim if it does not imply 'total accountability at all ranks' — or at the very least 'accountability at all ranks, with only a few justifiable exceptions'.

However, the strict application of the 'total accountability' principle leads to problems with certain classes of word. This has led to what might loosely be termed 'the rank scale debate', and I provide an account of this debate in Appendix C. Here I shall restrict the discussion to just those points that are central to establishing why I myself have abandoned the concept of the 'rank scale' in favour of a different concept.

As Matthews (1966) and others have pointed out, Halliday's principle of 'accountability at all ranks' requires that, in a clause such as *after we left Henry's*, the word *after* must be treated as a group, since it is an element of the clause. And the same would be true of the word *and* in ... *and we left Henry's* and *therefore* in *we therefore left Henry's*. In *IFG* Halliday introduces the concept of a 'conjunction group' to model structure within a Linker or a Binder, but see Section 1 of Appendix C for a dismissal of this concept as a possible solution to the problem of satisfying the principle of 'accountability at all ranks'. (For a start, it is highly unlikely that Halliday would wish to analyze every one-word Binder as a group with one element.) See Section 10.2.8 of Chapter 10 for how the Cardiff Grammar handles Binders with an internal structure (when they occur), and see Section 11.6.2 for the relevant concept of "variation in depth of exponence".

However, Halliday's most spectacular breach of the 'rank scale' principle is his treatment of the 'Finite' element (e.g., *did* in *Did he like it?*). Throughout *IFG* his analyses of the MOOD structure of clauses show the Finite as an element of the clause. The effect is that single words such as the 'modal verbs' and forms of *do, be* and *have* all regularly function as direct elements of the clause. In Fawcett (2000) and (forthcoming a) I demonstrate that the way to resolve this and the various other problems of the 'verbal group' is to promote not just the Finite but **all** of the elements of the supposed 'verbal group' to function as elements of the clause. This two-part paper sets out important evidence against the concept of the 'verbal group, and so against the concept of the 'rank scale'. (See Section 4 of Appendix C for a summary.)

The situation is therefore that Halliday seems on the one hand to wish to maintain the general principle of the 'rank scale' — and with it the view that "the guiding principle is exhaustiveness at each rank" (*IFG* p. 12 — and on the other to allow for exceptions. Indeed his statement of the "exhaustiveness" principle in *IFG* is closely followed by these words:

> At the same time, there is room for manoeuvre: in other words, it is an integral feature of this same guiding principle that there is indeterminacy in its application (Halliday 1994:12).

Thus the "exhaustiveness" principle seems to be one that can be breached. But the examples that Halliday cites are all cases of borderline judgements, and there will always be such cases in text analysis. The greater problem is the existence of many clear cases of exceptions, such as those cited above and in Appendix C. And even if the principle is only breached to the extent that I argue to be required in Fawcett (2000) and (forthcoming b), it is in effect dead.

Encouragingly, Halliday displays his usual willingness to allow for alternative approaches when he adds the following to the above passage:

> Such issues will be decided empirically. [...] The issue is whether, in a comprehensive interpretation of the system, it is worth maintaining the global generalization because of its explanatory power, even though it imposes local complications at certain places in the description (Halliday 1994:12).

This is sound advice on the question of how to go about describing a language. Let us see how it applies in the present case. The Cardiff Grammar certainly counts as a "comprehensive interpretation of the system", and there have been decades of "empirical" work by researchers using this framework. It has involved the exploration of alternative SF description of English (and other languages) for both the large scale analysis of texts and for the computer generation of language. The view to which it has led is that the "global generalization" that the 'rank scale' was intended to express has less "explanatory power" than the theory of syntax described here. So we who work in the framework of the Cardiff Grammar have, following the principles suggested by Halliday, "decided empirically" that the 'rank scale' is no longer needed. (For a fuller account of the 'rank scale' debates, see Appendix C.)

Is there a hint in the passage cited above that Halliday would now make a less strong claim for the 'rank scale' concept? If so, this might explain why it is omitted in "Systemic theory", and why it receives so little space in *IFG*.

The saying "Old habits die hard" holds for our habits of thought as linguists as well as for other sorts of habit, and the habit of thinking in terms of a 'rank scale' has been with most systemic functional linguists for all of their working lives. It seems to me that what Halliday did in setting up Scale and Category Grammar in 1961 and what other did in accepting it was to take over what was already to a large extent a tacit assumption in traditional grammar, and to formalize it as part of the new theory — just as he did with a number of other traditional concepts.[1] The concept of a 'rank scale of units' is therefore one which we may find particularly hard to hard to let go of. Indeed I allowed vestiges of it to remain in my own theory long after it had stopped playing any practical role in it (as I admitted in Chapter 8). So the general concept that there is indeed some sort of 'rank scale' — even if it is not exactly as Halliday describes it — is one that has been a background assumption about language for many linguists for most of the last half century — and probably longer.

If you are in this position, perhaps you might consider engaging in the following experiment. I would like to suggest that you try working with the approach that is proposed here for a couple of hours — or even a couple of days. First, let yourself drop the additional claims that the 'rank scale' makes over the more general concept of 'constituency'. Then make the model of 'constituency' more specific, using the concepts introduced in the next paragraph. Finally, examine the summary in Appendix B of what classes of unit can fill what elements of structure, and ask yourself whether this account of the relationships between classes of unit does not in fact give a more accurate picture of how the units of English syntax relate to each other than do the predictions of the 'rank scale' hypothesis.

For Halliday, it is upon the concept of the 'rank scale' that all of his generalizations as to what units may function at what elements rests. Since we

---

1. For example, consider the traditional concept of 'word class'. Halliday has incorporated this long-established concept into his theory of grammar, but given it a definition that I have found it necessary to change. See Section 10.5 of Chapter 10.

are about to meet the set of concepts which is proposed as a replacement for the 'rank scale', it may be useful to remind ourselves of just what the claims of the 'rank scale' hypothesis are. They are as follows:

1. that the elements of clauses will be filled by groups, the elements of groups will be filled by words and the elements of words by morphemes (though it is clear from the passage cited above that Halliday recognizes that there will be at least some exceptions);
2. that 'upward rank shift' does not occur (except, apparently, in the case of the 'Finite', as mentioned above);
3. that 'downward rank shift' is only permitted in the case of clauses and groups functioning as elements of groups (i.e., it is not the case that clauses may fill elements of clauses);
4. that the class of a unit is determined by the element or elements at which it occurs in the unit above it on the 'rank scale'.

(See Section 11.8.5 for the details of the very limited amount of embedding that Halliday allows, as specified in *IFG*.)

Here I propose a model in which none of the above four hypotheses has a place. The question therefore is: "What is wrong with the above set of generalizations, and what more useful alternative generalizations should replace them?"

Let us begin with the last of the four assumptions listed above. We have already seen in Section 10.2 of Chapter 10 the reasons why, in the new theory, we prefer to determine the class of a unit by its internal structure.

This leaves just the concept of the 'rank scale' itself. There are four interrelated reasons for dispensing with this concept. Firstly, the idea that there is a "consists of" relationship of 'constituency' between the units — which is what the concept of the 'rank scale' states — is not sufficiently precise to be useful. A unit does not in fact function directly as a constituent of another unit; as later sections of this chapter will demonstrate in detail. Instead, the concept of 'constituency' must be broken down into a number of other relationships. In the present theory we shall say that a **unit** is **composed** of a number of **elements**, and that any such element will be either **filled** by another unit or **expounded** by an **item**. (For the concepts of 'componence', 'filling' and 'exponence' see Sections 11.3, 11.5 and 11.6 respectively.) In other words, there is not in fact a 'consists of' relationship between units, but a rather more complex series of relationships.[2]

The second reason for dispensing with 'rank' is that in the present theory there are only two major candidates for 'ranks of unit' in the present description of English (and other languages): i.e., 'clause' and 'group', in contrast with the five 'units' of "Categories".[3] Can a 'rank scale' of which only two of the supposed 'ranks' occur in most instances really be regarded as a 'scale'?

The third reason for dispensing with the concept of 'rank' is that, while the 'rank scale' model raises problems even for Halliday's own description of English (as described in detail in Appendix C), the problems are far greater when we also take into account the extensions to the internal structure of groups that have been introduced in the Cardiff Grammar'. And the difficulty of sustaining he 'rank scale' hypothesis becomes even greater with the abolition of the 'verbal group' (the reasons for which are given in Fawcett 2000 and forthcoming b, and summarized in Section 4 of Appendix C).

The fourth reason for abandoning the 'rank scale' model is a positive one. It is that there is now an alternative model of relationships between units that enables us to predict much more accurately what units will occur within what other units in natural texts. Let us now see what this alternative model is.

## 11.2 Filling probabilities as a replacement for 'rank'

11.2.1 The principle concepts of the alternative approach

In the approach to 'constituency' proposed here the two key concepts are:

1. that the predictions are made in terms of the relationship of **filling** that holds between a **unit** and an **element of structure** in a higher unit in the tree (rather than being about relations between units), and

---

2. In due course we shall see that it would be even more precise to say that an element is located at a **place** in a unit, and only then that is it filled by a lower unit. For the concept of 'place' see Section 10.4 of Chapter 10.

3. There is also the 'cluster', as we saw in Section 10.2 of Chapter 10, but this occurs only infrequently and its existence is therefore an embarrassment for the 'rank scale' concept rather than a support for it. See Section 11.6.2 for the concept of 'variation in depth of exponence', which is often used in conjunction with the concept of the 'cluster' in the Cardiff Grammar.

2. the use of **filling probabilities**.4 (We shall look at the precise nature of 'filling probabilities' in Section 11.2.2.)

In this theory, then, there is no expectation that an element of a clause will necessarily be filled by a group. (For 'filling' as a theoretical concept, see Section 11.5.) Some clause elements are frequently filled by groups, a few are sometimes filled by groups, and some never are. And the same is true of groups. The frequencies vary greatly, so that in the question of what element a unit may fill is often better stated as a probability rather than as an absolute rule.

A further feature of the new theory is that, with respect to the groups, what matters most is not the fact that the unit is a group (as it is in the 'rank scale' model), but what **class of group** it is. Indeed, in the present framework the differences between the different classes of group (nominal, prepositional, quality and quantity) are just as important as the differences between them all, considered together as groups, and the clause. Indeed, each of the clause and the four classes of group recognized here for English may fill any one of various elements of structure in various classes of unit. Some of the constraints on what may fill what can be expressed by absolute rules, of course, but many others are better expressed as probabilities. In this version of SFL, then, the fact that a variety of different classes of unit may fill many of the elements of many on the units of a language such as English is not regarded as a problem (as it is in a 'rank-based' grammar) but as one of the great riches of human language.

It follows naturally from the statements which I have just made that there is no implication in the present theory of syntax that a unit is functioning in a highly marked manner when **embedding** occurs. In this theory it is expected that a clause will quite frequently occur as an element of another clause, or as an element of a group. This position is almost the opposite of that presented in *IFG*, where the picture is one of very severe limitations on the embedding of units within each other. Indeed, in *IFG* Halliday stipulates that it is not possible for a clause to fill an element of another clause (except indirectly, by filling the head of a nominal group that fills an element of the higher clause(*IFG* p. 242).

---

4. It may be significant that, although the concept of 'filling' was indirectly present in the S&C model (and so is still implicitly there in *IFG*), it has never been presented as one of the 'basic concepts' of the theory, as it is here (in Section 11.5 of Chapter 11). As we shall see, it is the concept of 'filling' that gives us a principled way to handle co-ordination as a phenomenon that is different from the usual 'componence' relationship of elements in a unit — a difference that all good grammars recognize but for which few have an adequate notation.

For a discussion of the concepts of 'embedding' and 'rank shift', see Sections 11.8.3 to 11.8.5.[5]


### 11.2.2 The two types of probabilities in filling

If we wish to make useful generalisations about what units are likely to fill what elements of what other units, we need to make statements about specific units and elements — initially for particular languages and then perhaps — though with great wariness — across languages and groups of languages. There are two ways of approaching such **filling statements**, and these can be characterized as 'top-down' and 'bottom-up'.

The 'bottom-up' approach is to ask, for each unit that is identified, (1) "What elements can it fill?", (2) "What is the degree of probability with which it fills each?" and (3) "What are its own elements?" A set of answers in these terms with respect to English is given in Appendix B, with the probabilities being stated in the list of elements at the top of the display of each unit. (This display is based on its 'potential structure', as far as that is possible; see Section 10.4.3 of Chapter 10 for the concept of 'potential structure'.)

The second way to make useful generalizations is the converse of this; i.e., the 'top-down' approach. Here we ask with respect to each element (1) "What units can fill it?" and (2) "What classes of items can expound it?" (We only rarely need to ask what unit it is an element of, since practically all of the

---

[5]. The clear implication of Halliday's concept of 'rank shift' that, when it occurs, the 'natural order' has in some sense been disrupted. The extensive use that he makes of 'hypotaxis' for modelling relations between units (and especially clauses) can be seen as a way of minimizing the role of embedding in the grammar. (See Section 2.6.1 of Chapter 2, Section 11.9 of this chapter and Section 3 of Appendix C for discussions of 'hypotaxis'.) I have never understood why Halliday should see embedding as something to be avoided in a model of language and its use. I suspect that a strong influence on the formation of his position has been the difficulty that users of any language have in processing texts — in either production or understanding — when the depth of embedding (especially non-final embedding) becomes a strain on short-term memory. So far as I know, Halliday has never discussed the reason for his distrust of the concept of embedding in any publication. This is perhaps not surprising, given the fact that he would regard himself, if pushed to choose, as a sociolinguist rather than a psycholinguist. Indeed, the substantial literature on embedding takes the viewpoint of the cognitive processing of language (and for good reasons). Halliday, then, leaves psycholinguistics and cognitive linguistics to others. However, this has not prevented some psycholinguists from using his insights in their own work in modelling language and its use, e.g., the excellent psycho-linguistics textbook by Clark & Clark (1977), now sadly out of print.

elements are unique to a given class of unit.)

Since Appendix B exemplifies the first approach, let us explore the second here, in order to get a flavour of the type of information that it gives us.

Let us start with the elements of the **clause**. Making use of the abbreviations introduced in the key at the start of Appendix B, we can say that:

(a) **S** is usually (over 99% of the time) filled by a ngp,
(b) **C** is quite frequently filled by a ngp, but also by a pgp, a qlgp or (with certain types of Process), a clause, and
(c) **A** is frequently filled by a pgp, qlgp or a clause, and occasionally by a ngp, with the probabilities varying greatly with the type of Adjunct (Manner, Place, Reason, etc.). However,
(d) many elements of clause structure are typically — and often obligatorily — expounded directly by items (e.g., **&**, **B**, **O**, the **Xs** and **M**). Moreover,
(e) many elements frequently follow more than one pattern, e.g., the **Mex** may be expounded directly by an item such as *out*, or filled by a ngp such as *a bath* in *He had a bath*. And some types of **A** may be (i) expounded by a single item *however*, or (ii) filled by a prepositional group such as *despite her absence*, or (iii) filled by a clause such as *although she was absent*..

The elements of the **nominal group** show a very similar variation. Thus:

(f) Many elements of nominal groups are typically — but not necessarily — filled by groups (e.g., **pd**, **qd**, and **m**), while
(g) others are obligatorily expounded by items (e.g., **&** and **v**).
(h) Some are filled by clauses (**q** often and **m** occasionally), while
(i) some follow more than one pattern, being both expounded by items and filled by units (e.g., **qd**, **dd**, **m** and **q**). Finally,
(j) two elements of the nominal group are typically expounded by items but are also quite often filled by clusters (**dd** and **h**).

Similar probabilisitc statements can be made for the three other classes of group and the clusters. Note that the 'top-down' approach can be made more sensitive by taking account of the surrounding text, e.g., as indicated in (b) above. The type of Process governs the likelihood of certain units occurring with it, particularly as the Complement (e.g., the strong probability of having a clause as the Complement with a mental process such as 'thinking'.

Notice that the 'filling probabilities' between an element and the unit below it are often different, depending on whether one is working 'top-down' (as in generating) or 'bottom-up' (as in the detailed stage of the hand analysis of texts). From the 'top-down' viewpoint, for example, the probability that a Subject will be filled by a nominal group is over 99%.[6] But, as Appendix B shows, in a 'bottom-up' approach the probability that a nominal group will fill the Subject is only around 45%) because it also frequently fills other elements.

When building a computer model that is capable of parsing incoming text, both types of information are useful, in the ways described in Weerasinghe & Fawcett (1993) and Weerasinghe (1994). However, for the detailed analysis of texts by hand, the best approach is first to identify the lowest units in the tree and then to ask about each "What function does this unit serve in the unit next above?", in the manner described in Fawcett (in press). For this purpose, then, the 'bottom-up' approach is the more useful, and this is why the probabilities in Appendix B are of this type.

In practical terms, then, the main use of the 'rank scale' concept has been as a model that makes predictions that guide the text analyst as to how the units of a text-sentence relate to each other — though these have sometimes caused problems for the analyst. However, statements of 'filling probabilities', as in Appendix B, meet the same need in a more effective manner.

All of the probabilities discussed so far are **instantial probabilities**, i.e., probabilities that certain patterns will occur in instances, i.e. in text-sentences. They are moreover probabilities at the level of **form**. In contrast with these are the probabilities on features in system networks, which we might refer to as **potential probabilities**, these being at the level of **meaning**. See Section 2 of Appendix C for a discussion of the relationship between the two.

11.2.3 The source of the probabilities given in Appendix B

The set of filling probabilities given in Appendix B are based on the syntactically analyzed corpus described in Fawcett and Perkins (1981), for which Michael Day has developed a query system called the Interactive Corpus Query

---

6. The other possibilities are that it will be filled a clause, as in *To err is human*, or directly expounded by the item *it* or *there*, i.e., in cases where there is an empty Subject, such as *It's nice to see you* and *There's something crawling up your back*.

Facility (ICQF), for which see Day (1993).[7] They are, as you would expect from the discussion in the last section, 'bottom-up' probabilities.

But how far, you may well be wondering, are those figures valid across different registers and dialects of English? Biber *et al.* (1999) demonstrate convincingly that there are significant grammatical variations between the four major registers that they cover, i.e., conversation, fiction, news (i.e., newspapers) and academic prose. Yet they also rightly emphasize the fact that there is also variation **within** each of these registers, i.e., between the 'sub-registers' (and indeed 'sub-dialects') that it is possible to recognize within them.[8]

Thus there is nothing sacred about the particular cut-off point chosen by Biber *et al.* on the scale of 'delicacy' for their study of grammatical variation according to register. And the corollary of this is that it is reasonable to suppose that there are certain broad probabilities that run right through all the registers of a language — so recalling the concept of a 'common core' of grammar, as used in Quirk *et al.* (1972) and (1985). I suggest that the probabilities that are given in Appendix B are unlikely to rise or fall by more than 10% with a change of register. However, it has to be said that no one has yet undertaken the detailed studies that would corroborate this prediction.[9]

---

7. The figures upon which those given in Appendix B are based were obtained through Day's ICQF from a corpus of approaching 20,000 words of syntactically analyzed casual and semi-formal conversation by 12-year old boys and girls from four different social classes, as described in Fawcett and Perkins (1981). Systems for interrogating parsed corpora that are stored in a computer are in their infancy, but ICQF has been described by a leading figure in the field as "possibly the best corpus query facility in existence" (Atwell, personal communication). The current version of ICQF can only be used on the corpus mentioned above, but Day is currently developing an improved version which will be adaptable to any parsed corpus, irrespective of the type of labelling of its tree structure.

8. Studies by students at Cardiff have shown again and again there are indeed great differences between, for example, the editorials of the *Sun* and the *Times* newspapers (both published for British readers by Rupert Murdoch). And there are also significant differences between the editorial in the *Sun* and its reporting of sports events (where more syntactic complexity is tolerated).

9. It is often stated that linguists have a lot to learn from the study of corpora, and this is undoubtedly true. However, it may be of interest to point out that the figures for twelve-year-old children upon which those in Appendix B are based correspond remarkably closely to my prior guesstimates, which I presented to Day before we interrogated the corpus. (These were in fact made for the probabilities in adult casual conversation, so some differences were expected.) My predictions for the probability of what elements a clause fills were within 1.2% of the figures from the corpus, though my figures for the nominal group were up to 12% different.

The variety in what elements may fill what elements of other units is a major factor in giving natural language its richness and flexibility —and it is this in turn that enables us to present both the observed world around us and the various worlds inside our minds to each other in the complex ways that we do.

In the next four sections we shall examine the three crucial relationships of **componence, filling** and **exponence** into which the 'consists of' relationship between units must be broken down — and also the concept that models in the syntax itself the multifunctional nature of language, i.e., conflation.

## 11.3 Componence

**Componence** is the part-whole relationship between a **unit** and the **elements** of which it is composed. Thus the componence of the nominal group *the man with a stick* is **dd h q**; the componence of the prepositional group *with a stick* is **p cv**, and that of the nominal group *a stick* is **qd h**. Componence is therefore not a relationship between a unit and its places. The role of 'places' is simply to enable the elements to be related to each other in the appropriate sequence, and it is the elements that are the 'components' of the unit. This is why, in a text-descriptive representation of a unit (as in Figure 10 in Chapter 7) there is no need to show the places.

There are two **realization operations** that introduce the relationship of componence to the structure. The first is Operation 2, i.e., "Locate an element at a place in a unit'. In English, this is the operation that builds the structure of the **clause**. The distinctive characteristic of this operation is that it is used to

(The twelve-year-olds had almost as many nominal groups that filled Complements (37%) as filled Subjects (40%), which was 12% more than I had predicted for adult conversation. It seems likely that this disparity reflect sthe fact that the task that the children were engaged in as they talked was building a house out of Lego bricks, so that the subject matter may biassed the texts towards action processes, in which the likelihood that a Complement will be filled by a nominal group is greater than it is with mental or even relational processes. (Even so, 7% of all the children's clauses filled Complements.) I have made a minor adjustment to reflect this probable bias by reducing the predicted percentage of nominal groups filling the Complement by 5%, and adding this 5% to the largest group, i.e., those filling the Subject. (I have not touched the figures for the clause.) The figures for the other units were broadly comparable with my predictions, and no other changes have been made. If my guesstimates for adults are roughly right (and I recognize that they may not be), it would seem that twelve-year-olds have already reached an adult pattern of probabilities, at least with respect to the aspects of grammar covered here. Other studies of this corpus have yielded similar findings, e.g. with respect to the maximum number of elements in a clause (which is around seven.)

insert an element in a clause at a specific, numbered place, e.g., "S at 35". This ability is vital in any grammar of the English clause that attains any degree of complexity, because the enormous variation in the sequence of its elements (especially the different types of Adjunct) requires the great flexibility that this method of sequencing elements brings.

However, in building the structure of **groups** and **clusters,** the operation that is used in practically all cases is Operation 4.[10] This operation is simply "Expound an element by an item." If Operation 2 has placed the element in the clause, the task is simply to expound the element. But if the element has not already been located, as occurs when generating a group, Operation 4 first consults the relevant **potential structure** (a list of the **elements** in a **fixed sequence** of numbered **places**, a simplified example of which is given in Appendix A). From this it discovers the place at which such an element goes, it places the element, and it then expounds it. Potential structures are, in principle, simply an economical way of identifying the places at which to locate elements in units with a relatively fixed sequence of elements, their effect being to simplify every realization rule for an element of group structure. But in practice they also provide the basis for useful summaries of the central aspects of syntax that are invaluable to the text analyst, as illustrated in Appendix B. (See Section 10.4.3 of Chapter 10 for a fuller account of potential structures and their status in the theory.)

We saw in Section 9.2.3 of Chapter 9 that the Sydney Grammar, according to the theoretical statements in each of the three summaries of its theory, uses two operations to accomplish the placing of an element in the structure of its unit, i.e., "Insert" and "Order". However, it seems from "Systemic theory" (p. 4505) that the "Order" operation may now have been extended to include "Order an element to some defined location", and this may signal the use of the concept of 'place', as originally introduced to SFL in Fawcett (1973/81). If this is so there is now little difference between the two models in this respect.

Componence is normally represented diagrammatically by lines going **down** the page, either vertically or diagonally. The lines start from the unit and branch out downwards to the elements below. Sometimes only one element of a unit is used, and in such cases of what is sometimes termed **singulary**

---

10. There are only a few cases of variation in the sequence of elements within groups, and these can be handled by having two versions of the same element at two places, e.g., "degree temperer 2" after the apex in the quality group, to handle *enough* as in *tall enough*; see Appendix B.

**branching** there is simply a vertical line from the unit down to the element.

Diagram (a) in Figure 14 illustrates the two types of componence, and Diagram (b) illustrates an alternative notation used by some grammarians for multiple branching (e.g., Halliday (1969/81:143), Hudson (1974/81), and Halliday (1994:17f.), in the chapter of *IFG* that discusses 'constituency'). For those with difficulties in drawing slanting lines (e.g., people using a word-processing package which lacks good line-drawing facilities), this second way of representing syntax may appear an attractive alternative.

However, there is in fact one fairly serious disadvantage in using a horizontal line as part of the representation of this major aspect of the syntax. This is that a horizontal line is required, as we shall see in a moment, to represent the 'filling' relationship — and the short vertical lines shown above in Diagram (b) can easily become less visible in a hurried pencil-and-paper analysis.

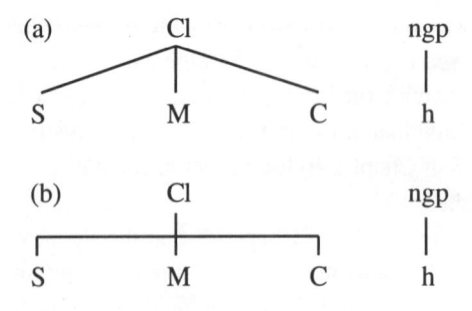

*Figure 14: Two notations for representing 'componence'*

This may appear to be a trivial point, but it is not. The diagrams that we draw to represent our models of language are the visual manifestation of the model's concepts, and the notations used in a theory are an important aspect of that theory. In the semiotic system of diagrams that represent linguistic structure — a semiotic system which most linguists use as a vital complement to our presentations of our theories through language — the notations that appear on paper or on the computer screen are the level of 'form'. And it helps to maintain effective communication through this semiotic system if we keep the **forms** that realize the different **meanings** clearly distinct from each other, just as it does in language. For this reason the notation used in the Diagram (a) is to be preferred.

In print, the use of diagrams can be sometimes be avoided by using brackets to represent 'constituency' relations, as in (c), and this can save the work and space of drawing or printing a diagram.

(c) ((The performer (of (this trick))) (requires) (an (absolutely silent) audience))

But such diagrams always require work to interpret them, and when linguists add superscript labels above each pair of brackets to show the beginning and end of the constituent, as is often done, they become even more complex than the equivalent tree diagram, while being much less readable.

However, there is one a linear notation that is easily readable:

(d) The performer of this trick [S] requires [M] a really silent audience [C].

The only limitation of this notation is that it cannot be expanded to show the full syntactic structure of a sentence, in the way that a tree diagram can. It is nonetheless very useful when the focus of interest is on just one layer of the structure.

The main notation used by Halliday in *IFG* consists of several lines of analysis, as exemplified in Figure 7 in Chapter 7. If we showed just the line that is the equivalent of what is shown here (the top line of the MOOD analysis), it would be as in Figure 15.

(e)

| He | would | visit | his gran | every Sunday |
|---|---|---|---|---|
| Subject | Finite | Predicator | Complement | Adjunct |

*Figure 15: A 'box diagram' representation of componence (as used in IFG)*

This gives essentially the same amount of information as the previous notation, and it has the same limitation that it does not lend itself to showing in the same diagram the lower layers of the structure. Moreover, it is not clear why it should be thought worth using the extra time and work of drawing boxes around categories in the diagram, rather than simply drawing single lines between categories, as in the first notation, i.e., (a) above.

The last notation to be presented is one that is used in the computer print-out from the COMMUNAL generator. It is a compromise between the limitations of print and the desire to show the componence visually. It operates on the simple principle of turning the conventional tree diagram through 90°. So here the lines showing componence run from left to right, in parallel, with an arrow pointing to the elements, thus:

(f)    Cl -> S
           -> M
           -> C

Other notations are sometimes found but, with one exception which we shall look at shortly, they are usually a variant of one or other of these.

All of the above notations represent exactly the same information — except (c), which is unlabelled, and (e), which simply uses the equivalent *IFG* terms. However, the clear visual image of the 'part-whole' relationship of componence that is given in the Type (a) is clearly preferable. And Type (d) is also useful as a way of saving time and space when attention is focussed on a single layer of structure. Both are used extensively in Fawcett (2000) and (in press).

Throughout this book I have assumed, as most linguists do, that the dominant relationship in modelling relationships in syntax is 'constituency'. And in spelling out the concepts that make up 'constituency' I have assumed that it is the concept of 'componence' that expresses the 'part-whole' relationship. However, there is an alternative concept that has at times attracted the support of a number of fine linguists. It is often called 'dependency grammar' — but, strictly speaking, it should instead be called "sister dependency grammar". This is because the traditional concept of 'dependency' is what is termed "mother dependency", i.e., the dependency between a category and the category above it in the tree diagram. The question is: "Is it either necessary or desirable to show 'sister dependency' relations in the syntactic representation of a text-sentence?" If it is either necessary or desirable, this would have a profound effect on the proposals set out here, and in particular on the place of 'componence' in the theory.[11]

---

11. Assuming that one wishes to express 'dependency' in a syntactic representation of a text-sentence — an assumption which we shall shortly examine further — it can be expressed in either of two ways: (1) by an arc leading from the 'dependent' category to the 'depended-upon' category, as in a sister-dependency representation, or (2) by labelling the elements of a tree diagram with words that reflect this dependence (such as, prototypically, the terms 'modifier' and 'head'). However, in Fawcett & Davies (1992) and Lin & Fawcett (1996), my colleagues and I have demonstrated (in terms of both visual diagrams and a computer implementation) that sister dependency relations can always be interpreted in constituency terms without loss of information. (Our discussion of the issue is in fact in terms of modelling the structure of exchanges in discourse, but the argument holds equally strongly for intra-sentential syntax.)

## A THEORY OF INSTANCES: RELATIONSHIPS

However, it can be shown that it is not in fact necessary — nor even desirable — to model sister dependency relations in syntax. As I pointed out in Section 10.3.3 of Chapter 10, the supposed 'dependency' of a "modifier" on the "head" on a unit (e.g., in a nominal group) is a 'second order' concept, and ultimately an uninsightful one. In a SF grammar the relationship between the two elements is more appropriately seen as an indirect one, because each element realizes its own aspect of the meaning of a referent, and the relationship is therefore at the level of meaning rather than form. In other words, in a SF grammar, any relationship of apparent 'syntactic sister dependency' is already expressed, in a natural manner, in the dependency relations by which one system is dependent on another in the system network of the language's meaning potential. For the systemic grammarian this is the true location of dependence (or 'dependency').

The question is therefore: "What is gained by modelling these dependency relations in the syntactic representation too?" The answer is that nothing is gained. In a SF grammar it is simply not the task of a syntactic structure to show that the presence of one element 'depends' on the presence of another. To attempt to do so leads one to ask inappropriate questions, since this is not where dependency is located. The type of 'dependency' that is important in syntax is the relationship of **componence**, i.e., that between the elements and the unit of which they are the elements. Without this theoretical concept no SF grammar would be complete — and nor could it be implemented in a computer.

## 11.4  Conflation

We come now to the concept of 'conflation'. Sometimes an **element** gets **conflated** with another **element** — as when an Auxiliary Verb is conflated with the Operator. If Element X is conflated with Element Y, X occurs in the structure immediately after and fused with Y, so that X and Y function as one

---

In purely syntactic terms, then, the difference between these two formal representations of syntax is not as great as is suggested in Hudson (1976) — and also in Martin (1992) when he is writing about exchange structure. Indeed, the major difference is that the 'sister-dependency' approach has certain disadvantages. Firstly, it lacks the concept of 'class of unit' (channelling all 'constituency' relations through the 'head'). Secondly, the sister dependency approach raises questions about which element 'depends on' which, when there is frequently not in fact any 'dependency' between them — even between the features in the system network from which the elements are generated. (See Section 10.3 of Chapter 10 for my view of elements.)

element. And, in an essentially similar manner, every Participant Role (PR) is introduced to the structure by being conflated with an element such as Subject. A PR is simply a particular type of element that is generated from the experiential component of the system network, and it is not a different order of phenomenon from an 'element'. A PR may appear to be more 'semantic' than an element such as Subject, but it is not. The presence of each in the structure directly expresses a meaning, and the only difference is that the meaning expressed by a PR (such as Agent) is overtly referred to in the name of the features in the system network, e.g., as [overt agent] and [covert agent], as in Figure 10 in Chapter 7.

In the realization operation that generates conflated elements in the Cardiff Grammar, the concept of 'immediately after and fused with' is expressed by "by", i.e., as "Ag by S". The notation for conflation is to place the element that is being conflated immediately after the element that it is being conflated with, separated by a slash, thus:

O/X    S/Ag

It is the concept of 'conflation' that expresses the multifunctional nature of language, and the same concept and notation are used in all versions of SFL.

One difference between the Cardiff and the Sydney Grammars is that the former does not mark the 'Theme' function of a Subject explicitly in the structure, while the Sydney Grammar does. It is in fact redundant to show this, in that the Subject's status is as a type of Theme is directly inferable from the fact that it is the Subject — i.e., the grammar specifies that any PR that is conflated with the Subject is thereby automatically also a "Subject Theme'. The fact that it must be a PR excludes "empty Subjects" (as in the underlined parts of *It was Ivy that did it*, *It's likely that she did* and *There's a fly in my soup*), which are not 'Themes'. (See Fawcett in press for such 'enhanced theme' constructions.)

The same notation is used in both tree diagrams and in print. So if we add 'conflation' to 'componence' we shall have a diagram such as that in Figure 16 (where 'Ag' = 'Agent' and 'Af' = 'Affected').

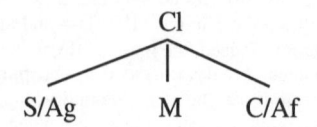

Cl
/ | \
S/Ag    M    C/Af

*Figure 16: The notations for representing 'componence' and 'conflation'*

## 11.5 Filling

**Filling** is the relationship between an **element** and the **unit** that 'operates at' it — this being the unit below it in a tree diagram representation. It can be argued that it is the fact that the Cardiff Grammar gives this concept a central position in the theory of syntax that enables it to solve a range of problems for which more complex solutions are proposed by Halliday. Thus it is filling that makes possible both co-ordination and embedding, and it is the extensive use of these that enables us to do without the somewhat problematical concepts of 'parataxis' and 'hypotaxis'.

Filling may introduce a single additional unit to the structure, or it may introduce two or more co-ordinated units. (For co-ordination see Section 11.8.2). For example, an Adjunct that expresses 'Time Position' may be filled by a nominal group such as *the day before yesterday*, a prepositional group such as *on Friday*, a quality group such as *quite recently,* or a clause such as *when I was last in London*. (In the last case it introduces a clause that is embedded in another clause; see Section 11.8.3 for 'embedding'.) Alternatively, an element may be filled by two co-ordinated units, as in *(I lost it) either last Monday or last Tuesday*.

The term "fill" was first introduced to SFL in Fawcett (1974-6/81), but it is also used in a broadly similar sense in Kenneth Pike's tagmemic linguistics (e.g., Pike & Pike 1982), where a "class of unit" such as "noun phrase" is said to "fill" a "slot" such as "Subject". Thus Pike's 'slot' is equivalent to our 'element' (not to our 'place').

In the Cardiff Grammar, the realization operation that introduces this relationship of filling to a structure is "Insert a unit to fill Element X". The most surprising fact about the Sydney Grammar's list of realization operations, as stated in their theoretical-generative publications, is the lack of any equivalent to this crucial operation (as discussed in Section 9.2.3 of Chapter 9).

Interestingly, there is an equivalent gap in the Sydney Grammar's notation for representing the outputs from the grammar. This arises from the surprising fact that there is no diagram in *IFG* — or in the equivalent diagrams in Matthiessen & Bateman (1991) or Matthiessen (1995) — that shows how such a relationship should be represented in the full analysis of a text-sentence. In all of these works each unit is analyzed in its own terms, almost as if the way in which they are to be related to the units above and below them in the structure is self-evident and has no complications. Filling is in fact a complex matter, and it very often happens that the possibilities as to what class of unit may fill an element depends, either in absolute or in probabilisitc terms, on choices in the generation of the unit above. The most obvious example is the restrictions on what may fill the Complements of particular Main Verbs (for which see Fawcett 1996). And, as we shall see in Section 11.8.2, the concept of 'filling' is central to modelling co-ordination.

However, the concept of 'filling' is not completely absent from the Sydney Grammar. It has been present from the start in the wording by which the relationship of a unit to an element is described, in the use of "operates at" (e.g., Halliday 1961/76:64). An alternative term is "function as". Thus a nominal group would be said to "operate at" (or "function as") the Subject or Complement of a clause. But it is not given a place as a central concept in the theory, as it is here. The term 'filling' seems to be preferable to "operating-at-ness" or "functioning-as-ness".

Its centrality in the theory of syntax is shown by the fact that it functions as the direct complement to 'componence'. In other words, as your eye moves down a full tree diagram representation of a text-sentence (e.g., Figure 25 in Section 12.6 of Chapter 12), you find that the relationships between categories are alternately those of **componence** and **filling**, and that these two are repeated until the point at which the analysis moves out of the abstract categories of **syntax** to the rather more concrete (but still abstract) category of **items** (via the relationship of **exponence**, to which we shall come in Section 11.6).

In a tree diagram, the notation for the relationship of filling is a horizontal line, as shown in Diagrams (a) and (b) in Figure 17. Note the way in which the line showing 'filling' extends to cover the two (or more) co-ordinated units. It is this use of a horizontal line in the representation of text-sentences that makes the use of representations of 'componence' that involve a horizontal line unsuitable (as I pointed out in Section 11.2).

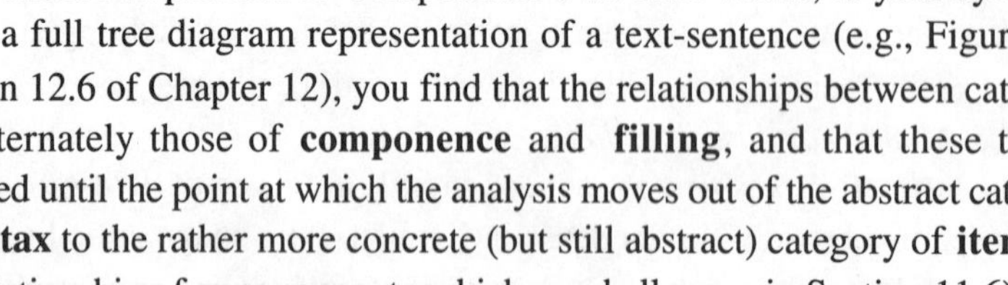

(a)    C/Af              (c)    C/Af|ngp
       ─────
        ngp

or, if there is co-ordination:

(b)      C/Af            (d)    C/Af|ngp
       ─────────                 |ngp
       ngp    ngp

*Figure 17: The notation for representing 'filling' in drawn diagrams and in print*

In print the relationship of 'filling' is shown by a vertical bar), as in (c) and (d) above. This is not to be confused with a slash, which shows conflation. If we now add **filling** to the representation in Figure 16, we have the diagram in Figure 18.

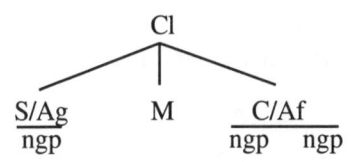

```
            Cl
      ┌─────┼─────┐
    S/Ag    M    C/Af
    ngp          ngp  ngp
```

*Figure 18:*
*The notations for representing 'componence', 'conflation' and 'filling'*

Up to this point I have been writing as if it was the Subject or the Complement that is filled by a nominal group. But it is, strictly speaking, the **Participant Role (PR)** that is conflated with the Subject or the Complement that the unit below fills. This is because, in generation, it is typically the PR which predicts what the unit will be, and the likely semantic features of the entity to be generated. (The configuration of PRs in a clause is in turn closely tied to the Process type, which is typically realized in the Main Verb.) However, from the viewpoint of drawing tree diagrams when analyzing text-sentences, it makes little difference whether you picture the unit as filling the PR or as filling the element with which it is conflated.[12]

The diagrams in Figures 16, 17 and 18 are beginning to resemble the generation of a text-sentence. But in fact the exponent of the Main Verb (i.e., the item *washed*, to which we shall come in the next section) would also be generated on the first traversal of the system network, and the three nominal groups shown in Figure 18 would not.[13]

---

12. This is why I have allowed myself to speak of the Subject being filled by a nominal group, etc. The fact that it is not seriously misleading to do so can be exploited in the initial analysis of a text (or in an introductory course in SFL), in which only the categories of 'Subject' and 'Complement' are inserted in the diagram, with the assignment of Participant Roles — whose identification can quite often be problematical — being left till later.

13. This is because the way in which a systemic functional grammar works is to generate, on each traversal of the system network, a unit, its elements and any direct exponent of any of those elements. It is the clause, its elements and their exponents that are generated on the first traversal. Each of the three nominal groups would be generated by the first realization rule to be applied on each of the subsequent traversals that generated them. For a similar but greatly simplified example, see Section 3 of Appendix A.

The introduction of the relationship of 'filling' as a complement to that of 'componence' is probably one of the Cardiff Grammar's main contributions to developing a theory of syntax for a modern systemic functional grammar.

## 11.6 Exponence and depth of exponence

11.6.1 The concept of exponence

The relationship between categories of **exponence** has a different theoretical status from any other, because it takes us out of the abstract categories of **syntax** and into the more concrete (but still abstract) phonological or graphological "shape" of **items**. Thus we may say that the head of a nominal group is **expounded** by the item *mountain*. As I pointed out earlier, the present use of the term is essentially a return to the sense in which it was used by Firth (1957/68), from whom Halliday borrowed it before greatly extending its meaning in "Categories". (Later, as we have seen, he re-named it 'realization').

In the Cardiff Grammar the realization operation that generates this relationship is "Expound an element by an item". Its notation is simply:

h < *mountain*.

Surprisingly, the equivalent operation in the Sydney Grammar is termed "Lexify". It is surprising because the traditional distinction between "grammatical" and "lexical" items has always been reflected in Halliday's work (e.g., what he does and does not cover in his system networks) so that it is odd to find the term "lexify" being used as the name of the operation that inserts **all** types of items, irrespective of where they come on the continuum from the most "lexical" to the most "grammatical". But the example in Halliday 1993:4505) shows that it really is intended to generate grammatical as well as lexical items.

Usually an item expounds a single meaning, as in the example above. But sometimes two meanings are realized in a single item, e.g., the meanings of [goose] + [plural] in *geese*. This is termed a **portmanteau realization**.

I have said that the category that is expounded is always an element. This statement is not inaccurate, but it should now be made more specific. There are in fact two types of 'exponence' operation. In the first, the element is simply expounded, as in the example cited above of "h < *mountain*". But sometimes a second item is added to the structure, and typically this is not a complete 'word' but a **suffix**. This uses a closely related type of realization operation, namely the "expound as suffix" operation — e.g., to generate the words *mountains*:

$$h < mountain, \ h <+ s$$

In traditional grammar, the existing element *mountain* in such an example would be described as the 'base' and the element *as* a "suffix". Here, however, we shall not use these terms. The reason is that there is no need (in English but not necessarily in other languages) to recognize the 'word' as a syntactic unit —though this was done in Scale and Category Grammar and in early Systemic Functional Grammar (e.g., as described in Berry 1975:85). In that approach each word consisted, in principle, of a base and potentially one or more affixes. So in the case of *mountains* the 'base' would have been said to be expounded by *mountain* and the 'suffix' by *s*. However, as I pointed out in Section 10.5.2 of Chapter 10, this would add an unnecessary extra layer to the generation and analysis of every text-sentence. In practice, all that the grammar of English needs is the ability to add a 'suffix' to an existing element, by the use of the "expound as suffix" operation — and, very rarely in English but commonly in some other languages, a prefix.[14] The term "suffix", then, is technically one that occurs within the name of a realization operation (though it can also be used as an informal label for a class of item that gets added to an element in this way, rather as we also make informal use the 'word class' labels when it is convenient). The 'suffix' is therefore not an integral part of the present theory (though it may be found useful for describing certain languages).

In addition to the 'plural' *-s* that is added to 'regular' nouns in English, the suffixes *-s*, *-ing* and *-ed* are added to 'regular' lexical verbs, and *-ly*, *-er* and *-est* to 'regular' adjectives. Diagram (a) in Figure 19 shows the usual way of showing exponence in a text-descriptive representation, and Diagram (b) shows how to represent an example with a suffix. However, it is not usual to show this degree of detail in a text analysis. Diagrams (c) and (d) show the representation in the printed format.[15]

---

14. In languages such as Japanese which require the introduction to the structure of a prefix (and in English in rare cases such as *great-great-grandfather*) a similar realization operation for adding a prefix is used, i.e., *great-* +> h.

15. There is only place that I can think of where a systemic functional linguist actually shows what the implications of placing the categories of 'word' and 'morpheme' on the 'rank scale' are for the representation of text-sentences. This is in Berry (1975:9), a work that provides a

256　　　A THEORY OF INSTANCES: RELATIONSHIPS

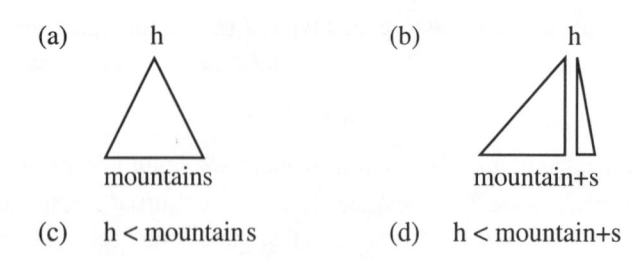

(a)　　h　　　　　　　(b)　　　h
　　　△　　　　　　　　　△|
　　mountains　　　　　　mountain+s

(c)　h < mountains　　(d)　h < mountain+s

*Figure 19: The notations for 'exponence' in drawn diagrams and in print*

11.6.2  Variation in depth of exponence

This section addresses, as we shall see, a question which would be a serious problem for a 'rank scale' grammar — and which has still not in fact been adequately addressed in the framework of such grammars. But the question is also relevant, in a modified form, in the present grammar. It concerns the point in a tree diagram at which the relationship of exponence should be introduced. We can approach it by asking "Is it the case that there are two types of element: (1) those that are always directly expounded by an item and (2) those that are always filled by another unit?"

In principle, the question should not arise in a grammar with 'accountability at all ranks', but in practice the examples to be considered below cause serious problems for a 'rank-based' grammar'. And in the present grammar it is still relevant to ask whether there should be an equivalent principle of 'total accountability at all possible layers of structure'.[16]

Consider the underlined portions of the following examples: _sixty_ books, _many_ books, _plenty_ of books, _a lot_ of books, _a very large number_ of books, _a huge heap_ of books, _two hundred_ books, _over sixty_ books and _over two hundred_ books. In each case the underlined portion expresses the 'quantity' of books. Sometimes this is marked by the presence of the item *of* (which

---

very useful 'fleshing out' of the concepts in Halliday's "Categories". Morphology is simply ignored in most other introductions to SFL. Indeed, this lack of discussion can be taken as indirect evidence for the rather different view of the 'word' and the 'morpheme' taken here — at least with respect to English. See the discussion in Section 10.5.2 of Chapter 10 of the problems for the 'rank scale' concept of languages such as Japanese, Mohawk and Swahili.

16. We might note that the data that we are about to consider are yet another serious source of embarrassment for the concept of the 'rank scale'.

expounds the **selector** in a nominal group) and sometimes it is not. (Thus here *of* is not a preposition; in a functional grammar such details of realization at the level of form should be fitted in around the major generalizations about the meanings of the elements.) In all of the above examples, then, we shall want to say that the quantifying expression functions as a **quantifying determiner** in a nominal group whose **head** is *books*.

This brings us to the question to be addressed here. If you work your way through the string of examples that I have just given, there is a point at which you will decide that the quantifying determiner is not directly expounded by an item, but is instead filled by a unit with its own internal structure. For me this would be *a lot of books* (because we must also allow for *a(n absolutely) huge lot of books*, etc.). Here we shall consider just the four examples where the quantifying expression is a cardinal number, i.e., *sixty books, two hundred books, over sixty books* and *over two hundred books*. Please look at the analyses of the first three examples in Figure 20.

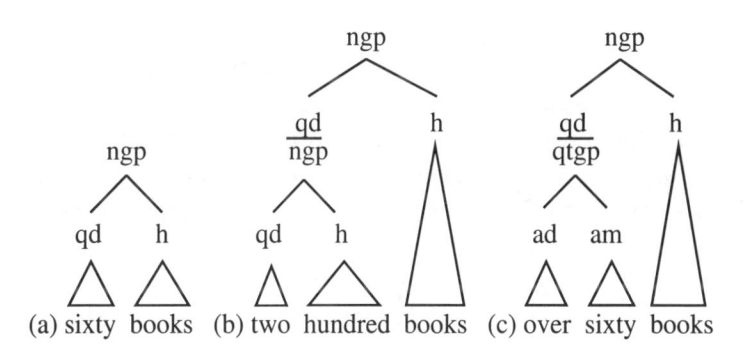

*Figure 20: Variation in the depth of exponence of a quantifying determiner*

In Example (a) the quantifying determiner (qd) is shown as directly expounded by the item *sixty*. But Examples (b) and (c), illustrate the fact that there are two frequent ways in which a quantifying determiner may be filled by a quantifying expression which itself has the internal structure of a group. Expressions of 'quantity' are frequently expressed through a **nominal group**, as in (b) above and in examples such as *a very large number* and *a huge heap*. Example (c) above illustrates the fact that the unit that fills a quantifying determiner is also frequently a **quantity group**, where the two elements are an **adjustor** and an **amount.** Moreover, the two constructions exemplified in (b) and (c) can be combined, as in *over two hundred books*, where the item *over* 'adjusts' the 'amount' of *two hundred* — so adding another layer of structure.[17]

The following important theoretical question now arises: "Should the analysis of (a) in Figure 20 show the potential of every quantifying expression that uses a cardinal number to be a nominal group? (Indeed, it can be two or more co-ordinated nominal groups, as in *five thousand, two hundred and fifty books*.) And should it additionally show the ability of the 'amount' to be 'adjusted', as in (c), and so for the two structures to be combined, as in *over two hundred books*? If we were to apply Halliday's principle of 'total accountability', we would have to show every occurrence of a simple cardinal number, as in *sixty books*, as embedded **two layers further down the tree**, i.e., as an element of a nominal group in a quantity group in a nominal group. And if this principle were extended to apply at every other point in the grammar where such issues arise (some of which we shall meet shortly), the work involved in both generating and analyzing a text would be enormously increased.

The solution to this problem proposed here — and already implemented in the computer model — is to build the relevant choices into the system networks. And the realization of the choices is **variation in the depth of exponence**.

In the system network for QUANTITY, for example, the feature [cardinal] leads to a system in which one of the options is [sub-hundred]. When this is chosen the grammar will generate a simple cardinal number such as *nine* or *ninety-nine*. The feature [sub-hundred], together with several other features, then enters a system in which the choice is between 'adjusting' the quantity and 'not adjusting' it. It is only if both of the features [sub-hundred] and [cardinal unadjusted] are chosen that the grammar will generate an item that directly expounds the qd. If they are not, the realization rules associated with the other features in the relevant systems trigger a re-entry to the system network to generate a new syntactic unit. So if 'adjustment' is required (e.g., to generate (c) in Figure 20) the generation of the cardinal is postponed till later. The re-entry to the network then generates a quantity group, which opens up the range of meanings that follow from choosing to 'adjust' the cardinal number.

If a feature other than [sub-hundred] is chosen (and there is no 'adjustment') the grammar is re-entered to generate a nominal group, as in (b). And of

---

17. Indeed, an adjustor can itself contain an embedded quantity group, such that the 'amount of adjustment' that it expresses is in turn adjusted, as in *well over two hundred books, a trifle over two hundred books*, etc.

course the two types of meaning may combine, as in *over two hundred* books.

A similar case arises with deictic determiners that express 'possession'. In examples such as *my books* and *his books* the items *my* and *his* are modelled as directly expounding the **deictic determiner** (dd). But in the case of *my friend's books* a **genitive cluster** fills the dd (its possessor being filled by the nominal group *my friend*). Another such case is the Main Verb Extension (Mex in Appendix B) — as in the example of the word *out* in *She threw it out into the yard*, because the Mex can be 'expanded' to *right out*. (Here the unit of the quantity group is borrowed to handle the structure.)

How far should this useful principle be extended? For example, should we say that the Subject of a clause that is ultimately expounded by a single pronoun such as *he* is to be directly expounded by it? Clearly, few linguists would wish to do this, but the criteria for not doing so are rarely stated clearly.

There are in fact several reasons for not extending the principle to such cases. The first is the sheer centrality of the choices in the nominal group in the grammar as a whole. It is the unit that is used for referring to 'objects', and within it we need to be able to choose between the three major ways of referring to objects that are exemplified by *my friend*, *she* and *Ivy* respectively. The second reason is the sheer frequency of all three types. And the third is the need to be able to co-ordinate different types (as in *my friend and I* and *Ivy and I*).

A more problematical case is the treatment of *tall* in *a tall man*. Since **modifiers** are quite frequently filled by **quality groups**, as in the underlined portion of *a very tall man*, we treat examples such as *a tall man* as cases where the modifier is filled by a quality group that has only an apex.

Ultimately, then, the criterion is a matter of economy. In other words, when a further layer of structure unit is required relatively frequently — as in the case of the nominal group that fills the Subject and the quality group that fills the modifier — we always introduce the additional unit. However, when the lower unit occurs only relatively infrequently — as in the case of the quantifying determiner cited above, we introduce a system to handle the choice that is manifested ultimately as variation in depth of exponence.

11.6.3   Exponence added to componence, conflation and filling

Let us now take the example analyzed in Figure 18, and add to it the one relationship of exponence that would be generated on the first traversal of the

260  A THEORY OF INSTANCES: RELATIONSHIPS

system network, i.e., the exponent of the Main Verb. This is the representation shown in Figure 21.

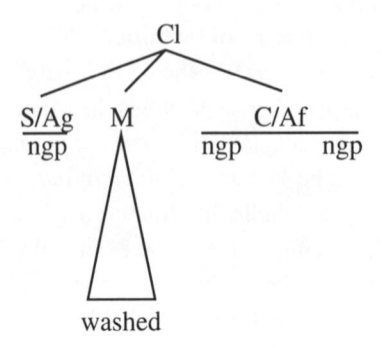

```
              Cl
      _____|_____
     /        |        \
   S/Ag       M        C/Af
   ngp                ngp   ngp
              /\
             /  \
            /____\
            washed
```

*Figure 21: The notations for 'componence, 'filling' conflation' and 'exponence'*

Let us now imagine that the system network has been re-entered three times more, to generate the three nominal groups shown in Figure 21, i.e. *Ike, his shirt* and the co-ordinated nominal group *and his jeans*. In Figure 22 I have also added the symbol for 'filling' to show the relationship between the clause and the topmost element in the structure, i.e., 'sentence' ($\Sigma$), and also the clause element Ender. (For the role of the sentence as the interface with discourse, see Section 10.1.2 of Chapter 10; for the Ender see Appendix B.)

The result of these additions to Figure 21 is a complete representation of a text-sentence at the level of form.

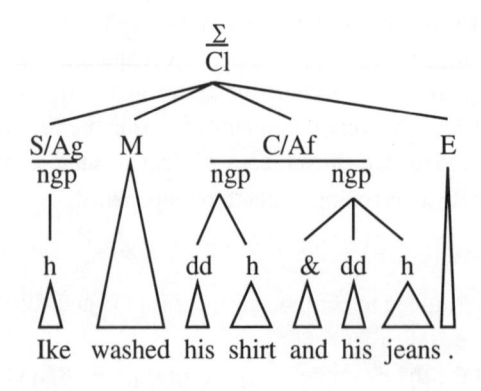

```
                  Σ
                  ─
                  Cl
         _____|_____
        /    |       |        \
      S/Ag   M      C/Af       E
      ngp          ngp  ngp
       |           /\    /\
       h         dd  h  & dd h
       Δ   /\   Δ  Δ    Δ  Δ  Δ
       Ike washed his shirt and his jeans .
```

*Figure 22: The complete syntactic analysis of a text-sentence*

Figure 22 can be taken as a summary of the four 'core' relationships in syntax, i.e., the relationships between syntactic categories that are the direct result of the application of realization operations.

However, there are two other important concepts that have a place in a theory of syntax, each of which can be best understood in relation to one or more of the realization operations, and we shall now look at these. The second of these — that of 'recursion' — itself contains two major concepts that are vital to explaining why syntax becomes as complex as it sometimes does: co-ordination and embedding.

## 11.7 Continuous and discontinuous relationships between 'sister' elements

Typically, the elements of a unit occur in an uninterrupted sequence. Such a unit can be said to be a **continuous** unit, and its elements are in the simple 'segmental' relationship of adjacency to each other. This conforms to the general principle that, once a performer has begun on the production of a semantic unit — and so on the production of the syntactic unit in which it is realized — it is helpful to the addressee to finish it before starting on another unit.

But sometimes this principle of "Finish the current unit" is in conflict with one or more other principles. Two of these are what we may call the "Get the pivotal element in soon" principle and the "End weight" principle. For a fuller presentation of these principles, which can be compared with those in Leech (1983), see Fawcett (in press).

In an example such as *The time has come when you must leave*, the nominal group filling the Subject is *the time* [...] *when you must leave*. But it is a **discontinuous** nominal group, with the qualifier *when you must leave* following the Main Verb *leave*. In such examples the combined influence of the "Get the pivotal element in soon" principle and the "End weight" principle is more powerful than the everyday "Finish the current unit" principle, and the clause moves to the pivotal element of the Main Verb *come* as quickly as it can, letting the semantically 'heavy' qualifier from the nominal group *when you must leave* follow, probably with its own information unit, i.e., in its spoken form:

‖ *the time has come* | *when you must leave* ‖

Within the structure of the nominal group, the same two principles lead to discontinuous quality groups such as the one indicated by the underlined portion of *a <u>more important</u> person <u>than he is</u>*. Here, the words *than he is* constitute a **finisher** in the discontinuous quality group *more* (t) *important* (a) [...] *than he is* (f). Figure 23 (taken from Fawcett in press) illustrates the notation for showing this type of discontinuity. Thus, whenever a line showing the relationship of componence crosses another representation of a relationship (here exponence) we have a case of discontinuity.[18]

```
                    ngp
           ┌─────────┬──────┐
          qd        m        h
                   ─────
                    qlgp
           │       ╱   ╲        │
           │      dt    a       f
           △     △    △    △
        (She is) a more important person than he is.
```

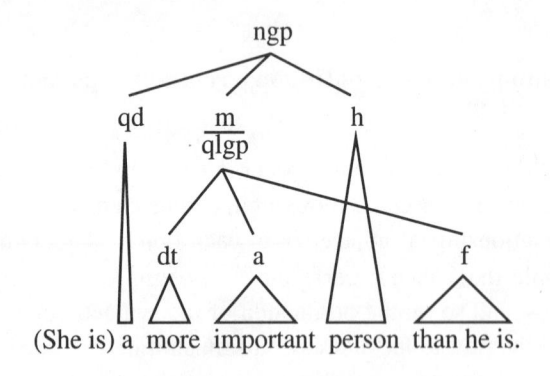

*Figure 23: The discontinuity of a quality group that fills a modifier*

However, discontinuity is most frequently the result of various types of **thematization**. Thus in *Who were you seen by?* the completive (cv) *who* is an element of the discontinuous prepositional group *by* [...] *who*. We saw in Section 10.4.4 of Chapter 10 (on the concept of 'place') that this type of discontinuity is sometimes called "raising", and an example of this type is given in Figure 13 in that section. Note that this type of discontinuity is different from the two earlier types, in that the thematized **completive** comes before rather than after the rest of the unit of which it is an element, and in a higher unit.

Thus the present theory of syntax provides for all types of discontinuity. See Fawcett (in press) for a fuller account of the various types of discontinuity that occur in English.

---

18. A completely different way of representing discontinuity is required for the computer implementation of the grammar. We mark with an asterisk both the separated element and the unit from which it is separated, so showing the componence of the discontinuous unit.

## 11.8 Recursion: co-ordination, embedding and reiteration

11.8.1 The general concept of 'recursion'

There are three types of recursive relationship in English: **co-ordination**, **embedding** and **reiteration**. Reiteration is much less central to the grammar of English than the other two, and it is used more in other languages. But do 'recursive structures' in fact occur in language? Strictly speaking, they do not.

Recursion occurs when a choice in the system network leads to a realization rule which specifies a **re-entry** to the system network and the choice of the same feature again. What we find at the level of syntax is two types of the 'repetition' of a class of unit and, in reiteration, the repetition of an item (as in *He's very very happy.*). All three of these are cases of the **realization** at the level of form of recursively selecting the same feature in the system networks. The effect of choosing such a feature is to generate a unit **alongside** an existing unit (this being is **co-ordination**) or **inside** another unit (this being second **embedding**. In the strict sense of embedding, a unit fills an element of the same class (most frequently a clause filling an element of a clause, as illustrated in Appendix B). In co-ordination the two or more co-ordinated units are typically of the same class — but not necessarily, as we will see in the next section. (We shall recognize a looser sense of 'embedding' in Section 11.8.3.)

It is the relationship of **filling** that makes possible the first two types of recursion, and the relationship of **exponence** that enables reiteration to occur.

11.8.2 The recursion of co-ordination

The first type of recursion is **co-ordination.** Here two or more units fill a single element of structure. It occurs between all units: clauses and all classes of groups and occasionally clusters. Typically the units are (or in the case of the genitive cluster, contain) potential **referring expressions**, because co-ordination is ultimately not between syntactic units but between mental referents.

Co-ordination is typically marked by an overt **Linker**, such as *and* or *or*, and these two Linkers can occur with all units. (The linker has a lower case "l" when it co-ordinates groups.) A Linker or linker may co-occur with intonational marking or a punctuation mark (e.g., the two commas in *Peter, his brother, his brother's wife and their children*).

While some co-ordinators (e.g., *and* and *or*) occur with all units, each class of unit has its own set, with its own probabilities. Thus there is not a single set of choices in co-ordination for all units, as some grammars imply.

Sometimes the meaning of 'co-ordination' is re-enforced by another linker that introduces the first unit, as in *both my wife and myself*. This suggests that the L/linker should be treated as an element of the unit that it introduces, rather than as a 'structural signal' that is not part of either unit (cp. Halliday 1966).

It is almost always the case that the two or more units that are co-ordinated belong to the same class of unit. But because the motivation to co-ordinate units occurs at a higher level of planning, we occasionally find the co-ordination of two units which serve the same semantic function but which differ syntactically — e.g., the nominal and prepositional groups in *(I lost it) either last Monday or during the previous weekend* which jointly fill a Time Position Adjunct.

Occasionally we need to allow for embedding in co-ordinated structures, as in examples such as *ten boys and girls* (where *ten* quantifies both the boys and the girls). The linker *and* is attached to *girls* (for the reasons given above) and the two nominal groups of (1) *boys* and (2) *and girls* jointly fill the head of a higher nominal group whose quantifying determiner is *ten*.

One notable characteristic of co-ordination is that the semantic and syntactic similarities between two units often result in a partial **syntactic parallelism** — and that this in turn often leads to **ellipsis**. Thus, in *The thieves have stolen our TV and drunk all my whisky*, the two elements of *they* (and not, it should be noted, *the thieves*) and *have* have been ellipted from the second clause. Ellipsis in co-ordinated clauses can become quite complex, as *in Ivy is going out with Paul and not Fred*. Here, to provide an adequate analysis, we need to reconstruct the ellipted elements, as follows: *Ivy is going out with Paul and (she is) not (going out with) Fred*. It is often the presence of the Negator *not* or an Adjunct that alerts the analyst to the presence of an ellipted clause.

11.8.3 The recursion of embedding

The second type of recursion is **embedding**. This occurs when a unit fills an element of the same class of unit — and also, in a looser sense, when a unit of the same class occurs above it in the tree structure. So we shall **not** say that we have a case of embedding in *on the table*, where the **nominal group** *the table* fills the completive of the **prepositional group** *on the table* (as

Halliday would; see p. 242 of *IFG*). However, if *the table* occurred in *the box on the table*, this is embedding in a looser sense of the term, because the nominal group *the table* fills the completive of the prepositional group *on the table*, and this in turn fills the qualifier of the higher nominal group *the box on the table*.

And, in an even looser use of the term, one could refer to any case in which a unit appears lower in the tree than the second layer as 'embedding'. Here, however, I shall normally use the term "embedding" in the sense of the occurrence (direct or indirect) of a class of unit within the same class of unit.

By far the most important type of embedding is the embedding of a clause as an element of a higher clause, or a clause as an element of a nominal, quality or quantity group — and so indirectly as an element of a higher clause. The reason why clause embedding is so important is, of course, that once one introduces an embedded clause at any point in a tree structure, many (but not all) of the vast set of meanings associated with a clause and its elements become available again, and additional layers of structure are necessarily added to the tree representation.

However, in the present grammar ir is not the concept of embedding *per se* that leads to the richness of syntax, but the grammar's ability to fill many elements of many units by many other units. Sometimes this results in the embedding of a unit inside another of the same class (e.g., a clause within a clause, as described above), but often it is one class of group within another — and so one that would, in *IFG* terms, be at the same 'rank' as the higher unit.

### 11.8.4 Embedding as a contribution to the richness of 'depth' in syntax

Let us consider an example of this crucial point. Figure 24, which is taken from Fawcett (in press), illustrates the important fact that nominal groups frequently contain other classes of groups within them. In this invented example, I have chosen to illustrate the use of units other than nominal groups, so that the only cases of 'embedding' are the two nominal groups that occur inside (1) the genitive cluster and (2) the prepositional group. It is well known, of course, that nominal groups frequently contain clauses that function as a qualifier ('relative clauses'), and Figure 24 complements this by illustrating the less widely-recognized fact that the richness in the layering of structure in the nominal group comes equally often from the occurrence of groups other than nominal groups.

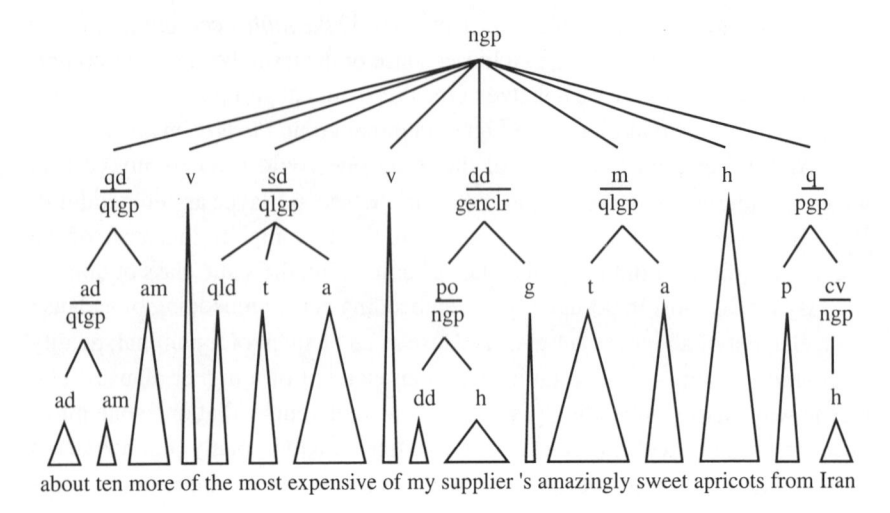

*Figure 24: An example of complexity in the nominal group*

Thus much of the very great richness in the syntax of English results from the fact that, when we come to fill the elements of the units of English, we very frequently do **not** take a step down the supposed 'rank scale', and so do **not** use embedding, in the proper sense of the term.

The concept of the 'rank scale' expresses a hypothesis about the 'natural' depth of layering in a structure (although Halliday himself has never suggested that this was a motivation for introducing it). Thus it predicts that, in the unmarked case, groups will occur at a depth of one, words at a depth of two, and morphemes at a depth of three. However, few natural texts conform to this pattern. In analyzing text in the framework of the Cardiff Grammar, we measure depth only down to the lowest structural unit, since words take us out of componence and into exponence. The evidence from the analysis of large quantities of text in terms of the description of English summarized in Appendix B is that we are able to manage up to about seven layers of depth, measured in such terms, and occasionally a couple more— and moreover that children of twelve seem to perform in a similar manner to adults in this respect.[19]

Since the processing of an unfinished unit is suspended when a lower

---

19. Specifically, the figure used was the mean of the five text-sentences which exhibited the greatest depth of a group in about ten minutes of interactive talk by each subject. See Section 11.2.2 for a brief account of the 'depth probabilities' implied in the diagrams of Appendix B.

layer of structure is encountered, there may well be a connection here with Miller's well-known finding that human short-term memory falls off steeply after processing seven units — plus or minus two, depending on individual variation (Miller 1956).[20]

The crucial notion, then, is not that of embedding in the strict sense of the term, but the amazing ability of human language to construct units that contain other units within them. This ability — of which the embedding of clauses within other clauses and within various classes of group is simply the most salient characteristic — is one of the chief glories of human language. Yet the use of terms such as 'rank scale' and 'rank shift' suggests a view of language in which embedding is regarded as an aberration from the right ordering of language — rather than being, as I believe it to be, a vital contribution to its elegant power to model our physical and mental worlds.

### 11.8.5 Halliday's position on 'rank shift' and 'embedding'

In "Categories" Halliday referred to the phenomenon of embedding as "rank shift". The concept of 'rank shift' is, of course, directly dependent on the concept of the 'rank scale', i.e., the general expectation that a unit will fill an element of structure of a unit higher on the 'rank scale' than itself. According to "Categories", 'rank shift' down the 'rank scale' is allowed (e.g., a clause can fill an element of another clause or of a 'lower' unit, but 'upward rank shift' is not allowed (i.e., a word cannot operate as an element of a clause, and a morpheme cannot operate as an element of a group or a clause).

---

20. Clearly, other factors are also relevant. Much of the discussion in the literature has been conducted in terms of distinctions between 'right-branching', 'self-embedded' and 'left-branching' structures. 'Right-branching' constructions such as those found in *This is the cat that chased the rat that ate the malt that lay in the house that Jack built* are generally held to be easier to process than 'left-branching' structures such as *his mother's friend's sister's handbag*. But another factor in making the processing easier is undoubtedly the fact that each qualifier in the 'house that Jack built' example extends a nominal group which could have finished after the head. It would be interesting to investigate this area of syntax in the framework of a functional model of language such as that suggested here. A related area of potential research concerns the number of elements in a clause. Interestingly, research on the developments in children's syntax (as described in Fawcett & Perkins 1981) shows that by the age of six — and across both sexes and four social classes — the mean length of children's longest five clauses in a ten-minute interaction is already between six and seven elements (assuming the model of the clause used in Appendix B). And there was little or no development in this respect in the eight-, ten- and twelve-year-old children.

Halliday later replaced the term "rank shift" by the more widely used term "embedding", and in my view this second term is indeed greatly preferable. This is because the term 'rankshift' can be interpreted in two ways that are misleading. The first is the implication that something has been "shifted", perhaps from its typical place in a structure to some other place, whereas in fact the unit has not been moved at all. The second possible misleading inference is that there is something unusual about a 'higher' unit filling an element of a 'lower' unit. But for virtually all linguists other than those who work in the *IFG* framework, embedding is a natural and frequently occurring phenomenon.[21]

What, then, is the place of embedding in Halliday's current theory? As we saw in Section 5.3 of Chapter 5, the concept is not mentioned at all in "Systemic theory". However, it is present in *IFG* — and in a version that is far more restrictive than in "Categories". Halliday's definition is as follows:

> Embedding is a mechanism whereby a clause or phrase comes to function as a constituent **within the structure of a group** [my emphasis], which is itself a constituent of a clause. Hence there is no direct relationship between an embedded clause and the clause within which it is embedded; the relationship [...] is an indirect one, with a group as intermediary. The embedded clause functions in the structure of the group, and the group functions in the structure of the clause. (Halliday 1994:242)

Unfortunately, Halliday does not explain why he thinks it desirable that a clause should not be permitted to fill an element of another clause. This omission is especially surprising, given that this was permitted in his earlier S&C grammar.

He then goes on to list the very small number of types of embedding that he does still allow (p. 242). These are (expressed here in both Cardiff Grammar and Sydney Grammar terms):

the occurrence of either a **clause** or a **prepositional group / phrase** (but no other class of unit, so not a nominal group) as:

---

21. It sometimes seems as if Halliday introduced the concept of 'hypotaxis' precisely to avoid having to embed one clause inside another — though Halliday nowhere explains why this phenomenon, which most other grammarians recognize as occurring with great frequency in many types of text, should be regarded as a Bad Thing. It is the fact that Halliday's grammar minimises embedding that forces him — or enables him, depending on your viewpoint — to interpret all of the types of direct 'clause within a clause' embedding recognized here as cases of a 'hypotactic' relationship. For an introduction to 'hypotaxis' see Section 2.6.1 of Chapter 2; for a critical discussion see Section 3 of Appendix C; and for the Cardiff Grammar alternatives see Section 11.9.

1. the **head** in a nominal group or
2. a **qualifier** in a nominal group (also referred to as a "postmodifier" in some sections of *IFG*), or
3. the **finisher** in a quality group (in *IFG* a "postmodifier" in an "adverbial group" (but note that in *IFG* there is no provision for a similarly structured quality group with an adjective as its apex).

Halliday then goes on to state categorically that "there are no further types". The above specification of what types of 'rank shift' are permitted is therefore extremely narrow. It provides for cases such as *what Jack built* and *for Jack to build a house* as embedded clauses that fill the Subject, but only by filling the head of a nominal group that in turn fills the Subject. And it even provides for rare cases such as *by the bridge* as the Subject — but again only as the head of a nominal group that fills a Subject. Why, one wonders, should the clause or prepositional group not fill the Subject directly? Halliday simply states his position and gives no reason. Yet this approach introduces an additional layer of structure, which runs against his general approach of reducing the number of layers of structure in the representation to the minimum.[22]

However, there is a further problem with Halliday's specification of the permitted types of embedding. This is that it excludes very many of the types of embedding that are recognized in the present grammar. These are shown in Appendix B, where the symbols at the top of the diagram for each class of unit show the elements of structure that it can fill.

It is of course precisely Halliday's purpose to exclude many of these — especially the ways in which a **clause** may occur within a **clause**). The reason is that he has changed his mind since "Categories" (as we saw in Section 2.6.1 of Chapter 2), so that he now wishes to handle such cases as 'hypotaxis' (in the way to be described in Section 11.9). Secondly, however, his specification excludes many of the ways in which a **clause** fills an element of a **group**, as is also shown in Appendix B. Finally, the specification excludes the many ways in which a **group** may fill an element of a **group** (or **cluster**), again as shown in Appendix B. In the last two cases the omissions may in part be due to the

---

22. In a footnote (p. 242) Halliday re-affirms that the embedded clause or prepositional phrase does indeed function as the head of a nominal group — while at the same time stating that in such cases "we may leave out the intermediate (nominal group) step in the analysis and represent the embedded clause or phrase as functioning directly in the structure of the outer clause, as Subject or whatever." I welcome this small concession, and I suggest that there is, in fact, no reason why a clause should not be permitted to fill an element of another clause.

great emphasis in *IFG* on the clause, so that groups are inadequately covered.

The overall picture that one gets from *IFG*, then, is that the concept of the 'rank scale' is just as central in *IFG* as it was in "Categories", but with far stricter conditions on 'rank shift'. The Sydney Grammar handles as 'hypotaxis' what other grammars treat as the embedding of clauses.

On the other hand, we should also recall the apparent diminution of the focus on 'rank' in Halliday's later descriptions of the theory, which we noted when surveying the basic concepts of "Systemic theory" and *IFG,* in Chapters 5 and 6 respectively. As we noted in Section 6.2.2 of Chapter 6, Halliday chooses to make the point, when discussing the concept of 'rank' in *IFG*, that

> the issue is whether, in a comprehensive interpretation of the system, it is worth maintaining the global generalization, because of its explanatory power, even though it imposes local complications at certain places in the description" (Halliday 1994:12).

In view of the changes to the SF model of syntax set out here, it is tempting to see this statement as an expression of Halliday's willingness to reconsider the concept of the 'rank scale' — though in reality such a change of position seems improbable. Yet it is hard to think of any other interpretation of the omission of the concept of the 'rank scale' from "Systemic theory" (Halliday 1993).

One of the major differences between the Sydney and the Cardiff frameworks is the fact that the coverage of groups is far fuller in the Cardiff Grammar than it is in the Sydney Grammar. See especially Tucker (1998) for a definitive description of the quality group and Fawcett (in press) for a fairly full account of all four of the classes of group that are recognized in the Cardiff Grammar. In large measure, it is the evidence from this mass of descriptive detail that has led us to replace the predictions of the 'rank scale' by probabilities as to what classes of unit fills what elements of structure.

Thus there is still considerable scope for the further development of the description of groups in the Sydney Grammar, and it may be that as this happens the over-narrow predictions set out in *IFG* will be replaced by a more wide-ranging statement — possibly expressed in terms of probabilities, as here.

### 11.8.6 The recursion of reiteration

The third type of recursion in language is much less frequent in English. It is **reiteration.** It occurs when a performer makes the choice to repeat an item for emphasis, and it therefore typically occurs with items that are themselves 'emphasizers', as in *She's very very nice.* The two occurrences of *very* are represented as jointly expounding a single temperer (using "<+").

## 11.9 How embedding and co-ordination can replace 'hypotaxis' and 'parataxis'

The twin concepts of 'parataxis' and 'hypotaxis' play such a large part in *IFG* (pp. 215-73) that it may be helpful to state how they are handled here.

Firstly, then, Halliday's two types of 'hypotactic projecting' clause ('locution' and 'idea') are handled as embedded clauses that fill a Phenomenon that is conflated with a Complement, thus:

John [S] said/thought [M] he was running away [clause filling C/Ph].

And his equivalent two types of 'paratactic projecting' clause are handled similarly — except that the embedded clause fills a sentence, which functions as an element in a simplified model of a 'move' in discourse (shown as "text"), and this in turn fills the Phenomenon/Complement (see Appendix B), thus:

He [S] said/thought [M] "I'll run away" [clause filling Σ in "text" filling C/Ph]

Within the 'expansion' type of 'hypotaxis', Halliday distinguishes 'elaboration', 'extension' and 'enhancement'. The last two are treated here as follows:

John [S] ran [M] away [Mex], whereas Fred stayed behind [A].
John [S] ran [M] away [Mex], because he was scared [A].

In other words, the two clauses embedded in an Adjunct express two of the many types of 'logical' relationship for which Adjuncts are used: the first is an Adversative Adjunct (cp. *in contrast, on the other hand*), while the second is a Cause Adjunct (cp. *therefore, for this reason*). And both are thematizable.

However, Halliday's third type of 'hypotactic expansion' is analyzed as a special type of co-ordination, termed a 'pseudo-relative', as follows:

[John[S] ran[M] away[Mex], [Cl]][which[S] surprised[M] everyone[C] [Cl]].

Here *which surprised everyone* is treated as equivalent to *and this surprised everyone*, and the two clauses jointly fill a sentence (which is omitted above).

Finally, *IFG*'s three types of 'paratactic expansion' (with clauses linked by a semi-colon, *and* and *so*) are simply three types of co-ordination.

To summarize: we treat four of Halliday's five types of 'hypotaxis' and two of his five types of 'parataxis' as embedding, and one type of 'hypotaxis' and his three 'expansion' types of 'parataxis' as co-ordination. Thus the features that generate these examples are found in various parts of the system network. This approach, then, is less novel than Halliday's, but it is equally systemic and functional. And it has all been implemented in COMMUNAL.

## 11.10 Summary of the relationships between categories in a modern systemic functional grammar

We have seen in this chapter that the three major relationships between categories are (1) the **componence** that relates a unit to its elements, (2) the **filling** that relates an element to a unit that functions at it, and — usually after one or more repetitions of the 'componence + filling' pattern — (3) the **exponence** that relates an element to the items that give the text its phonological or graphological shape. But there is also the relationship of **conflation**, which 'fuses' a new element (where the term 'element' includes 'Participant Role') with an existing one.

We have seen that the theory foregrounds the concept of **probabilities**, and we have focussed in particular on probabilities in **filling**. From the viewpoint of text analysis, it is these that are the nearest equivalent to the concept of the 'rank scale'.

We have also noted that there may occasionally be **discontinuity** in a unit, and that in some cases this may involve a 'raised' element, i.e., an element from a lower unit in the tree that is located at a **place** in a higher unit. Finally, we have noted three types of **recursion** that occur in the operation of the system networks — and which consequently generate structures that reflect these three types of recursion. These are **co-ordination**, **embedding** and (though only fairly infrequently in English) **reiteration**. But embedding, I have stressed, is simply a special case of the amazing general ability that human languages have to generate units that contain other units.

This set of relational concepts, then, together with the categories specified in Chapter 10, are what is needed for a modern theory of instances of syntax for Systemic Functional Linguistics.

# 12
# Summaries, conclusions and prospects

## 12.1 Introduction to the summaries: two models or one?

Chapters 9, 10 and 11 have described and discussed the concepts that are required in a modern SF grammar — together with a number of other concepts that have been proposed at various points in the development of SFL and that play no part in the new theory of syntax (such as the 'rank' and 'hypotaxis').

I suggest, therefore, that the concepts that are required in a modern systemic functional grammar are essentially the same as those found in the Cardiff Grammar (or some closely similar set). Moreover, as we saw in Chapter 7, the Sydney Grammar requires, to complete it, the concept of a single structure — i.e., a structure that is able to integrate the 'multiple structure' representations in *IFG* and the many derived works in a single structure. Thus any full account of a theory of SF syntax must recognize some such set of concepts associated with a single structure as those of the theory presented here.

However, we also saw in Chapter 7 that we cannot reconcile the two versions of the theory by simply adding the syntactic representation of the Cardiff Grammar to the 'multiple structures' of the Sydney Grammar, as a way to integrate them in a single structure. The first reason is that in the Cardiff Grammar it is simply not necessary to have any such 'intermediate' instantial representation between (1) the **selection expression** of features that are the output from the system networks and (2) the single, **integrated structure** that must be the final structural representation of any text-sentence (e.g., as shown in the upper half of Figure 10 in Chapter 7) — a fact that is demonstrated by the successful operation of the computer version of the Cardiff Grammar. The second reason why we cannot simply add the Cardiff representation of syntax to an *IFG*-style 'multiple structure' representation is that there are major (and probably insuperable) theoretical problems for the generative version of a model of language that is intended **first** to generate a set of five or more different structures for a clause and **then**, by the application of some type of 'structure conflation' rule that no SF theorist has yet attempted to formalize, to integrate them all into a single structure. It seems from the experience of those who have tried (in the Penman Project as reported in Matthiessen & Bateman 1991, and in the early stages of the COMMUNAL Project as described in Fawcett, Tucker & Lin 1993) that it is just not possible to incorporate 'multiple structures' in a generative SF grammar. The clear conclusion is that such grammars should be based on the concept of 'element conflation' rather than 'structure conflation'.

However, this leaves the long-established 'multiple structure' representations shown in the box diagrams of *IFG* and other works with no status in the theory. So the remaining question is whether the 'multiple structures' are nonetheless useful in text description — perhaps on the grounds that they are the best functional representations that are generally available at present (as it is arguably the case). This in turn raises the practical questions of how usable they in fact are in text analysis, and what alternatives are currently available, or soon will be. We shall return to these matters in the final section of this chapter.

Let us now look again at the two questions with which we began this book. The first was:

> What theoretical concepts are required for the description of syntax in a modern, large-scale systemic functional grammar?"

The short answer is that the concepts we need are specified in Chapters 10 and 11, and summarized in the last sections of those chapters. However, in the next three sections of this chapter I shall provide an integrated summary of the proposed new theory of syntax, and at the same time a comparison between it and the various other frameworks for syntax in SFL that I described in Part 1.

The subsidiary question with which we began was:

> How far are the founding concepts introduced by Halliday in "Categories" still valid in a modern, large-scale systemic functional grammar?

I shall return to this in Section 12.7 of this chapter.

The starting point for the summaries that follow must be the framework for a modern SF grammar that we established in Chapter 3. As Figure 4 in Section 3.2 of that chapter showed, its two principle characteristics are (1) that it consists essentially of the two levels of **meaning** and **form**, and (2) that there is at each level (a) a component that specified the **potential**, and (b) an 'output' from the grammar, i.e., the **instance** at that level.

As we have seen, an additional advantage of this formulation of the model is that it is at a sufficiently high level of generalization to provide a common framework in which we may compare the Sydney the Cardiff Grammars. Moreover, its ability to provide this common framework is not affected by Halliday and Matthiessen's increasing commitment, culminating in Halliday & Matthiessen (1999), to the idea of having a 'two-level' model of 'semantics' (as we saw in Section 4.6 of Chapter 4). In that model, you will recall, there is both the level of 'meaning potential' that Halliday recognized in the early 1970s as the semantics (e.g., Halliday 1971/73a:41-2), and a level of 'semantics' that is higher than this, roughly equivalent to Martin's (1992) 'discourse semantics'. The proposal that this common ground exists follows directly from statements of Halliday's from the late sixties to the present, such as:

> In a functional grammar, [...] a language is interpreted as a system of meanings, accompanied by forms through which the meanings can be expressed" (Halliday 1994:xix).

Indeed, it can be argued that all of the concepts that are required in a modern SF grammar follow from accepting the need to recognize the appropriate 'division of labour' between the two levels of semantics and form in such a model.

Section 12.2 will examine the 'categories', and Section 12.3 the 'scales' and the 'relationships' into which the 'scales' have developed. Then in Section 12.4 we will stand back from the comparison of individual concepts, and compare the Sydney Grammar and the Cardiff Grammar as two alternative models of language as a whole. The two have an enormous amount in common, of course, but they also have a number of important differences.

Can they be re-integrated into a single model? We who work in the framework of the Cardiff Grammar have learnt a tremendous amount from the work that is here characterized as the Sydney Grammar, and I have established in Chapter 3 that the two models have a sufficient amount in common to enable comparisons to be made. There is also, therefore, a basis for the exchange of concepts between the two models. Yet at the same time we who contribute to the Cardiff view of language have also found it valuable to make a number of changes, as this book shows. This should not be a matter of surprise — let alone resentment — because it is simply not reasonable to expect Halliday (or anyone else) to have 'got it right' at the first attempt (S&C) or even the second attempt (his SFL of the 1970s onwards). The purpose of writing this book is to try to contribute to the development of a more fully adequate systemic functional model of language, and I hope that the proposals made here will be considered by my fellow systemic functional linguists in that light.

There are two sorts of changes that we who contribute to the Cardiff

Grammar have made to the 'standard theory', as summarized in *IFG*. The first sort arises because the programme of exploration that Halliday sketched out had not been carried out in the Sydney framework, perhaps through a shortage of personnel. An example is the development of very large system networks for 'lexis as most delicate grammar' (1961/76:69) by Tucker and myself, assisted by others who have worked on the COMMUNAL Project such as Carlsen, Osman, Ball, and Neale. The work by Tucker, Lin and myself on incorporating probabilities into the system networks also falls into this category, in that Halliday has occasionally pointed out the importance of probabilities in language while leaving the implementation to others (one exception being Halliday & James 1993). In other cases, however, we have found it necessary to take a different approach Halliday's, in order to enable the model to reflect the data with greater coverage and, we think, more insightfully. It was for this reason that Tench developed his revised and extended version of Halliday's 1960s model of intonation (Tench 1996), and that Huang and I developed an explicitly functional approach to the **experiential enhanced theme** construction (Halliday's 'predicated theme' and formal grammar's '*it*-cleft' construction); see Fawcett & Huang (1995), Huang (1996) and Huang & Fawcett (1996).

In this book, then, I have set out an account of some of the major areas where we who work in the framework of the Cardiff Grammar wish to supplement or replace concepts relating to syntax proposed by Halliday. Moreover, I have tried to avoid merely presenting alternative approaches, and also to state the reasons for them. My hope is that those who work in the framework of the Sydney Grammar will resist the temptation to respond to this book as if it were an 'attack' on their model.[1] Instead, I hope that they might undertake the experiment suggested near the start of Chapter 11, and work with the approach suggested here for a couple of hours or days — or even weeks, months or years (which is of course what my colleagues and I have done with Halliday's proposals). It is only in this way that one really discovers the merits and demerits of a description, and so of the theory that underlies it.

If after making this small investment of time the reader's decision is that the original approach to, let us say, the 'rank scale' is superior to the approach taken here (in which the nearest equivalent is 'filling probabilities'), it would be

---

1. It is unfortunate that the overwhelmingly dominant metaphor for academic discussion is that of combat. Why should it not be a co-operative enterprise, such as building a house together? See Appendix C for examples of the problems that may arise is academic 'debate'.

helpful to future generations if the reasons could be given for maintaining that approach, in the light of the evidence offered here (and in Appendix C for the 'rank scale'). Indeed, we should not assume that the outcome to an exchange of views will necessarily be 'victory' or 'defeat'. One possible type of outcome is what has been called a 'transcending solution', i.e., the emergence from the discussion of a better idea than either party held at the start (so not a mere compromise), and this may well be a possibility in some areas. At other times, of course, we must hope for the humility, in both ourselves and our interactants, to say "Yes, I now see that the weight of the evidence is on your side, so I shall change my position."

It is my hope, then, that the effect of the publication of the work that has been developed in the framework described here will not be to separate further these two versions of the theory, but rather to provide ways of helping the theory as a whole to make the further improvements over the standard model (as represented currently by Halliday 1994 and Matthiessen 1995) that are clearly needed to make the theory stronger and more usable for the new century.

We turn now to the summaries, beginning with a summary of the categories found in the two models.

## 12.2 The categories of syntax: a summary and comparison

The first fundamental category in the present theory is the concept of **class of unit**. However, the criteria used for recognizing examples of classes of unit (and at the development stage of the grammar for setting up new units) are significantly different from those used in "Categories" and still used in *IFG*, so that it is effect a different concept from Halliday's 'class of unit'. In "Categories", the class of a unit is said to be determined by its potential for operation at given elements of the unit next above on the 'rank scale' — and in *IFG* classes of unit still appear to be assigned on the same principle (even though this leads to various anomalies, as pointed out in Section 10.2 of Chapter 10). Halliday has stuck by this criterion in spite of the fact that most of his grammatically-minded colleagues of the 1960s and 1970s (Huddleston, Hudson and Sinclair) seem to have given increasing weight to internal structure and semantics, as we saw in Section 10.2.2 of Chapter 10 — so effectively rejecting Halliday's criterion. In the present framework, as in Fawcett (1974-6/81), the class of a unit is identified solely by its internal structure, i.e., by its potential array of elements of structure. (But see below for their close relationship with the meanings that they realize.) For English five major classes of unit are recognized here: clause, nominal group, prepositional group, quality group and quantity group, together with the genitive cluster and a number of other classes of cluster that handle the internal structure of various types of 'name'.

We turn now from 'class of unit' to 'element of structure'. In "Categories" the "fundamental category" was said to be the concept of the 'structure' of a unit, but in the present theory it is recognized that the more specific and so more useful notion is the concept of **element of structure**. In Halliday (1956/76) **element** had been one of the key concepts, but in "Categories" it was curiously sidelined in favour of the less specific concept of the **structure** of a unit. The concept of 'element of structure' is nonetheless present throughout *IFG*, and it is impossible to envisage a SF grammar that did not give it a central role. This, then, is the second major category in the present theory of syntax.

A modern theory of SF syntax is — or should be — an explicitly functional theory of language, so that the criteria for recognizing an element of structure are — or should be — functional and semantic rather than formal and positional. Thus the elements of a unit are those that are required to realize the meanings that have been selected in the system networks for realization in this unit — ultimately, of course, as items (see below).

Halliday has surprisingly little to say in "Categories" (or indeed in any later writings) about the criteria for recognizing elements of structure (especially the elements of groups). Moreover, in his writings from the late 1960s onwards the emphasis is always placed on the concept that an element of a clause such as 'Subject' is not a single element but a conflation of three "functions" — and so the expression in structure of the concept that language simultaneously realizes several different types of meaning.

However, as we saw in Chapter 7, Halliday immediately extended the concept of the conflation of single coterminous elements to the much more ambitious concept that a whole unit such as the clause can be represented as a series of simultaneous but different structures. This implied in turn that the various structures, each roughly the length of a clause and each with 'elements' that were not coterminous with the elements in the other structures of the same clause, were to be unified, by the application of a final 'structure conflation' rule of an unspecified type, into a single, integrated structure. But the concept that five or more different clause-length structures can be 'integrated' is, as we have seen, theoretically untenable (except in the trivial sense that involves dismembering the structures into their 'lowest common denominators').

At this point we might remind ourselves that, in the new framework that is proposed here, the multifunctional nature of language is displayed in the analysis of a text **at the level of meaning**— so avoiding the problems that arise from the challenge of (1) generating and (2) integrating five or more different structures (as described in Chapter 7). This is achieved by arranging the features that have been chosen in generating it in separate lines, as in Figure 10 in Chapter 7. And we should also remind ourselves that the the application of the realization operations attached to the semantic features generates a single, integrated output structure, so making it both undesirable and unnecessary to generate 'intermediate' structures such as those found in *IFG*. .

The conclusion, therefore, is that single, coterminous elements are the only categories that can be conflated with each other — and this brings out yet more strongly the centrality in the theory of the concept of 'element of structure'.

The third major concept in the present theory of syntax is that of the **item**. This replaces the concepts of 'word' and 'morpheme' on the "Categories" 'rank scale' of units, these two now being simply types of item. The reasons for this major change are given in Section 10.5 of Chapter 10.

A fourth category that is required in the present theory is that of **place**, in the sense of the numbered position (or 'slot') in a unit at which an element is positioned. Interestingly, Halliday refers in passing to 'place' in "Categories", but it is not presented as a significant category, and nor is it given any role in his later work. Yet this concept has come to play an essential role in the generative versions of SF grammar — especially in providing the conceptual framework, with 'class of unit' and 'element of structure', for explaining the phenomenon known as 'raising' (as noted in Section 11.7 of Chapter 11). The first appearance of the concept of 'place' in the sense defined here was in Fawcett (1973/81) and it was later described formally in Fawcett, Tucker & Lin (1993). However, the concept was also used, it appears, in Mann and Matthiessen's computer implementation of Halliday's grammar (as explained in Section 10.4.2 of Chapter 10).

The fourth "fundamental category" in "Categories" was, of course, the concept of **system**. It was Halliday's re-interpretation of this term in 1966 as 'choice between meanings' that made it the fundamental concept of a new model of language, and so of a new theory of 'meaning' (as we saw in Chapters 3 and 4). It therefore has no role in the present model of syntax.[2]

The first "fundamental category" in "Categories" was that of a 'unit', but this concept, as will by now be abundantly clear, has no role to play in the theory of syntax proposed here, because it is inherently bound up with the concept of 'rank'. The word "unit" is used here, however, as a short form for the concept of 'class of unit'. Surprisingly, the concepts of 'unit' and its partner 'rank' occur only rarely in the recent writings of Halliday and Matthiessen. Yet it is clear that this pair of concepts still provides the general framework for the description of English set out in *IFG* — just as they underpinned the theory of syntax presented in "Categories".

We can summarize this section by recalling that, while 'unit', 'class of unit' and 'element of structure' can still be recognized in essentially their "Categories" senses in *IFG*, none of them is included as a "basic category" in Halliday's "Systemic theory" (1993). The only "Categories" concept that continues in essentially the same sense in the theory of syntax proposed here is 'element of structure'.

We turn next to the relationships between the categories (so including the three 'scales' introduced in "Categories").

## 12.3 The relationships of syntax: a summary and comparison

Since this is a comparison as well as a summary, we shall take as our starting point one of the 'scales' of "Categories": the highly generalized concept of 'exponence'. The problem with 'exponence' in its "Categories" sense is that it covers a very larger number of different concepts — i.e., every relationship between "the categories of the highest degree of abstraction" (by which Halliday

---

2. It would be possible to envisage a model with a set of system networks that represented choices at the level of 'pure' form such that these were 'predetermined' by choices made at a higher level of 'semantics'. Hudson's work (e.g., Hudson 1971) is presented as a systemic model of syntax of just this type (with no ambition to model choices between meanings), but this is not the direction in which Halliday has led Systemic Functional Linguistics. I would claim that the fact that the Cardiff Grammar can indeed operate with system networks that are explicitly intended to model choices in meaning and that can be directly realized in syntax at the level of form vindicates Halliday's original hunch in the 1960s that the system networks of TRANSITIVITY, MOOD, THEME etc. should be regarded as modelling choices between meanings.

means the features in the system networks) and "the data" (Halliday 1961/76:71). However, when in the 1960s Halliday introduced the concept that systems are choices between meanings, he also introduced the term **realization** as a replacement for "exponence", and it quickly came to be used as the standard general term for referring to the relationship between different levels (or strata) of language. In the context of the present discussion it refers to the relationship between **meaning** and **form** (as described in Chapter 3 and as summarized in Figure 4 in Section 3.2 of that chapter).

The general concept of 'realization' is made specific through five major types of **realization operation**. As we saw in Section 9.2 of Chapter 9, it is they, together with the potential structures, that specify the 'form potential' of a language.

Notice, however, that when they are applied (i.e., to a **selection expression** of features generated on a traversal of a system network, as described in Appendix A), they generate syntactic structures. The first four operations directly generate four of the relationships in syntax to be described below. And the last two provide the framework for generating structures with the recursion of co-ordination, embedding or re-iteration. Thus the **realization operations** in the grammar are directly related to the **relationships** in the syntax of an output from the grammar — while not, as I emphasized in Chapter 9, being the same as them. In other words, we need both a theory of 'syntax potential' and a theory of syntactic instances'.

The specification of the realization operations that follows is essentially the same as that given in Section 9.2.1 of Chapter 9, the difference being that this list additionally identifies the type of relationship that corresponds to the operation. In their typical order of application, the major realization operations are:

1. **Insert** a **unit** (e.g., "ngp") into the structure to 'fill' (or 'function at') an **element or Participant Role** (e.g., "cv") — so introducing to the structure the relationship of **filling**. (The topmost clause in a text-sentence fills the 'Sentence'.)
2. **Locate** an **element** (e.g., "S") at a given **place** in a **unit** — so introducing the relationship of **componence**.
3. Insert an element or Participant Role to be **conflated** with an existing element, i.e., to be located immediately after it and to be at the same **place** (e.g., "S/Ag") — so introducing the relationship

of **conflation**.
4 **Expound** an **element** by an **item** — so introducing the relationship of **exponence**.
5 Re-set the **preferences** (i.e., the percentage probabilities on features in certain specified systems), including the **preselection** of **features** by the use of 100% and 0% probabilities — these probabilities being reset to their original percentages after the next traversal of the network.
6 **Re-enter** the **system network** at a stated feature — so possibly also introducing the recursion of **co-ordination, embedding** or **reiteration**.

The result of applying Operation 6 (and so in turn Operation 1) is to introduce to the structure either a **single unit** or two or more **co-ordinated units**. In either case the resulting structure may additionally involve the addition of more layers of unit, including the **embedding** of a unit inside another unit of the same class — depending on what choices have been made in the system network.

Thus, the highly general concept of 'exponence' from "Categories" was first re-interpreted by Halliday as the second highly general concept of interstratal 'realization'. Then the researchers at London who were developing generative SF grammars specified the particular types of operation required in realization. These have been refined over the years, and those set out above can be seen to specify, in their turn, the relationships between categories that are found in the syntax. It is somewhat ironic that the term "exponence" is re-introduced here with roughly the sense that it was originally given by Firth (1957/68:183), before Halliday borrowed it and stretched — indeed over-stretched — its meaning in "Categories".

Let us now turn to Halliday's concept of the 'rank scale', as presented in "Categories". This predicts that every element of the clause will be filled by a group or by a 'rankshifted' clause, and that every element of a group will be expounded by a word (unless filled by a 'rankshifted' group or clause). Thus what Halliday terms "upward rank shift" is permitted, but "downward rank shift" is not. However, we saw in Chapter 7 that the picture changes in *IFG*, so that Halliday now only permits embedded clauses to function within groups (at least, in English).

But how well does the 'rank scale' way of generalizing about relationships between units reflect the patterns of syntax found in English texts? The theory presented here is based on the well-tested assumption that we can make more useful generalizations in terms of the concept of **class of unit** (in its present sense) and **element of structure**, together with the concept that the relationship between a unit and the element that it fills is **probabilistic** rather than absolute. Thus the present theory of syntax makes much weaker claims as to what is and is not permitted than the *IFG* version of the theory does. Indeed, it is designed to enable the overall description of a language to celebrate the flexibility and richness of structure in language. We replace the 'rank scale' claim by the statement that (1) the five major classes of unit (i.e., the clause and the four classes of group) all occur quite frequently at a number of different elements of structure within a number of different classes of unit; (2) that they do so with varying degrees of probability, and (3) these probabilities (and others) need to be represented in the grammar. Thus 'absolute' rules can be seen as extreme cases of probability. It is an interesting side-effect of defining classes of unit by their internal structure that it becomes impossible to apply Halliday's criterion of the unit's potential for operation in the unit above it on the 'rank scale'. One must choose one criterion or the other. The generalizations captured in the diagrams in Appendix B suggest the value of basing classes of unit on their internal structure, and the corollary is that the description is able to show that all the major classes of unit (the clause and the four groups) can all fill several different elements.

Appendix B summarizes the main facts of what **filling** relationships are possible. In other words, statements about where a unit can and cannot occur have to be made for each unit and for each element that it may fill. This approach to the relations between units seems to correspond more closely to the patternings that we find in naturally-occurring texts than the picture that emerges when one tries to apply the 'rank scale' hypothesis that is embodied in "Categories" and *IFG*. In Appendix B, the differences in the probability that a unit will fill one element or another are indicated for conversation, and we must expect that some adjustments will be needed for other registers, such as academic writing.

However, the ultimate source of these probabilities is in the generative grammar. Here the probabilities are shown as percentages on features in systems, so that the theoretical-generative version of the model is capable of great refinement. Indeed, the probabilities can be changed in the light of specific contextual or systemic contexts. (See Fawcett, Tucker & Lin 1993 for a fuller picture.)

One can, of course, still find within the present theory traces of the phenomena that suggested the original 'rank scale' concept. Firstly, there is the fact that the clause (or "clause complex" when co-ordination occurs) is the only unit that can occur as the highest unit in a tree representation of a text-sentence. Secondly, we can say — for what it is worth — that, for each word that the analyst identifies in a text, there is a fairly good possibility that it will be functioning as an element of a group, and that if one has successfully identified a group there is a fairly good possibility that it is filling an element of a clause. But there is also quite a strong possibility in each case that the supposed generalization will not hold. (See the fuller discussion in Section 10.2.1 of Chapter 10).

Finally, Halliday's term **delicacy** is, in the present theory, restricted solely to relationships within the system networks. However, Halliday continues to use the concept in his structural descriptions of clauses in *IFG* (as pointed out in Section 2.4 of Chapter 2 and Section 7.2 of Chapter 7). The disadvantage of this is that it adds one or more extra lines of structure to a clause, so introducing unnecessary complexity to the analysis.

However, each of the two current theories has added new structural concepts of its own. The Sydney Grammar has added the concept that a clause (and, potentially, each of the other units) has a **multiple structure**, i.e., it has several structures, each of which corresponds to a different broad type of meaning (roughly, to each 'metafunction', but with two for the 'textual' 'metafunction'). A second new concept in the Sydney Grammar is **'hypotaxis'**, which is contrasted with 'parataxis' (i.e., co-ordination in a broad sense of the term). As we saw in Section 2.6.1 of Chapter 2, 'hypotaxis' is a relationship between two units in which one is said to be 'dependent' on the other, but without being embedded in it (i.e., without filling one of its units). It is noteworthy that, while quite a number of Halliday's ideas have been adopted by other grammarians who are writing functionally-oriented descriptions of English such as Quirk and his colleagues, they have not taken over either of these ideas. And here, in the appropriate sections, I have explained why they are not used in the present theory. See Section 12.6 for a discussion of an example that in *IFG* would be analyzed as containing 'hypotaxis' rather than embedding.

However, the present theory introduces several concepts that are not found explicitly in any of "Categories", "Systemic theory" or *IFG*. These include the central roles given to the three key relationships of 'componence', 'filling' and 'exponence'; the recognition that classes of unit are determined by their internal structure; the fact that many units fill many elements of many other units (so that 'embedding' is seen as a valuable resource for constructing meanings). In addition the theory incorporates a number of well-recognized concepts that are not mentioned in those works, such as 'discontinuity' in units. The familiar concept of 'co-ordination' occurs in both theories, but in *IFG* it is included in 'parataxis' (which is contrasted systemically with "hypotaxis").

In summary, we can say that in the theory proposed here the concept of the 'rank scale' has been abandoned, together with its associated predictions about 'rank shift, and so also has 'delicacy' (in the sense of 'primary' and 'secondary' structure in syntax (as opposed to 'delicacy' in the system networks). "Exponence" has been re-defined in a way that enables it to be used in what is broadly its original Firthian sense, and the important new structural concepts of 'componence', 'filling' and 'exponence' have been introduced.

## 12.4 A comparison of the two frameworks as integrated wholes

In any comparison between the two versions of the theory up to this point, we have compared first the 'categories' of the two theories and then the 'scales' or 'relationships'. For our final comparison we shall look at each theory as a whole, integrating the categories and the relationships.

Clearly, Halliday sees the concepts of "Categories" as also being the concepts that underlie *IFG* — but with certain additions such as the concepts of 'multiple structures' and the two relationships between units of 'parataxis' and 'hypotaxis'. Let us now compare the two frameworks — i.e., the one that is derived from "Categories" and exemplified most fully in *IFG* (which we shall call "the *IFG* framework") and the one proposed here.

First, in both theories the original "Categories" concept of 'system' has been removed from the theory of syntax, as a result of its elevation to the role of modelling meaning potential. However, even though both theories are derived from the remaining concepts of "Categories", the conceptual core of each is quite different.

The core of the *IFG* framework still appears to be the concept of **units** on the **'rank scale'** — even though it is mentioned only occasionally in *IFG* and not at all in "Systemic theory". Moreover, the concept of **class** (which is always 'class of unit') is tied into the 'rank scale' too, in that it is defined in terms of its patterns of operation in the unit next above on the 'rank scale'. The concept of **element of structure** continues to serve a vital role in the theory, though it receives little overt recognition. The concept of **delicacy** seems to hover between being a theoretical category and a descriptive convenience. Systemically the more important concept is **dependence**, and structurally, as I suggested in Section 10.3.4 of Chapter 10, showing structures with varying degrees of delicacy adds unnecessary complexity to the representation of texts.) And **exponence** in "Categories" was a concept waiting to be redefined as **realization**, and then needing to be split up into specific **realization operations**. The original concept of 'exponence' has no role in the theory of syntax that underlies *IFG,* though 'realization' is used as the general term for the interstratal relationship. To these concepts from "Categories" Halliday has added three further ones: 'multiple structures' in the clause, and 'parataxis' and 'hypotaxis'. The concepts underlying *IFG* are therefore the 'rank scale' of 'units', 'class of unit' defined in terms of the 'rank scale', 'paratactic' or 'hypotactic' relations between units on the 'rank scale', and 'element of structure' — together with 'multiple structures' and the absolute minimum of 'rankshift'. According to the 'rank scale' prediction, clauses should consist of groups, groups of words, and words of morphemes — all in the same 'ranked' relationship to each other.

The theory proposed here is rather different. The key categories are **class of unit, element of structure** and **item**. But a 'class of unit' is defined by its internal structure, the major classes (of English) being the clause and the nominal, prepositional, quality and quantity groups. Moving down the layers of a tree diagram representation of a text-sentence, we find that 'unit' and 'element' occur alternately (these being related to each other by the similarly alternate relationships of **componence** and **filling**), until the lowest element in the tree is reached and the relationship of **exponence** relates that element to an **item**. There is no place in the formal representations for the concept of 'word class' (although terms such as "noun" and "adjective' are used as convenient short forms for referring to classes of item that are ultimately defined by the part of the system network from which they are generated). To this core framework must be added the general concept of **probability**. More specifically, the theory provides that the likelihood that a given unit will fill a given element should be expressed in probabilistic terms (as well as absolute terms where it has a zero probability). The claim is that probabilistic statements about the potential of each class of unit to fill an element are more accurately predictive than the 'rank scale' predictions — and so more useful when the theory is being employed for the analysis of text-sentences (whether by a human or by a computer).

Finally, we should return to the *IFG* framework in order to note that it requires, as well as 'multiple structures' such as those found in *IFG*, a way of modelling the integration of these different structures in a final, integrated structure, i.e., one in which the five or more structures of an *IFG*-style representation must be integrated. It currently lacks this, so that it requires a theory of syntax such as that outlined here to model this integrated structure.

Thus, even though the two theories of syntax share a common origin in "Categories", they are now very different. The two theories are equally 'systemic' and 'functional', in that they both operate within the generalized model of level of language that was presented in Chapter 3 and summarized in Figure 4 in Section 3.2 of that chapter. However, as we saw in Section 7.4 of Chapter 7, the Sydney Grammar appears to need an additional component in order to integrate its multiple structures.

## 12.5 'Autonomous syntax', 'grammaticality' and 'probability'

As we saw in Section 4.3 of Chapter 3, there is no claim that the present framework is sufficient to specify all and only the grammatically acceptable sentences of English. It is not an 'autonomous' theory of syntax. In a systemic functional grammar the system network and the realization rules jointly specify what is 'grammatical' and what is 'ungrammatical', as exemplified in the little grammar in Appendix A.[3] Since the system network is at the level of meaning, there is no attempt to specify what is 'grammatical' in terms of 'syntax rules', as there is in a typical 're-write rule' grammar (i.e., what is often termed a 'context free grammar' or a 'phrase structure grammar').[4]

---

3. We should also note that there are other types of unacceptability, which it is appropriate to control from the belief system and other higher components.

4. The assumption made here is that there are two aspects of English syntax that render the 're-write rule' approach to syntax so seriously inadequate that it is not regarded as a good starting point for specifying syntax. These are (1) the enormous number of variations in the sequence of elements in the clause — especially for the many different types of Adjunct — and (2) the great variation in the potential for the co-occurrence of elements in **all** units. In SFL it is the system networks and the realization rules that handle these matters.

This theory therefore accepts the challenge that a model of language should be generative (in a model that integrates meaning and form). But it also adds to the sterile opposition of 'grammaticality' vs. 'ungrammaticality' the more flexible concept of 'probability'. As with other concepts, the need for this is suggested in Halliday's early writings (e.g., 1961/76:63). This gives the model the ability to show that an example such as *if that book you haven't read* is relatively unlikely (rather than ungrammatical). Corpus linguistics is increasingly clearly showing the need for a theory of language that has the concept of probability built into its core — and SFL is just such a theory. However, while probabilities can be used in conjunction with the theory of syntax specified here in applications such as the computer parsing of text-sentences (as in Weerasinghe & Fawcett 1993, and Weerasinghe 1994), the concept of 'probability' belongs ultimately in the system networks. The concepts necessary for the semantic component of a generative systemic functional grammar are described in full in Sections 2.4 and 2.5 of Fawcett, Tucker & Lin (1993). The goal of the present work is simply to provide a statement of the theoretical concepts that underpin the descriptive framework for English syntax provided in summary form in Appendix B and more fully in Fawcett (in press).

## 12.6 The importance of clear and usable representations

A theory of syntax has a responsibility to provide a notation for representing the structure of text-sentences. Throughout this book I have emphasized that we need **two** representations of each text-sentence, one at the level of form — where the main problem is that of how to represent a functional syntax — and one at the level of meaning — where I have shown that the question of how to display meaning can be resolved by bringing in the concept that lies at the core of the theory, i.e., the features from the system networks themselves.

In Figure 10 in Chapter 7 I showed an example of an analysis in these terms. The purpose at that point was to show that there is an alternative way to represent, in an easily interpretable form, the concept that a clause realizes in one structure several different types of meaning — with some elements realizing two or three such types of meaning. It was important, at that point in the argument, to demonstrate that there is an alternative way of representing this important aspect of language, because I had just shown that representations of the type used in *IFG* have no status in the theory. Clearly, if it is possible, it is

# SUMMARY AND CONCLUSIONS 289

preferable to use representations that are fully consistent with the theory, and the purpose of Figure 10 is to demonstrate that it is.

In the rest of this section we shall see how the present theory addresses a second problem of the representations in *IFG*. This is the problem that the 'box diagram' way of representing structure does not lend itself to showing, in the same diagram, the internal structure of a text-sentence. Indeed, it is one of the more surprising facts about *IFG* that it never provides us with a diagram that relates one layer of structure to another (e.g., a clause to a nominal group).[5]

As an illustration of the way in which the different layers of a tree structure are related to each other in the framework of the present theory, consider Figure 25. As you can see, the tree diagram notation lends itself naturally to modelling the relationships between the various layers of structure within the text. The key to Appendix B can be used to interpret the symbols used in the diagram to represent the various classes of unit and their elements of structure, and Chapter 11 explains the symbols representing the relationships between the categories.

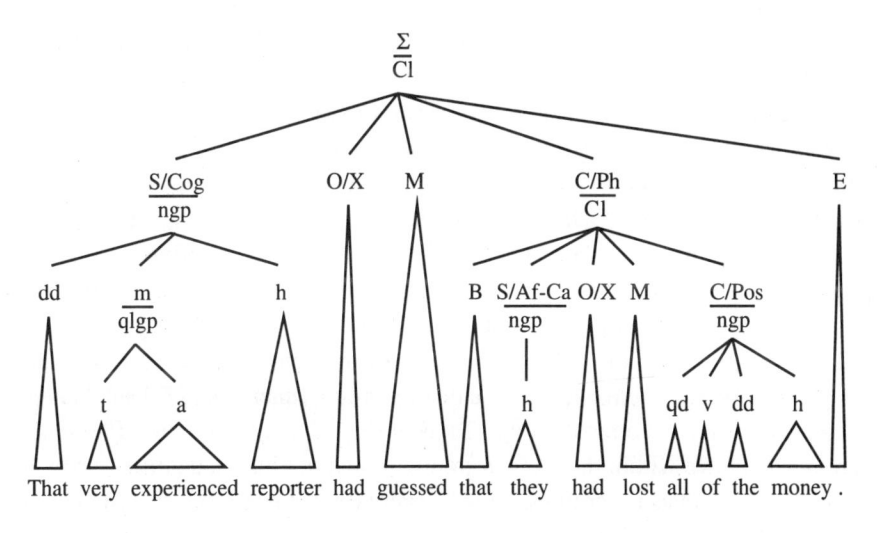

*Figure 25: The analysis of a sentence with an embedded clause*

This is not the place for a full explanation as to why the analysis in Figure 25 is as it is. (For this level of detail, see Fawcett in press.) But it may be help-

---

5. This leads to a lack of clarity on a number of central issues, those that relate to the supposed 'verbal group' being discussed in Fawcett (2000 )and (forthcoming b).

ful, in the task of understanding precisely how the present theory differs from the Sydney Grammar, if I comment on a couple of points.

Firstly, this sentence contains just one case of embedding, in the strict sense of the term. This is the embedded clause *that they'd lost all the money*, which functions as the Phenomenon of the Process of 'guessing'. This is conflated with the Complement, so filling an element of the higher clause. In *IFG* the clause *that they'd lost all the money* would be described as serving the general logical function of 'modifying' the supposed 'head' clause of *That very experienced reporter had guessed*. Thus this second string of words would be said to be 'dependent' on the former **without being embedded in it** — even though the clause *That very experienced reporter had guessed* is clearly incomplete when it stands, alone i.e., without the Phenomenon that it "expects". It is not clear how Halliday would answer the criticism that the clause which this string of words initiates is incomplete, and that it can only be completed by modelling the dependent clause as a part of the overall clause of *That very experienced reporter had guessed that they'd lost all the money*.

In the Cardiff Grammar's view of the TRANSITIVITY of the main clause, the Process of the main clause is 'guessing' and the Phenomenon (which is conflated with the Complement) is *that they'd lost all the money*. Notice that the Phenomenon could also be *the nature of the problem*. In a functional grammar the way in which the Phenomenon happens to be filled on a given occasion should surely not lead to a different analysis of the structure of the clause, since the Process is, in both cases, 'guessing'.) For the full descriptive framework and a fuller explanation of why this approach to such examples has been adopted, see Fawcett (1997) on 'complementation' and Fawcett (in press).

The second part of Figure 25 that I shall comment on is the quality group *very experienced.* Here one group, a quality group, functions to fill an element of another group, a nominal group. Texts in English are in fact full of nominal groups that have within them other groups — and not just as qualifiers, which is all that *IFG* states is permitted. See Tucker (1998) for the fullest treatment in any theory of language of adjectives and the structures into which they enter. He demonstrates conclusively the value of the approach taken here to this major and hitherto understudied area of syntax — an area for which he has now provided the definitive description in SFL terms.

In the last analysis, it is the value of a theory in making principled descriptions of languages and texts that provides one of the two most telling types of evidence for or against it — together with the test of a principled, large-scale computer implementation. But it is not enough to provide a theory of syntax; one must also provide a complementary theory and description of the meanings of many types that the syntax expresses (together with the items and the intonation or punctuation). This is a topic to which we shall return in the final section of this chapter.

## 12.7 A final evaluation of the significance of "Categories" for a modern systemic functional grammar

Before we conclude, I would like to pay tribute to the role of Halliday's "Categories' in the development of the modern "theory of syntax for Systemic Functional Linguistics" that has been presented here. This tribute is richly deserved in spite of the fact that, as we have seen, only one of the seven original concepts of "Categories" has anything like its original meaning in the new theory of syntax. Indeed, even though Halliday still holds to his original 'rank scale' concept in *IFG*, in practice the concepts of 'rank' and 'unit' place little part in the description of English offered there.

However, such changes are surely no more than one should expect — given the influences on the theory in the intervening period. The first of these was directly theoretical, i.e., the revolutionary set of changes to the theory summarized in Chapter 4, of which the most fundamental was the elevation of the concept of 'system' to the semantics. The second was the widespread application of the theory to descriptions of a variety of languages, and then in turn the application of these descriptions to the task of describing large quantities of text (especially, however, texts in English) — all of which had the potential to stimulate modifications to the theory. And the third major influence on the theory was the demanding requirements of the large scale computer implementations of SFL, which have led to further advances.

In terms of the development of the present theory of syntax, it was the elevation of the system networks to model **meaning** that led to the reassessment of the role in the new framework of the existing syntactic categories. But it was the work in describing very large quantities of text that led to the establishment of the new meaning for **class of unit,** and so the recognition of the central place in the theory of the concept of **filling** (together with the other changes introduced in Fawcett 1974-6/81). And it took the challenge of the computer implementation of the lexicogrammar to show that the concept of a 'rank scale of units' had no role to play in the generative grammar — and so also no role in the use of the theory for describing languages or analyzing texts.

Was the theory described in "Categories", which had such an effect on so many linguists in the subsequent years, completely misguided? Of course not. The impressive thing about it is that it has proved sufficiently bendable (and mendable) for a new and more comprehensive theory to emerge from it. It is perhaps surprising that **any** of its concepts should have survived, given the fundamental nature of the change brought about by the elevation of the system networks to a higher level. Just as in language *tout se tient* (Meillet 1937), so it is also true that, in the models that we build to represent language, the function of every part depends upon the function of every other part. So it would be natural to expect that this major change would result in changes throughout the rest of the grammar. And this has happened — more clearly, however, in the present theory of syntax than in the Sydney Grammar.

However one concept, that of **element of structure**, has survived virtually unchanged from its initial appearance, in 1956, in Halliday's "Grammatical Categories in Modern Chinese" (1956/76). It has survived via its slight demotion in "Categories" — and its apparently even greater demotion in "Systemic theory" — to be used in essentially the same sense in *IFG* as it originally had, and to become one of the two principle categories in the present theory. Perhaps this is not surprising, since it is the 'element' that most clearly corresponds to the concept of 'function' in syntax — so much so that it is often used instead of it.

What is certain is that, if the framework for grammar set out in "Categories" had not existed, there would not have been a 'base framework' from which to explore the alternative approaches to the problems of modelling language that have been developed in the years since then within the framework of SFL. And if these explorations had not occurred, the theory of syntax presented here would not have evolved as it has. From this viewpoint, the impressive thing about "Categories" is that it provided a framework of concepts, each of which could be adapted, tested and either adapted further or discarded as a significant part of the developing theory.

The changes in the theoretical apparatus for expressing the categories and relationships of functional syntax that are described in this book reflect, I believe, our growing understanding of what a systemic functional model of language should be like. But these categories no longer constitute the full theoretical apparatus of the grammar, as they did in 1961. They are just the theoretical apparatus that is required at the level of form. But they are the type of theory that is required for a syntax that realizes the meaning potential of a language, i.e., the meanings of TRANSITIVITY, MOOD, THEME and so on.

All in all, we can say that a theory of the type described here — together with the theory of system networks and their realization as illustrated in Appendix A and in Fawcett, Tucker & Lin (1993) — provides a principled analysis of English syntax that is at every point explicitly functional. It therefore continues the line of development that extends from "Categories" through "Language as choice in social contexts" and, in some measure "Systemic theory". And since the theory of system networks and of the realization component are clearly quite close in the Sydney and the Cardiff Grammars — at least, so long as Halliday continues to regard the networks of TRANSITIVITY, MOOD, THEME etc. as modelling the 'meaning potential' — it is in the theory of syntax that one of the major differences between the two is to be found.

The other great difference, of course, is the answer to the question "What further components does each model have above the system networks for TRANSITIVITY, MOOD, THEME etc? But that must await another book!

## 12.8 From theory to description: the prospects

As we end the present book, I should remind you that Appendix A describes a very small generative grammar that illustrates the 'two-level' model whose essential structure is common to both theories. Appendix B gives you a much fuller — though still incomplete — picture of the central units of English syntax, their internal structures, and the probabilities for each of filling various elements of a higher unit in the tree. In their different ways, the two appendices give a foretaste of two of the further books that are expected to appear soon.

Appendix B is taken from my *Functional Syntax Handbook: Analyzing English at the level of form.* (Fawcett, in press), and it can be regarded as a summary of some of the central parts of that work. However, before you try to use it for the analysis of texts, it would be better to have available the clarifications and explanations given in the full work. This consists of a full description of English syntax in terms of the theory presented here. It is both (1) a 'fast track' course book and (2) a reference work that can be consulted by those analyzing the structure of text-sentences in functional terms at all levels, including the level of postgraduate research. It provides a very full coverage of

English, including several aspects of syntax that are not covered in other frameworks (some of which are introduced here in Chapter 10).

This 'syntax handbook' will be complemented in due course by a 'semantics handbook', i.e., my *Functional Semantics Handbook: Analyzing English at the level of meaning*. (Fawcett forthcoming a). This 'semantics handbook' will build on the syntactic analyses provided in the 'syntax handbook', to provide an equivalent framework for the analysis of texts in terms of eight 'strands of meaning'. In the past, users of systemic functional grammars have often found it hard to locate and interpret system networks, so it may be useful to add that those in the *Functional Semantic Handbook* are designed to be easy to consult and to intepret — both as an introduction to the systemic-semantic level of language (here English), and for use when analyzing a text in systemic-semantic terms. This approach to text analysis solves the difficulty of how to show the multifunctional nature of language in a representation of a text without using the theoretic-ally problematical 'multiple structures' used in *IFG*.

We have seen an example of an analysis that draws on the two handbooks in Figure 10 in Chapter 7. In such a representation, the multifunctional nature of language is shown in terms of the features that have been chosen at the level of meaning (rather than as 'multiple structures' that lie somewhere between meaning and form, as in *IFG*). The major feature of the *Functional Semantics Handbook* will be a full set of system networks that define the meaning potential of English, presented in such a way that they can be used for text analysis.

In due course I intend to publish, with colleagues, at least three further books. One will give a full account of the generative version of the Cardiff Grammar, as implemented (in Prolog) in the computer. The other, to be jointly written with Huang Guowen, will provide an in-depth treatment of the generation of one of the more challenging constructions in English. It is the one exemplified in *It is this book that gives you the best picture of how we see the various components of language generation working together in the production of a text-sentence*, and it describes every component that is required, from the belief system, through the discourse planner to the sentence planner that incorporates the lexicogrammar. In due course I also hope to write an introductory book about the Cardiff Grammar with Gordon Tucker, drawing especially on Tucker (1998) and the two handbooks. Our hope is that this set of books will provide both a full guide to analyzing texts in functional terms at the levels of both form and meaning, and a theoretical-generative account of a modern systemic functional model of language.

# Appendices

# Appendices

# Appendix A:
# a fragment of a generative systemic functional grammar

## 1 The purpose and scope of this appendix

The little example of how a systemic functional grammar works that is presented here is taken from a vastly fuller lexicogrammar for "things" in English. As we have seen in the main text, a **thing** is a semantic unit that is typically expresses an **object** in the belief system and that is realized at the level of form by a **nominal group**. While the source grammar for "things" has over 150 systems that are realized grammatically (and many thousands more that are realized lexically), the present grammar has just four systems that are realized in grammar and two that are realized in lexis. The highly simplified model to be presented here therefore includes only a very small number of the many meanings and structures that are expressed in the nominal group. Specifically, they will be restricted to a few that use the two elements of the **head** and the **deictic determiner**. Nonetheless this will be sufficient to illustrate the main principles of how a systemic functional grammar works. For a much fuller example of how a systemic functional grammar works, see Fawcett, Tucker & Lin (1993).

What this little grammar does **not** show is the clause in which the nominal group might occur. To provide a context of situation for it, let us say that two overworked lecturers in a university meet briefly in a corridor, and the following conversation takes place:

A: *Where have you been for the last half hour? I've been looking for you everywhere.*
B: *I've been discussing .... with Peter.*

The row of dots gives us the context of the nominal group to be generated. And B's **planner** has already prepared the representation of the object in **logical form** that is the input to the system network.

## 2 The system network

The key concept of a systemic functional grammar is a **system** — this term being used here in a technical sense where it means a 'choice between two or more semantic features'. The heart of the grammar is therefore the system network of semantic features. Consider the little example shown in Figure 1.

SYSTEM NETWORK OF MEANINGS

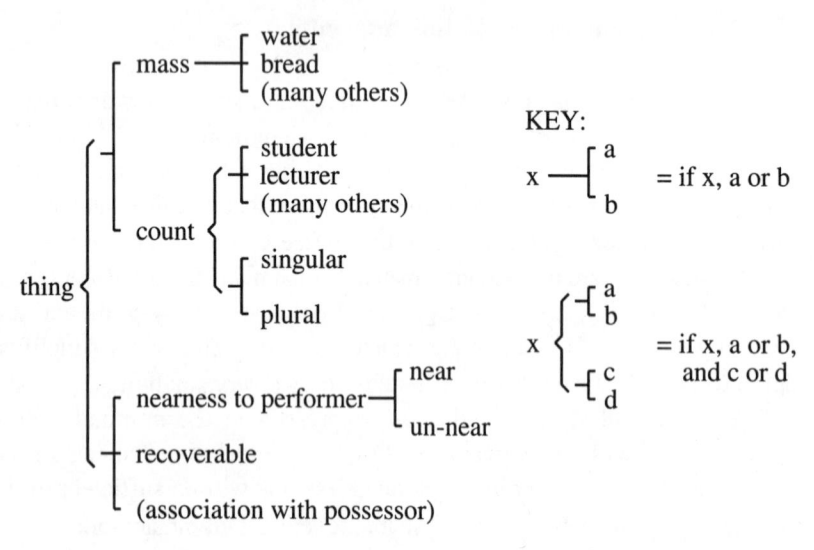

```
                    ┌ water
         ┌ mass ────┤ bread
         │          └ (many others)
         │                                KEY:
         │         ┌ student                        ┌ a
         │   ┌─────┤ lecturer          x ───────────┤      = if x, a or b
         │   │     └ (many others)                  └ b
         └ count ┤
thing ┤          │   ┌ singular
         │   └───┤                               ┌─ ┌ a
         │       └ plural                        │  └ b
         │                         x ────────────┤              = if x, a or b,
         │   ┌ nearness to performer ┌ near      │  ┌ c           and c or d
         │   │                       └ un-near   └─ └ d
         └ ──┤ recoverable
             └ (association with possessor)
```

*Figure 1: A highly simplified system network for 'thing' in English*

Each system in the system network has an **entry condition** and, since this is typically a feature in another system, a number of systems of related features typically combine to create a **system network**. Furthermore, as Figure 1 shows, there can be parallel entries to more than one system. **It is the system network of semantic features that models the meaning potential of a language.**

The system network corresponds to the top left box in Figure 4 (in Section 3.2 of Chapter 3). The way to use a system network is to 'traverse' it, starting with the leftmost feature. Whenever an 'and' bracket is encountered, all the systems to its right must be entered, so that the pathway through the network typically becomes a set of branching pathways.

# A GENERATIVE SF GRAMMAR

When you have completed a traversal of the network, you will have collected a **selection expression** of semantic features such as:

[thing, count, plural, student, nearness to performer, un-near].

Notice that features are typically written in square brackets, to show their status as features. This **output** from the network corresponds to the top right box in Figure 4 (in Chapter 3) — i.e., it is an **instance** of this little lexicogrammar's **meaning potential**. This small network of six systems will generate eighteen different selection expressions, each of which constitutes a representation at the level of meaning of a different nominal group. While eighteen is not a large number of potential instances, it could clearly be quickly scaled up by the addition of a few other systems. The full network for 'things' in the Cardiff Grammar (from which this mini-network is adapted) currently has around 120 semantic features — most of which have an associated realization rule — and it generates many millions of different nominal group structures.[1]

## 3 The realization component

This selection expression of features becomes the **input** to the **realization** component. This is the bottom left box in Figure 4 (in Chapter 3), and it contains two main types of statement: (1) **realization rules**, as given in Figure 2, and (2) **potential structures**, which simply show the sequence in which those elements that are fixed in sequence must appear (such as those in the nominal group). Here we shall introduce a highly simplified potential structure, which can be summarized as:

ngp: dd m h q.

This simply means that when any of the four elements of a **deictic determiner (dd)**, a **modifier (m)**, a **head (h)** and a **qualifier (q)** occur in a

---

[1]. In the Cardiff Grammar, the general probabilities for each of the features in a system would be shown as a percentage. For example, we know that the general probability is that the feature [singular] will be chosen far more often than the feature [plural], so that the picture of this part of the grammar can be refined by writing 95% before [singular] and 5% before [plural]. Similarly, it is a part of our 'knowledge' of our grammar that the item *the* is very much more frequent than any of *this*, *that*, *these* and *those*, and the grammar can show this by placing 95% before [recoverable], leaving 5% to be split between [nearness to performer] and [association with possessor].

**nominal group** (**ngp**), they come in this sequence. A fuller nominal group has many more elements. These facts about the nominal group apply potentially to all nominal groups, and the realization rules given in Figure 2 use the potential structure to ensure that the elements occur in the right sequence.2

| FEATURE | CONDITIONAL FEATURE(S) | REALIZATION |
| --- | --- | --- |
| thing | | insert ngp |
| water | | h < "water" |
| bread | | h < "bread" |
| student | | h < "student" |
| lecturer | | h < "lecturer" |
| near | singular or mass<br>plural | dd < "this"<br>dd < "these" |
| un-near | singular or mass<br>plural | dd < "that"<br>dd < "those" |
| recoverable | | dd < "the" |
| plural | | h < "+s" |

*Figure 2: Some simplified realization rules for the 'thing' in English*

The first rule in Figure 2 inserts the nominal group itself into the structure being built. Nominal groups typically occur in clauses, so let us assume that this one occurs in the context of *I've been discussing ... with Peter*. At this point, then, we are generating a nominal group to fill the Complement following the Main Verb, i.e., *discussing*.

Each of the next four rules assigns one of the four representative examples of nouns given here to the 'head'. Specifically, the realization rule for the feature [water] says: "The head of the nominal group is *water*" — or, more technically and so more precisely, "The head of the nominal group is ex-

---

2. I should perhaps remind you that there is no equivalent potential structure for the clause, because very few elements occur at fixed places in sequence. (See p. 305 of Appendix B.)

pounded by the item *water*".[3]

Those rules generated lexical items. The rest of the rules all generate grammatical items: five words and a morpheme.

The next two rules illustrate the way in which a systemic functional grammar handles the important fact that **often there is not a simple one-to-one relationship between meaning and form**. The first rule, which is for the feature [near], states that, if the 'thing' is either a 'singular' thing or a 'mass' thing (such as 'water' or 'bread', each of which is viewed in English as an uncountable 'stuff'), then the deictic determiner will be *this* — but that, if it is a 'plural' thing, the determiner will be *these*. And there is a similar pattern for the realization rule for the feature [un-near]. However the next rule, which is for the feature [recoverable], is simpler, in that this feature is always realized by the item *the*. The meaning of *the* is roughly 'If you inspect the rest of this nominal group, you will know which instance of the class of objects specified in the head I am referring to', and it is this meaning that the feature [recoverable] summarizes.

The final realization rule is another simple one, and it says "If the 'thing' is 'plural' the head is given the morpheme *s* as a suffix." (See Section 11.4.2 of Chapter 11 for a discussion of the way in which the term "suffix" is used in the present theory.) Notice that there is no need to specify that this rule does not apply to 'mass' things such as 'bread', because the system network itself ensures that 'mass' things do not enter the system in which 'singular' or 'plural' is chosen.[4]

If we now apply these realization rules to the selection expression given

---

3. To characterize the 'core' meaning of the item *water*, we could have used an abbreviated version of a dictionary definition (e.g., 'a clear, tasteless liquid essential for life') or even (in this case) an expression such as '$H_2O$'. But such methods do not ultimately advance the characterization of the meaning, and the aspects hinted at here must ultimately be expressed in terms of the belief system of a user of the language. At the present level of language (i.e., the intra-linguistic level of meaning) we simply borrow the form of the word and place it in single quotation marks to indicate that this is a meaning (i.e., a 'sense') of the word and not its form. (For further discussions of these issues, see Fawcett 1994b and Tucker 1996a).

4. The system of NUMBER can be handled in this way quite satisfactorily in an introductory grammar, but in a fuller grammar it is in fact handled differently. This is not because of irregular plurals (such as *men* and *women*), but because of the existence of other NUMBER categories, such as 'plural only' and 'pair only', e.g., as realized in *clothes* and *police*, and *trousers* and *scissors*. See Fawcett (1994b) for a description of how we handle the full NUMBER system.

earlier, we shall generate a nominal group with two elements. The first is a deictic determiner, and it is expounded by *those,* and the second is a head that is expounded by *student + s.* If we then strip away the syntax, we are left with the sort text of *those students.*

## 4  Summary

Clearly, this little grammar leaves out a rather large proportion of the many complex meanings that can be expressed through the nominal group in English. Equally clearly, it ignores various problems, such as the plurals of words like *box* and the irregular plurals of *men* and *women,* etc. All of these matters are covered in the full lexicogrammar from which this simplified one has been taken. The fact that this little lexicogrammar is very limited in its coverage of English nominal groups is unimportant, because our purpose here is simply to illustrate the **basic principles** of how a grammar that is founded on the concept of 'choice between meanings' actually works. The key concept, then, is that the system network of a language (or any other sign system) defines the **meaning potential** of that language, and the realization component defines the **form potential**. But when such a lexicogrammar is set to work it also specifies the **instances** that are possible at the levels of both **meaning** (in the selection expression of semantic features) and **form** (in the structured strings of word forms that are the output).

The brief summary given here shows only what happens **for one unit**. If the output is to be a sentence with more than one layer of structure — as is typically the case — then the network will first be entered to generate a **clause** and its elements, and then re-entered to generate any 'lower' unit that is required. This may be a **nominal group**, as here, or one of the other various types of group. The important point is that each such re-entry to the network adds a new unit to the structure, each with its own internal structure. And, as I have pointed out on numerous occasions in the main part of the book, language has an amazing ability to generate **units within units** — clauses within clauses, groups within groups, clauses within groups, and so on. Yet the simple principles for generating structure that have been illustrated here are sufficient (with a small number of extensions) to cover all of these cases.

# Appendix B:
# A summary of English syntax
# for the text analyst

The figures in this Appendix are taken from my *Functional Syntax Handbook: Analyzing English at the level of form.* London: Continuum. (Fawcett in press).

# Notes

1. This summary is organized round the main syntactic units of English. For each unit the diagram shows: (1) which elements of structure each unit can fill, (2) the probability of filling each named element (if over 0.5%), and (3) which elements of structure occur within the unit.
2. In each diagram, the 'pivotal element' is shown vertically below the unit. The item that expounds it is typically - but not absolutely always - present in the text.
3. The key below gives the full forms of the abbreviations used on the next three pages, and it explains the symbols. For all units except the clause, the elements are listed in their typical sequence. For the clause (in which sequence varies greatly) they are listed alphabetically.
4. For each unit, the elements expounded in punctuation or intonation are listed last. (The full model of intonation has additional elements.)

# KEY

## Units

| | | |
|---|---|---|
| Cl | = | Clause |
| ngp | = | nominal group |
| pgp | = | prepositional group |
| qlgp | = | quality group |
| qtgp | = | quantity group |
| genclr | = | genitive cluster |
| 'text' | = | text (simplified model) |

## Elements of the Clause

| | | |
|---|---|---|
| A | = | Adjunct (many types, including the Inferential Adjunct (IA) |
| B | = | Binder |
| C | = | Complement |
| F | = | Formulaic Element |
| I | = | Infinitive Element |
| L | = | Let Element |
| M | = | Main Verb |
| Mex | = | Main Verb Extension |
| N | = | Negator |
| O* | = | Operator or O/X or O/M (where / = 'is conflated with') |
| S | = | Subject |
| V | = | Vocative |
| X | = | Auxiliary Verb (several types) |
| Xex | = | X Extension (several types) |
| & | = | Linker |
| St | = | Starter |
| E | = | Ender (a final comma, full stop, question mark, exclamation mark, semi-colon or colon, or the equivalent in intonation) |

## Elements of the nominal group

| | | |
|---|---|---|
| rd | = | representational determiner |
| v | = | selector (always *of*, = [v]) |
| pd | = | partitive determiner |
| fd | = | fractionative determiner |
| qd | = | quantifying determiner |
| sd | = | superlative determiner |
| od | = | ordinative determiner |
| qid | = | qualifier-introducing determiner |
| td | = | typic determiner |
| dd | = | deictic determiner |
| m | = | modifier (many types) |
| h | = | head |
| q | = | qualifier (several types) |

## Elements of the prepositional group

| | | |
|---|---|---|
| p | = | preposition (or postposition, if *ago*) |
| pt | = | prepositional temperer |
| cv | = | completive |

## Elements of the quality group

| | | |
|---|---|---|
| qld | = | quality group deictic |
| qlq | = | quality group quantifier |
| et | = | emphasizing temperer |
| dt | = | degree temperer |
| at | = | adjunctival temperer |
| a | = | apex |
| s | = | scope |
| f | = | finisher |

## Elements of the quantity group

| | | |
|---|---|---|
| ad | = | adjustor |
| am | = | amount |
| qtf | = | quantity finisher |

## Elements of the genitive cluster

| | | |
|---|---|---|
| po | = | possessor |
| g | = | genitive element |
| o | = | own element |

## Elements found in all groups

| | | |
|---|---|---|
| & | = | linker (e.g., *and, or*, etc) |
| i | = | inferer (e.g., *even, only*) |
| st | = | starter (an initial comma, or the equivalent in intonation) |
| e | = | ender (a final comma, or the equivalent in intonation) |

## Elements of a text (simplified model)

| | | |
|---|---|---|
| Σ | = | Sentence |
| OQ | = | Opening Quotation mark |
| CQ | = | Closing Quotation mark |

## Other symbols

x(70%) y(30%) means: 'The probability that unit 'zgp' fills 'x' is 70% and that it fills 'y' is 30%.'

(...) means: 'Also consider examples without this element'.

[...] means: 'Typical co-text' OR 'Preceding item is this element.'

# SUMMARY OF ENGLISH SYNTAX

## THE CLAUSE

Elements that it fills: Σ (85%) C (7%) A (4%) q (2%) f (0.5%) or s, qtf, S, Mex, m, cv, po

| & B | A | A | C or A | O* | S | O* | N | A | I | X | X | X | M | Mex | C | Mex | C | A | V | E |
|---|---|---|---|---|---|---|---|---|---|---|---|---|---|---|---|---|---|---|---|---|
| | In fact | | | | Fred | ought | not | | | | | | meet | | Ivy | | to Ivy | by himself | | just yet |
| If | | | | | they | | | really | to | | | | gave | up | a loan | | one | instead | | today |
| or if | | | | would | you | were | | perhaps to | | | | | give | | her | | | again | | |
| But | | | | | she | could | | then | | | | | take | up | skiing | | | seriously | , Mum ? | |
| [He says] that, sadly, | | | when will | | she | | | ever | | | | | take | | skiing | up | | unexpectedly, aged eighty | , Dr Idle ? | |
| And | Being ill, | | | | Ian | | | | | | be | | passed away | | | | | very much | , do you | |
| | | | | | they | | | | | | | | sending | | you | | out to Tokyo | for two years | , y'know | |
| So | by now | | | | you | don't | | | | have been | | | want | | to (go) | | | for an hour | , I reckon | |
| | | | | | Ivy | will | | | soon | | | | going | out | with like | | | these days | , please | |
| | | | | | this | must | | | | have been being discussed | | | | | | (by them) | | near me | , however | |
| | Till now, though, | | | | Ivy | | | | | | | | have | | a row with Ivy | | | in the Alps | with him | |
| | | | | | I | 've | | never | | | | | gone | | walking | | | in here | , right | ? |
| And | | | who [cv] did | | You | mustn't | | ever | | | | | fall | | asleep | | | first | , d'you think | ? |
| (when | | | | | she | | | | | | | | fall | | in love | with [p] | | | | (.) |
| (for | | | | | he | was) | | | to | | | | reading | | this | | | like that | | ! |
| | | | | | Fred) | | | Yes/No | | | | | look | | at Ivy | | | please/thanks | | |

## NOTES

1. S and C (and cv in a pgp when a PR) may be **covert**, and any element may be **ellipted**. In both cases, insert the unexpressed elements in round brackets.
2. Subjects and Complements typically have a **Participant Role** (such as Agent, Affected, Carrier or Attribute) conflated with them. These are omitted here.
3. The diagram shows many of the most frequent patterns - but see Notes 4-11.
4. Up to **THREE Main Verb Extensions** can co-occur, if one is *back* or a group. Some Mexs can be thematized, e.g. *Off* [Mex] *he* [S] *went* [M] *to China* [C].
5. A fairly frequent element that is omitted above is the **Auxiliary Extension (Xex)**. They occur after Xs and are typically followed by an additional **Infinitive Element (I)**, as in *You* [S] *have* [O/X] *got* [Xex] *to* [I] *eat* [M] *it* [C], and *Are* [O/X] *you* [S] *able* [Xex] *to* [I] *swim* [M] *500 metres* [C] ? Two or occasionally more may occur together, as in *He* [S] *isn't* [O/X] *going* [Xex] *to* [I] *be* [X] *willing* [Xex] *to* [I] *eat* [M] *that* [C].
6. There are many types of **Adjunct**. The diagram shows two occurring together, both early and late in the clause. Occasionally three or more may co-occur.
7. There are many other possible positions for **Adjuncts** besides those shown. These include: between S and O, between any two of O, I, X, Xex and M, and between M or Mex and C. While some of these positions are very infrequent, all are possible. When an Adjunct occurs between M or Mex and C, the Process is usually 'locational' or 'directional', as in *Ivy* [S] *walked* [M] *slowly* [A] *(out* (Mex)) *to the car* [C]. Occasionally two (and very occasionally more) Adjuncts may occur in these less frequent positions, as in *I* [S] *have* [O/X] *honestly* [A] *never* [A] *wittingly* [A] *lied* [M] *to you* [C].
8. **Vocatives (V)** can occur in the **Let element (L)**, as in *Do* [O] *let* [L] *'s all* [S] *go* [M] *for a swim* [Mex].
9. An occasional element is the **Formulaic Element (F)**, e.g. *Thanks* [F], *mate* [V], *for your help with that* [A].
10. When a clause contains a segment that is not analyzable syntactically, it is a **Starter (St)**, and it is often matched by an Ender (E).
11. Sometimes there is an initial **Starter (St)**, and it is often matched by an Ender (E). In writing it is usually a comma (as in clauses in some late As above).

## SUMMARY OF ENGLISH SYNTAX

### THE NOMINAL GROUP

Notes 1 A **fractionative determiner [fd]** may occur, preceding qd, with an intervening v. The two don't usually occur together, but if they do fd precedes qd, as in *two thirds* [fd] *of* [v] *all* [qd] *my* [dd] *friends* [h].
2 A **qualifier-introducing determiner [qid]** may also occur, preceding v dd. Again, the two don't often co-occur, but if they do qid precedes dd, as in *those* [qid] *of* [v] *our* [dd] *friends* [h] *who know her* [q].
3 Sometimes a compound noun or even two ngps may fill h, e.g. ten [qd] <u>boys and girls</u> [h] from Iran [q].

Elements that it fills: <u>S (45%) C (32%) cv (15%) A (3%) m (2%) or Mex, V, rd, pd, fd, qd, td, q, dt, po</u>

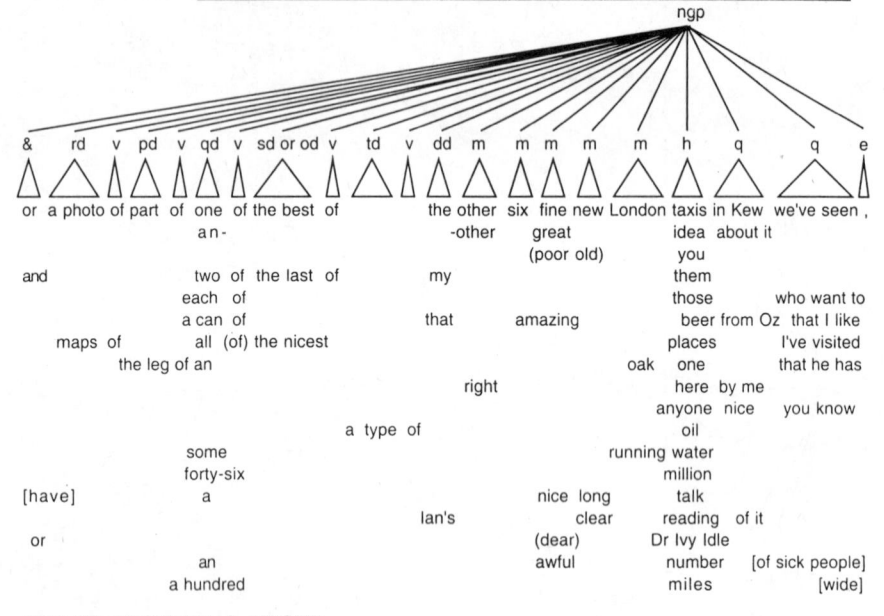

```
                                                         ngp
        &    rd    v   pd   v   qd   v  sd or od  v   td   v   dd    m    m   m   m       m      h         q          q      e
```

| & | rd | v | pd | v | qd | v | sd or od | v | td | v | dd | m | m m m | m | h | q | q | e |
|---|----|----|----|----|----|----|----|----|----|----|----|----|----|----|----|----|----|----|
| or | a photo | of | part | of | one | of | the best | of | | | the other | six | fine new London | | taxis | in Kew | we've seen | , |
| | an- | | | | | | | | | | -other | great | (poor old) | | idea | about it | | |
| and | | | two | of | the last | of | | | | | my | | | | them | | | |
| | | | each | of | | | | | | | that | amazing | | | those | | who want to | |
| | maps | of | a can | of | | | | | | | | | | | beer | from Oz | that I like | |
| | | | all (of) | the nicest | | | | | | | | | | | places | | I've visited | |
| | | | the leg | of an | | | | | | | | | | | oak | one | that he has | |
| | | | | | | | | | | | | right | | | | here | by me | |
| | | | | | | | | | | | | | | | anyone | nice | you know | |
| | | | | | | | a type | of | | | | | | | | oil | | |
| | | | some | | | | | | | | | | | | running water | | | |
| | | | forty-six | | | | | | | | | | | | million | | | |
| [have] | | | a | | | | | | | | | nice long | | | talk | | | |
| | | | | | | | Ian's | | | | | clear | | | reading | of it | | |
| or | | | | | | | | | | | | (dear) | | | Dr Ivy Idle | | | |
| | | | an | | | | | | | | | awful | | | number | [of sick people] | | |
| | | | a hundred | | | | | | | | | | | | miles | [wide] | | |

### THE PREPOSITIONAL GROUP

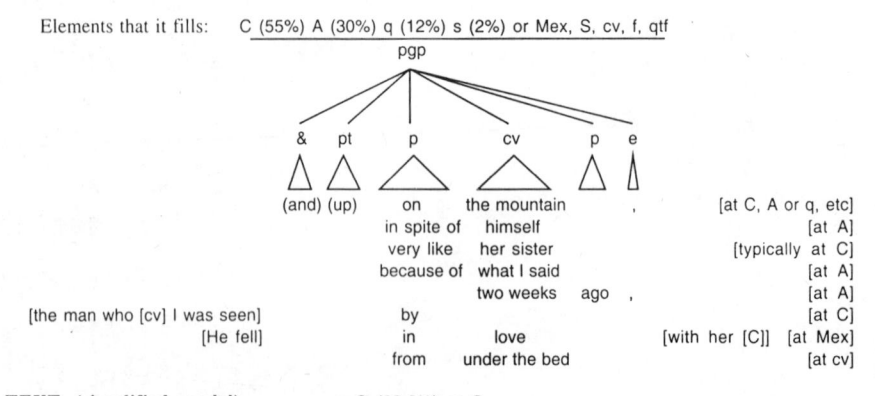

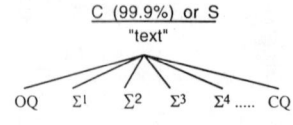

Elements that it fills: C (55%) A (30%) q (12%) s (2%) or Mex, S, cv, f, qtf

```
                              pgp
              &    pt    p    cv    p    e
```

| & | pt | p | cv | p | e |
|---|----|----|----|----|----|
| (and) | (up) | on | the mountain | , | [at C, A or q, etc] |
| | | in spite of | himself | | [at A] |
| | | very like | her sister | | [typically at C] |
| | | because of | what I said | | [at A] |
| | | | two weeks | ago , | [at A] |
| [the man who [cv] I was seen] | | by | | | [at C] |
| [He fell] | | in | love | | [with her [C]] [at Mex] |
| | | from | under the bed | | [at cv] |

**TEXT** (simplified model)      <u>C (99.9%) or S</u>
                                    "text"

```
              OQ    Σ¹    Σ²    Σ³   Σ⁴ ..... CQ
```

# SUMMARY OF ENGLISH SYNTAX    307

## THE QUALITY GROUP

Elements that it fills: C (38%) m (36%) A (24%) sd (0.5%) or Mex, Xex, od, q, dt, at, p, S

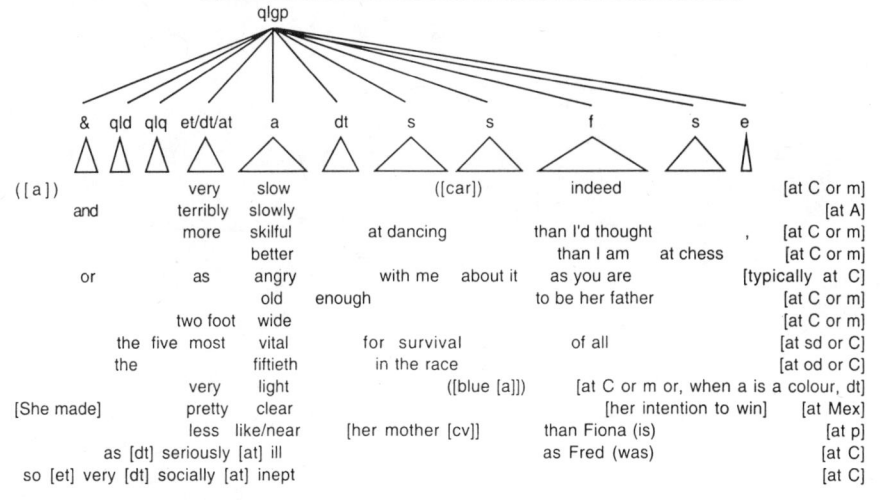

```
                                    qlgp
        &   qld  qlq  et/dt/at   a       dt      s           s          f            s      e
```

| & | qld | qlq | et/dt/at | a | dt | s | s | f | s | e |
|---|---|---|---|---|---|---|---|---|---|---|
| ([a]) | | | very | slow | | ([car]) | | indeed | | [at C or m] |
| and | | | terribly | slowly | | | | | | [at A] |
| | | | more | skilful | | at dancing | | than I'd thought | , | [at C or m] |
| | | | | better | | | | than I am | at chess | [at C or m] |
| or | | | as | angry | | with me | about it | as you are | | [typically at C] |
| | | | | old | enough | | | to be her father | | [at C or m] |
| | | | two foot | wide | | | | | | [at C or m] |
| | the | five | most | vital | | for survival | | of all | | [at sd or C] |
| | the | | | fiftieth | | in the race | | | | [at od or C] |
| | | | very | light | | ([blue [a]]) | | | | [at C or m or, when a is a colour, dt] |
| [She made] | | | pretty | clear | | | | [her intention to win] | | [at Mex] |
| | | | less | like/near | | [her mother [cv]] | | than Fiona (is) | | [at p] |
| as [dt] seriously [at] ill | | | | | | | | as Fred (was) | | [at C] |
| so [et] very [dt] socially [at] inept | | | | | | | | | | [at C] |

## THE QUANTITY GROUP

Elements that it fills: qd (85%) A (8%) dt (6%) or B, p, ad, fd, sd

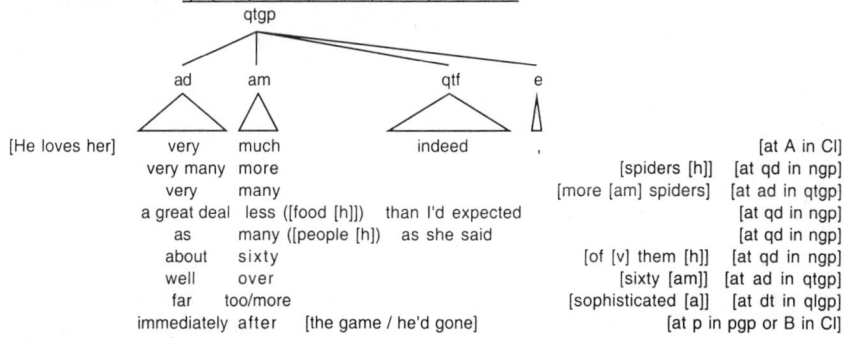

```
                qtgp
        ad     am         qtf      e
```

| | ad | am | | qtf | e | | |
|---|---|---|---|---|---|---|---|
| [He loves her] | very | much | | indeed | | | [at A in Cl] |
| | very many | more | | | | [spiders [h]] | [at qd in ngp] |
| | very | many | | | | [more [am] spiders] | [at ad in qtgp] |
| | a great deal | less | ([food [h]]) | than I'd expected | | | [at qd in ngp] |
| | as | many | ([people [h]]) | as she said | | | [at qd in ngp] |
| | about | sixty | | | | [of [v] them [h]] | [at qd in ngp] |
| | well | over | | | | [sixty [am]] | [at ad in qtgp] |
| | far | too/more | | | | [sophisticated [a]] | [at dt in qlgp] |
| | immediately | after | [the game / he'd gone] | | | | [at p in pgp or B in Cl] |

## THE GENITIVE CLUSTER

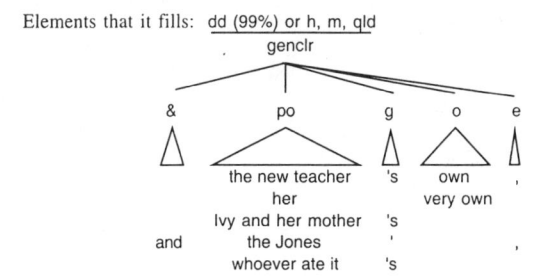

Elements that it fills: dd (99%) or h, m, qld

```
                genclr
        &    po        g    o    e
```

| | & | po | g | o | e |
|---|---|---|---|---|---|
| | | the new teacher | 's | own | , |
| | | her | | very own | |
| | and | Ivy and her mother | 's | | |
| | | the Jones | ' | | , |
| | | whoever ate it | 's | | |

# Appendix C:
# The 'rank scale' debate

## 1 The first phase of the debate: the 1960s and 1970s

Huddleston has rightly described the concept of 'rank' as both "a salient and controversial feature of Halliday's model" (1988:140). Over the last forty years this concept has attracted more criticisms than any other aspect of Systemic Functional Linguistics (SFL) — and additional reasons for abandoning it are given in Sections 11.1 and 11.2 of Chapter 11, and also in Fawcett (2000) and (forthcoming b). (For a summary of these two see Section 4 of this appendix.)

As we consider the question of whether a grammar should or should not include a 'rank scale of units', we should be clear that if it does so this logically entails having 'total accountability at all ranks' — or, in a weaker version of the same principle, 'accountability at all ranks, with a few clearly justifiable exceptions'. As we have seen, the concept of the 'rank scale' entails a 'consists of' relationship between its 'units', and if in a description a unit on the 'rank scale' can be omitted the concept of 'consists of' is lost. Thus 'accountability at all ranks' is simply a more formal statement of the 'consists of' relationship..

Butler (1985) provides the fullest history so far of the development of SFL, and he includes an excellent summary (on pp. 29-33) of what we may term the first phase of the 'rank scale' debate. However, he does not refer to what was, in its quiet way, the most significant of all of the criticisms of the concept that were made in that period, as we shall see in the next section.

In practice there was not a 'debate', in the true sense of the word. The first contribution was a set of criticisms by Postal (1964), claiming that Halliday's framework did not rule out certain types of 'rank shift' that he thought it should. However, as Butler points out (1985:29), Postal's points were based on misunderstandings of Halliday's claims, so I shall not discuss them further.

While Matthews also misunderstands the nature of some of Halliday's statements (as is pointed out in Huddleston 1988:141), his criticisms are more substantial. The only 'debate' is in fact Matthews' short article in the *Journal of Linguistics* (1966) and Halliday's fairly brief 'reply' in the same issue. Matthew unfortunately scatters his highly critical paper with expressions such as "facile" (p. 101) and "irremediably unsound" (p. 102), the effect of which is to make it harder to accept that some at least of his points deserve a detailed response. Judging by later references to this 'debate' in the literature of SFL (e.g., in Berry 1975 and Butler 1985), some systemic linguists found Halliday's 'reply' more persuasive than others. I myself was somewhat disappointed with it because I wanted to know how he would handle the various problems raised by Matthews, on the grounds that theoretical concepts depend ultimately on their value as a framework for making detailed descriptions. But Halliday did not indicate how he would resolve these problems.

When Matthews' pejorative evaluations and misunderstandings are stripped away, five specific problems for Halliday's proposals on 'rank' remain. The first concerns *Yes* and *No*, but I see these as functioning outside the main grammar, so I shall set them aside. The second problem is that a **Binder** such as *after* in *after we left Henry's* clearly invites analysis as a word rather than a group. Yet according to the 'accountability at all ranks' principle it should be a group, since it is an element of the clause. And the same is true of those types of **Adjunct** that cannot be 'expanded' such as *therefore*. Fourthly, a **Linker** such as *and* and *or* is similarly a direct element of the clause (for me but not for Matthews). For Matthews (p. 107) it "cannot reasonably be said to go with" either the preceding or the following clause. Fifthly, Matthews points out that the unit that is here called the **genitive cluster** (e.g., *my father's*) is a serious embarrassment for the concept of the 'rank scale'. The reason (though this is not how Matthews presents it) is as follows. While any such expression is clearly a unit that consists of more than one word, the 'rank scale' principle denies it 'group' status because it cannot function as a direct element of the clause. In fact it always fills an element of a group (usually the deictic determiner in a nominal group), and this suggests that it must be 'lower' on the 'rank scale' than the group. However, while one of its main elements is expounded by a morpheme (almost always *'s*), its other principal element is always filled by one or more nominal groups (and occasionally by a clause, as in *whoever ate it's mistake*). The existence of the genitive cluster is therefore a serious problem for the concept of the 'rank scale'. (See Section 10.2.11 of Chapter 10 and Appendix B for the straightforward approach to this unit that is taken here.)

In his reply to Matthews' paper, Halliday (1966:110-8) accepts that it is at least worth considering one idea floated by Matthews, i.e., that items such as *and* and *or* might be treated as "markers" (as he suggest punctuation might be) rather than as "constituents".[1] However, the main thrust of his defence of the 'rank scale' is to make a set of claims for the general insightfulness of working with the concept of the 'rank scale' — as a means of relating units and their associated system networks to each other, as a hypothesis that raises interesting questions about language, and as a tool that may be useful in fields of applied linguistics such as translation and others that involve text analysis. In other words, the defence is an empirical one: if the concept proves to be useful in advancing our understanding of how language works, it is a hypothesis that is worth making. And it has to be said that, whatever one's view of the 'rank scale' today, there is little doubt that, for those doing descriptive work in the theory and those using it in various fields of application in the 1960s and 1970s, the 'rank scale' did indeed provide a framework for describing languages that was an advance over unrestricted constituency relations. And, despite the drawbacks of its excessively strong claim, it has for several decades provided one dimension of the 'matrix' model of Systemic Functional Grammar (the other dimension being Halliday's four 'metafunctions', i.e., the 'experiential', the 'logical', the 'interpersonal' and the 'textual'). From this viewpoint, it may seem to some that it is 'politically' important to defend the 'rank scale' concept.

We have seen that, in his response to Matthews' comments, Halliday (1966) allows that Matthews may have a valid point with respect to Linkers such as *and*. In *IFG*, however, he makes an alternative proposal (p. 211). He introduces a new class of group, the 'conjunction group', which is to fill a Linker or Binder. He is right that this is needed (at least for Linkers), but one wonders whether the proposal has the additional attraction of enabling him to handle Linkers within the 'rank scale' rather than as 'markers', and so to defend the original 'rank scale' concept. However, while Binders occasionally require

---

1. In his 1988 review of *IFG*, Huddleston suggests (ironically, presenting the idea as a possible source of support for the 'rank scale' concept) that, Halliday may have taken up Matthews' suggestion, and that he would analyze the genitive element *'s* in *my father's* as a "structural signal rather than a constituent" (Huddleston 1988:141), and that "the same probably holds for co-ordinators such as *and* and *or*." But there is no indication in Halliday's analyses in *IFG* that this would be his solution to any of the four types of problem mentioned above. There he classifies both 'linkers' and 'binders' (together with 'continuatives') as types of 'adverbial', and so as 'constituents' rather than as 'structural signals' (p. 214). The problem of how best to handle these four cases in a 'rank scale' grammar therefore remains unresolved.

an internal structure (as Appendix B shows), Linkers do not. (I assume here that Halliday would treat *and so*, etc. as a single item, as I would). Halliday's new class of group does not help here, nor does it help with Adjuncts that express logical relations such as *therefore* and *however*. Moreover, the structure that he suggests for the 'conjunction group' is simply "β α". The problem here is that this makes it a 'hypotactic' relationship, so that an example such as *immediately after* is treated as a 'word complex' rather than a group. In other words, such a structure does not constitutes a group in Halliday's theory, but a 'unit complex' that occurs between a simple word and a simple group.

Before we leave Phase 1 of the debate, I should remind you that Halliday's concept of 'class of unit' and his concept of the 'rank scale' are mutually interdependent, since a 'class of unit' is defined by its potential for operation in the unit above it on the 'rank scale'. So the debate about the meaning of 'class of unit' (as described in Butler (1985:33-4) and in Section 10.2.2 of Chapter 10) is also in effect a debate about the 'rank scale'.

What does Butler himself think of the concept of the 'rank scale'? In Butler (1995) he writes, in carefully chosen words, that "there are considerable advantages to be gained from a rank-based grammar, if we accept the aims of Halliday's theorizing" (p. 32). Butler in fact appears to accept these aims, but he continues (referring to the first phase of the 'rank scale' debate): "we have seen that there are points at which it [a 'rank scale' grammar] breaks down." He then suggests, from a broader perspective, that "it is of great value to pursue a theoretical concept to the point where it begins to break down, so that we find out how much it accounts for and how much remains to be explained". Now, over fifteen years after writing those words, I wonder if Butler would agree that the concept of the 'rank scale' has now "broken down" in additional important ways, and so come to the end of its life as a useful concept?

We need to ask why there has been so little discussion of alternative systemic functional solutions to problems in SFL. The reason is partly the example that is set by Halliday himself. He, like many others, has a strong dislike for the type of supposedly 'hard-nosed' combative argumentation that was so popular in the heyday of Chomskyan linguistics. This may be at least part of the reason why Halliday has only rarely responded to criticisms, and why he hardly ever comments adversely on alternative proposals from within SFL — and so why there is so little 'debate' in SFL. On the rare occasions when he does reply to a criticism, his typical response is to concede courteously that the point needs consideration (as he did with respect to Matthews' idea of treating Linkers such as *and* as "markers"), while at the same time continuing to assert the value of the original concept. The problem is that, with the passage of time and the repeated re-presentation of the original concept (both his own works and, often, in the various introductions to his ideas by others) the criticism gets forgotten and the original concept, despite its weaknesses, survives.[2]

The general sense that the theory does not change is also fostered by the fact that Halliday only rarely states publicly that he has changed his mind on some aspect of his model of language— even though he has often done so, as is of course inevitable. Indeed, he takes the view (as we saw in Chapter 4) that the way in which the theory has developed over the last forty years is through expansion rather than change. SFL has certainly expanded, but it has also changed in an evolutionary manner — and the sum of these changes was in effect revolutionary, in that they led to the creation of a new theory of language.

As we shall see in Section 3, Halliday himself takes no part in the second phase of the 'rank scale' debate, which we shall come to in Part 3.

## 2 Hudson's *de facto* contribution to the debate

First, however, we must look at what was, in my view, the most telling criticism of the 'rank scale' in the early period. It came from Hudson, one of Halliday's closest colleagues in the sixties. Surprisingly, perhaps, his book *English Complex Sentences: an Introduction to Systemic Grammar* (Hudson 1971) is still the fullest account of an attempt to build a generative grammar based on systemic principles to be published in book form (though very large SF grammars are available in the form of computer programs). Yet the significance of Hudson (1971) is not usually acknowledged by SF linguists.

What, then, was Hudson's view of the 'rank scale'? The way in which he expressed his view was to construct a systemic grammar in which it had no place at all. In other words, he did not argue against the 'rank scale', like Matthews, and simply presented his alternative concept. Indeed, it may be this

---

[2]. I am not suggesting that Halliday (or any presenter of his version of the theory) adopts this strategy consciously, but it seems to me a fair description of what in fact often happens. However, although Halliday's attitude to discussion may avoid unpleasantly wounding encounters, it also reduces the chance of the fruitful exchanges that may lead to improvements in the model. It seems likely that this has been the cause of the departure from the theory of a number of fine scholars over the years, including most obviously his two main colleagues of the 1960s, Hudson and Huddleston, and, in the 1990s, Butler.

that explains why his views are not cited in summaries of the 'rank scale' debate such as those in Berry (1975) and Butler (1979) and (1985).[3]

Hudson's alternative proposal is an interesting one, and it is expressed in the form that it is because his system networks are at the level of form rather than meaning. He suggests (1971:70) that "'clause', 'phrase' and 'word' are simply the names of classes of grammatical items" and, since his grammar models language at the level of form, he is able the treat the relationship between the 'ranks' as a systemic one, and so to say that "the relation between them is simply a system rather than some other unique kind of grammatical relation "— by which he presumably means the 'rank scale'. He therefore dispenses with the 'composed of' relationship between 'ranked units'. He then goes on to specify the mechanism that provides the constraints on what units can occur at what elements of other units, as follows:

> Thus if some [structural] environment allows a word but not a clause or phrase then the only part of the total network which is thereafter available to be chosen from will be the part extending rightwards from 'word'. (Hudson 1971:70)

In other words, a feature that is chosen on a traversal of the network to generate a clause may have a realization rule attached to it which specifies that, when the network is re-entered to generate the next layer of structure, it must select the feature [word], rather than [clause] or [phrase].

In the very large SF grammar that is implemented in the computer in the COMMUNAL Project at Cardiff, a broadly similar mechanism is used to determine what units can fill what elements in higher units — except that here it is interpreted in terms of a model in which the choices are between **semantic features** (rather than syntactic ones, as in Hudson's model).[4]

---

3. One of the main reasons why Hudson (1971) is referred to less than it deserves is the fact that, by the time it was published, Halliday had moved on to create 'systemic functional grammar'. Moreover, Hudson himself soon moved on to another version of his own developing theory of language called 'daughter dependency grammar' (Hudson 1976), and from this he in turn developed 'word grammar' Hudson 1984). All three of Hudson's models have been centred on the level of form, perhaps in part under the influence of the Chomskyan paradigm. Hudson (1971) remains, in many ways, his finest achievement, and it has had a considerable influence on both my own work and on what was the finest natural language generation system of the 1970s (and arguably for a decade more), Davey's Proteus (Davey 1978).

4. Thus an early system offers a choice between 'situation', 'thing', quality of thing', etc. A further difference between Hudson's model and the Cardiff Grammar is that there is no semantic equivalent of 'word' in the latter. This is because a word in not a potential referring expression in the sense that a clause or a group is. In the Cardiff Grammar, then, the items

A second major difference between the Cardiff Grammar and Hudson (1971) is our introduction of the concept of **probabilities on features** in systems. These are inherently paradigmatic probabilities, of course. It is from these probabilities in the specification of the meaning potential by system networks that, after the application of the realization rules to generate structural representations, we can derive a set of statements as to the likelihood that a given element will be filled by any one of several classes of unit. If these probabilities are right, they will match the 'filling' probabilities found in natural texts. And it is from the latter — i.e., from the occurrences of vast numbers of instances in natural texts the natural texts — that we derive our statements about syntagmatic probabilities such as those stated in Appendix B. These, then, are the 'instantial probabilities' that we referred to in Section 11.2.2 in Chapter 11.

Thus it is these instance-based 'filling probabilities' (as summarized in Appendix B) that provide the nearest equivalent in the Cardiff Grammar to the 'rank scale' concept, i.e., to the set of predictions as to what units can occur within what other units that follow from the acceptance of this concept. (But even this requires supplementing by a list of exceptions, i.e., when 'rank shift' or 'embedding' is permitted, as we saw in Section 11.8.5.)

It is important to emphasize that the source of these structural probabilities is, as I have said, ultimately the semantic features in the system networks. It is only when these are translated, as it were, from the systemic-semantic to the structural-formal that they become directly useful to the text analyst. For example, if in the course of analyzing a text you have identified a nominal group, it is extremely useful to know what elements of what units it may fill, and what the rough probability is that it will fill each of those elements — i .e., exactly the information that is provided in Appendix B.

## 3  The second phase of the debate: the 1980s and 1990s

However, there was to be a further phase to the debate about the 'rank scale' (as part of a more general debate about the merits and demerits of Halliday's approach to language in *IFG*).

---

that expound the Operator, the Auxiliaries and the Main Verb, are generated on the same traversal of the network that generates the overall structure of the clause. And the items that expound the head and most determiners in the nominal group are similarly generated on the traversal of the network that generates the nominal group.

The paper that re-ignited the debate was the lengthy review article of *IFG* by Huddleston in the *Journal of Linguistics* (1988). Sadly, however, the word "debate" is again not fully appropriate — but this time for a different reason.

Huddleston's review of *IFG* begins fairly positively, including the early statement "I would emphasize that the book contains innumerable original insights and valuable observations". And he adds in a footnote: "I acknowledge my own deep indebtedness to Halliday, with respect to his influence on my thinking in linguistic theory and the grammar of English" (p. 140). Moreover the sheer length of the review (37 pages) can itself be seen as an expression of the importance that he attaches to Halliday's work. The overall tone of the review, however, is quite severely critical, and it is particularly unfortunate that it ends with two negative points. First he suggests — justifiably, it must be said — that "the absence of clear grammatical criteria will make the analysis difficult to apply for the students for whom the book is primarily intended" (p. 173). And his final remark is a complaint about the lack of an index (a lack that was rectified in the 1994 edition). How different the overall effect would have been if he had concluded with one of his initial appreciative statements!

At any event, the review led, three years later, to a long and strongly-worded rebuttal by Matthiessen and Martin (1991) in *Occasional Papers in Systemic Linguistics* — and then to an immediate reply by Huddleston (1991), and in due course to further replies to replies.[5] Here I shall focus on (1) those aspects of Huddleston's 1988 review that concern the 'rank scale' and (2) the relevant parts of the reply by Matthiessen and Martin. Huddleston's review covers many points, often in considerable detail, and he frequently introduces additional examples that he considers to present problems for *IFG* (for which he naturally offers his own analyses). The section on 'rank' occupies almost half of the review (pp. 140-55), and its importance for us is that it points to several problems which were not mentioned in the earlier debate and which deserve

---

5. As the 'debate' progressed, mutual misunderstanding and point-scoring came increasingly to dominate the discourse. The later exchanges provided few further insights — except perhaps into the ways in which the genres of the 'journal review article' and the 'journal reply' should and should not be used (including the perhaps unconscious use of the well-known 'straw man' technique for downgrading the persuasiveness of one's opponent's position). Here, then, I shall therefore ignore the later stages of this increasingly unproductive debate. Important academic, educational and political issues were (and still are) at stake, namely the question of what model of language is most helpful to those working in the education systems of the various Australian states. No doubt this helped to fuel the row, but the scholars on both sides of the debate deserve to be read by the other(s) with much greater sympathy that they were in this acrimonious exchange.

careful attention. Here I shall focus on the three most important of these.

Firstly, Huddleston suggests that in *He assumed that she was guilty*, the clause *that she was guilty* functions as a Complement, just as *too much* is a Complement in *He assumed too much*.[6] Similarly, he suggests that in *He left before the vote was taken*, the clause *before the vote was taken* functions as an Adjunct, just as *before the debate* does in *He left before the debate*. Huddleston's point is that Halliday should treat the dependent clause in such examples as functioning as an element of the matrix clause (i.e., as embedded) and not as a clause that is 'hypotactically' related to the rest of the main clause in a 'modifier-head' relationship. The relevance of this for the 'rank scale' is that, if his position is accepted, the amount of 'rank shift' in the grammar is thereby increased enormously, and the predictions made by the 'rank scale' concept are consequently weakened. We shall shortly consider more closely both Huddleston's reasons for taking the position that he does on this matter, and Matthiessen and Martin's reply. As you may have noticed, Huddleston's position is essentially the same as my own, as described in Section 11.9 of Chapter 11.

Secondly, Huddleston discusses in considerable detail certain problems that result from the concept of 'layered univariate structures' within 'parataxis' and 'hypotaxis'. We first met these concepts in Section 2.6.1 of Chapter 2. Figure 2 in that section (which is taken directly from Halliday 1965/81) illustrates in a simplified form the concept that 'hypotactic' structures add new layers to the overall structure. Moreover, the top halves of the diagrams in Figures 7-2 and 7-3 on p.217 of *IFG* similarly suggest that each 'hypotactic' relationship adds a further layer of structure. And the 'paratactic' structures of Halliday's model, with their elements of "1 2 3", necessarily also add more layers to the overall structure.[7]

Let us therefore now consider the implications for the concept of the 'rank scale' of the fact that 'parataxis' and 'hypotaxis' introduce further 'layers' to the structure of a text-sentence. Huddleston (1988) brings out some of these, but

---

6. We should not let doubts about the rightness of Huddleston's analysis of *too much* as a nominal group detain us. (In the present framework it is a quantity group; see Section 10.2.8 in Chapter 10.) An equivalent pair of examples that raise no such problems would be *She announced that she was retiring* and *She announced her retirement*.

7. In the Cardiff Grammar, however, co-ordination only rarely adds a layer to the overall structure, because the first layer of co-ordination between units — which accounts for well over 99% of cases — is handled by the 'filling' relationship, in which two or more units jointly fill an element (for which see Section 11.8.2 of Chapter 11).

he does not pursue them all the way to what I see as their logical conclusions.

Firstly, then, we need to note that in Halliday's current model any such "unit complex" is located above the equivalent "basic unit" on the 'rank scale'. (These terms were introduced by Huddleston himself, in his important contribution in Huddleston 1965/81:46.) In other words, Halliday's model states (1) that above the clause there is the 'clause complex' (the term "sentence" being permitted as an equivalent when referring to written rather than spoken text); (2) that between the clause and the group/phrase there is the 'group/phrase complex'; (3) that between the group/phrase and the word there is the 'word complex'; and (4) that between the word and the morpheme there is the 'morpheme complex'. In principle, then, the introduction of 'unit complexes' to the theory doubles the number of 'units' on the 'rank scale'. Moreover, there is no doubt that a unit complex is a type of 'unit' in Halliday's theory, because he refers to it as a 'unit' — writing, for example, that "the clause complex is the only grammatical unit that we shall recognize above the clause" (*IFG* p. 216).

However, so far as the two 'rank scale' concepts of (1) 'accountability at all ranks' and (2) 'rank shift' are concerned, Halliday treats the 'unit complexes' as if they were **not** part of the 'rank scale'. He does **not** consider, therefore, that every clause should be analyzed as serving a function in a clause complex, that every group should be seen as filling an element in a group complex, and so on. (And yet, as we shall shortly see, this is precisely what he does say, at some points.) Although he does not state in *IFG* why it is undesirable to treat 'unit complexes' as 'units' on the 'rank scale', we can infer that the reason is the additional layers of 'singular branching' that would occur — because one of his reasons for introducing 'hypotaxis' in 1965 was to avoid the "somewhat artificial increase in 'depth' in number of layers [introduced by embedding]."[8]

But matters are in fact even more complex, because recursive structures canoccur within 'unit complexes' of both the 'paratactic' and the 'hypotactic' types (as is illustrated on pp. 216-9 of *IFG*). Thus there can be **more than one** layer of structure between each 'basic rank', e.g., as in the three layers of hypotactically related clauses in the two examples in Figure 2 in Section 2.6.1

---

8. A defender of Halliday's position might be tempted to offer a modified model of the standard column of units on the 'rank scale', in which each type of unit complex was placed **beside** its equivalent basic unit rather than above it. But this would not resolve the problem, because it would leave the relationship between a 'unit' and its equivalent 'unit complex' undefined. There is in fact no alternative, in Halliday's framework, to accepting unit complexes as additional units on the 'rank scale'.

of Chapter 2, and similarly in Halliday's example of *I don't mind if you leave as soon as you've finished*, shown in Figure 7-2 on p. 217 of *IFG*. (This example would have essentially the same representation as (a) in Figure 2.)

I should add, however, that Halliday would probably not agree that every additional element in a 'hypotactic' unit complex (after the first two) adds a new layer of structure — even though diagrams such as those referred to above clearly imply that they do. In Halliday (1965/81:34) he says that "a hypotactic structure is better thought of as a chain of dependencies". Indeed, 'box diagrams' such as those in the lower halves of Figures 7-2 and 7-3 on p. 217 of *IFG* show the elements "α β γ" as a set of adjacent symbols — so implying that they are all elements of the same unit. This in turn raises the question of whether it is possible to have a recursive 'modifier-head' relationship between three elements α, β and γ, because the β element has to function as **both** a head (to γ) **and** a modifier (to α), which is arguably illogical. Halliday certainly intends this interpretation (1965/81:36), but I find his reasons for its desirability unpersuasive, and I would analyze all of his examples in terms of embedding. I agree with Huddleston (1988:148-9), therefore, when he says that "hypotactic univariate structures do not lend themselves satisfactorily to the minimal bracketing principle", i.e., to a representation of such structures as "α β γ". Huddleston devotes four pages to a discussion of 'maximal' vs. 'minimal' bracketing and an examination of Halliday's illustrative analyses (pp. 148-51), and his strongly worded conclusion (which seems to be justified) is that "the α β γ structure is unmotivated and inconsistently applied" (1988:151).

However, it makes little difference which way one decides on this matter, because my essential point stands in either case. This is that the effect on the concept of the 'rank scale' of introducing 'parataxis' and 'hypotaxis' is that it greatly increases the number of units on the 'rank scale'. Indeed, since in Halliday's model there can be unit complexes of both the 'paratactic' and the 'hypotactic' types above each basic unit, the number of units on the 'rank scale' is increased to at least twelve. Moreover, since either the 'paratactic' or the 'hypotactic' structure may come above the other (or indeed between two instances of the other) there may be even more layers still. The model with which Halliday's account of ' univariate' structures leaves us is therefore one which has, in principle, potentially very many layers of unit complexes (either 'paratactic' or 'hypotactic' or both) above each of the four basic 'units' of the 'rank scale'. (In any one instance, of course, the number of layers would be constrained by the limits of human short-term memory.)

We come now to the theoretical core of the problem that 'unit complexes' raise for the concept of the 'rank scale'. Halliday's descriptions of these additional layers of structure are always in terms of what he terms their "elements", e.g., the 'hypotactic' ones are said to be in a series of 'modifier-head' relationships to each other (*IFG* p. 217-8), represented by the symbols "α β γ" etc. But these elements are not treated as elements of a **unit** (as in the case of the modifier and head of a nominal group), but as elements that are somehow able to function in relation to each other **without the use of the concept of 'unit'**. Yet in SFL the concepts of 'unit' and 'element' are mutually defining. In other words, an element is by definition an element of the structure of something, and in SF theory that "something" is a unit. Yet in *IFG* we are presented with 'elements' that are shown in the diagrams as relating directly to each other, without any indication of the unit of which the element is a component — or indeed of the unit that fills the element. In other words, the concept of a 'unit' is in fact covertly present, even through it is not referred to at any point.[9]

Is there any reason why Halliday should not include in his representations the 'unit-complexes' that the description implies? The reason why he does not address this question is, I would guess, that the additions to the 'rank scale' that such structures imply would threaten its viability because of the unacceptable quantity of 'singular branching' that the maintenance of the principle of 'accountability at all ranks' would introduce. They are therefore unwelcome in Halliday's theory, both as 'units on the rank scale' and as the representation of such units on paper.[10]

The above argument goes rather further in exploring the implications for the concept of the 'rank scale' of Halliday's proposals than does Huddleston's review, perhaps in part because he concentrates on different matters (relations

---

9. This practice is reminiscent of that followed in some presentations of S&C grammar, in which the units are omitted to simplify the representation. Examples are found in Berry (1975:84-5 and 91), Muir (1972:82-8) and, more recently, in Morley (2000:156-62) All three scholars follow the "Categories" pattern rather than the *IFG* pattern, i.e., they recognize the sentence as a unit on the 'rank scale', so that they all have a unit of which the α and β elements can be components. Thus Berry's, Muir's and Morley's analyses of clause complexes are unlike those of Halliday in *IFG*.

10. A possible alternative answer might in principle be that, while this would suit 'hypotactic' structures quite well, it would not suit 'paratactic' structures, because co-ordination does not involve a 'modifier-head' relationship (as is recognized in all theories). However, given Halliday's view of the centrality of the 'rank scale' in the theory, it seems more likely that the reason suggested in the main text is the right one.

between words and groups, and issues of left and right branching). While I shall not attempt to summarize these here, I shall cite his interesting concluding words. These deserve attention because he was, as we noted in Section 5.1 of Chapter 5, one of the small team (with Halliday, Hudson and Henrici) who worked on these problems in the 1960s. Indeed, it was Huddleston who wrote one of the key S&C papers on this topic (Huddleston 1965/81). Since he was so closely involved, we should give due weight to his statement that

> historically, the layered univariate structure was introduced in the context of an attempt to solve certain problems stemming from the total accountability requirement of the rank model. [...] "The problems we have been discussing [layering in 'paratactic' and 'hypotactic' structures] are created by the [rank scale] model". (Huddleston 1988:151)[11]

The clear implication of this revealing statement is that the purpose of introducing the concepts of 'paratactic' and 'hypotactic' relations in structure to the theory was less their inherent insightfulness than to shore up the ailing concept of the 'rank scale'. This is therefore secondary evidence for the position taken here, i.e., that the concept of the 'rank scale' is ultimately not a useful one. Moreover we now have a replacement for it, i.e., the concept of a set of units, each of which is capable of filling several elements of one or more higher units in a tree representation, supplemented for text analysis by filling probabilities.[12]

Finally, we should note that the position taken by Halliday himself on this issue is exploratory rather than dogmatic. He writes that "hypotaxis is in some ways intermediate between parataxis and [...] rankshift; in fact all hypotaxis could be regarded as rankshift" (1965/81:40). And over twenty years later (*IFG* p. 216) he introduces this aspect of his model with hedging expressions such as "the tendency is [...]", "we shall assume [...]", "we shall interpret [...]".

The third problem for the 'rank scale' that Huddleston's review brings out is the fact that the **completive** of a 'prepositional group/phrase' is practically

---

11. We saw in Section 11.8.2 of Chapter 11 how 'layering' within 'paratactic' structures can be represented, like layering in 'hypotactic' structures, through embedding. For further discussion see Fawcett (in press).

12. Many of those who accept Halliday's approach to 'paratactic' and 'hypotactic' relations in structure would claim that the categorizations of relations between clauses (and other units) into 'projection' and 'expansion' (and then of the latter into 'elaboration', 'extension' and 'enhancement') are independently self-justifying. But there are in fact different ways of analyzing all of these phenomena that many others, including myself, consider to be more insightful. See Section 11.9 of Chapter 11 and Fawcett (1996) and (in press) for examples of these.

always filled by one or more nominal groups. The problem is that 'phrase' and 'group' are at the same 'rank' on the 'rank scale'. As Huddleston says (1988:154), "for the prepositional phrase always to involve rankshift is contrary to the spirit of rankshift, since rankshift represents a departure from the normal or unmarked state of affairs".

However, there are many aspects of Huddleston's views on syntax with which I disagree, and some that I find surprising. Firstly, I find surprising his tendency to interpret all group structures in terms of what is essentially the 'hypotactic' relationship of 'modifier-head'. This is perhaps to be explained by the fact that such interpretations reflect broadly the same theoretical concepts as those in his major project of the 1990s, *The Cambridge Grammar of English*. (Huddleston and Pullum forthcoming). This very full description of English grammar uses what are essentially 'modifier-head' relations (and their variants in 'determiner-head' and 'head-complement' relations), together with the multiple layering of constituents (Huddleston, personal communication, 2000).[13]

It is also surprising that Huddleston should take Halliday to task for having "completely different structures for the nominal group, the verbal group and the prepositional phrase" (p. 155). After all, he is well aware that Halliday is a functional grammarian, and it is natural, as I emphasized in Section 10.3 of Chapter 10, that in a functional description of a language different elements of different units should be seen as serving different functions.[14]

But Huddleston goes even further, apparently dismissing the concept of the 'group' (or 'phrase') altogether. So it is yet more surprising that he states:

---

13. Thus his framework is not very far from that used in current Chomskyan linguistics, where the concepts of 'head,' 'adjunct' (= Huddleston's 'modifier'), 'complement' and 'specifier' are used for all such relationships. Interestingly, these can be seen as highly generalized functional elements. Can it really be the case that the generative-formalist linguists are beginning to think in slightly more functional terms?

14. It is equally surprising that Huddleston continues as follows: "Nor, as far as I am aware, does the group provide the domain for any system network" (1988:155). Huddleston must surely be as aware as anyone of the existence of Halliday's system networks for both the supposed 'verbal group' and the nominal group, e.g. as published in Halliday (1976) and (1977/78), since they were available at the time when he worked with Halliday. It is more understandable that he should not be aware of the system networks for groups of other systemic linguists (e.g., those for the nominal group in Fawcett 1980). And it is a particular matter of regret that he could not have seen, at the time when he wrote his review, the system networks for the quality group (i.e., the 'adjectival group', to use the term with which he would be familiar from the 1960s) in Tucker (1998).

Clause, word and morpheme are commonplace categories in syntactic theory; it is the group, among Halliday's basic ranks, that has no significantly close analogue in non-rank grammars, and it is difficult to see that this innovation has anything to recommend it" (Huddleston 1988:155).

Here Huddleston seems to be denying the value of the concept of the group (or 'phrase'). Presumably he would replace them with various types of 'word complex', each built up of simple 'modifier-head' relationships.[15] Yet he himself uses the concept of 'phrase' throughout Huddleston & Pullum (forthcoming). It is therefore hard to understand what prompted him to make the statement cited above, unless he has moved from that position to a more conventional one in the period since 1988. But if the above remarks stand, he would not only do away with the 'rank scale', but also with any units other than the clause, the word and the morpheme. This would indeed be radical.[16]

15. This passage reads as if Huddleston is suggesting that the concept of the 'group' (or 'phrase') is an "innovation" by Halliday, whereas it is in fact a commonplace of descriptive grammars — including Huddleston's own current grammar of English. Perhaps the "innovation" is intended to be the placing the group on the 'rank scale'? In any case, the syntax in Huddleston & Pullum (forthcoming) makes full use of familiar concepts such as 'noun phrase', 'adjectival phrase' and 'prepositional phrase' (Huddleston, personal communication 2000). It is interesting to see that it has in common with Systemic Functional Grammar the fact that each node in a tree diagram is labelled twice: i.e., with both a **function** label and a **class** label. For example, the three immediate constituents of the NP (Noun Phrase) *a very young boy* would be labelled first with the function labels of 'Det(erminer)','Mod(ifier)' and Head, and then with the class labels of 'D(eterminative)', 'Adj(ectival) P(hrase)' and 'N(oun)'. The constituents of the' AdjP' would then in turn be labelled as 'Mod' and 'Head', with the 'Mod' being filled by the word class 'Adv(erb)' and the 'Head' by 'Adj(ective)'. The analysis is thus a mixture of the highly traditional (e.g. treating *very* as an adverb) and an approach that apparently seeks to combine at least some of the insights of functional syntax (the double labelling of nodes) with the current approach of formal grammarians (using a minimal set of quasi-functional labels).

16. As with many other concepts, the idea that all groups can be handled as word complexes is one for which at least some support can be gleaned from Halliday's writings (e.g., "a group is in some respects equivalent to a word complex (*IFG* pp. 179-80), and "a group is the expansion of a word" (p. 180). Indeed, Halliday sometimes gives the concept of a group as a word complex more weight than the concept of a group as the expression of a semantic unit with its own set of functional elements. One clear case is his treatment of quality groups when they fill the modifier in a nominal group, as in the case of *very small* in *some very small ones* (*IFG* pp. 192 and 194). Thus *very small* is said to be a 'complex' of two words that are 'hypotactically related' rather than a group of words. Yet the same words would be a group for Halliday if they filled a Complement, as in *The egg was very small.* We can guess that the reason why he adopts this somewhat inconsistent position is that it at least has the virtue (from his viewpoint but not mine) that it avoids having to recognize such examples as yet another cased of the unwanted phenomenon of 'rank shift' — which, if acknowledged, would be further evidence against the concept of the 'rank scale'.

There is much in Huddleston's review, therefore, with which I disagree. However, it will be clear that I share his conclusion that most of the uses to which 'hypotaxis' has been put by Halliday are better handled by a simple embedding relationship (but one by co-ordination; see Section 11.9 of Chapter 11). And I also share his view (though for a set of reasons that only partly overlap with his) that "the constraints this [i.e., the requirement of 'accountability at all ranks'] imposes on the grammar have numerous unsatisfactory consequences" (Huddleston 1988:141). Indeed, I would also agree with his statement (though again for reasons that only partly overlap with his) that

> the unsatisfactory nature of the constituent structures given in [*IFG*] derives in very large measure from their foundation in rank theory. (Huddleston 1988:155)

Where I part company most drastically from Huddleston (and indeed from Hudson too) is that I, unlike them, find great value in Halliday's concept that the heart of a functional model of language is a system network of choices between meanings — and that these meanings are realized systematically, though not in a one-to-one manner, in forms. This is the fundamental reason why I first became and still remain a systemic functional linguist. The differences between Halliday and myself that I have discussed in this book are important but, unlike the differences between myself and Huddleston or Hudson, they are differences between two students of language who both subscribe to the basic principles of systemic functional linguists.

In fundamental matters, then, I have far more in common with Matthiessen and Martin (M&M) than I have with Huddleston. Indeed, I agree with most (though not all) of the "general considerations" in the first ten pages of their "Response to Huddleston" (Matthiessen & Martin 1991). The core of their criticism of Huddleston's review is less that they wish to claim that Halliday's analyses are 'right' and that Huddleston's are 'wrong', than that Huddleston should recognize Halliday's right to do his linguistics in the framework of a different philosophy of science from his. They emphasize the limitations of argument by counter-example, and the value of exploring alternative analyses — especially ones that take account of an example's discourse context — and they suggest that Halliday's proposals often provide new and insightful analyses.

However, it seems to me that a linguist has an obligation to assemble the evidence from the data in whatever theoretical framework he or she is using, to decide which examples should be shown to be similar to each other in their meanings and their structure, and then to explain why. In specifically SF terms, one should seek the answer by considering other text-sentences (and potential text-sentences) that have a close systemic relationship to the problem example. Grammarians working in other frameworks (including ex-systemicists such as Huddleston) in fact often take an essentially similar approach, so in effect adopting an informal systemic approach. Moreover M&M appear to agree with this approach, since they state (1991:25) that the question is that of "what to treat as the basic agnation" (where "agnation' means 'systemic relationship').

However, when it comes to the nitty gritty of M&M's responses to Huddleston's comments and proposals, I am too often left unpersuaded by the ways in which they seek to rebut his criticisms. While it would be impossible to summarize their 69-page "Response", I should perhaps illustrate this comment. I shall do so by discussing an area of the grammar where M&M accept that one may legitimately agree with Huddleston's argument and still be a SF linguist — and indeed where one of them has already come half way to accepting the position advocated here (Martin 1988, referred to in M&M 1991:29). The proposal that we shall consider is the idea that a grammar benefits from including Halliday's concept of 'hypotaxis' (i.e., 'dependence' without embedding') in addition to the standard concept of embedding, and that it should be used for modelling the set of 'dependent' clauses found in the summary table on page 220 of *IFG* and discussed in the following fifty pages. But in Halliday's model this is coupled with a second claim, namely that the same set of logico-semantic relations (which can be expressed in a system network) are found in clauses that are related by 'parataxis' (co-ordination). My rather different analyses of these supposed 'hypotactic' and 'paratactic' clauses, most of which I locate in significantly different parts of the overall network from Halliday, are given in Section 11.9 of Chapter 11.

M&M exemplify the above claims by offering a defence of the view that (1a) below should be analyzed as two clauses related by 'hypotaxis' — i.e., that *He left the room* is the 'alpha' (head) clause and *before they voted* is the 'beta' (modifier) clause. On this basis, the second claim is that (1a) is systemically closer to its 'paratactic' equivalent in (3a) than it is to (2a). (In both (1a) and (3a) the relationship is said to be the 'enhancement' type of 'expansion', and more specifically the 'temporal' type; see pp. 232-4 of *IFG*). Thus, while Huddleston argues that (1a) is more like (2a) than (3a), M&M claim that the reverse is the case. (I have slightly altered the wording of Huddleston's examples to create 'minimal pairs' that make the relevant contrasts fully explicit.)

(1a) He left the room before they voted.
(2a) He left the room before the vote.
(3a) He left the room, then they voted.

Huddleston's grammatical analysis of (1a) — which is broadly similar to mine — is to treat it as a single clause in which the embedded clause *before they voted* functions as an Adjunct that identifies the 'time position' of the event of 'leaving' by relating it to an event that is already known to the addressee (the 'voting' event), in the same way that *before the vote* does in (2a). Indeed, Halliday and M&M would agree with Huddleston and me that, when the event of 'voting' is nominalized as in (2a), it serves this function and is therefore an Adjunct. So why, we might ask, do they not also treat *before they voted* in (1a) as an Adjunct? Essentially, their approach is to interpret (1a) as a relating of two events (rather than as a 'main' event that is located in time by relating it to another event) — and to claim that this 'relating' can be achieved either 'paratactically', as in (3a), or 'hypotactically' as in the second interpretation of (1a).

Here Halliday's suggestion for this non-standard analysis alerts us to the important fact that the construction exemplified in (1a) can be used to state the temporal relationship between two events that are both integral parts of a narrative, **as well as** to identify the position in time of an event. In a SF grammar it is often possible to show two or more meanings simultaneously in a structure (as we have seen in the main text of this book), but here the grammar forces us to choose between them — at least, at the level of the system networks within the lexicogrammar. Thus I agree with M&M that the structure in (1a) does indeed often serve the purpose of relating two events temporally (as in a narrative), but I consider, as I shall show below, that this aspect of its meaning belongs at a higher level of analysis. And this then predetermines, non-congruently, the choices in the lexicogrammar analysis. Thus the final syntactic output would be more like Huddleston's than Halliday's.

I suggested earlier that a SF linguist should approach a problem of this sort by asking: "What evidence is there that we should give priority in the system networks to one of these relationships over the other?" Specifically, one should first collect together a body of examples that are closely related systemically to each of (1a), (2a) and (3a). Then one should examine them to see how far they provide evidence (1) that the relationship in (1a) is one of 'hypotaxis' rather than embedding, and (2) that the grammar does indeed make similar options available when relating clauses 'paratactically' to the options that are available when the relationship is 'dependent' (whether interpreted as 'hypotaxis' or embedding). Next, one should make a judgement as to which systemic relations should be given priority in the system networks (i.e., those that model meaning potential within the lexicogrammar), and finally one should make proposals as to how any relationship that has not been modelled in the grammar should be handled in the overall model.

I shall now illustrate this approach — quite briefly — and then we shall ask how far each of Huddleston (1988) and M&M (1991) carry out equivalent explorations of the systemically related data.

Here is a set of examples, all of which are potential text-sentences (though these too have been adapted from the original example in order to create 'minimal pairs'). I suggest that they provide a useful basic set of data for exploring this area of the grammar.

(1a, i-iii) He left the room before / after / while they voted.
(2a, i-iii) He left the room before / after / during the vote.
(1b, i-iii) Before / after / while they voted, he left the room.
(2b, i-iii) Before / after / during the vote he left the room.
(3a, i-v) He left the room, then / (,) and then / (,) and they voted.
(3b, i-n) He left the room, but earlier (on) / first / before that / before his departure / etc. they (had) voted.
(3c, i-n) He left the room and in that period / during that time / during his absence / etc. they voted.
(3a, v-n) He left the room, and later (on) / afterwards / after that / after his departure / etc. they voted.

Firstly, I suggest that all linguists would agree that (1a, i) — which was earlier labelled simply (1a) — has a close systemic relationship with (1a, ii-iii). Notice, though, that one result of recognizing this rather obvious fact is to show us that the parallel between (1a) and (3a) is less close than one might otherwise assume. Thus, if we wish to express the meaning of 'subsequent time' in a 'paratactic' structure (i.e., by co-ordination) we can use the grammatical items *then* or *and then* as the Linker, such that these correspond in meaning to the Binder *after*, as used in (1a, i), but if we wish to express the meaning of 'antecedent time', there is no co-ordinating Linker that corresponds to the Binder *before*. And neither is there a Linker that expresses 'simultaneous time' and that therefore corresponds to the Binder *while*. It is always possible, of course, to express a roughly equivalent meaning by a **combination** of the

Linker *and* and an Adjunct such as *afterwards* or *during that time*, etc., these Adjuncts being shown by underlining in (3b,1-n) and (3c, i-n). But this is a very different matter, in terms of the systemic choices that are available, as these examples show — because the introduction of the Adjunct opens up a very much larger range of possibilities than is available within the Linker. (Indeed, the use of "n" in the numbering of the examples symbolizes the open-endedness of the available options.) Moreover, a similar range of options to those shown in (3b, i-n) and (3c, i-n) is also available to express the concept of 'subsequent time', as (3a, i-n) demonstrates. Thus the system of choices within 'paratactic' relations is significantly different from that when the relationship is one of 'dependence' (whether this is interpreted as 'hypotaxis' or as embedding). The lists of examples given in each of Tables (7(6) and 7(7) on pages 216 and 217 of *IFG* in fact illustrate precisely this difference. (These tables cover not just temporal relations but the full range of types of embedded clause that express a Circumstance, and in so doing they provide further evidence for the position taken here.) Halliday must therefore be aware that the parallels are limited.

One the other hand, the grammar should — and can — capture the fact that we can thematize both *before they voted* and *before the vote*, as in (1b, i) and (2b, i) — a possibility which suggests that the same element (which we may term a Time Position Adjunct) is involved in both (1a, i-iii) and (2a, i-iii). And equivalent variants can be generated, of course, for (1b, ii-iii) as in (2b, ii-iii), if the option to thematize the Time Position Adjunct is exercised.

Thus the lexicogrammatical evidence begins to mount up that, on the one hand, (1a, i) belongs systemically with (1a, ii-iii), and that, on the other, it belongs with (1b, i). Moreover, these two pairs of systemic relationships can both be handled in a natural way in the lexicogrammar. (We know this because we have implemented this approach in the generative grammar in COMMUNAL.) On the other hand, the lexicogrammatical evidence is that a different range of choices is available for modelling **co-ordination** between clauses ('parataxis') from the range for modelling **'dependent'** relations (whether these are viewed as 'hypotaxis' or embedding). The case for foregrounding the parallels between 'parataxis' and 'hypotaxis' in the system networks therefore looks rather less convincing than it may have at the start of this study of the data.

If we put this evidence together with that of my alternative analyses of the examples of Halliday's ten major categories for 'paratactic' and 'hypotactic' relations between clauses (as set out in Section 11.9 of Chapter 11), we have two separate pieces of evidence that the grammar should **not** in fact foreground the contrast between 'parataxis' vs. 'hypotaxis' as a system that is to be entered simultaneously with one for 'expansion' vs. 'projection', etc. The alternative is that each type of 'co-ordination' and each type of 'dependence' should be modelled in terms of the systemic choices that are available to it, so avoiding the ever present temptation to the grammarian, i.e., that of modifying the description to conform to the theory.

Let us now look at how Huddleston tackles the problem (1988:145-6). He presents partially similar arguments for treating (1a) as being functionally like (2b). They are grammatical arguments, though they are not, of course, expressed in explicitly systemic terms. He cites (a) the 'thematizability' of the Time Position Adjunct in both (1a) and (2a); (b) the parallels as "focus of an interrogative" between *Did he leave before they voted?* and *Did he leave before the vote?* and (c) the fact that it is possible to co-ordinate a clause and a nominalized event, as in *He left before the debate or (at least) before the vote was taken.*[17] (We shall consider the weight to be attached to Huddleston's third piece of evidence when we come to M&M's response to it.)

The main rhetorical thrust of M&M's "Response to Huddleston" is a forceful rejection of almost all of what he says. Yet often, as we shall see, they do not show why we should reject arguments such as these, even sometimes accepting Huddleston's analysis. Instead, their major point is (following Halliday in his 'reply' to Matthews in the first stage of the 'rank scale' debate) that it is a virtue of Halliday's model that it raises questions about grammatical struct-ure, rather than to establish that the *IFG* approach is 'right' and that the more traditional analysis that Huddleston offers is 'wrong'. This approach is fully justifiable at the exploratory stage, but systemic functional linguists have now had well over a quarter of a century to explore English in the systemic functional framework. Even though Halliday may be right that language is ultimately "ineffable" (Halliday 1984/88), it seems to me that, as SF linguists, it is our task to carry out the research programme outlined earlier, i.e., to assemble the available evidence; to decide which relationships between examples should be given systemic priority in the model of the lexicogrammar; and to

---

17. It is not clear how Huddleston's second pair of examples is relevant. It surely cannot be the case that he believes that anything significant follows from the fact that a 'beta' clause may have a separate information unit (and so intonation unit). An example such as *Did he leave, before they voted?* is unusual but not unacceptable. But if Huddleston's example of the 'polarity seeker' type of "interrogative" was a slip and he actually intended to draw attention to the fact that *When did he leave?* is the "*wh*-interrogative" equivalent of both (1a) and (2a), then his point would clearly be relevant.

explain our decisions.

As we have seen, M&M accept this goal too, recognizing that the question is that of "what to treat as the basic agnation" (M&M 1991:25). So how far do they do this? On the 'thematizability' evidence for treating (1a) as being like (2a) rather than (3a), M&M simply state that "Halliday points out that the thematic principle is not limited to [elements within] the clause; it is also in operation in the clause complex" (1991:26). But one's inevitable response is that, since they start from a position of commitment the concept of 'hypotaxis', they are bound to take this position, so that this it is not independent evidence in support of their argument. Their reply to Huddleston leaves two problems unaddressed. The first is that, if we do not treat both *after they voted* in (1a) and *after the vote* in (2a) as Adjuncts, our grammar will require two different rules to model a generalization that patently invites expression in a single rule. And the second is that it is not clear how such a rule can in fact be formalized (unless the 'alpha' and 'beta' clauses are admitted as full elements of an as yet unnamed unit, so that the 'beta' element can be thematized in the same way that an Adjunct is.

Having only partially rejected the 'thematizability' criterion, M&M then add (1991:26): "by itself, the recurrence of the thematic principle [e.g., (1a) as (1) and (2a) as (2b)] does not constitute an argument that thematic elements must all have the same grammatical function [e.g., an Adjunct]". But Huddleston's 'thematizability' argument does not in fact stand "by itself" because, as we have seen, he gives two further types of evidence for his position. M&M have little to say about his second argument, perhaps having difficulty in interpreting it, as I have. Here we shall consider M&M's response to Huddleston's "co-ordination" argument.

This begins, perhaps surprisingly, with M&M's agreement that his analysis is indeed a possible one (i.e., the analysis in which *before the vote was taken* is treated as a clause embedded as an Adjunct). However, they move quickly on from this apparent olive branch to a robust defence of what they take to be the *IFG* position on this matter — claiming that Huddleston is wrong to criticize *IFG* for ruling out his analysis, because "there is nothing in Halliday's system to block this analysis" (p. 27). But on this matter Huddleston is right and M&M are wrong, as is shown by Halliday's own specification of the types of rankshift that his model permits. Thus he states (*IFG* p. 242) that "the relationship of an embedded clause to the 'outer' clause is an indirect one" — i.e., the embedded clause must fill an element of a group, not a clause. (See Section

11.8.5 of Chapter 11 for a summary of Halliday's statement on this matter.)

In the second part of their case, M&M suggest a second analysis of Huddleston's example, i.e., as two co-ordinated clauses with ellipsis in the second, thus: *He left before the debate or (he left) (at least) before the vote was taken.* But again, I am afraid, I have to point out a problem. While their analysis appears at first to be another possible one, we need to take account of the fact that one can insert *either* to the left of *before the debate*, so that it becomes *He left <u>either</u> before the debate <u>or</u> (at least) before the vote was taken.* And this fact demonstrates clearly that the grammar must allow for the possibility of generating the prepositional group and the clause as jointly filling an Adjunct.

Thus M&M suggest that two possible analyses should be allowed (the first being Huddleston's and mine). They therefore do **not** address the question of which of the two is systemically preferable, and why. Moreover, Huddleston's criticism of *IFG* stands. In other words, he is right that Halliday's decision to treat all clauses embedded directly in clauses as 'hypotaxis' means that the Sydney Grammar cannot handle examples such as Huddleston's.

Finally, to demonstrate that Huddleston's example is not a 'special case', consider the following example with a simple 'additive' Linker: *On average, people died earlier in those days, <u>both</u> from diseases such as diphtheria <u>and</u> because they worked such dreadfully long hours.* Notice that here (as in Huddleston's example) the item *both* prevents the M&M analysis in terms of two co-ordinated clauses with ellipsis. The conclusion, then, must be that we should treat all such 'beta' clauses as embedded clauses.

To summarize so far: M&M's main complaint about Huddleston's review is less that his proposed alternative analyses are 'wrong' than that he does not allow for the possibility that Halliday's analyses may be equally insightful. Moreover, while M&M's rhetoric leads us to interpret them as arguing against Huddleston's analysis, they actually allow it as a possible one (even though in the case considered here Halliday would not). And their alternative solution of clause co-ordination with ellipsis does not cover all cases. Withe respect to the areas of the grammar described here, then, M&M fail to rebut Huddleston's critical comments.

However, M&M can still point out that the question remains of where, in the overall model, we should express the similarity between (1a) and (3a). My answer is that the place to handle the choice that is realized by these examples is in a higher component of the generation process than the lexicogrammar. This is the component which plans the **rhetorical structure** relations of the discourse, and so how best to present the relations between any two events. (For the key proposals for this component see Mann and Thompson 1987, and for a useful introductory discussion see Martin 1992.) Indeed, the choice that is realized in (1a), (2a) or (3a) must also be extended to include a realization such as (4), so that for this reason too it is appropriate to handle it outside the lexicogrammar.[18]

(4)  He left the room. Then they voted.

An important principle is involved here. It is that, when one is deciding which patterns of similarity and contrast to assign to the system network of meaning potential within the grammar, one should give **priority to those choices which are realized directly at the level of form**. And one should recognize that other similarities and contrasts may first need to be modelled at a higher level in the process of generation, and then at a later point be mapped, often incongruently, onto the choices in the grammar itself. Thus, when a text-sentence such as (1a) is used to express a relationship between two events in a narrative, that decision should be modelled as part of the rhetorical structure, and predetermination rules should then ensure that the relationship gets mapped onto the choices in the grammar that present one event as locating the position in time of another.

M&M then go on to consider, much more briefly, examples such as the clause *he'd go* in *He said he'd go*. For Halliday (and so M&M) this is a case of the 'hypotactic' relationship of 'projection', with *he'd go* being a 'beta' clause to the supposed 'alpha' clause *he said*. As we saw at the start of this section, for both Huddleston and me this example has an embedded clause that fills a Complement of the higher clause *He said he'd go*. (Strictly speaking, for me it fills the Participant Role of Phenomenon, this being conflated with the Complement.) As M&M very fairly point out, "Fawcett (1980), [...] working within a theoretical framework closely related to Halliday's, treats all of Halliday's hypotactic clauses through embedding, the very position which Huddleston espouses." After also indicating that Martin (1988) suggests an analysis of such examples in which the experiential analysis at clause rank is in these terms, they go on: "The theory can thus be seen to accommodate a range of approaches

---

18. In fact, it is also at this stage in generation that the planner needs to consider choosing other conceptually equivalent choices realized in forms which M&M do not mention but which express the same basic temporal relationship of successivity between events, such as *They voted after he left the room* and *After he left the room they voted*.

to the question of subordination" (M&M 1991:29).[19]

Quite so. In other words, the analyses of dependent clauses that Huddleston advocates in his review of *IFG* are indeed possible ones within SFL. But the fact that SF linguists agree that we should explore the value of both 'hypotaxis' and alternative concepts within the theory does not absolve us from the obligation to try to decide whether 'hypotaxis' is needed in all or some or none of the cases for which Halliday proposes its use. The key point for the present debate is that, if we replace 'hypotaxis' by embedding in the examples discussed here (as Huddleston and I advocate), the case for retaining the concept of the 'rank scale' is greatly weakened. Thus it is not the case, as M&M suggest (p. 28), that "Huddleston's objections are descriptive, not theoretical".

M&M make many valuable points in their "Response to Huddleston". The main weakness in the case that they present in the sections of their "Response" summarized above is this: they do not show how the generalizations that Halliday gives up in order to foreground the similarities between the 'hypotactic' and 'paratactic' analyses are to be handled in the grammar. If M&M are to 'defend' the position taken in *IFG* successfully, they need to address this question. But perhaps there should be less 'attacking' and 'defending', and more accepting of genuine 'problem examples', together with more exploring of comprehensive solutions to such problems, in the framework of a multi-component model?

## 4 The third phase of the debate: the 2000s

Interestingly, none of the previous critics of the concept of the 'rank scale' (except Hudson 1971, implicitly) have discussed the role of the 'verbal group' as either supporting or undermining the concept of the 'rank scale'. Yet the reasons for abolishing the 'verbal group' and promoting its elements to function as elements of the clause are so persuasive that this set of reasons alone is sufficient to cause one to re-think the viability of the concept of 'accountability at all ranks', and so the 'rank scale' itself. In the present section, therefore, I

---

19. However, I am surprised to find Martin advocating this idea, because it involves an insuperable problem. This is that the second part of his proposal is that there should be a "simultaneous analysis" (showing the 'logical' structure) **at the 'rank' of the "clause complex"**. This is, as we have seen, a different 'unit' on the 'rank scale' from the clause, so that if Martin's idea were to be adopted there would even more serious problems for the concept of conflating these two structures than those already specified in Section 7.4 of Chapter 7. It may be that Martin would now wish to reconsider this proposal.

shall provide an outline of the argument set out in my two-part paper "In place of Halliday's 'verbal group'" (Fawcett 2000 and forthcoming b).[20]

This substantial paper is published in two parts. Here I cannot present its many arguments in their full, compelling detail, but I can try to indicate its major points.

Part 1 begins by pointing out a number of inconsistencies, from the functional viewpoint, in the way in which Halliday labels the elements of his 'verbal group' in *IFG*. It then demonstrates the way in which these problems are resolved in the alternative approach taken in the Cardiff Grammar.

The most obvious of these inconsistencies is the way in which *IFG* presents the Finite (which is very roughly equivalent to the Cardiff Grammar's Operator). At one point (p. 72) Halliday describes the Finite as "**part of** the verbal group [my emphasis]", while at another (p. 79) he says that "the predicator ... is realized by a verbal group **minus the Finite** [my emphasis]". And the Finite is in fact shown in the analyses of clauses throughout *IFG* as part of the more delicate of the two analyses of 'interpersonal' meaning in the clause, i.e., as an element of the clause. (However, if it really is to be modelled an element of the clause **as well as** an element of the 'verbal group', this would bring horrendous problems in its train for a generative SF grammar.)

In a rather similar manner, Halliday analyzes the word *off* in *They will call the meeting off* as an Adjunct in *IFG*, i.e., as an element of the clause rather than as an element of the 'verbal group'. Yet we might have expected him to have analyzed it as an element of the 'verbal group' since it is the co-realization, with *call*, of the meaning of the single Process of 'calling off', and *called* is unequivocally an element of the 'verbal group' in *IFG*.

The paper demonstrates that the solution to these problems is to treat all of the elements of the supposed 'verbal group' as direct elements of the clause, as is done in the Cardiff Grammar. Indeed, to do so is simply to carry through to its logical conclusion the change already initiated by Halliday in promoting the Finite to function as an element of the clause (a change that in fact dates back to Halliday 1967:218), and echoed in his treatment of *off* as an Adjunct in *They called the meeting off*. The paper then sets out four major types of reason why this approach in both more workable (e.g., in a generative version of the

---

20. While earlier works such as Hudson (1971), Fawcett (1973/81), Fawcett (1980) and subsequent works in the framework of the Cardiff Grammar have all presented models that assumed that the elements of the supposed 'verbal group' were elements of the clause, the full case for abolishing the 'verbal group' has not been made until now.

grammar) and more insightful (e.g., for purposes of text-analysis).

The first reason is that, if the Finite is to be promoted to function as an element of the clause, the other 'major' elements of the 'verbal group' must be promoted too. This is because, under the appropriate circumstances, **each of the Auxiliaries or the Main Verb can be conflated with the Finite**. And it would be a highly illogical grammar that treated an Auxiliary, let us say, as an element of the clause when it is conflated with the Finite and as an element of the 'verbal group' when it is not. Part 1 of the paper then introduces three other elements which must clearly also be promoted to the clause if the Auxiliaries and the Main Verb are, i.e., the Auxiliary Extension, the Infinitive (*to*) and the Negator (*not*). All of these are introduced in Appendix B.

Part 2 of the paper begins by presenting a set of reasons for dispensing with the 'verbal group' that are all based on the generation of the internal **morphology** of the elements concerned (e.g., *be* + *en*) and the **portmanteau** forms of some of the elements (e.g., *is* can function simultaneously as both Operator and Auxiliary, or as Operator and Main Verb). So this evidence too shows that the Operator, Auxiliaries and Main Verb should be in the same unit. In principle this could be either the 'verbal group' or the clause, but after the decision to promote the Finite to the clause it must clearly be the clause.

The third major type of evidence is the fact that virtually every element of the supposed 'verbal group' needs to be generated in close conjunction with an established element of the clause — very much as the Operator needs to be generated as an element of the same unit as the Subject, as the co-realization of meanings of MOOD. This was, of course, Halliday's reason for promoting the Finite (or Operator) in the first place. A well-constructed systemic functional grammar should provide for the interdependencies between, let us say, the 'tense' of the Operator or Main Verb and a Time Position Adjunct, preferably by (1) generating them on the same traversal of the system network and (2) realizing them in the same unit. There are seven other similar types of interdependency between elements of the supposed 'verbal group' and well-established elements of the clause.

The fourth type of evidence is that the 'full' version of the 'verbal group' (i.e., the version that includes the Finite) is so liable to interruption by other clause elements (the Subject, Complements and Adjuncts) that its status as a grammatical unit should be questioned on these grounds alone. Alternatively, if we interpret the 'verbal group' as consisting of what remains when the Finite and the Main Verb Extension are treated as elements of the clause, there is so little left that we might as well promote these elements to the clause as well (and so avoid the various problems with the 'verbal group' that the paper describes).

Thus the paper presents four major, mutually supportive types of evidence, such that each provides an independent set of reasons why the elements of the supposed 'verbal group' should be treated as elements of the clause. Moreover, each set of reasons applies not merely to one element, but to many of the relevant elements — and in some cases to all of them. In other words, the paper makes the case for abolishing the 'verbal group' four times over, so that even if only one of the four types of evidence were to be deemed to be admissible the case still stands.

Clearly, the abolition of the 'verbal group' seriously affects the standard claim of the concept of the 'rank scale' that there should be 'accountability at all ranks'. While it might just possibly be arguable that we should treat Linkers such as *and*, Binders such as *because* and even perhaps Adjuncts such as *therefore* as 'minor' exceptions (leaving aside for the moment the various other problems for the 'rank scale' concept that we have noted) it is simply not possible to claim that the elements of the clause are always (or even typically) filled by groups, once the Operator, the Auxiliaries and the Main Verb are all recognized as clause elements, because these are clearly not filled by groups. The abolition of the 'verbal group' therefore leaves a considerable hole in any description of a language that is expected to illustrate the 'rank scale' concept.

## 5  A possible end point to the debate: from 'rank' to 'filling probabilities'

Even if we set aside the case for abolishing the 'verbal group' set out in the last section, as well as the more general evidence of the value of a description of English such as that summarized in Appendix B, it is surprising that the evidence produced by Matthews, Huddleston and others summarized above has not persuaded Halliday to reconsider the status of the 'rank scale' concept. After all, it is clear that the strongest claim that can be made for it is that it characterizes a tendency towards a pattern to which there are in fact a great many exceptions. One sometimes gets the impression that support for the 'rank scale' is maintained simply because of a general perception that 'there is no alternative'.[21] But there now is an alternative: a simple unordered set of **classes of unit**, each of which is capable of filling several elements of one or more higher units, as presented in Section 10.2 of Chapter 10.

Interestingly, the concept of the 'rank scale' plays no role in a generative SF grammar. Its main practical value has always been as a model (if a problematical one) that makes predictions that guide the text analyst in how the units in a text-sentence relate to each other. And for this purpose we can now use the set of units supplemented by the concept of **filling probabilities** that is described in Section 11.2 of Chapter 11 and exemplified in Appendix B. From one viewpoint they are simply a drastic re-interpretation of the 'rank scale' concept, but in essence they are a replacement for it, as a guide for use in text analysis.

We can summarize the relevant arguments from the main part of the book by saying that the essence of the new proposal for modelling syntax is (1) that **classes of unit** are defined in terms of their internal structures (this being quite different from the way in which Halliday defines 'classes of unit'), (2) that each of these classes of unit (or simply 'units') has an internal structure that reflects as directly as possible the types of **meaning** that they are required to realize, and (3) that for each such unit there is a set of statements about the general probability that it will **fill** each of the **elements** of each of the various units that are recognized in the grammar. In other words, it makes predictions as to what units will function as elements of what other units — rather as the 'rank scale' concept of 'accountability at all ranks' does, but in a far more flexible manner. Many of these predictions are absolute (just as the strong version of the 'rank scale' concept is), in the sense that many combinations are ruled out by not being mentioned as possibilities in summary diagrams such as those in Appendix B, but the vast majority of the statements in Appendix B are probabilistic. An important feature of this approach is that it allows for very low probabilities as well as for the high ones — so that it shows that a clause, for example, may occur occasionally (though typically in a truncated form) as a pre-head modifier in a nominal group, e.g., the underlined portion of *her recently married sister* and *a very slowly running river*.

Unlike the predictions made from the 'rank scale' framework, the probabilities that the new model suggests can be changed. Such changed may be triggered by the **context of co-text** (which includes the specific point in the

---

21. This is the 'TINA' attitude to change that is close to the heart of many a right-wing politician — and so not, one would assume, Halliday's.

structure), or by some aspect of the **context of situation**. And, interestingly, there can also be variation within the model itself (across time or in alternative versions). This dimension of variation may well be introduced to future systemic functional grammars, taking data either directly from corpora or indirectly from corpus-based source grammars such as Sinclair (1990), Francis, Hunston and Manning (1996 and 1998), and Biber *et al* (1999).

In a systemic functional grammar, then, the probabilities are ultimately the probability of choosing a given meaning in a given context. This is formalized in the Cardiff Grammar by associating a percentage with the likelihood that, in any system, one feature will be chosen rather than another. These probabilities often get changed, sometimes by the choice of other features elsewhere in the system network, and sometimes by influences external to language itself, including aspects of the context of situation which trigger **register** variations, e.g., in MODE (spoken or written text) and TENOR (degrees of formality).

These systemic probabilities and the model's ability to vary them play a major role in the computer generation of text in the Cardiff Grammar. But from the viewpoint of the text analyst — whether a human or a computer — what is needed is the 'realization' of these **systemic** probabilities as **structural** probabilities. In other words, probabilities that are ultimately **semantic** and **paradigmatic** have to be expressed in terms of probabilities that are **formal** and **syntagmatic**. And, within the wide range of syntagmatic probabilities at the level of form, is the particular set which states the relative likelihood that a given unit will fill a given element of another unit (or an element of the same class of unit higher in the structure). It is this aspect of the syntagmatic probabilities that replaces the concept of the 'rank scale'.

Thus the present book, together with Fawcett (2000) and (forthcoming b), contributes to the 'rank scale debate' in two ways: one negative and one positive. On the negative side, it provides a fuller set of reasons than is given by any previous presentation of the case for **not** building into the grammar the concept of the 'rank scale' (and its accompanying concept of 'accountability at all ranks'). On the positive side, it states clearly what the nearest equivalent concept is — i.e., that the model is built around the concept of a set of units, each of which is capable of filling several elements of one or more higher units in a tree representation of a text-sentence (including a unit of the same class). But the 'filling probabilities' vary greatly, and these probabilities are as much a part of the grammar as the bare fact that a unit may fill an element.

I rest my case that it is now time to replace the concept of the 'rank scale'.

# References

Asher, R.E. (ed.-in-chief). 1993. *Encyclopaedia of Languages and Linguistics.* Oxford: Pergamon Press.

Ball, Fiona C., 1995. *In Search of the Perfect Advertisement: An INvestigation into the Relationship between Effectiveness and the Lexicogrammar in Paper Media Advertising.* Year 3 Dissertation. Cardiff: Cardiff University, Centre for Language and Communication Research.

Benson, J.D., & Greaves, W.S., 1973. *The Language People Really Use.* Agincourt, Canada: Book Society of Canada.

Berry, Margaret., 1975. *Introduction to Systemic Linguistics, Vol 1: Structures and Systems.* London: Batsford.

Berry, Margaret., 1977. *Introduction to Systemic Linguistics, Vol 2: Levels and Links.* London: Batsford.

Berry, Margaret., 1996. "What is Theme? - a (nother) personal view". Berry *et al.* 1996. 1-64.

Berry, Margaret, Butler, Christopher, Fawcett, Robin, & Huang, Guowen (eds.) 1996. *Meaning and Form: Systemic Functional Interpretations.* Meaning and Choice in Language: Studies for Michael Halliday. Norwood, N. J.: Ablex.

Biber, Douglas, Johansson, Stig, Leech, Geoffrey, Conrad, Susan & Finegan, Edward, 1999. *Longman Grammar of Spoken and Written English.* Harlow: Pearson.

Bloor, Tom, & Bloor, Meriel, 1995. *The Functional Analysis of English: a Hallidayan Approach.* London: Arnold.

Bolinger, Dwight., 1977. *Meaning and Form.* London: Longman.

Butler, Christopher S., 1979. "Recent work in systemic linguistics". *Language Teaching and Linguistics Abstracts* 12. 71-89.

Butler, Christopher S., 1985. *Systemic Linguistics: Theory and Application.* London: Batsford.

Butler, Christopher S., 1993a. "Scale and Category Grammar". Asher 1993. 4500-4.

Butler, Christopher S., 1993b. "Systemic Grammar in Applied Language Studies". Asher 1993. 4500-4.

Butler, Christopher S., forthcoming a. *Structural-functional Grammars, Volume 1: Approaches to the Simplex Clause.* Amsterdam: Benjamins.

Butler, Christopher S., forthcoming b. *Structural-functional Grammars, Volume 2: From Clause to Discourse and Beyond.* Amsterdam: Benjamins.

Butt, D., Fahey, R., Spinks, S., & Yallop, C., 1995. *Using Functional Grammar: An Explorer's Guide.* Sydney: National Centre for English Language Teaching and Research, Macquarie University.

Chomsky, N., 1957. *Syntactic Structures.* The Hague: Mouton.

Chomsky, N., 1995. *The Minimalist Program.* Cambridge, Mass: MIT Press.

Clark, H. H., & Clark, E. V., 1977. *Psychology and Language.* New York: Harcourt Brace Jovanovich.

Collerson, John, 1994. *English Grammar: A Functional Approach.* Newtown, NSW: Primary English Teaching Association.

Davey, Anthony, 1978. *Discourse Production: a Computer Model of some Aspects of a Speaker.* Edinburgh: Edinburgh University Press.

Day, Michael D., 1993. *The Interactive Corpus Query Facility and Other Tools for Exploiting Parsed Natural Language Corpora.* MSc Dissertation. Cardiff: Dept. of Computer Science, Cardiff University.

Dik, Simon C., 1997a. *The Theory of Functional Grammar, Part 1: The Structure of the Clause,* 2nd edn. Hengeveld, K. (ed.). Berlin: Mouton de Gruyter.

Dik, Simon C., 1997b. *The Theory of Functional Grammar, Part 2: Complex and Derived Constructions.* Hengeveld, K. (ed.). Berlin: Mouton de Gruyter.

Downing, Angela, & Locke, Philip, 1992. *A University Course in English Grammar.* New York: Prentice Hall.

Eggins, Suzanne, 1994. *Systemic Functional Linguistics: Basic Concepts and Techniques for Analysing Texts.* London: Pinter.

Fawcett, Robin, 1973/81. "Generating a sentence in systemic functional grammar". University College London (mimeo). Reprinted in Halliday & Martin 1981. 146-83.

Fawcett, Robin, 1974-6/81. "Some proposals for systemic syntax: Parts 1, 2 & 3". *MALS Journal* 1.2 1-15, 2.1 43-68, 2.2 36-68. Reprinted 1981 as *Some Proposals for Systemic Syntax.* Pontypridd: Polytechnic of Wales.

Fawcett, Robin, 1975. "Some issues concerning levels in systemic models of language". *Nottingham Linguistic Circular* 4.1. 24-37.

Fawcett, Robin, 1980. *Cognitive Linguistics and Social Interaction: Towards*

# REFERENCES

*an Integrated Model of a Systemic Functional Grammar and the Other Components of an Interacting Mind*. Heidelberg: Julius Groos & Exeter University.

Fawcett, Robin, 1983. "Language as a semiological system: a re-interpretation of Saussure". Morreall, J., (ed.) 1983, *The Ninth LACUS Forum 1982*, Columbia: Hornbeam Press. 59-125.

Fawcett, Robin, 1987. "The semantics of clause and verb for relational processes in English". Halliday & Fawcett 1987a. 130-83.

Fawcett, Robin, 1988a. "Language generation as choice in social interaction". Zock, Michael, & Sabah, Gérard, (eds), *Advances in Natural Language Generation Vol 1*. London: Pinter. 27-49.

Fawcett, Robin, 1988b. "What makes a good system network 'good'? - four pairs of concepts for such evaluations". Benson, J. D., & Greaves, W. S., (eds.) 1988, *Systemic Functional Approaches to Discourse: Selected Papers from the 12th International Systemic Workshop*, Norwood, N.J.: Ablex. 1-28.

Fawcett, Robin, 1990. "The computer generation of speech with semantically and discoursally motivated intonation". *Proceedings of 5th International Workshop on Natural Language Generation*, Pittsburgh. 164-73.

Fawcett, Robin P., 1992. *Felicity Conditions and Predetermination Rules for the Lexicogrammar: The Generation of Referring Expressions as a Test Case*. COMMUNAL Technical Report No. 13. Cardiff: Computational Linguistics Unit, Cardiff University.

Fawcett, Robin, 1993. "Language as program: a reassessment of the nature of descriptive linguistics". *Language Sciences* 14.4. 623-57.

Fawcett, Robin, 1994a. "A generationist approach to grammar reversibility in natural language processing". Strzalkowski 1994, 365-413.

Fawcett , Robin, 1994b. "On moving on on ontologies: mass, count and long thing things". McDonald, D. (ed), *Proceedings of the Seventh International Workshop on Natural Language Generation* (Association for Computational Linguistics). Waltham, Mass: Computer Science, Brandeis University. 71-80.

Fawcett, Robin, 1996. "A systemic functional approach to complementation in English". Berry *et al.* 1996. 297-366.

Fawcett, Robin, 1997. 'Invitation to Systemic Functional Linguistics: The Cardiff Grammar as an Extension and Simplification of Halliday's Systemic Functional Grammar'. *Helicon 22*. 55-136. Nara, Japan.

Fawcett, Robin, 1998. *The COMMUNAL Project and the Cardiff Grammar: an Annotated Bibliography of Selected Publications.* COMMUNAL Working Papers No. 9. Cardiff: Computational Linguistics Unit, Cardiff University.

Fawcett, Robin, 1999. "On the subject of the Subject in English: two positions on its meaning (and on how to test for it). *Functions of Language* 6.2. 243-273.

Fawcett, Robin, 2000. "In place of Halliday's 'verbal group', Part 1: Evidence from the problems of Halliday's representations and the relative simplicity of the proposed alternative". *Word* 51.2. 157-203.

Fawcett, Robin, in press. *Functional Syntax Handbook: Analyzing English at the Level of Form.* London: Continuum.

Fawcett, Robin, forthcoming a. *Functional Semantics Handbook: Analyzing English at the Level of Meaning.* London: Continuum .

Fawcett, Robin, forthcoming b. "In place of Halliday's 'verbal group', Part 2: Evidence from generation, semantics and interruptability". *Word* 51.3.

Fawcett, Robin, forthcoming c. "In place of Halliday's 'verbal group complex".

Fawcett, Robin, & Davies, Bethan, 1992. "Monologue as a turn in dialogue: towards an integration of exchange structure and rhetorical structure theory". Dale, R., Hovy, E. H., Roesner, D., & Stock, O., (eds.) 1992, *Aspects of Automated Natural Language Generation.* Berlin: Springer. 151-66.

Fawcett, Robin, & Huang, Guowen, 1995. "A functional analysis of the enhanced theme construction in English". *Interface: Journal of Applied Linguistics* 10.1. 113-44.

Fawcett, Robin, & Huang, Guowen, in preparation. *Explaining Enhanced Theme (the 'Cleft' Construction): a Test Case for Systemic Functional Linguistics - and Every Theory of Language.* London: Continuum.

Fawcett, Robin, & Perkins, Michael, 1981. "Project report: Language development in 6- to 12-year-old children. *First Language* 2. 75-9.

Fawcett, Robin, & Tucker, Gordon, 1990. "Demonstration of GENESYS: a very large, semantically based systemic functional grammar". *Proceedings of COLING 90*, Vol 1. Morristown N. J.: Bell Communications Research. 47-49.

Fawcett, Robin, Tucker, Gordon, & Lin, Y.Q., 1993. "How a systemic functional grammar works: the role of realization in realization". Horacek, Helmut, & Zock, Michael, (eds.), 1993, *New Concepts in Natural Language Generation,* London: Pinter. 114-86.

# REFERENCES

Fawcett, Robin, Tucker, Gordon, & Young, David, 1988. *Issues Concerning Levels and Channels in a Generator with Both Graphological and Phonological Outputs.* COMMUNAL Technical Report No. 8. Cardiff: Computational Linguistics Unit, Cardiff University.

Fawcett, Robin, & Young, David, (eds.) 1988. *New Developments in Systemic Linguistics, Vol 2: Theory and Application,* London: Pinter.

Firth, J. R. 1957. *Papers in Linguistics 1935-1951.* London: Oxford University Press.

Firth, J. R. 1957/68. "A Synopsis of Linguistic Theory, 1930-55". *Studies in Linguistic Analysis.* 1-31. Special volume of the Philological Society. Oxford: Blackwell. Reprinted in Palmer, F.R. (ed.) 1968, *Selected Papers of J.R. Firth* 1952-59, London: Longman. 169-205.

Firth, J.R., 1968. *Selected Papers of J.R. Firth* 1952-59 (ed. F.R. Palmer). London: Longman.

Francis, Gillian, Hunston, Susan, & Manning, Elizabeth, 1996. *Grammar Patterns 1: Verbs.* The COBUILD Series. London: HarperCollins.

Francis, Gillian, Hunston, Susan, & Manning, Elizabeth, 1998. *Grammar Patterns 2: Nouns and Adjectives.* The COBUILD Series. London: HarperCollins.

Gerot, Linda, & Wignell, Peter, 1994. *Making Sense of Functional Grammar.* Cammeray, NSW: Antipodean Educational Enterprises.

Givon, T., 1993a & b. *English Grammar: A Function-Based Introduction: Volumes I and II* Amsterdam: Benjamins.

Gregory, M., 1987. "Meta-functions: aspects of their development, status and use in systemic linguistics". Halliday & Fawcett 1987, 94-106.

Gregory, Michael. unpublished work. *Patterns of English.*

Haegeman, Liliane, & Guéron, Jacqueline, 1999. *English Grammar: A generative perspective..* Oxford: Blackwell.

Halliday, M. A. K., 1956/76. "Grammatical categories in Modern Chinese". *Transactions of the Philological Society* 1956. 177-224. Reprinted in part in Halliday 1976. 36-51.

Halliday, M. A. K., 1959. "Some aspects of systematic description and comparison in grammatical analysis". *Studies in Linguistic Analysis* (Special volume of the Philological Society). Oxford: Blackwell. 54-67.

Halliday, M. A. K., 1959. *The Language of the Chinese 'Secret History of the Moguls'.* Oxford: Blackwell (Publications of the Philological Society 17).

Halliday, M. A. K., 1961/76. "Categories of the theory of grammar". *Word* 17,

241-92. Reprinted as Bobbs-Merrill Reprint Series No. Language-36, and in part in Halliday 1976. 84-7.

Halliday, M. A. K., 1963/76. "Class in relation to the axes of chain and choice in language". Linguistics 2, 5-15. Reprinted in part in Halliday (1976), 84-7.

Halliday, M. A. K., 1964/76. "English system networks". Course given at Indiana University 1964. Reprinted in Halliday 1976, 101-35.

Halliday, M. A. K., 1964/81. "Syntax and the consumer". Stuart, C.I.J.M. (ed.), 1964. *Report of the Fifteenth Annual (First International) Round Table Meeting on Linguistics and Language Study*. Monograph Series in Languages and Linguistics 17. Washington DC: Georgetown University Press, 11-24. Reprinted in part in Halliday & Martin 1981, 21-8.

Halliday, M. A. K., 1965/81. "Types of structure". Working paper for the OSTI Programme in the Linguistic Properties of Scientific English. University College London, mimeo. Reprinted in Halliday & Martin 1981 29-41.

Halliday, M. A. K., 1966. "The concept of rank: a reply". *Journal of Linguistics* 2.1, 110-118.

Halliday, M. A. K., 1966/76. "Some notes on 'deep' grammar". *Journal of Linguistics* 2.1, 241-92. Reprinted in part in Halliday 1976, 88-98.

Halliday, M. A. K., 1967-8. "Notes on transitivity and theme in English, Parts 1-3". *Journal of Linguistics* 3.1, 37-81; 3.2, 199-244 & 4.2, 179-215.

Halliday, M. A. K., 1969/76. "Systemic Grammar". *La Grammatica: La Lessicologia.* Roma: Bulzoni (Atti del I e del II Convegno di Studi, Società di Linguistica Italiana), Reprinted in part as "A brief sketch of systemic grammar". Halliday 1976, 3-6.

Halliday, M. A. K., 1969/81. "Options and functions in the English clause". *Brno Papers in Linguistics 8*, 81-8. Reprinted in Householder, F.W., (ed.) 1972, *Syntactic theory 1: Structuralist,* Harmondsworth: Penguin, 248-57, and in Halliday & Martin 1981, 138-45.

Halliday, M. A. K., 1970. "Language structure and language function". Lyons, J. (ed.) 1970. *New Horizons in Linguistics*, Harmondsworth: Penguin. 140-65.

Halliday, M. A. K., 1970/76a. "Functional diversity in language, as seen from a consideration of modality and mood in English". *Foundations of Language* 6. 322-61. Reprinted in part in Halliday 1976. 189-213.

Halliday, M. A. K., 1970/76b. "The form of a functional grammar". Read to the Seminar on the Construction of Complex Grammars, Cambridge, Mass, 1970. Revised version published in Bernstein, B., (ed.), 1973, *Class, Codes and Control Vol II*, London: Routledge & Kegan Paul. Original version published in Halliday 1976. 7-25.

Halliday, M. A. K., 1971/73a. "The functional basis of language". Bernstein, B., (ed.) 1971, *Class, Codes and Control 1: Theoretical Studies Towards a Sociology of Language*. London: Routledge & Kegan Paul, and Halliday 1973, 22-47.

Halliday, M. A. K., 1971/73b. "Linguistic function and literary style: an inquiry into the language of William Golding's *The Inheritors*". Chatman, S., (ed.) 1971, *Literary Style: a Symposium*, New York: Oxford University Press (330-65), and in Halliday, M. A. K., 1973. 103-43.

Halliday, M. A. K., 1973. *Explorations in the Functions of Language*. London: Arnold.

Halliday, M. A. K., 1976. *System and Function in Language: Selected Papers by M. A. K. Halliday* (ed. Gunther Kress), London: Oxford University Press.

Halliday, M. A. K., 1977/78. "Text as semantic choice in social contexts". Van Dijk, T. A., & Petöfi, J. S., (eds.), 1978. *Grammars and Descriptions*. Berlin: de Gruyter, 176-225). Reprinted in part (without the grammatical detail) in Halliday, M. A. K., 1978, *Language as Social Semiotic: the Social Interpretation of Language and Meaning*. London: Arnold, 128-51.

Halliday, M. A. K., 1979. "Modes of meaning and modes of expression: types of grammatical structure and their determination by different semantic functions". Allerton, D. J., Carney, E., & Holdcroft, D. (eds.) *Function and Context in Linguistic Analysis: Essays Offered to William Haas*. Cambridge: Cambridge University Press.

Halliday, M. A. K., 1981. "Introduction". Halliday & Martin 1981, 13-16.

Halliday, M. A. K., 1984. "Language as code and language as behaviour: a systemic-functional interpretation of the nature and ontogenesis of dialogue". Fawcett, Robin, Halliday, M. A. K., Lamb, Sidney M., & Makkai, Adam, (eds.) 1984, *The Semiotics of Culture and Language, Vol 1 Language as Social Semiotic*. London: Pinter. 3-35.

Halliday, M. A. K., 1984/88. "On the ineffability of grammatical categories". Manning, A., Martin, P. & McCalla, K., 1984. *The Tenth LACUS Forum 1983*, Columbia S. C.: Hornbeam Press. 3-18. Reprinted in Benson, J. D., Cummings, M & Greaves, W. (eds.), 1988, *Linguistics in a Systemic*

*Perspective*, Amsterdam: Benjamins. 26-51.
Halliday, M. A. K., 1985. *An Introduction to Functional Grammar*. London: Arnold.
Halliday, M. A. K. 1993. "Systemic Theory". Asher 1993. 4505-8.
Halliday, M. A. K., 1994. *An Introduction to Functional Grammar (Second Edition)*. London: Arnold.
Halliday, M. A. K., 1996. "On grammar and grammatics". Hasan *et al.* 1996, 1-38.
Halliday, M. A. K., & Fawcett, Robin (eds.) 1987a. *New Developments in Systemic Linguistics, Vol 1: Theory and Description*. London: Pinter.
Halliday, M. A. K., & Fawcett, Robin 1987b. "Introduction". Halliday & Fawcett 1987. 1-13.
Halliday, M. A. K., & Hasan, Ruqaiya, 1976. *Cohesion in English*. London: Longman.
Halliday. M. A. K., McIntosh, A., & Strevens, P., 1964. *The Linguistic Sciences and Language Teaching*. London: Longman. Republished 1966, Bloomington, Indiana: Indiana University Press, & 1970, English Language Society.
Halliday. M. A. K., & James, Zoe, 1993. "A quantitative study of polarity and primary tense in the English finite clause". Sinclair, J. McH., Hoey, M, & Fox, G., (eds.) 1993 *Techniques of Description: Spoken and Written Discourse*. London and New York: Routledge. 32-66.
Halliday, M. A. K., & Martin, J. R., 1981 (eds.), *Readings in Systemic Linguistics.*, London: Batsford.
Halliday, M. A. K., & Matthiessen, C. M. I. M., (1999) *Construing Experience through Meaning: A Language-Based Approach to Cognition*. London: Cassell Academic.
Hasan, Ruqaiya, 1987. "The grammarian's dream: lexis as most delicate grammar". Halliday, M. A. K., & Fawcett, Robin (eds.) 1987a, *New Developments in Systemic Linguistics, Vol 1: Theory and Description*, London: Pinter (184-211), and in Hasan, Ruqaiya, 1996, *Ways of Saying, Ways of Meaning* London: Cassell Academic. 73-103.
Hasan, Ruqaiya, 1992. "Meaning in sociolinguistic theory". Bolton, K. & Kwok, H., (eds.)*Sociolinguistics Today: International Perspectives*. London: Routledge & Kegan Paul. 80-119.
Hasan, Ruqaiya, & Cloran, Carmel, 1990. "A sociolinguistic interpretation of everyday talk between mothers and children". Halliday, M. A. K., Gib-

bons, J., & Nicholas, H., 1990, *Learning, Keeping, and Using Language: Selected Papers from the Eighth World Congress of Applied Linguistics*, Amsterdam: Benjamins. 67-99.

Hasan, Ruqaiya, & Martin, J. R., (eds.) 1989. 'Introduction' to *Language Development: Learning Language, Learning Culture*. Meaning and Choice in Language: Studies for Michael Halliday. Norwood, N. J.: Ablex. 1-9.

Hasan, Ruqaiya, & Martin, J. R., 1989. "Introduction" to Hasan & Martin 1989. 1-9.

Henrici, A., 1966/81. "Some notes on the systemic generation of a paradigm of the English clause". University College London, mimeo. Reprinted in Halliday & Martin 1981, 76-98.

Huang, Guowen, 1996. "Experiential Enhanced Theme in English". Berry *et al.* 1996. 65-112.

Huang, Guowen, & Fawcett, Robin, 1996. "A functional approach to two "focussing" constructions in English and Chinese". *Language Sciences* Vol. 18.1-2, 179-94. Also in Jaszczolt, K., & Turner, K., (eds.), 1996, *Contrastive Semantics and Pragmatics,* Amstersdam: Elsevier.

Huddleston, Rodney D., 1965/81. "Rank and depth". *Language* 41. 574-86. Reprinted in Halliday & Martin 1981. 42-53.

Huddleston, Rodney D., 1966/81. "A fragment of a systemic description of English". University College London, mimeo. Reprinted in Halliday and Martin 1981. 222-36.

Huddleston, Rodney D., 1988. 'Constituency, multi-functionality and grammaticalization in Halliday's Functional Grammar'. *Journal of Linguistics* 24. 137-74.

Huddleston, Rodney D., 1991. 'Further remarks on Halliday's Functional Grammar: a reply to Matthiessen and Martin'. *Occasional Papers in Systemic Linguistics* Vol. 5. 75-129.

Huddleston, Rodney D, & Pullum, Geoffrey K., (principle authors) forthcoming. *The Cambridge Grammar of English.* Cambridge: Cambridge University Press.

Hudson, R. A., 1967/81. "Constituency in a systemic description of the English clause". *Lingua* 18. 225-50. Reprinted in Halliday & Martin 1981. 103-21.

Hudson, R. A., 1971. *English Complex Sentences: An Introduction to Systemic Grammar.* Amsterdam: North Holland.

Hudson, R. A., 1974/81. "Systemic generative grammar". *Linguistics* 139, 5-

42. Reprinted in Halliday & Martin 1981, 190-217.

Hudson, R. A., 1976. *Arguments for a Non-transformational Grammar.* Chicago: Chicago University Press.

Kasper, Robert T., 1988. "An Experimental Parser for Systemic Grammars". *Proceedings of COLING-88: 12th International Conference on Computational Linguistics* (Budapest). Morristown N.J.: Bell Communications Research.

Kress, Gunther, 1976. "Introduction" and section "Introductions". Halliday 1976, vii-xxi, 33-5, 99-100.

Kress, Gunther, & van Leeuwen, Theo, 1997. *Reading Images.* London: Macmillan.

Lamb, S., 1966. *Outline of Stratificational Grammar.* Washington: Georgetown University Press.

Leech, G. N., 1966. *English in Advertising: A linguistic study of advertising in Great Britai*n. London: Longmans.

Leech, Geoffrey, 1983. *Principles of Pragmatics.* London: Longman.

Lin, Y. Q., & Fawcett, Robin, 1996. "Implementing an Integration of the Systemic Flowchart Model of Dialogue and Rhetorical Structure Theory". Scott, D. (ed), *Proceedings of the Eighth International Natural Language Generation Workshop*, Vol 2. (SIGGEN, Association for Computational Linguistics). Brighton: ITRI, Brighton University. 41-44.

Lock, Graham, 1996. *Functional English Grammar: An Introduction for Second Language Teachers.* Cambridge: Cambridge University Press.

Lyons, John, 1977. *Semantics* (Vol 1). Cambridge: Cambridge University Press.

Mann, W. C., & Matthiessen, C. M. I. M., 1983/85. "A demonstration of the Nigel text generation computer program". Mann, W. C., & Matthiessen, C. M. I. M., *Nigel: A Systemic Grammar for Text Generation.* Marina del Rey, Calif: ISI/USC. Reprinted in Benson, J. D., & Greaves, W. S., (eds.), *Systemic Perspectives on Discourse, Vol 1: Selected Theoretical Papers from the Ninth International Systemic Workshop,* Norwood, N.J., Ablex, 50-83.

Mann, W. C., and Thompson, S. A., 1987. "Rhetorical structure theory". Polyani, L., (ed.) *Discourse Structure.* Norwood, N. J., Ablex.

Martin, J. R., 1981. Linking material in Halliday & Martin, 1981 (eds.). 18-20, 56-7, 100-2, 134-7, 186-9, 220-1.

Martin, J. R., 1988. "Hypotactic recursive relations in English: towards a functional explanation". Benson, J. D., and Greaves, W. S., (eds.) 1988. *Systemic Functional Approaches to Discourse: Selected Papers from the 12th International Systemic Workshop.* Norwood, N. J.: Ablex. 240-70.

Martin, J. R., 1992. *English Text: System and Structure.* Amsterdam: Benjamins.

Martin, J. R., Matthiessen, C. M. I. M., & Painter, Clare, 1997. *Working with Functional Grammar.* London: Arnold.

Matthews, P. H., 1966. "The concept of rank in neo-Firthian Linguistics". *Journal of Linguistics* 2.1. 101-09.

Matthiessen, C. M. I. M., 1995. *Lexicogrammatical Cartography: English Systems.* Tokyo: International Language Sciences Publishers.

Matthiessen, C.M.I.M., 1999. "The system of TRANSITIVITY: an exploratory study of text-based profiles". *Functions of Language* 6.1. 1-51.

Matthiessen, C. M. I. M., & Bateman, J. A., 1991. *Text Generation and Systemic Functional Linguistics.* London: Pinter.

Matthiessen, C. M. I. M., & Martin, J. R., 1991. "A response to Huddleston's review of Halliday's Introduction to Functional Grammar". *Occasional Papers in Systemic Linguistics* Vol. 5. 5-74.

Miller, George A., 1956. "The magical number seven, plus or minus two: some limits on our capacity for processing information". *Psychological Review* 63.2.

Monaghan, James, 1979. *The Neo-Firthian Tradition and its Contribution to General Linguistics.* Tubingen: Niemeyer.

Morley, G. David, 2000. *Syntax in Functional Grammar: An Introduction to Lexicogrammar in Systemic Linguistics.* London: Continuum.

Muir, James, 1972. *A Modern Approach to English Grammar: An Introduction to Systemic Grammar.* London: Batsford.

O'Donnell, Mick, 1994. *From Theory to Implementation: Analysis and Generation with Systemic Functional Grammar.* PhD thesis. University of Sydney.

O'Donoghue, Timothy F., 1994. "Semantic interpretation in a systemic grammar". Strzalkowski 1994, 415-447.

O'Toole, Michael. 1994. *The Language of Displayed Art.* London: Pinter.

Patten, Terry, 1988. *Systemic Text Generation as Problem Solving.* Cambridge: Cambridge University Press.

Pike, K. L., & Pike, E. G., 1982. *Grammatical Analysis.* Dallas: The Summer Institute of Linguistics and the University of Texas at Arlington.

Pollard, C., & Sag, I. A., 1994. *Head-driven Phrase Structure Grammar*. Chicago: Chicago University Press.

Postal, P. M., 1964. *Constituent Structure*. (Publication 30 of the Research Center in Anthropology, Folklore, and Linguistics.) *IJAL* 30.1. Part III.

Quirk, R., Greenbaum, S., Leech, G., & Svartvik, J., 1972. *A Grammar of Contemporary English.*. London: Longman.

Quirk, R., Greenbaum, S., Leech, G., & Svartvik, J., 1985. *A Comprehensive Grammar of the English Language*. London: Longman.

Scott, F. S., Bowley, C. C., Brockett, C. S., Brown, J. G., & Goddard, P. R., 1968. *English Grammar: A Study of its Classes and Structures*. London: Heinemann Educational Books.

Sinclair, John. 1972. *A Course in Spoken English: Grammar*. Oxford: Oxford University Press.

Sinclair, John, (ed.), 1990. *Collins COBUILD English Grammar*. London: Collins.

Smith, Neil., and Wilson, Deirdre, 1979. *Modern Linguistics: The Results of Chomsky's Revolution*. Harmondsworth: Penguin.

Souter, D. Clive, 1996. *A Corpus-based Parser for Systemic Syntax*. PhD Thesis. Leeds: University of Leeds, School of Computer Studies.

Steiner, Erich, 1983. *Die Entwicklung des Britischen Kontextualismus*. Heidelberg: Julius Groos Verlag.

Steiner, Erich, Eckert, Ursula, Roth, Birgit, & Winter-Thielen, Jutta, 1988. "The development of the EUROTRA-D system of Semantic Relations". Steiner, Erich, Schmidt, Paul, & Zelinsky-Wibbelt, Cornelia (eds.) 1988, *From Syntax to Semantics: Insights from Machine Translation*. London: Pinter. 40-104.

Steiner, Erich, Bateman, John, Maier, Elizabeth, Teich, Elke, & Wanner, Leo, 1990. *KOMET: Department Plan*. Technical report. Darmstadt, Germany: GMD/Intitut fur Integrierte Informations- und Publikationssysteme.

Tatsuki, Mas-aki, 1998. "On the definition of 'Finiteness': a contrastive study of English and Japanese". *Doshisha Daigaku* 69. Kyoto: Doshisha University.

Teich, Elke, 1999. *Systemic Functional Grammar and Natural Language Generation*. London: Cassell Academic.

Tench, Paul, 1990. *The Role of Intonation in English Discourse*. Frankfurt-am-Main: Peter Lang.

Tench, Paul, 1996. *The Intonation Systems of English*. London: Cassell

Academic.
Thibault, Paul, 1997. *Re-reading Saussure: The Dynamics of Sign in Social Life.* London: Routledge.
Thompson, G., 1996. *Introducing Functional Grammar.* London: Arnold.
Tucker, Gordon, 1996a. "Cultural classification and system networks: a systemic functional approach to lexis". Berry *et al.* 1996a. 533-536.
Tucker, Gordon, 1996b. "So grammarians haven't the faintest idea: reconciling lexis-oriented and grammar-oriented approaches to language". Hasan, Ruqaiya, Butt, David, & Cloran, Carmel, (eds.) 1996. *Functional Descriptions: Theory in Practice*, Amsterdam: Benjamins. 145-78.
Tucker, Gordon, 1997. "A functional lexicogrammar of adjectives". *Functions of Language* 4.2, 215-250.
Tucker, Gordon, 1998. *The Lexicogrammar of Adjectives: a Systemic Functional Approach to Lexis.* London: Cassell Academic.
Turner, G. J., & Mohan, B. A., 1970. A Linguistic description and Computer Program for Children's Speech. London: Routledge & Kegan Paul.
van Leeuwen, Theo, 1999. *Speech, Music, Sound.* London: Macmillan.
Van Valin, R., 1993. "A synopsis of role and reference grammar". Van Valin, R., (ed.) *Advances in Role and Reference Grammar.* Amsterdam: Benjamins. 1-164.
Weerasinghe, A. R., 1994. *Probabilistic Parsing in Systemic Functional Grammar.* PhD Thesis. Cardiff: Dept. of Computer Science, Cardiff University.
Weerasinghe, A. R., & Fawcett, Robin, 1993. "Probabilistic incremental parsing in Systemic Functional Grammar". Bunt, H., & Tomita, M., (eds.) *Proceedings of the Third International Workshop on Parsing Technologies (PT3)*, Association for Computational Linguistics Special Interest Group on Parsing. Tilburg, Netherlands: Institute for Language Technology and Artificial Intelligence, University of Tilburg, 349-367.
Winograd, Terry, 1972. *Understanding Natural Language.* Edinburgh: Edinburgh University Press.
Young, David, 1980. *The Structure of English Clauses.* London: Hutchinson. Reprinted by NELL, Department of English, University of Nottingham, 1992.

# Index

Page numbers in **boldface** indicate the main discussion(s) of this entry. Single quotation marks round an entry mean that this term is not a part of the theory proposed here, and that it is normally also placed in single quotation marks in the text. Page numbers include the footnotes on that page. If there is a run of mentions of an entry with a single intervening page that does not mention it, that page is included in the run of pages.

'accountability at all ranks': 233-4. See also 'rank (scale)'.
'adjectival group/phrase': 322-3.
Adjunct (in clause): 19, 29-30, 114-5, 126, 154, 161, 199-200, 208, 214-5, 219, 221, 225, 241-2, 245, 251, 264, 271, 287, **304-5**, 310, 312, 317, 326-31, 334-6.
adjustor (in quantity group): 231, 257-8, **304**, **307**.
'adverbial group': 164, 199, 202-3, 207-8.
agglutinating languages: 4, 227-8.
'agnation' (= systemic relationship'): 325.
amount (in quantity group): 202, 223, 230, 257, **304**, **307**.
apex (in quality group): 203, 206, 214-5, 222, 230, 245, 259, 269.
'autonomous syntax': 33, **44**, 287.
Auxiliary Verb (in clause): 200, 219, 231, 249, 325, **304-5**, 314, 335.
Auxiliary Verb Extension (in clause): 325, **304-5**.
availability, (scale of): 51, **109-11**, 144, 274, 294.

Ball: 150, 276.
Bateman: ixx, 7, 36, 78-9, 88, 93, 116, 129-38, 143, 175, 179-84, 251, 273. See also Steiner, Bateman, Maier, Teich & Wanner.
belief system: 3, 197, 201-2, 209-10, 287, 294.
Benson & Greaves: 26.

Berry: 22-3, 25-6, 31, 40, 93, 110, 157, 160, 197, 229, 255, 310, 314, 320.
Biber, Johansson, Leech, Conrad & Finegan: xvii, 5, 15, 50, 80, 243, 328, 338.
Binder (in clause): 196, 200, 208-9, 230, 234, **304-5**, 310-12, 327, 336.
Bloor & Bloor: 108, 145.
Bolinger: 50.
Butler: v, xvii, 1-2, 5, 9, 31, 80, 162, 165, 197-9, 309-14.
Butt, Fahey, Spinks and Yallop: 108.

Cardiff Grammar: **6-9**, references throughout.
Carlsen: 276.
category: ixx, xx, 11, 16, **18-20**, 21, 24, 27, 31-2, 46, 74-5, 82-3, 90-1, 96-7, 99, 101-3, 160, **163-5**, 167, 173, 185-6, **187-232**, 236, 248, 252, 254, 264, **277-80**, 286.
Chomsky: vii, xv, xvii, 78, 97, 110, 268, 314, 322.
Clark & Clark: 240.
class of item: 225-232, 340, 286.
'class of unit' (Sydney Grammar sense): 18, **20**, 31, 83, 90, 95, 97, 99, 101-3, 105, 159-60, 163-5, 176, 178, 201, 237, 311, 313, 337.
class of unit (Cardiff Grammar sense): **193-200**, **277-8**, refer-

# INDEX

ences throughout. See also unit (= class of unit).
'class of word': see 'word class'.
clause: **200-1**, **304-5**, references throughout.
clause complex: **318-30**. See also text-sentence.
'clefting', '*it*-cleft construction': see experiential enhanced theme.
cluster: 163-4, 176, 179, 186, 190-1, 194, 203, **211-2**, 213-4, 223, 238, 241, 245, 263, 270-2, 278.
Collerson: 108.
COMMUNAL (Project): **7-8**, references throughout.
Complement: 10, 20, 25, 29, 31, 114-5, 154, 161, 185, 192, 198-200, 214, 225, 227, 234, 241-3, 251-4, 271, 290-300, **304-5**, 317, 332, 335.
completive (in prepositional group): **204**, 225, 242, 262, 265, 270, **304-6**, 321.
componence: **165**, 175, 199, 237, 239, **244-9**, 250-53, 259-60, 262, 272, 281, 284-5.
conflation (typically = element conflation): 87-90, 97, **113**, 116-7, 122-157, 176-7, 185, 244, **249-50**, 252-3, 259-60, 272, 278, 281. See also element conflation, and cp. 'structure conflation'.
'conjunction group': 202, **208-9**, 311.
constituency: 27-8, **84-5**, 92, 96, 98-101, 111-4, 140, 188, 191, 210, 218, **233-7**, 246-8.
context of co-text: 70, 337.
context of situation: 17, 38, 48, 55, 297, 337.
'co-ordination': 26-7, **263-4**, 284-5, 239, 251-2, 258-61, **263-4**, 271-2, 281-5, **317-33**.

Davey: 179, 314.
Day: 243.
delicacy in system networks: **22-3**, 84, 100, 284-6.
delicacy in structure: 19, **22-3**, 84, 100, 184, 284-6. See also structure ('primary' and 'secondary' etc).
dependence/dependency in structure: **28**, 30, 192, 194, 200-1, **216-7**, 221-2, 248-9, 270, 284, 290, 313, **317-33**. For 'dependence without embedding' see 'hypotaxis'.
dependence in system networks: **23**, 38, 43, 84, 249, 286.
dependence in realization rules: 68.
depth (in structure): 28, **31**, **265-7**, 317. See also variation in depth of exponence.
determiner, deictic (in nominal group): 211-2, 216, 259, 300-301, **304**, **306**, 310.
determiner, general (in nominal group): 204, 219, **304**, **306**, 315.
determiner, quantifying (in nominal group): 257, 259, 264, **304**, **306**.
Dik: vii, xv, xvi, 1, 42.
discontinuity: 127, 166, 204, 225, **261-2**, 272.
Downing & Locke: 108.

Eggins: 108, 145.
element (of structure): references throughout, **18-21**, **203-20**.
element conflation: 113, 124, 127, **129-31**, 135-7, 142, 149, 161-6, 175-87, 190-232, 273-4, 278. See also conflation, and cp. 'structure conflation'.
ellipsis, ellipt: 190, 202, 222, **264**, 305.
embedding: 27-30, 99-100, 102, 166, 176, 189, 192-3, 211, 233, 237, 239-40, 258, 261-4, **265-72**, 282, 285-6, 302, **315-33**.
Ender: **304-5**.
ender; **304**, **306-7**.
evaluative enhanced theme: 128.
'exhaustiveness (at each rank)': **233-4**. See 'rank (scale)'.

experiential enhanced theme (= 'predicated theme', clefting): **128**, 250, 276.
exponence, exponent: **21-2**, 74, 84-5, 92, 100, **165**, 176-7, 181-2, 192, 212, 216, 226, 228, 237, 244, 252-3, **253-6**, 259-60, 263, 272, 280-6, 280. See also variation in depth of exponence, and cp. realization.
'extraposition': see evaluative enhanced theme.

Fawcett: xvii, ixx, xxi, 2, 5-7, 11, 16, 20-3, 29-30, 33-6, 39, 49, 51, 55-9, 64, 78, 80-1, 89, 92-3, 97, 105, 108-9, 114, 120, 129-33, 150-1, 158-9, 162-5, 171-3, 177, 179, 181, 185-7, 194-6, 198-9, 201-4, 207-16, 222-32, 235, 238, 242-5, 248-57, 262, 265, 267, 270, 276-9, 288-94, 300, 334, 338. See also Fawcett & Davies; Fawcett, Tucker & Lin; and Lin & Fawcett.
Fawcett & Davies: 248.
Fawcett, Tucker & Lin: ixx, 7, 9, 39-41, 59, 67-8, 78, 81, 92-3, 135-6, 171, 173, 175, 178, 183, 185, 220, 228, 273, 279, 283, 288, 293, 297, 309, 321-2, 334, 338.
filling: **27**, **251-3**, references throughout.
filling probabilities: **238-44**, 276, 315, 337-8.
finisher (in quality group): 207, 262, 279.
'Finite (operator)': 37, **114**, 132-3, 184-5, 218, 227, 234-5, 237, 334-5, cp. Operator.
Firth: 2-3, 18, 20, 22, 29, 43, 177, 226, 254, 282, 285.
form (level of): **33-5**, references throughout.
form potential: 40, **103-4**, 172, 281, 301, cp. meaning potential.
formula, Formulaic Element: 222, 304-5.
Francis, Hunston & Manning: 5, 50, 80, 328, 338.
function (= element): see element.
function (= 'metafunction'): see 'metafunction'.
function in general sense: references throughout.
genitive cluster: 164, 191, 194, **212**, 214, 259, 263, 266, 278, **304**, **307**.
Gerot & Wignell: 108.
Givon: 42.
Gregory: 26, 51.
grammar: references throughout.
grammaticality: 44, **287-8**.
group as 'rank': 19-21, 100-1, 147, 163, 165-6, 198, 228-9, 232-4, 237, 318, 322-3.
group as unit: 163-4, 176, 179, 183-4, 190-201, **201-9**, 210-2, 217, 222-4, 222-4, 226-7, 238-45, 257, 263-271, 278, 282-6, 289, 301-3, 314, 323. See also entries under nominal, prepositional, quality and quantity groups.
'group-complex': 318.

Haegeman and Guéron: 110.
Halliday: references throughout.
Halliday, McIntosh & Strevens: 15.
Halliday & James: 276.
Hasan: 2, 6, 24. See also Hasan & Cloran.
Hasan & Cloran: 55-6.
head (in nominal group): 179, 194-6, 200, **203-4**, 211-9, 222-31, 234, 239, 254, 257, 264, 267, 269, 297-301, **304**, **306**, 315.
'head' (in general sense): 195-6, 201, 207, 217, 248-9, 320-2, 325, cp. pivotal element.
Henrici: 47, 77-8, 93, 321.
Huang: 6, 129, 276, 294.
Huddleston: xvii, 24-6, 31, 47, 77-8, 93, 116, 197-9, 270, 277, 309-11, 313, 316-33, 336. See also

Huddleston & Pullum.
Huddleston & Pullum: 322-3.
Hudson: vii, 21, 24-5, 40, 47, 53, 55, 69, 77-8, 87, 93, 96, 130, 135, 175, 194, 197-9, 216, 246, 248, 277, 280, 313-5, 318, 321-6.
human proper name cluster: 164, 194, 203, **213**, 230.
'hypotaxis', 'hypotactic' relations: **26-30**, 101-2, 114, 192, 240, 268, 270, **271**, 273, 284-5, 263, 312, **317-33**.

Inferential Adjunct: 304.
inferer: 304.
Infinitive element (in clause): 323, **304-5**, 335.
inflectional languages: 227.
instance (in general): **35-6**, 42, 58, 62-3, 74, 105-6, 123-4, 153, 242.
instance of form / syntax: 10, **35-6**, 41-3, 65, 86, 90-1, 94, 100-5, 172, 174, 185-6, **187-232**, 233-7, 303, 315.
instance of meaning: see selection expression.
instantiation: **36**, **48-9**, 61-4, 74, 86, 90-1.
integrated structure: 21-3, **70-3**, 94, 102, 123-4, 128, 135-6, 143-51, 155, 157, 173, 273, 278, 287, cp. 'multiple structure'.
intonation: 6, 7, 35, 37, 39, 43, 51, 59, 96, 132, 136, 138, 163, 184, 186, 215-6, 226, 263, 276, 291, cp. punctuation.
item (= word or morpheme): 23, 33, 35, 37, 39, 58, 66, 68-9, 87, 152, 163-5, 176-8, 181-2, 184, 191-3, **226**, 227-232, 237, 240-1, 245, 252-9, 263-4, 271-2, 278-9, 282, 286, 291.
'item' (= 'unit on the rank scale'): 119, 314.

Kaspar: 7, 105.
Kress: v, 2, 18, 21, 31, 49, 52, 205.

Lamb: 22, 48, 71.
Langacker: vii.
Leech: xvii, 26, 261. See also Biber, Johansson, Leech, Conrad & Finegan; and Quirk, Greenbaum, Leech & Svartvik.
'left-dislocation': 200.
Let element: 305.
lexis: 7, 17, **23-4**, **37**, 59, 70, 186, 220, 254-5, 276, 287.
Lin: 4, 6, 32, 40, 276. See also Fawcett, Tucker & Lin.
Lin & Fawcett: 248.
Linker (in clause): 200, 234, **263-4**, **304-5**, 310-2.
linker (in group or cluster): **263-4**, **304**, **306-7**.
logical form: 202, **209-10**.
Lock: 108.
Lyons: 203, 217.

M&M: see Matthiessen & Martin.
Main Verb (in clause): 196, 200-1, 222, 227, 231, 251, 253-4, 261, 300, **304-5**, 314, 335.
Main Verb Extension (in clause): 200, 259, **304-5**, 335.
Mann: 7, 30, 67, 77, 79, 116, 131, 221-2, 279.
Mann & Thompson: 332.
Martin: v, 2, 6, 16, 25, 31, 47-8, 56, 187, 248, 275, 325, 343-3. See also Martin, Matthiessen & Painter; and Matthiessen & Martin.
Martin, Matthiessen & Painter: 108, 145.
Matthews: 21, 234, 309-13, 329, 336.
Matthiessen: ixx, 7-8, 30, 52-3, 56-7, 66-7, 77-9, 85, 88-9, 93, 106, 108, 113, 116, 129, 1245, 129-35,175, 179-80, 182-4, 189, 192, 197, 200, 221-2, 226, 251, 273-4, 277-80, 316, 321. See also Martin, Matthiessen & Painter; and Matthiessen & Martin.
Matthiessen & Martin: 316, 324-35.

# INDEX

meaning (level of): **33-5**, references throughout.
meaning, Halliday's 'two-level' model: 45, **55-6**, 89, 274, 293.
meaning potential: **38-9**, **48-50**, references throughout after p. 47.
'metafunction': xxii, 9, 16, **51**, 89, 98, 112-5, 124-5, 139-40, 142, 147, 153-4, 187, 284, cp. strands of meaning.
Miller: 267.
modifier (in nominal group): 198, 204-5, **212-7**, 219, 242, 259, 262, 269, **304**, **306**, 315, 337.
modifier (in general sense): 194-5, 207, 214, 248-9, 320-2, 325.
Monaghan: 2.
MOOD: general references throughout; for realizations of MOOD see Subject and Operator.
Morley: 108, 320.
morpheme: 19, 21, 27, 33, 96, 164-6, 184, 191-2, **226-9**, 232, 233, 237, 255, 268, 279, 286, 301, 310, 318.
'morpheme-complex': 318.
morphology: 3, 4, 7, 17-8, 70, 226. 228-9, 333.
Muir: 26, 160, 320.
multifunctional nature of language: 16, **50-1**, 108, 112, 117, 121-2, 139, 141, 143, 146-52, 157, 177, 244, 250, 279, 294.
'multiple structure': xxii-xxiii, 26, 51, 71, 77, 95, 99, 107-8, **111-8**, 125, 128, 135-6, 140, 142-3, 154-6, 161-2, 174, 284-7, 294.
'multiple theme': 184.
'multivariate' structures: 27, 30.

Neale: 276.
Negator: **304-5**, 335.
nominal group: **203-4**, **297-302**, **304**, **306**, references throughout.
nominal group, discontinuous: 262.
'noun phrase': 323, cp. nominal group.

O'Donnell: 7.
O'Donoghue: 7, 105, 150.
Operator: 135, 184, 200, 218, 220, 222, 227, 231, 249, **304-5**, 314, 334-5, cp. 'Finite'.
Osman: 276.
O'Toole: 49.

paradigmatic relations: 23, **42-3**, 47, 49, 61-2, 82, 90, 118, 157, 159, 315, 338.
'parataxis', 'paratactic' relations: **26**, 30, 101-2, 114, 192, 263, **271-2**, 284-6, **317-33**.
Participant Roles: 29, 57, 175-7, 192, 200, 227, 250, 253, 272, 281, 290, 332.
parser/parsing: 5, 7, 104-5, 167, 172, 174, 185, 190, 196, 211, 215, 224, 232, 242-3, 288.
Patten: 7, 131.
'phrase' (as 'rank'): 318, 322-3.
'phrase-complex': 318.
Pike: 251.
pivotal element: 195-6, 201, 203-4, 206-9, 261.
planner, planning: 43, 64, 129, 194, 209, 204, 294, 323.
Pollard & Sag: 110.
portmanteau realization: 254, 335.
potential structure: 40, 87, **176-7**, 178-9, 181, **223-4**, 232, 240, 245, 281, 297.
predetermination rules: 332.
'predicated theme': see experiential enhanced theme.
'Predicator': 19-20, 72, 114-5, 135, 137, 153-4, 161, 322.
preposition (in prepositional group): 196, 202, 204, 209, 212-3, 230, **304**, **306**.
'preposition group': 202, 208-9.
prepositional group: 164, 194, 198, 202, **204-6**, 209, 241-2, 244, 251, 262-5, 269-70, 278, 286, **304**, **306**, 321-2.
prepositional group, discontinuous:

255, 262.
'prepositional phrase': 202, 204-5, 321-3.
probabilities (systemic and structural): 7, 44, 79, 144, 166, 176, 178, 182, 190, 193, 222, 232, **238-43**, 264, 266, 272, 276, 282-3, 286-8, 293, **315**, 337-8.
proper name: see human proper name cluster.
punctuation: 7, 35, 37, 39, 43, 59, 163, 184, 186, 215-6, 226, 260, 263, 291, cp. intonation.

qualifier (in nominal group): 205, 217, 219, 261, 265-7, 269, 290, 297, **304**, **306**.
quality group: 164, 179, 194, 196, 202-5, **206-7**, 208, 212, 215-6, 222, 230, 245, 251, 259, 262, 265, 269, 271, 278, 290, **304**, **307**, 322-3.
quality group, discontinuous: 262.
quantity group: 164, 190, 194, 196, 202, 204, **207-9**, 230, 257-8, 265, 278, 286, **304**, **307**, 317.
'quantity-quality group': 164, 208.
Quirk, Greenbaum, Leech & Svartvik: xvii, 15, 26, 50, 80.

'raising': see discontinuity.
'rank (scale)': xx, 19-20, **21**, 23-6, 31, 83-8, 92, 96, 99-102, 163-4, **165-6**, 167, 182, 185, 187-98, 197-8, 200, 203, 207-8, 217, 225-9, 232, **233-8**, 239-40, 256, 264-8, 270-3, 276-86, 291, **309-38**.
'rank shift': see embedding.
realization (as process / relationship): xxii, 22, **34**, 35, 42, 48-9, 61-3, 67-9, 74-81, 84-7, 90-3, 100, 160, 122, 139, 147, 157, 254, 256, 263, 278, 281-2, 286, 293, **297-301**.
realization (as product): 7, 33, 39, 54, 66, 69, 71, 117-8, 147-8, 150, 153, 157, 166, 201, 207, 217, 220, 222, 228, 332, 338.
realization operation / operator: 79, **87**, 89-91, 93, 103,113, **175-8**, 179-85, 218, 244, 250-1, 254-5, 261, 279-82, 286, **297-301**, 314-5.
realization rule / statement: 39-42, 50, 59-71, 75, **86-7**, 88-90, 94, 103, 105, 112-3, 120-1, 130, 133, 140, 149, 162, 167, 171, **175**, 176, 185, 222, 224, 229, 245, 253, 258, 263, 287, **297-301**, **304-7**, 314-5.
recursion **263**, 166, 176, **263**, 264, 272, 281-2, 318-9.
referring expression: **202**, 211, 263, 314.
register: 338.
reiteration: 176, 178, 263, **271**, 271.
relationship (between categories): xx, 11, 21, 139, **163**, 165-6, 173, 175-7, 185-6, 191, 228, **233-72**, 275, **280-5**, 286, 289, 292, 300, 312, 315-6, 318, 320.
rhetorical structure: 331-2.
'right-dislocation': 200.

Saussure: 2, 33, 35, 41-2.
'scale': 11, 18, **21-4**, 31-2, 46, 75, 83-6, 95-100, 165, 186, 275-80, 283, 285. See also 'rank (scale)'.
scale of availability: see availability, scale of.
scope (in quality group): 207, **304**, **307**.
Scott, Bowley, Brockett, Brown & Goddard: 26, 160.
selection expression (= instance of meaning): 39, 40-2, 58, 65, 67, 86, 90-4, 297, 303, cp. instance of form / syntax.
selector (in nominal group): **304**, **306**.
semantic(s): references throughout, especially after 47, cp. meaning.
semantic interpreter: 8, 105, 149-50.
sentence: see text-sentence.

Sinclair: xvii, 5, 26, 50, 80, 160, 199, 277, 328.
single (= integrated) structure: see integrated structure and cp. 'multiple structure'.
Smith & Wilson: xv.
Souter: 105, 167, 185.
Starosta: vii.
Starter: 304-5.
starter: 304.
Steiner: 2, 6, 31. See also Steiner, Eckert, Roth; and Steiner, Bateman, Maier, Teich & Wanner.
Steiner, Eckert, Roth, & Winter-Thielen: 7, 131.
Steiner, Bateman, Maier, Teich & Wanner: 131.
strands of meaning: xxii, 3, 51, 72-3, 75, 98, 105, 187, 218-9, cp. 'metafunctions'.
Strang: 26, 160.
structure (in general, e.g., contrasted with 'system'): references throughout, cp. syntax potential.
structure (of a unit): **18-19, 195-200**, references throughout. See also integrated structure, multiple structure, potential structure.
structure ('primary', 'secondary' etc.): 84, 102, **114-5**, 133, 154, 114-5, 133, 154, 184, **217-9**, 285-6.
'structure conflation': 113, **123-9**, 136-7, 142-3, 149, 185, 273-4, 278, cp. element conflation.
Subject: 16, 19-20, 73, 87-9, 91, 96-7, 103, 113-5, 128-50, 153, 181-5, 198-200, 218, 220, 222, 227, 242, 250-3, 259, 261, 269, 278, **304-5**, 335.
Subject Theme: 147.
Sydney Grammar: **6-9**, references throughout.
syntagmatic relations: 3, **42-3**, 47, 49, 61-2, 87, 90, 118, 157, 338.
syntax: references throughout.
syntax potential (= part of form potential): 103, 201, **171-2**, 174, 178, 201, 223, 281, cp. meaning potential.
system: 18, **20**, 22-3, 37, 43, 47, 48-9, 82, 84, 91, 99, 106, 118-22, 144, 149, 160-1, 165, 176, 178, 190, 201, 220, 249, 258-9, 281-5, 291, 297, 298-9, 301, 338.
system (as a level): 70-1, 118, 121-2, 160, 273.
system (contrasted with 'structure'): 61, 82, 89.
system (= semiotic system): 5, 33-4, 43, 50, 61, 95, 99-100, 103, 105, 108, 178, 194, 235, 246, **271**, 301, 314.
system network: **38-9, 47-50, 298-9**, 311, 314-5.
systemic functional grammar / linguistics: references throughout.

Tatsuki: 6, 228-9.
Teich: 7, 131. See also Steiner, Bateman, Maier, Teich & Wanner.
temperer (in quality group, three types): **214-5,** 230, 245, 271, **307**.
Tench: 6, 39, 216, 276.
text-descriptive work: **78-81**, 107, 110, 186, 173-4, 223, 231, 233, 244, 255.
text-sentence: **24**, **177**, references throughout.
theme: 72, 77, 87-9, 98, 112-6, 128, 130, 132, 135-7, 147-9, 184, 218-9, 250, 276.
thematizability: 328-30.
theoretical-generative work: **78-81**, 110-1, 116, 119, 121-4, 126, 128-9, 135, 137, 142-3, 146, 152, 154, 157, 173-4, 179, 185-6, 233, 244, 255.
Thibault: 33.
Thompson, G: 26, 145.
'total accountability at all ranks': 233-4. See also 'rank (scale)'.
TRANSITIVITY: general references

throughout. See also Participant Roles.
Tucker: v, ixx, 6-7, 9, 23-4, 39, 80, 109, 150, 164, 206-7, 271, 290, 294, 300, 322. See also Fawcett, Tucker & Lin.
Turner & Mohan: 26, 160.
'type' (of unit): 31, 187.

unit (= class of unit): **187-9, 193-213**, references throughout.
'unit' (= unit on the rank scale'): **16-19**, references throughout.
'unit-complex': 318-20.
'univariate' structures: 26-7, 317, 321.

van Leeuwen: 49.
van Valin: vii, xv, 1, 42.
variation in depth of exponence: 234, 238, **256-9**.

'verbal group': 20, 30, 65, 135, 164, 194-5, 202, 209, 235, 238, 289, 309, 322, **333-6**.
Vocative: 304-5.

Weerasinghe: 7, 35, 105, 167, 185.
Winograd: 79.
'word class' (= 'class of word'): 20, 99, 194, 204, 206, 208, 228, **229-32**, 234, 236, 255, 320.
word (as item): 3, 96, 104-5, 133, 147, 164-6, 177, 191-2, 204, 211, **226-9**, 254-5, 259, 262, 268-9, 284, 290, 301, 314.
'word' (as 'rank'): 19, 95, 233-7, 279, 282, 310, 318.
'word-complex': 318.

'X-bar syntax': 201.

Young: 5-6, 108.

# CURRENT ISSUES IN LINGUISTIC THEORY

E. F. K. Koerner, Editor
Department of Linguistics, University of Ottawa
OTTAWA, Canada K1N 6N5
koerner@uottawa.ca

The *Current Issues in Linguistic Theory* (CILT) series is a theory-oriented series which welcomes contributions from scholars who have significant proposals to make towards the advancement of our understanding of language, its structure, functioning and development. CILT has been established in order to provide a forum for the presentation and discussion of linguistic opinions of scholars who do not necessarily accept the prevailing mode of thought in linguistic science. It offers an alternative outlet for meaningful contributions to the current linguistic debate, and furnishes the diversity of opinion which a healthy discipline must have. In this series the following volumes have been published thus far or are scheduled for publication:

1. KOERNER, Konrad (ed.): *The Transformational-Generative Paradigm and Modern Linguistic Theory.* 1975.
2. WEIDERT, Alfons: *Componential Analysis of Lushai Phonology.* 1975.
3. MAHER, J. Peter: *Papers on Language Theory and History I: Creation and Tradition in Language.* Foreword by Raimo Anttila. 1979.
4. HOPPER, Paul J. (ed.): *Studies in Descriptive and Historical Linguistics. Festschrift for Winfred P. Lehmann.* 1977.
5. ITKONEN, Esa: *Grammatical Theory and Metascience: A critical investigation into the methodological and philosophical foundations of 'autonomous' linguistics.* 1978.
6. ANTTILA, Raimo: *Historical and Comparative Linguistics.* 1989.
7. MEISEL, Jürgen M. & Martin D. PAM (eds): *Linear Order and Generative Theory.* 1979.
8. WILBUR, Terence H.: *Prolegomena to a Grammar of Basque.* 1979.
9. HOLLIEN, Harry & Patricia (eds): *Current Issues in the Phonetic Sciences. Proceedings of the IPS-77 Congress, Miami Beach, Florida, 17-19 December 1977.* 1979.
10. PRIDEAUX, Gary D. (ed.): *Perspectives in Experimental Linguistics. Papers from the University of Alberta Conference on Experimental Linguistics, Edmonton, 13-14 Oct. 1978.* 1979.
11. BROGYANYI, Bela (ed.): *Studies in Diachronic, Synchronic, and Typological Linguistics: Festschrift for Oswald Szemérenyi on the Occasion of his 65th Birthday.* 1979.
12. FISIAK, Jacek (ed.): *Theoretical Issues in Contrastive Linguistics.* 1981. Out of print
13. MAHER, J. Peter, Allan R. BOMHARD & Konrad KOERNER (eds): *Papers from the Third International Conference on Historical Linguistics, Hamburg, August 22-26 1977.* 1982.
14. TRAUGOTT, Elizabeth C., Rebecca LaBRUM & Susan SHEPHERD (eds): *Papers from the Fourth International Conference on Historical Linguistics, Stanford, March 26-30 1979.* 1980.
15. ANDERSON, John (ed.): *Language Form and Linguistic Variation. Papers dedicated to Angus McIntosh.* 1982.
16. ARBEITMAN, Yoël L. & Allan R. BOMHARD (eds): *Bono Homini Donum: Essays in Historical Linguistics, in Memory of J.Alexander Kerns.* 1981.
17. LIEB, Hans-Heinrich: *Integrational Linguistics. 6 volumes. Vol. II-VI n.y.p.* 1984/93.
18. IZZO, Herbert J. (ed.): *Italic and Romance. Linguistic Studies in Honor of Ernst Pulgram.* 1980.
19. RAMAT, Paolo et al. (eds): *Linguistic Reconstruction and Indo-European Syntax. Proceedings of the Colloquium of the 'Indogermanischhe Gesellschaft'. University of Pavia, 6-7 September 1979.* 1980.
20. NORRICK, Neal R.: *Semiotic Principles in Semantic Theory.* 1981.

21. AHLQVIST, Anders (ed.): *Papers from the Fifth International Conference on Historical Linguistics, Galway, April 6-10 1981.* 1982.
22. UNTERMANN, Jürgen & Bela BROGYANYI (eds): *Das Germanische und die Rekonstruktion der Indogermanischen Grundsprache. Akten des Freiburger Kolloquiums der Indogermanischen Gesellschaft, Freiburg, 26-27 Februar 1981.* 1984.
23. DANIELSEN, Niels: *Papers in Theoretical Linguistics. Edited by Per Baerentzen.* 1992.
24. LEHMANN, Winfred P. & Yakov MALKIEL (eds): *Perspectives on Historical Linguistics. Papers from a conference held at the meeting of the Language Theory Division, Modern Language Assn., San Francisco, 27-30 December 1979.* 1982.
25. ANDERSEN, Paul Kent: *Word Order Typology and Comparative Constructions.* 1983.
26. BALDI, Philip (ed.): *Papers from the XIIth Linguistic Symposium on Romance Languages, Univ. Park, April 1-3, 1982.* 1984.
27. BOMHARD, Alan R.: *Toward Proto-Nostratic. A New Approach to the Comparison of Proto-Indo-European and Proto-Afroasiatic. Foreword by Paul J. Hopper.* 1984.
28. BYNON, James (ed.): *Current Progress in Afro-Asiatic Linguistics: Papers of the Third International Hamito-Semitic Congress, London, 1978.* 1984.
29. PAPROTTÉ, Wolf & René DIRVEN (eds): *The Ubiquity of Metaphor: Metaphor in language and thought.* 1985 (publ. 1986).
30. HALL, Robert A. Jr.: *Proto-Romance Morphology. = Comparative Romance Grammar, vol. III.* 1984.
31. GUILLAUME, Gustave: *Foundations for a Science of Language.*
32. COPELAND, James E. (ed.): *New Directions in Linguistics and Semiotics.* Co-edition with Rice University Press who hold exclusive rights for US and Canada. 1984.
33. VERSTEEGH, Kees: *Pidginization and Creolization. The Case of Arabic.* 1984.
34. FISIAK, Jacek (ed.): *Papers from the VIth International Conference on Historical Linguistics, Poznan, 22-26 August. 1983.* 1985.
35. COLLINGE, N.E.: *The Laws of Indo-European.* 1985.
36. KING, Larry D. & Catherine A. MALEY (eds): *Selected papers from the XIIIth Linguistic Symposium on Romance Languages, Chapel Hill, N.C., 24-26 March 1983.* 1985.
37. GRIFFEN, T.D.: *Aspects of Dynamic Phonology.* 1985.
38. BROGYANYI, Bela & Thomas KRÖMMELBEIN (eds): *Germanic Dialects:Linguistic and Philological Investigations.* 1986.
39. BENSON, James D., Michael J. CUMMINGS, & William S. GREAVES (eds): *Linguistics in a Systemic Perspective.* 1988.
40. FRIES, Peter Howard (ed.) in collaboration with Nancy M. Fries: *Toward an Understanding of Language: Charles C. Fries in Perspective.* 1985.
41. EATON, Roger, et al. (eds): *Papers from the 4th International Conference on English Historical Linguistics, April 10-13, 1985.* 1985.
42. MAKKAI, Adam & Alan K. MELBY (eds): *Linguistics and Philosophy. Festschrift for Rulon S. Wells.* 1985 (publ. 1986).
43. AKAMATSU, Tsutomu: *The Theory of Neutralization and the Archiphoneme in Functional Phonology.* 1988.
44. JUNGRAITHMAYR, Herrmann & Walter W. MUELLER (eds): *Proceedings of the Fourth International Hamito-Semitic Congress.* 1987.
45. KOOPMAN, W.F., F.C. Van der LEEK , O. FISCHER & R. EATON (eds): *Explanation and Linguistic Change.* 1986
46. PRIDEAUX, Gary D. & William J. BAKER: *Strategies and Structures: The processing of relative clauses.* 1987.
47. LEHMANN, Winfred P. (ed.): *Language Typology 1985. Papers from the Linguistic Typology Symposium, Moscow, 9-13 Dec. 1985.* 1986.
48. RAMAT, Anna G., Onofrio CARRUBA and Giuliano BERNINI (eds): *Papers from the 7th*

*International Conference on Historical Linguistics.* 1987.
49. WAUGH, Linda R. and Stephen RUDY (eds): *New Vistas in Grammar: Invariance and Variation. Proceedings of the Second International Roman Jakobson Conference, New York University, Nov.5-8, 1985.* 1991.
50. RUDZKA-OSTYN, Brygida (ed.): *Topics in Cognitive Linguistics.* 1988.
51. CHATTERJEE, Ranjit: *Aspect and Meaning in Slavic and Indic. With a foreword by Paul Friedrich.* 1989.
52. FASOLD, Ralph W. & Deborah SCHIFFRIN (eds): *Language Change and Variation.* 1989.
53. SANKOFF, David: *Diversity and Diachrony.* 1986.
54. WEIDERT, Alfons: *Tibeto-Burman Tonology. A comparative analysis.* 1987
55. HALL, Robert A. Jr.: *Linguistics and Pseudo-Linguistics.* 1987.
56. HOCKETT, Charles F.: *Refurbishing our Foundations. Elementary linguistics from an advanced point of view.* 1987.
57. BUBENIK, Vít: *Hellenistic and Roman Greece as a Sociolinguistic Area.* 1989.
58. ARBEITMAN, Yoël. L. (ed.): *Fucus: A Semitic/Afrasian Gathering in Remembrance of Albert Ehrman.* 1988.
59. VAN VOORST, Jan: *Event Structure.* 1988.
60. KIRSCHNER, Carl & Janet DECESARIS (eds): *Studies in Romance Linguistics. Selected Proceedings from the XVII Linguistic Symposium on Romance Languages.* 1989.
61. CORRIGAN, Roberta L., Fred ECKMAN & Michael NOONAN (eds): *Linguistic Categorization. Proceedings of an International Symposium in Milwaukee, Wisconsin, April 10-11, 1987.* 1989.
62. FRAJZYNGIER, Zygmunt (ed.): *Current Progress in Chadic Linguistics. Proceedings of the International Symposium on Chadic Linguistics, Boulder, Colorado, 1-2 May 1987.* 1989.
63. EID, Mushira (ed.): *Perspectives on Arabic Linguistics I. Papers from the First Annual Symposium on Arabic Linguistics.* 1990.
64. BROGYANYI, Bela (ed.): *Prehistory, History and Historiography of Language, Speech, and Linguistic Theory. Papers in honor of Oswald Szemérenyi I.* 1992.
65. ADAMSON, Sylvia, Vivien A. LAW, Nigel VINCENT and Susan WRIGHT (eds): *Papers from the 5th International Conference on English Historical Linguistics.* 1990.
66. ANDERSEN, Henning and Konrad KOERNER (eds): *Historical Linguistics 1987.Papers from the 8th International Conference on Historical Linguistics,Lille, August 30-Sept., 1987.* 1990.
67. LEHMANN, Winfred P. (ed.): *Language Typology 1987. Systematic Balance in Language. Papers from the Linguistic Typology Symposium, Berkeley, 1-3 Dec 1987.* 1990.
68. BALL, Martin, James FIFE, Erich POPPE &Jenny ROWLAND (eds): *Celtic Linguistics/ Ieithyddiaeth Geltaidd. Readings in the Brythonic Languages. Festschrift for T. Arwyn Watkins.* 1990.
69. WANNER, Dieter and Douglas A. KIBBEE (eds): *New Analyses in Romance Linguistics. Selected papers from the Linguistic Symposium on Romance Languages XVIIII, Urbana-Champaign, April 7-9, 1988.* 1991.
70. JENSEN, John T.: *Morphology. Word structure in generative grammar.* 1990.
71. O'GRADY, William: *Categories and Case. The sentence structure of Korean.* 1991.
72. EID, Mushira and John MCCARTHY (eds): *Perspectives on Arabic Linguistics II. Papers from the Second Annual Symposium on Arabic Linguistics.* 1990.
73. STAMENOV, Maxim (ed.): *Current Advances in Semantic Theory.* 1991.
74. LAEUFER, Christiane and Terrell A. MORGAN (eds): *Theoretical Analyses in Romance Linguistics.* 1991.
75. DROSTE, Flip G. and John E. JOSEPH (eds): *Linguistic Theory and Grammatical*

*Description. Nine Current Approaches.* 1991.
76. WICKENS, Mark A.: *Grammatical Number in English Nouns. An empirical and theoretical account.* 1992.
77. BOLTZ, William G. and Michael C. SHAPIRO (eds): *Studies in the Historical Phonology of Asian Languages.* 1991.
78. KAC, Michael: *Grammars and Grammaticality.* 1992.
79. ANTONSEN, Elmer H. and Hans Henrich HOCK (eds): *STAEF-CRAEFT: Studies in Germanic Linguistics. Select papers from the First and Second Symposium on Germanic Linguistics, University of Chicago, 24 April 1985, and Univ. of Illinois at Urbana-Champaign, 3-4 Oct. 1986.* 1991.
80. COMRIE, Bernard and Mushira EID (eds): *Perspectives on Arabic Linguistics III. Papers from the Third Annual Symposium on Arabic Linguistics.* 1991.
81. LEHMANN, Winfred P. and H.J. HEWITT (eds): *Language Typology 1988. Typological Models in the Service of Reconstruction.* 1991.
82. VAN VALIN, Robert D. (ed.): *Advances in Role and Reference Grammar.* 1992.
83. FIFE, James and Erich POPPE (eds): *Studies in Brythonic Word Order.* 1991.
84. DAVIS, Garry W. and Gregory K. IVERSON (eds): *Explanation in Historical Linguistics.* 1992.
85. BROSELOW, Ellen, Mushira EID and John McCARTHY (eds): *Perspectives on Arabic Linguistics IV. Papers from the Annual Symposium on Arabic Linguistics.* 1992.
86. KESS, Joseph F.: *Psycholinguistics. Psychology, linguistics, and the study of natural language.* 1992.
87. BROGYANYI, Bela and Reiner LIPP (eds): *Historical Philology: Greek, Latin, and Romance. Papers in honor of Oswald Szemerényi II.* 1992.
88. SHIELDS, Kenneth: *A History of Indo-European Verb Morphology.* 1992.
89. BURRIDGE, Kate: *Syntactic Change in Germanic. A study of some aspects of language change in Germanic with particular reference to Middle Dutch.* 1992.
90. KING, Larry D.: *The Semantic Structure of Spanish. Meaning and grammatical form.* 1992.
91. HIRSCHBÜHLER, Paul and Konrad KOERNER (eds): *Romance Languages and Modern Linguistic Theory. Selected papers from the XX Linguistic Symposium on Romance Languages,University of Ottawa, April 10-14, 1990.* 1992.
92. POYATOS, Fernando: *Paralanguage: A linguistic and interdisciplinary approach to interactive speech and sounds.* 1992.
93. LIPPI-GREEN, Rosina (ed.): *Recent Developments in Germanic Linguistics.* 1992.
94. HAGÈGE, Claude: *The Language Builder. An essay on the human signature in linguistic morphogenesis.* 1992.
95. MILLER, D. Gary: *Complex Verb Formation.* 1992.
96. LIEB, Hans-Heinrich (ed.): *Prospects for a New Structuralism.* 1992.
97. BROGYANYI, Bela & Reiner LIPP (eds): *Comparative-Historical Linguistics: Indo-European and Finno-Ugric. Papers in honor of Oswald Szemerényi III.* 1992.
98. EID, Mushira & Gregory K. IVERSON: *Principles and Prediction: The analysis of natural language.* 1993.
99. JENSEN, John T.: *English Phonology.* 1993.
100. MUFWENE, Salikoko S. and Lioba MOSHI (eds): *Topics in African Linguistics. Papers from the XXI Annual Conference on African Linguistics, University of Georgia, April 1990.* 1993.
101. EID, Mushira & Clive HOLES (eds): *Perspectives on Arabic Linguistics V. Papers from the Fifth Annual Symposium on Arabic Linguistics.* 1993.
102. DAVIS, Philip W. (ed.): *Alternative Linguistics. Descriptive and theoretical Modes.* 1995.

103. ASHBY, William J., Marianne MITHUN, Giorgio PERISSINOTTO and Eduardo RAPOSO: *Linguistic Perspectives on Romance Languages. Selected papers from the XXI Linguistic Symposium on Romance Languages, Santa Barbara, February 21-24, 1991.* 1993.
104. KURZOVÁ, Helena: *From Indo-European to Latin. The evolution of a morphosyntactic type.* 1993.
105. HUALDE, José Ignacio and Jon ORTIZ DE URBANA (eds): *Generative Studies in Basque Linguistics.* 1993.
106. AERTSEN, Henk and Robert J. JEFFERS (eds): *Historical Linguistics 1989. Papers from the 9th International Conference on Historical Linguistics, New Brunswick, 14-18 August 1989.* 1993.
107. MARLE, Jaap van (ed.): *Historical Linguistics 1991. Papers from the 10th International Conference on Historical Linguistics, Amsterdam, August 12-16, 1991.* 1993.
108. LIEB, Hans-Heinrich: *Linguistic Variables. Towards a unified theory of linguistic variation.* 1993.
109. PAGLIUCA, William (ed.): *Perspectives on Grammaticalization.* 1994.
110. SIMONE, Raffaele (ed.): *Iconicity in Language.* 1995.
111. TOBIN, Yishai: *Invariance, Markedness and Distinctive Feature Analysis. A contrastive study of sign systems in English and Hebrew.* 1994.
112. CULIOLI, Antoine: *Cognition and Representation in Linguistic Theory. Translated, edited and introduced by Michel Liddle.* 1995.
113. FERNÁNDEZ, Francisco, Miguel FUSTER and Juan Jose CALVO (eds): *English Historical Linguistics 1992. Papers from the 7th International Conference on English Historical Linguistics, Valencia, 22-26 September 1992.* 1994.
114. EGLI, U., P. PAUSE, Chr. SCHWARZE, A. von STECHOW, G. WIENOLD (eds): *Lexical Knowledge in the Organisation of Language.* 1995.
115. EID, Mushira, Vincente CANTARINO and Keith WALTERS (eds): *Perspectives on Arabic Linguistics. Vol. VI. Papers from the Sixth Annual Symposium on Arabic Linguistics.* 1994.
116. MILLER, D. Gary: *Ancient Scripts and Phonological Knowledge.* 1994.
117. PHILIPPAKI-WARBURTON, I., K. NICOLAIDIS and M. SIFIANOU (eds): *Themes in Greek Linguistics. Papers from the first International Conference on Greek Linguistics, Reading, September 1993.* 1994.
118. HASAN, Ruqaiya and Peter H. FRIES (eds): *On Subject and Theme. A discourse functional perspective.* 1995.
119. LIPPI-GREEN, Rosina: *Language Ideology and Language Change in Early Modern German. A sociolinguistic study of the consonantal system of Nuremberg.* 1994.
120. STONHAM, John T.: *Combinatorial Morphology.* 1994.
121. HASAN, Ruqaiya, Carmel CLORAN and David BUTT (eds): *Functional Descriptions. Theorie in practice.* 1996.
122. SMITH, John Charles and Martin MAIDEN (eds): *Linguistic Theory and the Romance Languages.* 1995.
123. AMASTAE, Jon, Grant GOODALL, Mario MONTALBETTI and Marianne PHINNEY: *Contemporary Research in Romance Linguistics. Papers from the XXII Linguistic Symposium on Romance Languages, El Paso//Juárez, February 22-24, 1994.* 1995.
124. ANDERSEN, Henning: *Historical Linguistics 1993. Selected papers from the 11th International Conference on Historical Linguistics, Los Angeles, 16-20 August 1993.* 1995.
125. SINGH, Rajendra (ed.): *Towards a Critical Sociolinguistics.* 1996.
126. MATRAS, Yaron (ed.): *Romani in Contact. The history, structure and sociology of a language.* 1995.
127. GUY, Gregory R., Crawford FEAGIN, Deborah SCHIFFRIN and John BAUGH (eds): *Towards a Social Science of Language. Papers in honor of William Labov. Volume 1: Variation and change in language and society.* 1996.

128. GUY, Gregory R., Crawford FEAGIN, Deborah SCHIFFRIN and John BAUGH (eds): *Towards a Social Science of Language. Papers in honor of William Labov. Volume 2: Social interaction and discourse structures.* 1997.
129. LEVIN, Saul: *Semitic and Indo-European: The Principal Etymologies. With observations on Afro-Asiatic.* 1995.
130. EID, Mushira (ed.) *Perspectives on Arabic Linguistics. Vol. VII. Papers from the Seventh Annual Symposium on Arabic Linguistics.* 1995.
131. HUALDE, Jose Ignacio, Joseba A. LAKARRA and R.L. Trask (eds): *Towards a History of the Basque Language.* 1995.
132. HERSCHENSOHN, Julia: *Case Suspension and Binary Complement Structure in French.* 1996.
133. ZAGONA, Karen (ed.): *Grammatical Theory and Romance Languages. Selected papers from the 25th Linguistic Symposium on Romance Languages (LSRL XXV) Seattle, 2-4 March 1995.* 1996.
134. EID, Mushira (ed.): *Perspectives on Arabic Linguistics Vol. VIII. Papers from the Eighth Annual Symposium on Arabic Linguistics.* 1996.
135. BRITTON Derek (ed.): *Papers from the 8th International Conference on English Historical Linguistics.* 1996.
136. MITKOV, Ruslan and Nicolas NICOLOV (eds): *Recent Advances in Natural Language Processing.* 1997.
137. LIPPI-GREEN, Rosina and Joseph C. SALMONS (eds): *Germanic Linguistics. Syntactic and diachronic.* 1996.
138. SACKMANN, Robin (ed.): *Theoretical Linguistics and Grammatical Description.* 1996.
139. BLACK, James R. and Virginia MOTAPANYANE (eds): *Microparametric Syntax and Dialect Variation.* 1996.
140. BLACK, James R. and Virginia MOTAPANYANE (eds): *Clitics, Pronouns and Movement.* 1997.
141. EID, Mushira and Dilworth PARKINSON (eds): *Perspectives on Arabic Linguistics Vol. IX. Papers from the Ninth Annual Symposium on Arabic Linguistics, Georgetown University, Washington D.C., 1995.* 1996.
142. JOSEPH, Brian D. and Joseph C. SALMONS (eds): *Nostratic. Sifting the evidence.* 1998.
143. ATHANASIADOU, Angeliki and René DIRVEN (eds): *On Conditionals Again.* 1997.
144. SINGH, Rajendra (ed): *Trubetzkoy's Orphan. Proceedings of the Montréal Roundtable "Morphophonology: contemporary responses (Montréal, October 1994).* 1996.
145. HEWSON, John and Vit BUBENIK: *Tense and Aspect in Indo-European Languages. Theory, typology, diachrony.* 1997.
146. HINSKENS, Frans, Roeland VAN HOUT and W. Leo WETZELS (eds): *Variation, Change, and Phonological Theory.* 1997.
147. HEWSON, John: *The Cognitive System of the French Verb.* 1997.
148. WOLF, George and Nigel LOVE (eds): *Linguistics Inside Out. Roy Harris and his critics.* 1997.
149. HALL, T. Alan: *The Phonology of Coronals.* 1997.
150. VERSPOOR, Marjolijn, Kee Dong LEE and Eve SWEETSER (eds): *Lexical and Syntactical Constructions and the Construction of Meaning. Proceedings of the Bi-annual ICLA meeting in Albuquerque, July 1995.* 1997.
151. LIEBERT, Wolf-Andreas, Gisela REDEKER and Linda WAUGH (eds): *Discourse and Perspectives in Cognitive Linguistics.* 1997.
152. HIRAGA, Masako, Chris SINHA and Sherman WILCOX (eds): *Cultural, Psychological and Typological Issues in Cognitive Linguistics.* 1999.
153. EID, Mushira and Robert R. RATCLIFFE (eds): *Perspectives on Arabic Linguistics Vol. X. Papers from the Tenth Annual Symposium on Arabic Linguistics, Salt Lake City, 1996.* 1997.

154. SIMON-VANDENBERGEN, Anne-Marie, Kristin DAVIDSE and Dirk NOËL (eds): *Reconnecting Language. Morphology and Syntax in Functional Perspectives.* 1997.
155. FORGET, Danielle, Paul HIRSCHBÜHLER, France MARTINEAU and María-Luisa RIVERO (eds): *Negation and Polarity. Syntax and semantics. Selected papers from the Colloquium Negation: Syntax and Semantics. Ottawa, 11-13 May 1995.* 1997.
156. MATRAS, Yaron, Peter BAKKER and Hristo KYUCHUKOV (eds): *The Typology and Dialectology of Romani.* 1997.
157. LEMA, José and Esthela TREVIÑO (eds): *Theoretical Analyses on Romance Languages. Selected papers from the 26th Linguistic Symposium on Romance Languages (LSRL XXVI), Mexico City, 28-30 March, 1996.* 1998.
158. SÁNCHEZ MACARRO, Antonia and Ronald CARTER (eds): *Linguistic Choice across Genres. Variation in spoken and written English.* 1998.
159. JOSEPH, Brian D., Geoffrey C. HORROCKS and Irene PHILIPPAKI-WARBURTON (eds): *Themes in Greek Linguistics II.* 1998.
160. SCHWEGLER, Armin, Bernard TRANEL and Myriam URIBE-ETXEBARRIA (eds): *Romance Linguistics: Theoretical Perspectives. Selected papers from the 27th Linguistic Symposium on Romance Languages (LSRL XXVII), Irvine, 20-22 February, 1997.* 1998.
161. SMITH, John Charles and Delia BENTLEY (eds): *Historical Linguistics 1995. Volume 1: Romance and general linguistics.* 2000.
162. HOGG, Richard M. and Linda van BERGEN (eds): *Historical Linguistics 1995. Volume 2: Germanic linguistics.Selected papers from the 12th International Conference on Historical Linguistics, Manchester, August 1995.* 1998.
163. LOCKWOOD, David G., Peter H. FRIES and James E. COPELAND (eds): *Functional Approaches to Language, Culture and Cognition.* 2000.
164. SCHMID, Monika, Jennifer R. AUSTIN and Dieter STEIN (eds): *Historical Linguistics 1997. Selected papers from the 13th International Conference on Historical Linguistics, Düsseldorf, 10-17 August 1997.* 1998.
165. BUBENÍK, Vit: *A Historical Syntax of Late Middle Indo-Aryan (Apabhraṃśa).* 1998.
166. LEMMENS, Maarten: *Lexical Perspectives on Transitivity and Ergativity. Causative constructions in English.* 1998.
167. BENMAMOUN, Elabbas, Mushira EID and Niloofar HAERI (eds): *Perspectives on Arabic Linguistics Vol. XI. Papers from the Eleventh Annual Symposium on Arabic Linguistics, Atlanta, 1997.* 1998.
168. RATCLIFFE, Robert R.: *The "Broken" Plural Problem in Arabic and Comparative Semitic. Allomorphy and analogy in non-concatenative morphology.* 1998.
169. GHADESSY, Mohsen (ed.): *Text and Context in Functional Linguistics.* 1999.
170. LAMB, Sydney M.: *Pathways of the Brain. The neurocognitive basis of language.* 1999.
171. WEIGAND, Edda (ed.): *Contrastive Lexical Semantics.* 1998.
172. DIMITROVA-VULCHANOVA, Mila and Lars HELLAN (eds): *Topics in South Slavic Syntax and Semantics.* 1999.
173. TREVIÑO, Esthela and José LEMA (eds): *Semantic Issues in Romance Syntax.* 1999.
174. HALL, T. Alan and Ursula KLEINHENZ (eds): *Studies on the Phonological Word.* 1999.
175. GIBBS, Ray W. and Gerard J. STEEN (eds): *Metaphor in Cognitive Linguistics. Selected papers from the 5th International Cognitive Linguistics Conference, Amsterdam, 1997.* 1999.
176. VAN HOEK, Karen, Andrej KIBRIK and Leo NOORDMAN (eds): *Discourse in Cognitive Linguistics. Selected papers from the International Cognitive Linguistics Conference, Amsterdam, July 1997.* 1999.
177. CUYCKENS, Hubert and Britta ZAWADA (eds): *Polysemy in Cognitive Linguistics. Selected papers from the International Cognitive Linguistics Conference, Amsterdam, 1997.* n.y.p.

178. FOOLEN, Ad and Frederike van der LEEK (eds): *Constructions in Cognitive Linguistics. Selected papers from the Fifth International Cognitive Linguistic Conference, Amsterdam, 1997.* 2000.
179. RINI, Joel: *Exploring the Role of Morphology in the Evolution of Spanish.* 1999.
180. MEREU, Lunella (ed.): *Boundaries of Morphology and Syntax.* 1999.
181. MOHAMMAD, Mohammad A.: *Word Order, Agreement and Pronominalization in Standard and Palestinian Arabic.* 2000.
182. KENESEI, István (ed.): *Theoretical Issues in Eastern European Languages. Selected papers from the Conference on Linguistic Theory in Eastern European Languages (CLITE), Szeged, April 1998.* 1999.
183. CONTINI-MORAVA, Ellen and Yishai TOBIN (eds): *Between Grammar and Lexicon.* 2000.
184. SAGART, Laurent: *The Roots of Old Chinese.* 1999.
185. AUTHIER, J.-Marc, Barbara E. BULLOCK, Lisa A. REED (eds): *Formal Perspectives on Romance Linguistics. Selected papers from the 28th Linguistic Symposium on Romance Languages (LSRL XXVIII), University Park, 16-19 April 1998.* 1999.
186. MIŠESKA TOMIĆ, Olga and Milorad RADOVANOVIĆ (eds): *History and Perspectives of Language Study.* 2000.
187. FRANCO, Jon, Alazne LANDA and Juan MARTÍN (eds): *Grammatical Analyses in Basque and Romance Linguistics.* 1999.
188. VanNESS SIMMONS, Richard: *Chinese Dialect Classification. A comparative approach to Harngjou, Old Jintarn, and Common Northern Wu.* 1999.
189. NICHOLOV, Nicolas and Ruslan MITKOV (eds): *Recent Advances in Natural Language Processing II. Selected papers from RANLP '97.* 2000.
190. BENMAMOUN, Elabbas (ed.): *Perspectives on Arabic Linguistics Vol. XII. Papers from the Twelfth Annual Symposium on Arabic Linguistics.* 1999.
191. SIHLER, Andrew L.: *Language Change. An introduction.* 2000.
192. ALEXANDROVA, Galina M. and Olga ARNAUDOVA (eds.): *The Minimalist Parameter. Selected papers from the Open Linguistics Forum, Ottawa, 21-23 March 1997.* n.y.p.
193. KLAUSENBURGER, Jurgen: *Grammaticalization. Studies in Latin and Romance morphosyntax.* 2000.
194. COLEMAN, Julie and Christian J. KAY (eds): *Lexicology, Semantics and Lexicography. Selected papers from the Fourth G. L. Brook Symposium, Manchester, August 1998.* 2000.
195. HERRING, Susan C., Pieter van REENEN and Lene SCHØSLER (eds): *Textual Parameters in Older Languages.* n.y.p.
196. HANNAHS, S. J. and Mike DAVENPORT (eds): *Issues in Phonological Structure. Papers from an International Workshop.* 1999.
197. COOPMANS, Peter, Martin EVERAERT and Jane GRIMSHAW (eds): *Lexical Specification and Insertion.* 2000.
198. NIEMEIER, Susanne and René DIRVEN (eds): *Evidence for Linguistic Relativity.* 2000.
199. VERSPOOR, Marjolijn H. and Martin PÜTZ (eds): *Explorations in Linguistic Relativity.* 2000.
200. ANTTILA, Raimo: *Greek and Indo-European Etymology in Action. Proto-Indo-European \*aġ-.* 2000.
201. DRESSLER, Wolfgang U., Oskar E. PFEIFFER, Markus PÖCHTRAGER and John R. RENNISON (eds.): *Morphological Analysis in Comparison.* 2000.
202. LECARME, Jacqueline, Jean LOWENSTAMM and Ur SHLONSKY (eds.): *Research in Afroasiatic Grammar. Papers from the Third conference on Afroasiatic Languages, Sophia Antipolis, 1996.* 2000.
203. NORRICK, Neal R.: *Conversational Narrative. Storytelling in everyday talk.* 2000.
204. DIRVEN, René, Bruce HAWKINS and Esra SANDIKCIOGLU (eds.): *Language and Ideology. Volume 1: cognitive theoretical approaches.* n.y.p.

205. DIRVEN, René, Roslyn FRANK and Cornelia ILIE (eds.): *Language and Ideology. Volume 2: cognitive descriptive approaches.* n.y.p.
206. FAWCETT, Robin: *A Theory of Syntax for Systemic Functional Linguistics.* 2000.
207. SANZ, Montserrat: *Events and Predication. A new approach to syntactic processing in English and Spanish.* n.y.p.
208. ROBINSON, Orrin W.: *Whose German? The ach/ich alternation and related phenomena in 'standard' and 'colloquial'.* n.y.p.
209. KING, Ruth: *The Lexical Basis of Grammatical Borrowing. A Prince Edward Island French case study.* n.y.p.
210. DWORKIN, Steven N. and Dieter WANNER (eds.): *New Approaches to Old Problems. Issues in Romance historical linguistics.* n.y.p.
211. ELŠÍK, Viktor and Yaron MATRAS (eds.): *Grammatical Relations in Romani. The Noun Phrase.* n.y.p.
212. REPETTI, Lori (ed.): *Phonological Theory and the Dialects of Italy.* n.y.p.
213. SORNICOLA, Rosanna, Erich POPPE and Ariel SHISHA HALEVY (eds.): *Stability, Variation and Change of Word-Order Patterns over Time.* n.y.p.